Autonomy and Cooperation Within the International Criminal Court and United Nations Security Council

Dimitris Liakopoulos

Autonomy and Cooperation Within the International Criminal Court and United Nations Security Council

Dimitris Liakopoulos

W. B. Sheridan Law Books

Academica Press
Washington - London

Library of Congress Cataloging-in-Publication Data

Names: Liakopoulos, Dimitris, author.
Title: Autonomy and cooperation within the International Criminal Court and United Nations Security Council / Dimitris Liakopoulos.
Description: Washington : Academica Press, [2020] |
Identifiers: LCCN 2020932879 | ISBN 9781680531305 (hardcover) LC record available at https://lccn.loc.gov/2020932879

Dedicated to Irene and Sofia

Contents

Workplan

The present study takes the perspective of the International Criminal Court (ICC) in analyzing the relationship between ICC and Security Council (SC). Moreover, if the main interest of the research is to study the rules aimed at regulating the relations between the two bodies, the starting point could only be the Treaty of Rome, the only tool within which it is possible to trace specific rules of coordination.

The perspective of SC and more generally of United Nations in interaction with ICC will not be directly investigated. For example, it will be only incidentally and for the most relevant purposes for the investigation of the SC's powers to affect the content of the Treaty establishing the Court. More generally, any limits to the action of SC will be observed only in light of the repercussions that may have on the jurisdictional activity of ICC. From an internal perspective, so to speak, to the Court itself, it should be emphasized that the autonomy referred to is only that of the ICC with respect to another institution, a political body, the SC. As relevant, therefore, the rules of operation of the Court that guarantee a certain degree of impartiality and independence of the individual judicial bodies, such as for example the mechanisms relating to the election of judges and Prosecutor, the duration of the mandates or the rules will not be analyzed on the withdrawal of the same[1].

The division of the chapters and the overall structure of the work respond to the need to first investigate the content of the relevant statutory rules, in an attempt to determine their functioning and resolve some of the interpretative issues that characterize them. Once completed, through the chapters dedicated to the intervention powers of SC recognized by the Statute, this first complex operation will help understanding what the forms and coordination tools of the action of the two organizations are.

The survey has five parts. Four of them are dedicated to reconstructing the content of powers attributed by the Statute of Rome to SC. Thus the first chapter will be devoted to the power to activate the investigations of the Prosecutor; the second chapter will instead have the power to suspend the judicial

[1]O. DE FROUVILLE, Les juridictions pènales internationales et hybrides, in H. RUIZ-FABRI, J.M. SOREL, Indèpendance et impartialitè des juges internationaux, ed. Pedone, Paris, 2010, pp. 154ss. E. DECAUX, O. DE FROUVILLE, Droit international public, ed. Dalloz, Paris, 2018. H. BLAISE NGAMENI, Le droit international pènal à l'èpreuve des règimes politiques africaines, in Revue Quèbècoise de Droit International, 29 (1), 2016, pp. 10ss.

activity, the third will deal with defining the characteristics of SC intervention in the context of cooperation and judicial assistance and the fourth examines the prerogatives recognized to the politician body regarding the crime of aggression. These four chapters will in turn be organized in order to trace some of the problems that emerged in the path that led to the drafting of the relevant provisions, i.e. reconstruct the practice of SC in the exercise of those powers and offer an analysis of the main legal issues raised by the choices drafting of the statutory rules and their concrete application. A final fifth chapter aims to examine on the one hand the impact of SC action on the jurisdictional activity of ICC and on the other, the power of ICC to exercise a union on the decisions of SC aimed at influencing its functioning. The final considerations aim to examine the relevance of the possible coordination models of the action of the two bodies, proposed during this introduction, in defining the forms that the interactions between ICC and SC take. Some reflections aimed at highlighting the effects resulting from the dynamics of the relationship between the two organizations on the legitimacy and effectiveness of the ICC action close the investigation.

1. Introduction

It does not seem possible until today that the establishment of a permanent criminal court at international level represents a success for the international community. If the high number of States that have acceded to the Treaty of Rome is an undoubted and perhaps unexpected sign of a general and shared will to repress the most serious international crimes by any means, in practice however they seem to go in the opposite direction because of the practical difficulties encountered by ICC in dealing with certain cases and situations, i.e. in the execution of some of its decisions and more generally in the search for effective cooperation of States and in certain contexts of the United Nations (UN) and its bodies. The uncertainty about the role that the ICC will be called to play in the coming decades is also the result of the not always harmonious relationships that it has had in recent years with SC. The sometimes uncooperative attitude of SC with respect to the action of the Court undoubtedly falls among the reasons why the latter does not seem to have reached the authoritativeness and centrality that the task assigned to it should guarantee them.

Keeping in mind the importance that these relationships have in determining the success or failure of the international criminal repression system created through the Treaty of Rome, this investigation aims to investigate the legal problems that arise in international level by ICC and SC.

The need to coordinate the action of SC and ICC derives above all from the very close connection existing between the material situations on which the two institutions are called to exercise their functions. In practice, the large-scale Commission on international crimes has been associated with the existence of a threatening situation for peace and international security. This material connection is explicitly referred to in the same preamble of the ICC Statute (StICC) where it is recognized that the crimes under ICC jurisdiction: "Threaten the peace, security and well-being of the world (...)"[2].

These possible interferences between the functions and objectives that guide the two institutions have led to the introduction of forms of connection to the activities of the two organizations within the Statute of Rome. In the discipline of relations between ICC and SC, two distinct needs take on particular importance, the need for protection of which can sometimes generate tensions or be at the origin of real conflicts (i.e. the safeguarding of the two bodies autonomy in their political and judicial spheres of competence) and that for collaboration between the two organizations in order to pursue two fundamental objectives of the international order, i.e. peace and justice.

The difficulties of coordination between SC and ICC and the possibilities between necessary protection of their respective prerogatives and cooperation needs, derive precisely and more generally from the intricate relationships that entertain the two essential values of the international order pursued by these institutions. As far as peace and justice are purposes commonly considered fundamental by all the subjects operating in the international legal system, the risk of colliding with each other and the need for some form of reconciliation is constant. Reconciling peace and justice is an operation that can prove extremely complex, also in light of the various priorities that inevitably guide the behavior of an international criminal court and that of a political body responsible for maintaining peace.

The StICC tries to offer some coordination tools, whose correct and careful use should in principle favor a harmonious and effective interaction between the two organs and avoid the emergence of conflicts. As we will try to highlight, despite these intent of the statutory provisions, the margin of discretion inevitably granted to ICC and SC in interpreting the extension of the powers recognized to them, can lead to tensions and contrasts of not easy solution.

At least in theories autonomy and cooperation can be guaranteed jointly. On the one hand the autonomy of the judicial body in the repression of international crimes and the execution of the decisions taken in a given conflictual context are not necessarily hindered by the parallel intervention of SC[3]. On the contrary, the work of SC can in some cases be the foundation and decisive support for the prosecution of international criminal proceedings. On the other hand, and at the same time, the needs of SC to guarantee the effectiveness of its action and preserve the discretion of its choices, are not always and automatically endangered by any judicial activity of ICC. The goal of peacekeeping may in some cases instead be supported or even depend on an intervention by ICC.

Despite the danger of conflicts between political initiatives and the correct administration of justice, the idea that the persecution of international crimes represents an important means for the maintenance of peace and security has long been consolidated and inspired in various historical contexts, i.e. the UN

---

[2] 3rd recital of preamble of StICC.

[3] See the ultimate sentence of VI Trial Chamber, Bosco Ntaganda, ICC-01/04-02/06, CR 2019_03568 of 8 July 2019.

action. The establishment of international criminal courts for the former Yugoslavia (International Criminal Tribunal for the Former Yugoslavia) and for Rwanda (International Criminal Tribunal for Rwanda) by SC testifies tangibly a conception of the international criminal instrument as one of the means for the achievement of peace[4]. In this same perspective, the StICC provides that the SC can take advantage of ICC action when it considers it instrumental to the restoration of international peace and security (art.13 b)[5]. It deals more generally with the idea that the action of the two organs can in some cases be complementary and even indissoluble. In short, there is no peace without justice[6].

---

[4]For further details see: V. GOWLLAND-DEBBAS, The Security Council and issues of responsibility under international law, in Recueil des cours, ed Brill, Bruxelles, vol. 353, 2012, pp. 298ss. M.P. MOELLE, The international responsibility of international organizations, Cambridge University Press, Cambridge, 2017, pp. 7ss. V.J. PROULX, Institutionalizing state responsibility: Global security and UN organs, Oxford University Press, Oxford, 2016. D. WHITTLE, The limits of legality and the United Nations Security Council: Applying the extralegal measures model to chapter VII action, in European Journal of International Law, 26 (3), 2015, pp. 674ss.

[5]In the first debate within SC, the idea of a functional role of ICC with respect to the maintenance of international peace and security emerged clearly. See in particular: Concept note of the open debate of the Security Council on peace and justice with a special focus on ICC, 17 October 2012, S/PV.6849. Part of the doctrine pointed out how the impact of the ICC action on armed conflicts in progress-by virtue of the numerous and complex repercussions it can have and the political reasons that led to its activation-is actually "not only largely unpredictable but also non-linear. See, P. KASTNER, Armed conflicts and referrals to the International Criminal Court, in Journal of International Criminal Justice, 12 (3), 2014, pp. 482ss. P. KASTNER, International criminal law in context, Routledge, London & New York, 2017.

[6]No peace without justice is the motto that supported the establishment of the first international criminal courts in the 1990s. For some considerations on the complementary nature of the two organs and more generally on the different forms that the interaction between peace and justice can assume, see the contributions of V. GOWLLAND-DEBBAS, The role of the Security Council in the new international criminal court from a systemic perspective, in L. BOISSON DE CHAZOURNES, V. GOWLLAND-DEBBAS, The international legal system in quest of equity and universality. Liber amicorum Georges Abi-Saab, ed. Brill & Martinus Nijhoff Publishers, Bruxelles, The Hague, 2001, pp. 632ss. D. RUIZ VERDUZCO, The relationship between the ICC and the United Nations Security Council, in C. STAHN, The law and practice of the International Criminal Court, Oxford University Press, Oxford, 2015, pp. 32ss. T. MALUWA, M. DU PLESSIS, D. TLADI, The pursuit of a brave new world in international law. Essays in honor of John Dugard, ed. Brill, Bruxelles, 2017, pp. 256ss. N. SHAMSI, The International Criminal Court: A political toll? How the Rome statute is susceptible to the pressures of more power states, in Willamette Journal of International Law and Dispute Resolution, 24 (1), 2016, pp. 88ss. N. HOGAN, Five sides of justice. The dangerous and disproportionate influence of the permanent five members of the United Nations Security Council in the International Criminal Court, in Brigham University of Prelaw Review, 32, 2018, pp. 234ss. J.E. MENDEZ, J. KELLEY, Peace making justice and the International Criminal Court, Cambridge University Press, Cambridge 2015, pp. 480ss. In this last contribution three

One cannot help remembering the role recognized by the board of administration to the international criminal justice over time as it has raised many problems with respect to some fundamental principles of criminal law. Here we want to recall the selectivity exercised by SC in the choice of contexts, worthy of attention by international or mixed courts, and the potential contrast of this selective approach with the principle of equality of individuals before the law. Many of the criticisms of past experiences insist on these aspects. Criminal action, carried out internationally, would often be nothing more than a different and certainly more acceptable but problematic declination of the justice exercised in Nuremberg and Tokyo. It is evident, however, that if criminal justice is perceived in these terms by part of the conflict, the work of reconciliation that the courts themselves should favor is far from being accomplished. ICC has in some cases been the subject of criticisms not so dissimilar from those of the past, to the point of suggesting that some of the historical distortions just mentioned are not completely overcome[7].

These last (real) reflections or presumed tensions between peace and justice are rather frequent in international legal experience. It is undeniable that in some contexts the judicial activity may have a negative impact on the complex process of restoring peace and conciliation of the parties in conflict[8]. The

---

different possible relationships are reconstructed: The ICC as a tool available to SC for peacekeeping; the idea, not fully realized of a total institutional autonomy and a clear separation of mandates and functions; and the SC as executive body and implementation of judicial decisions. From a different, wider and political viewpoint, the division that some have made is between liberals, which highlight the positive effects of the creation of criminal courts for the re-establishment of a peaceful coexistence between peoples and realists, which tend to see its destabilizing effects more than anything else. See in argument: G.Y. BASS, Stay the hand of vengeance. The politics of war crimes tribunals, Princeton University Press, Princeton, 2001, pp. 284ss. The author, while considering the results achieved in the past experiences of repression of international crimes, calls for the victims of crimes not to be the weapon of revenge (whatever form it may take) and to preserve the role of mediator in some way that can be played by the courts International: "a great advantage of international legalism is that it institutionalizes and moderates desires for revenge" (pag. 304). C. DE VOS, S. KENDALL, C. STAHN, Contested justice: The politics and practice of International Criminal Court interventions, Cambridge University Press, Cambridge, 2015. I. NNABUIKE MALU, The International Criminal Court and peace processes. Côte d'Ivoire, Kenya and Uganda, ed. Springer, Berlin, 2019. A. DUURSMA, T.R. MÜLLER, The International Criminal Court indictment against Al-Bashir and its repercussions for peacekeeping and humanitarian operations in Darfur, in Third World Quarterly, 40 (5), 2019.

[7]D. BUTT, Victor's justice? Historic injustice and the legitimacy of international law, in L.H. MAYER, Legitimacy, justice and public international law, Cambridge University Press, Cambridge, 2009, pp. 164ss.

[8]K. PESCHKE, The ICC investigation into the conflict in norther uganda: beyond the dictotomy of peace versus justice, in B.S. BROWN, Research handbook on international criminal court, Edward Elgar Publishers, Cheltenham, 2011, pp. 178ss. J.N. CLARK, Peace, justice and the international criminal court, in Journal of International Criminal

hypothesis of a contrast between criminal justice and peacekeeping is also explicitly taken into consideration by StICC. At least in certain specific and provisional circumstances, the pursuit of justice is expected to hinder the restoration of peace and compromise the stability of international relations itself. To this end, and here emerges a certain pre-eminence of the value of peace over that of justice among the fundamental objectives of the international order, SC can ask the ICC to stop for a limited period of time its judicial activity, which may be resumed when peacekeeping needs permit (art.16)[9]. In this particular area of

---

Justice, 9 (3), 2011, pp. 522ss.G. WERLE, F. JESSBERGER, Principles of international criminal law, Oxford University Press, Oxford, 2014, pp. 35ss. R. CRYER, H. FRIMAN, D. ROBINSON, E. WILMSHURST, An introduction to international criminal law and procedure, Cambridge University Press, Cambridge, 2014, pp. 231ss. See also the case: ICTR, Prosecutor v. Kayishema and Ruzindana, Trial Judgment, TC-II, ICTR-95-1-T, 21 May 1999, par. 138-140. For further details see: J. KNOOPS, An introduction to the law of international criminal Tribunals. A comparative study, ed. Brill. The Hague, 2014. J. NICHOLSON, Strengthening the validity of international criminal Tribunals, ed. Brill, The Hague, 2018. H. VAN DER WILT, C. PAULUSSEN, Legal responses to transnational and international crimes, Edward Elgar Publishing, Cheltenham, 2017. G. BOAS, P. CHIFFLET, International criminal justice, Edward Elgar Publishing, Cheltenham, 2017. J. MCKNIGHT, Accountability in Northern Uganda: Understanding the conflict, the parties and the false dichotomies in international criminal law and transitional justice, in Journal of African Law, 59 (2), 2015, pp. 196ss. L. REYNAMS, J. WOUTERS, C. RYNGAERT, International prosecutors, Oxford University Press, Oxford, 2012, pp. 538ss. B. KRZAN, International Criminal Court facing the peace vs. justice dilemma, in International Comparative Jurisprudence, 2 (2), 2016, pp. 84ss. A. MACDONALD, In the interests of justice? The International Criminal Court, peace talks and the failed quest for war crimes accountability in Northern Uganda, in Journal of Eastern African Studies, 11 (4), 2017, pp. 630ss. C. GEGOUT, The International Criminal Court: Limits, potential and conditions for the promotion of justice and peace, in Third World Quarterly, 34 (5), 2014, pp. 800ss. M. STERIO, M. SCHARF, The legacy of ad hoc tribunals in international criminal law, Cambridge University Press, Cambridge, 2019. In relation to the activity of the ICC and in particular on its effective ability to affect the re-establishment of the country, in the Democratic Republic of Congo, see: J. KAZADI MPIANA, La cour pènale international et la Rèpublique dèmocratique du Congo: 10 ans après. Ètude de l'impact du statut de la cour pènale international dans le droit interne congolais, in Revue Quèbècoise de Droit International, 26 (1), 2012, pp. 59ss. C. STAHN, The geometry of transitional justice, in Leiden Journal of International Law, 18 (3), 2005, pp. 426ss. E. VAN SLIEDREGT, S. VASILIEV, Pluralism in international criminal law, Oxford University Press, Oxford, 2014.

[9]The request to suspend the judicial action does not necessarily imply that the SC is materially and actively dealing with that particular situation. For this reason he speaks of a possible and dangerous paralysis given by the joint inaction of the UN and the ICC. For further details see: K. ELABY, The role of the Security Council and the independence of the International Criminal Court. A challenge of impunity, Taylor & Francis, New York, 2017. Some reflections, in M. POLITI, G. NESI, The International Criminal Court: A challenge to impunity, Ashgate Publishing, Aldershot, 2001, pp. 46ss. S.E. DAVIES, J. TRUE, The oxford handbook of women, peace and security, Oxford University Press, Oxford, 2018.

relationship between the two organs emerges not only the possible conflict for peace and justice but also the need to make the effectiveness and discretion of political action of SC prevail in some contexts, albeit limited with respect to the criminal repression and autonomy of the Court. Here the cooperation or rather the coordination between the two bodies, is expressed in the withdrawal of one, i.e. ICC in favor of SC[10].

In other contexts, an attitude of active cooperation on the part of SC can be decisive for allowing ICC to perform its function effectively. The need for the judicial activity of the Court to be supported by a prompt and incisive use of the powers of intervention of SC emerges clearly in the context of cooperation and mutual legal assistance (Chapter IX of the Statute). The StICC does not provide ICC with the coercive tools necessary to make its judicial action effective. In the collection of evidence in the capture of the accused and more generally in the execution of some of its own decisions, ICC depends entirely on the assistance of the States, if the latter do not intend to cooperate with the action of SC. In the particular sphere of judicial assistance and collaboration, the discretion and autonomy of SC decision can end up hindering or totally preventing the effective functioning of ICC. The lack of effective cooperation by the States and SC was also the cause of numerous problems in the repressive action of the ad hoc courts.

It should also be noted that the crucial role that the SC could be called upon to play in matters of cooperation and mutual legal assistance in the event that States do not spontaneously intend to collaborate with ICC may have some impact on the decision-making autonomy of the Court. It is difficult to imagine that the Prosecutor and the ICC judges, aware of being able to find a coercive intervention of SC, oppose the requests coming from the latter and take direct decisions to crack the relationships with an organ whose work it can be decisive to guarantee the effectiveness of one's action.

In other spheres of interaction between ICC and SC, the possible tensions between claims for autonomy and cooperation needs emerge in different forms. The suppression of the crime of aggression falls within these distinct areas of possible encounter between the activities of the two institutions. At the conference of Rome the definition of the crime of aggression for the purpose of exercising ICC's competence was postponed to a subsequent revision of the Statute which took place in Kampala in 2010, after years of intense negotiations. Following ratification of these amendments by more than 30 States and the decision of the Assembly of States to activate ICC's jurisdiction over this particular crime[11], the ICC will be able to prosecute individuals suspected of having committed an

[10]G.M. LENTNER, The role of the United Nations Security Council towards the International Criminal Court. Resolution 1970 (2011) and its challenges to international criminal justice, in International Criminal Law Review, 14 (2), 2014, pp. 9ss.

[11]Assembly of States Parties, Draft Resolution proposed by the Vice-President of the Assembly activation of the jurisdiction of the Court over the crime of aggression, ICC-ASP/16/L-10, 14 December 2017.

aggression crime since 17 July 2018[12]. Although there are still no elements of practice in the light of which to evaluate the attitudes assumed by the two bodies, the evolution of the statutory discipline on the crime of aggression and the role attributed to ICC and SC in the matter offer some food for thought. In principle, an attempt was made to ensure a form of coordination between the action of the two institutions by providing that the Prosecutor, before acting on its own motu, is required to verify that the SC has not already ascertained the existence of a state act of aggression against the UN Secretary General, attaching all the necessary information and documents of the situation investigated. The judicial organ's autonomy needs re-emerge to the crime for a certain period of time (6 months), after which, even in the absence of an investigation by SC, the Prosecutor is free to act. Also in this context it can be observed how the StICC tries to find a coordination between the two bodies, called to intervene in identical material circumstances (the aggression by one State towards another), albeit in distinct areas (state and individual responsibility) and with different consequences (possible intervention of SC and criminal repression). However appreciable the considerable autonomy guaranteed to ICC towards the statutory changes may be considered, it is worth underlining that the scope of this modification of StICC could have rather limited effects. In this regard it is sufficient here to remember that States can make use of the opt-out clause and not accept ICC's jurisdiction over this single crime.

Finally, as with any other international organization, the autonomy and effectiveness of ICC action are largely linked to the financial support that will be guaranteed to it by the Member States[13]. As regards financial liability, StICC has also proposed the possibility that UN will bear the costs of the judicial activity of ICC, at least in the event that SC requests the exercise of the criminal action and makes use of ICC. If a certain degree of autonomy of ICC is guaranteed by the funds that the States Parties make available to the organization, requests to open investigations from SC may require a further and additional sacrifice in terms of costs and resources used. This is why it is hoped that the UN, with a view to collaborating with ICC, will undertake to finance those expenses of the ICC's judicial activity occasioned by the requests of SC. On this point two conflicting needs of autonomy clash: The one necessary to guarantee the effective operation of ICC, through an economic support that allows ICC to perform the functions assigned to it (from SC itself) and that of UN, and in particular from the General Assembly on budget matters.

As we have tried to highlight in these first pages, the investigation is aimed at studying how the possible interactions between ICC and SC, summarily

---

[12]In argument see also the Resolution adopted by the General Assembly on 4 November 2009 in relation to the difference and scope of ICC in the future and the work finished until know for the impunity of the crimes ((GA, A/RES/74/6) of 12 November 2019).

[13]T. INGADOTTIR, The financing of international adjudication, in C.P.R. ROMANO, K.J. ALTER, Y. SHANNY, The oxford handbook of international adjudication, Oxford University Press, Oxford, 2014, pp. 596ss.

illustrated here, move between claims of autonomy and cooperation needs. It seems essentially to investigate in which hypotheses judicial independence and political discretion are legitimate prerogatives claimed by the two bodies and when the implicit reference to these needs also comes from the harmonic dynamic relationship of ICC and ICC that is in contrast with the rules and principles governing relations between the two bodies.

In evaluating all the critical issues that the possible interactions between ICC and SC raise, it is worth making two final general considerations. A first element that the statutory regulations highlights and that should be made explicit now is the need of ICC to support SC in order to be able to carry out its judicial function fully and effectively. This emerges clearly and has already been noted in the field of cooperation and of mutual legal assistance. Since States on whose territory international crimes have been committed or citizens are suspected of being perpetrators, ICC will necessarily must be able to carry out its own investigations, to hear the witnesses capture the defendants. It is possible that the prosecution also requires an active and decisive commitment of SC, the only body that through its coercive powers can force the reticent States to engage in collaborative behavior towards the international tribunal.

The second consideration somewhat mitigates the effects of the first. Despite being in a second position, SC in the choice of how to interact with ICC exposes itself to some risks that cannot be underestimated. Particularly, ICC could be perceived by States (or at least by some States) as an instrument that SC can dispose[14]. The belief could essentially consolidate and in this sense there are already many criticisms that the permanent members of SC (and among them the United States, China and the Russian Federation that are not part of the StICC) claim to enjoy some, hardly acceptable, privileges: Selectively criminalize the ruling classes of the other states of the international community through the rhetoric of the fight against impunity and at the same time protect their citizens and those of allied countries from ICC action[15]. The arbitrary and improper use of powers assigned to it by the UN Charter and the exercise of which StICC relates some important consequences on the action of ICC, can however significantly affect the authoritativeness of SC decisions. If some of the limits imposed by the right to discretion in politics are clearly overstepped and distorted, SC could see

---

[14]B. GRAEFRATH, International crimes and collective security, in E. SUY, K. WELLES, International law, theory and practice essays in honor of Eric Suy, Martinus Nijhoff Publishers, Hague, 1998, pp. 238ss. T. SQUATRITO, O.R. YOUNG, A. FOLLESDAL, G. ULSTEIN, The performance of international Courts and Tribunals, Cambridge University Press, Cambridge, 2018. F. BAETENES, Legitimacy of unseen actors in international adjudication, Cambridge University Press, Cambridge, 2019. T. SUQATRITO, Resourcing global justice: The resource management design of international courts, in Global Policy, 8 (5), 2017, pp. 67ss.

[15]M. DRUMBL, Atrocity, punishment and international law, Cambridge University Press, Cambridge, 2007, pp. 152ss. R. THAKUR, The United Nations, peace and security: From collective security to the responsibility to protect, Cambridge University Press, Cambridge, 2010, pp. 280ss.

its action delegitimized in the context of international criminal justice and perhaps more generally in the composite dispute of the government for collective security[16].

2. ICC as an autonomous and distinct organization compared to UN. The relationship agreement of 2004

The autonomy of the political sphere assumes an absolute centrality for any Court. It is in fact an essential characteristic and inherent in the function that the Courts are called upon to perform[17] one of the most important variations of this autonomy. It was International Criminal Tribunal for the Former Yugoslavia (ICTY) himself who reminded us the Kompetenz-Kompetenz principle, that is, the prerogative of each jurisdictional body to determine the scope of its competence[18]. It is an inherent and intrinsic power to the same judicial function that indeed, "does not need to be expressly provided for in the constitutive documents"[19].

---

[16]R. THAKUR, The United Nations, peace and security: From collective security to the responsibility to protect, op. cit.

[17]H. RUIZ-FABRI, J.M. SOREL, Indèpendence et impartialitè des juges internationaux, ed. Pedone, Paris, 2010. A.M. THÉVENOT-WERNER, Le droit des agents internationaux à un recours effectif: Vers un droit comun de la procèdure administrative international, ed. Brill, Bruxelles, 2016. A. VON BOGDANDY, I. VENZKE, In whose name? A public law theory of international adjudication, Oxford University Press, Oxford, 2014.

[18]An investigation into the powers inherent in the judicial function, including at least the interpretation offered by various international jurisdictions, the Kompetenz-Kompetenz principle is that of P. GAETA, Inherent powers of international courts and tribunals, in L.C. VOHRAH, Man's inhumanity to man. Essays on international law in honor of Antonio Cassese, Martinus Nijhoff Publishers, The Hague, London, New York, 2003, pp. 354ss. See also in argument: C. BROWN, The inherent powers of international courts and tribunals, in British Yearbook of International Law, 76 (1), 2005, pp. 196ss. E. LAUTERPACHT, Partial judgments and the inherent jurisdiction of the international court of justice, in V. LOWE, M. FITZMAURICE, Fifty years of the international court of justice. Essays in honor of Sir Robert Jennings, Cambridge University Press, Cambridge, 1996, pp. 466ss. J. LIANG, The inherent jurisdiction and inherent powers of international criminal courts and tribunals: An appraisal of their application, in New Criminal Law Review. An International and Interdisciplinary Journal, 15 (3), 2012, pp. 378ss. L. CRUSZCZYNSKI, W. WERNER, Deference in international courts and tribunals: Standard of review and margin of appreciation, Oxford University Press, Oxford, 2014. Interesting on the proposed examination of the permanent court of arbitration, The Republic of Croatia and the republic of Slovenia, in the matter of an arbitration under the arbitration agreement between the government of the republic of Croatia and the government of the Republic of Slovenia signed on 4 November 2009, Partial award, 30 June 2016, parr. 145ss.

[19]ICTY, Prosecutor v. Tadić, decision on the defence motion for interlocutory appeal on jurisdiction, Appeals chamber, IT-94-1-AR72, 2 October 1995, par. 18. The first to define the concept even if in the different context of the division of competences between states

Within the Rome Statute there are indeed at least two provisions which seem to make this principle explicit. On the one hand art. 119 states that ICC: "Shall satisfy itself the jurisdiction in any case brought before it", on the other hand among the final clauses, there is a rule that provides, in more general terms that: "Any dispute concerning the judicial functions of the Court shall be settled by its decision"(art. 119 (2))[20].

In addition to being a judicial body by its independent nature, the ICC is also from a formal point of view an autonomous organization with its own legal personality as expressly sanctioned by art. 4 of the same founding treaty. The ICC unlike the ad hoc tribunals-subsidiary bodies of the SC created through the powers exercised by the latter on Chapter VII of the UN Charter-was established through a special international treaty, the Rome statute.

It is interesting to observe that as emerges from the work of the International Law Commission (ILC), the conclusion of an international treaty is generally considered "the normal method of setting up an international institution". In the opinion of ILC, even if it had been wished to make the Court part of the UN system, the structure and functioning of this institution would still have required "to be agreed on by States". Ultimately compared to a decision of SC or from the General Assembly (GA) only the conclusion of a founding treaty would have ensured "a sufficient degree of international support"[21].

Over time, the hypotheses of a ICC institution as the main or subsidiary body of UN have been discarded[22]. Their direct to create a criminal chamber within the ICC through a complex charter modification process of UN or to establish a new subsidiary body of the Organization, through a SC or of GA

---

and the Bund was H. BÖHLAU, Competenz-competenz? Erörterungen zu artikel 78 der Verfassung des Nordeutschen Reichs, ed. Veit, Leipzig, 1869. C.R.F. AMERASINGHE, Jurisdiction of international tribunal, Martinus Nijhoff Publishers, The Hague, London, New York, 2003. I.F.I. SHIHATA, The power of the international court of determine its own jurisdiction, ed. Springer, The Hague, 1965. L. BOISSON DE CHAZOURNES, The principle of compètence de la compètence in international adjudication and its role in an era of multiplication of courts and tribunals, in M.H. ARSANJANI, J.K. COGAN, S. WIESSNER, Looking to the future. Essays on international law in honor of W. Michael Reisman, Martinus Nijhoff Publishers, Leiden, 2011, pp. 1028ss.

[20]F. BAETENES, Legitimacy of unseen actors in international adjudication, op. cit.,

[21]Report of the international law commission on the work of its forty-fourth session, official records of the General Assembly, forty-seventh session, Supplement n. 10, UN doc. A/47/10, 4 May-24 July 1992, pp. 64ss.

[22]These hypotheses emerge from the analysis of several documents including. Report of the International Law Commission to the General Assembly on the work of its forty-sixth session, in Yearbook of International Law Commission, 1994, vol. II, pp. 27-28 and Report of the Preparatory Committee on the establishment of an International Criminal Court, vol. II, UN doc. A/51/22, 13 September 1996, p. 4. If a third party was taken into consideration, that is to say, to frame the ICC as a specialized institution through a liaison agreement pursuant to art. 57 and 63 with the Economic and Social Council. For further details see: J. DUGARD, Obstacles on the way of an international criminal court, in Cambridge Law Journal, 56 (2), 1997, pp. 330ss.

resolution have not been successful. The reasons why it was decided not to travel these different roads have already been highlighted in doctrines and can be found in the work of the ILC itself. The impracticability of the first hypothesis was associated with the difficulty of proceeding with an amendment to the Charter, while the second way would have according to many considerably compromised the autonomy and capacity of ICC action, whose jurisdictional activity would have been excessively linked the will of the UN political bodies[23]. The choices made appear to be dictated by practical reasons (the difficulties in changing the Charter) and by the need to preserve the independence and autonomy of the international tribunal as much as possible. Finally, as recalled by the Commission itself, the institution through a special international treaty would have more guaranteed the necessary support from the States and a more solid consensual basis[24].

A fundamental element that emerges from the regulatory framework drawn up by the StICC is therefore that the ICC as an independent body with its own international legal personality is not formally subject to the UN Charter. Some principles enshrined in the Charter are undoubtedly universal in nature and ICC has also committed itself through the relationship agreement which will shortly be respected but the international tribunal is not part of that system. The jurisdiction and functioning of ICC as required by art. 1 of the treaty of Rome: "Shall be governed by the provisions of this Statute"[25]. This is the regulatory parameter that defines and measures the legitimacy of the Court's repressive action.

The ICC has a permanent and universal character. It does not have that

---

[23]See in particular: Report of the Preparatory Committee on the establishment of an International Criminal Court, vol. I, UNJ doc. A/51/22, 13 September 1996, par. 26. report of the International Law Commission to the General Assembly on the work of the International Law Commission to the General Assembly on the work of its forty-fifth session, in Yearbook of International Law Commission, 1993, pp. 16ss. For further details see: L. CONDORELLI, L. VILLALPANDO, Relationship of the court with the United Nations, in A. CASSESE, P. GAETA, J.R.W.D. JONES, The Rome statute of the international criminal court. A commentary, Oxford University Press, Oxford, 2002, pp. 220ss. L.S. WEXLER, The proposed permanent international criminal court. An appraisal, in Cornell International Law Journal, 29 (3), 1996, pp. 667ss. D. H. KRIEGER, A permanent international court and the United Nations systems, in N. AL-NAUMI, R. MEESE, International legal issues arising under the United Nations decade of international law, Martinus Nijhoff Publishers, Hague, 1995, pp. 774ss. M. VAGIAS, J. DUGARD, The territorial jurisdiction of the International Criminal Court, Cambridge University Press, Cambridge, 2014, pp. 46ss. F. BENEDETTI, K. BONNEAU, J. WASHBURN, Negotiating the International Criminal Court: New York to Rome 1994-1998, Martinus Nijhoff Publishers, The Hague, 2013.

[24]See also: Report of the International Law Commission on the work of its forty-fourth session, Official records of the General Assembly, forty-seventh session, supplement n. 10, UN doc. A/47/10, 4 May-24 July 1992.

[25]F. BENEDETTI, K. BONNEAU, J. WASHBURN, Negotiating the International Criminal Court: New York to Rome 1994-1998, op. cit.

special and transitory nature that characterized the experiences of the nineties. The permanent character has several effects of no small importance. Permanence offers the possibility to the Commission of International Crimes, at least in theory, of an immediate reaction, since the UN States do not have to devise new and appropriate mechanisms of criminal repression. Even more important for the purposes of this investigation is the fact that the ICC action is governed by pre-established statutory rules that should not at least in theory be adapted or modified according to the different political contexts in which the Court is called to operate. As mentioned in part, SC activity effects on ICC's action are regulated even with the difficulties that such regulation entails in StICC. In other words, we wanted to give a stable and as far as possible foreseeable shape to the role that the SC can play with respect to ICC action[26]. The difficult task to which we tried to carry out was essentially to trace a legal framework that would allow us to reconcile the contingency of political action with the continuity and stability of the judicial function.

Despite the nature of an autonomous organization that the Treaty of Rome confers on ICC, the need to coordinate the judicial activity of ICC with the powers recognized to SC in matters of peacekeeping has been felt since the very first codification work of StICC. It was in fact difficult to imagine that the ICC action in such a delicate area, which produces various effects both on the exercise of some sovereign prerogatives of the States and potentially on the maintenance of international peace and security, could leave aside some connection with the UN and in particular with the SC. Already at the origins of the creation of a permanent tribunal for the suppression of international crimes, an agreement was concluded between this new jurisdiction and UN. This idea emerges clearly in the draft statute drawn up by the ILC on 1994[27] and even earlier in the work of the various UN Committees which have dealt with the issue since the 1950s[28]. So art. 2, StICC provides that ICC "shall be brought into relationship with the UN through an agreement"[29].

This relationship agreement was concluded in 2004 through an articulated procedure that first saw approval by the assembly of States that are part of ICC, the UN General Assembly and then by the UN Secretary General and the ICC President. The pact between the two organizations should have clarified and governed in more detail the nature and content of the different legal relationships that may be established between ICC and UN (and in particular for

[26]L. CONDORELLI, L. VILLALPANDO, Les Nations Unies et les juridictions penales internationales, in J.P. COT, M. FORTEAU, A. PELLET, La charte des Nations Unies commentaire article par article, LGDJ, Paris, 2005, pp. 202ss.

[27]Draft statute for an international criminal court, in Yearbook of the International Law Commission, 1994, vol. II, part two.

[28]Report of the committee on international criminal jurisdiction, UN GAOR, 7th session, supp.n. 11, 1-31 August 1951, UN doc. A/2136 (1952).

[29]F. BENEDETTI, K. BONNEAU, J. WASHBURN, Negotiating the International Criminal Court: New York to Rome 1994-1998, op. cit.

what matters most here, the SC). Several relevant provisions of StICC relating to the coordination mechanisms between the two bodies would have required some clarifications and specifications. Expectations in this regard have largely been disappointed. A single provision art. 17 of the agreement, expressly deals with the cooperation between ICC and SC without however adding much to what is already governed by StICC[30]. The scope of the agreement is not to be underestimated. It establishes some important general principles which should inspire the interactions between ICC and UN organs. In particular, the relationship agreement insists on the need for close cooperation between the two institutions and for constant coordination of their respective actions in compliance with the different purposes that they aim to achieve and with the international treaties that established them[31].

Among the provisions that should be recalled to fully understand the scope and meaning of the agreement there is undoubtedly art. 3. Its content, although of a general nature, consecrates the centrality of the principles of collaboration and coordination in the relationship between ICC and UN and represents the ultimate goal of the understanding between the two institutions in the light of which the statutory provisions should be read and interpreted. The law states that in order to facilitate the effectiveness of their action, the two institutions "shall cooperate closely, whenever appropriate, with each other and consult each other on maters of mutual interest"[32]. In particular, cooperation between organizations must take place "in conformity with the respective provisions of the Charter and Statute"[33].

Before even art. 2 of the agreement states the importance of recognizing and respecting each other's prerogatives and responsibilities. On the one hand, UN recognizes "the Court as an independent permanent judicial institution" (art. 2 (1)). On the other, ICC recognizes the UN responsibilities under the Charter (art. 2 (2)). Finally, this principle can play a decisive role in the reconstruction of the meaning and ratio of the relevant statutory rules and in the determination of the limits of the action of the two bodies, UN and Court respect each other's status and mandate (art. 2 (3))[34].

3. Security Council role in the administration of international criminal justice. The powers attributed by StICC

StICC has granted SC a series of powers aimed at producing various

---

[30]See art. 17 of the statute entitled: Cooperation between the Security Council of the United Nations and the Court.

[31]Even from a purely material and organizational point of view, the two organizations are in close contact with one another. The statute provides, for example, that the assembly of the states parties may hold its sessions in the UN headquarters (art. 112, par. 6).

[32]F. BAETENES, Legitimacy of unseen actors in international adjudication, op. cit.,

[33]F. BAETENES, Legitimacy of unseen actors in international adjudication, op. cit.,

[34]F. BAETENES, Legitimacy of unseen actors in international adjudication, op. cit.,

effects of no small importance on the jurisdictional activity of ICC in order to regulate the relations between the two institutions.

The prerogatives attributed to SC respond to different needs. On the one hand, there are powers clearly inspired by the desire to ensure greater effectiveness of the ICC's action. This is the possibility that the SC activates the investigations of the ICC prosecutor allowing the prosecution even in contexts where this could not be founded in other statutory rules. Also in support of the ICC action there is also the possibility that the SC intervenes to impose obligations of cooperation towards States that do not fulfill their duties of mutual assistance towards ICC. On the other hand, at least one of the most important prerogatives among those recognized by SC and StICC reflects strictly political needs and more particularly the need to protect the discretion of SC in determining the most suitable measures to maintain peace and international security. This refers to the power to suspend ICC's business. Other prerogatives were built with the intention of preserving both spheres of competence of the two bodies as much as possible. In the specific case of the crime of aggression, in fact, an attempt was made to guarantee the prosecutor an independent investigation power over individual crime while at least to some extent protecting the discretion of SC in the assessment provided for by art. 39, UN Charter.

It is now appropriate to specify some of the characteristics of the powers attributed to SC to which reference is being made in general terms. For the moment, we will simply define the essential aspects in order to offer a first picture of the possible relations between the two bodies.

The analysis of the powers recognized to SC by the StICC highlights the various areas in which the need for coordination between the action of the political body and ICC is manifested. SC can through the powers of activation and suspension as well as through its assessment of the Commission of a state act of aggression affect the exercise of jurisdiction by ICC. In the area of judicial assistance and cooperation, the possible intervention of SC can play a crucial role in the execution phase of ICC decisions. Finally, if SC takes advantage of the repressive action of ICC, the UN can make important decisions in financial terms and in material support for the activity of ICC.

The power to activate ICC jurisdiction falls within the so-called trigger mechanisms of prosecution by the Prosecutor. Art. 13 StICC provides that ICC Prosecutor can undertake its investigation activity in three distinct hypotheses. The reporting of a particular situation in which one or more of the crimes subject to ICC jurisdiction ratione materiae may have been committed, may come from a Member State of the Statute (art.13, letter a) of SC (art. 13, letter b) or the Prosecutor may decide on its own motu to open an investigation (art.13, letter c)[35].

Of course, the second hypothesis is of interest here even if it is convenient to make some considerations on the discretion granted to the Prosecutor to act autonomously as it assumes an important importance with a view to safeguarding the independence of ICC. Although limited by the judicial control

---

[35]F. BAETENES, Legitimacy of unseen actors in international adjudication, op. cit.,

of the preliminary chamber that must authorize the investigations (art.15), the attribution to the Prosecutor of the faculty to proceed ex officio concentrates on the hands of this ICC body a power of considerable importance, which increases autonomy of the whole institution but whose exercise is at the same time extremely delicate. Here we limit ourselves to observing that the exercise of this power, however independent, is inevitably conditioned by the political dimension of the situations potentially investigated. In other words, a further example emerges of the possible intertwining between the demands of criminal repression and the political dimension of the conflictual contexts in which ICC operates. The Prosecutor cannot ignore the possibility that its action leads to an escalation of the conflict or somehow negatively affects, the re-establishment of a peaceful coexistence between the parties[36].

For this reason art. 53 (2) (c) StICC provides that the Prosecutor for the purpose of opening an investigation must take into account the various factors of the seriousness of the situation and the interest of the victims and verify in light of these latter elements, which there are substantial reasons to believe that an investigation would not serve the interests of justice. The office of the Prosecutor made clear that the decision not to proceed should be a course of last resort[37]. Although the primary interest of the victims is seeing justice done, the same Prosecutor considers that other essential interests such as their protection must also be taken into consideration[38]. All this to underline that the protection of the

---

[36]See in argument: M.M. DE GUZMAN, Choosing to prosecutor. Expressive selection at the international criminal court, in Michigan Journal of International Law, 33, 2012, pp. 267ss. J.D. OHLIN, Peace, security and prosecutorial discretion, in C. STAHN, G. SLUITER, The emerging practice of the international criminal court, ed. Brill, Bruxelles, 2009, pp. 186ss. W.A. SCHABAS, Prosecutorial discretion v. Judicial activism at the International Criminal Court, in Journal of International Criminal Justice, 6 (4), 2008, pp. 732ss. A.K.A. GREENWALT, Justice without politics? Prosecutorial discretion and the international criminal court, in International Law & Politics, 39, 2007, pp. 584ss. H. OLASOLO, The prosecutor of the ICC before the initiation of investigations. A quasi judicial or a political body?, in International Criminal Law Review, 3 (2), 2003, pp. 88ss. R.J. GOLDSTONE, N. FRITZ, In the interests of justice and independent referral. The ICC prosecutor's unprecedent powers, in Leiden Journal of International Law, 13 (3), 2000, pp. 667ss. C. DE VOS, S. KENDALL, C. STAHN, Contested justice: The politics and practice of International Criminal Court interventions, op. cit., W.A. SCHABAS, The International Criminal Court: A commentary on the Rome statute, Oxford University Press, Oxford, 2016, pp. 846ss. L.E. CARTER, M.S. ELLIS, C. CHERNOR JALLOH, The International Criminal Court in an effective global justice system, Edward Elgar Publishers, Cheltenham, 2016, pp. 176ss.

[37]Office of the Prosecutor, Draft Policy Paper on case selection and prioritarisation, 29 February 2016, p. 11.

[38]Office of the Prosecutor, Policy Paper on the interests of justice, ICC-OTP, September 2007. In making an assessment of the broader political context, the Prosecutor will naturally maintain its own independence even if it will inevitably take into account the positions eventually taken by other subjects and in particular SC: "(...) In situation where the ICC is involved, comprehensive solutions addressing humanitarian security, political

victims (or their family members) as well as other essential interests, can in some cases be better guaranteed through an arrest of the criminal action. In essence, the Prosecutor may believe that the interests of justice can be compressed or temporarily suspended in favor of contingent needs for peace and security[39]. In view of the interactions between ICC and SC it can be observed how the Prosecutor can decide to renounce his investigative activity also in light of SC decisions or measures that are not directly aimed at suspending the criminal action. In other words, the office of the Prosecutor could believe that some resolutions of SC, although they do not manifest themselves in a formal request for suspension of the criminal action, are however indicative of possible impedimental repercussions to the peacekeeping process, deriving from the potential start o continuation of the investigation[40]. More generally, the high rate of politicity of many of the decisions taken in the international criminal justice field whether they are taken by the Prosecutor or SC reveals all the complexity of the function assigned to ICC (and to the Prosecutor in particular) and more generally confirms the idea that this Court is undoubtedly part of a broader global diplomatic network of international politics[41].

As regards more specifically the activation power exercised by SC, the essential element is the legal basis on which the request sent to ICC Prosecutor must necessarily rest. SC action must be attributable to Chapter VII of the UN Charter[42] and have as its presupposition the existence of a threat to peace, a violation of peace or an act of aggression. Another central element on which we

---

development and justice elements will be necessary. The office will seek to respect the mandate of those engaged in other areas but will pursue its own judicial mandate independently (...)". The same policy paper of the Prosecutor, has declared that: "(...) Were viewed ads clearly separate from the interests of peace with the latter falling outside of the ICC's mandate (...)". See in argument: J. KYLE, The "new legal reality"? Peace, punishment and Security Council referrals to the ICC, in Transational Law and Contemporary Problems, 109, 2015, pp. 134ss.

[39]Indeed, some words of the Prosecutor Bensouda do not seem to go in this direction but rather keep the needs of peace and those of justice distinct, with the ICC called upon to safeguard only the victims: "As the ICC, is an independent and judicial institution, it cannot take into consideration the interests of peace, which is the mandate of other institutions, such as the United Nations Security Council (...)". F. BENSOUDA, International justice and diplomacy: Partnering for peace and international security, in Acadèmie Diplomatique Internationale-Forum for new diplomacy, 20 March 2013.

[40]M.R. BRUBACHER, Prosecutorial discretion within the international criminal court, in Journal of International Criminal Justice, 2 (1), 2004, pp. 84ss.

[41]A. CASSESE, Is the ICC still having teething problems?, in Journal of International Criminal Justice, 4, 2006, pp. 434ss. D. BOSCO, Rough justice, Oxford University Press, Oxford, 2014. K.A. RODMAN, P. BOOTH, Manipulated commitments: The International Criminal Court in Uganda, in Human Rights Quarterly, 35 (2), 2016, pp. 274ss. N.N. JURDI, The International Criminal Court and national court: A contentious relationship, ed. Routledge, London & New York, 2016.

[42]D. WHITTLE, The limits of legality and the United Nations Security Council: Applying the extralegal measures model to chapter VII action, op. cit.

will focus during the investigation is the subject of the referral expressed in the drafting of art. 13 through the term situation. It is clear that determining the content of this notion is crucial for defining the limits of the scope and nature of the activation of investigations by SC.

StICC also asks UN to assume its own financial responsibility towards ICC, in the event that it is precisely the SC that activates its jurisdictional activity. The relevant provision, art. 115, lett. b) StICC establishes that the UN must follow up requests for triggering investigations from SC, i.e. financial support for the Court. To this end, the same statutory provision however recognizes the need for prior authorization of GA. The problem of coordination between the action of the two organizations derives here from the budgetary role that within the UN is reserved to GA. The risk that lies ahead is the compression of the prerogatives of this body in matters of budget through a provision contained in an international treaty establishing a new and distinct organization. Trying to preserve the powers of GA on expenses of the UN, art. 115 StICC seems more than anything else to propose to encourage a correct coordination between the requests that the SC can legitimately make towards the ICC and the needs for its effective functioning with respect to which the financial component plays a fundamental role[43].

A further area of interaction concerns SC power to suspend the jurisdictional activity of ICC. This is the power of deferral, governed by art. 16 StICC. This is one of the most controversial provisions of the Treaty of Rome and on which there were more discussions and contrasts during the preparatory work. The controversial are the first elements of practice relating to the use of this power. Central aspect of the exercise of the deferral is once again the fact that SC decision to request the interruption of the criminal action must be based on the powers provided by Chapter VI of the UN Charter and on the assumption therefore that one of the conditions contemplated exists in art. 39. Moreover, the suspension of the criminal action can be of a temporary nature only, the request being limited to a period of 12 months. By express statutory provision, this request can be renewed. SC should in practice check at the end of 12 months, if the conditions that led to the arrest of the prosecution of the main perpetrators of serious international crimes in the name of peace and security maintenance needs still exist.

The possible exercise of SC referral and deferral powers plays a crucial role in the functioning of ICC jurisdictional activity and characterizes the interactions between the two bodies. Both these provisions are characterized by a rather concise drafting which leaves the interpreter the solution to a series of anything but marginal questions. The particular drafting of articles (13 (b) and 16) in question is the result of complicated political compromises. More generally, in addition to the hermeneutical issues concerning the individual provisions, the parameters and boundaries of a possible judicial control of ICC on SC's requests are not clear in StICC. Equally indeterminate are the limits to the discretion of SC political decisions made on the basis of Chapter VII of the UN Charter and which

---

[43]F. BAETENES, Legitimacy of unseen actors in international adjudication, op. cit.,

in the light of the statutory provisions can produce effects on ICC action. The delimitation of these boundaries lends itself to different interpretations and can be at the origin of claims for autonomy and spaces of political or judicial freedom in potential conflict with the needs of cooperation and the effectiveness of the action of the two bodies. And this in the event that the goals of peace and justice cannot find a point of convergence.

In this perspective of collaboration and convergence between the action of the two institutions, an entire chapter of StICC (IX) is then dedicated to cooperation and judicial assistance and provides in some of its provisions an important role of SC. In this particular area, the discipline of relations between ICC and SC takes on a more than anything else and inevitably exhortative character. The StICC cannot directly impose cooperation obligations on UN bodies. These have been assumed although in rather generic terms through the relationship agreement between ICC and UN.

If in the matter of mutual assistance the relationships between the two bodies are inspired by the need for coordination and cooperation, the relevant provisions necessarily give the discretion and decision-making autonomy of SC the power to give or not follow up to possible ICC requests for help. ICC can only inform SC following an exercise of the referral power by the latter in the event that a State not part of StICC does not comply with an ad hoc agreement or a cooperation agreement previously reached with ICC (art 87 (5)). In this regulatory context, ICC cannot do anything else in practice than to exert through its requests and decisions a series of pressures to convince SC of the necessity and importance of its intervention. In essence, in the absence of cooperation from States, the framework drawn up by StICC limits the possibility of implementing the decisions of the Court and making their requests effective to the voluntary (and inevitably discretionary) assistance of SC. A problem that arises in this particular area is that of understanding whether the legal regime established by StICC regarding cooperation and mutual legal assistance obligations can be changed and how by SC decisions.

Still to be verified are the effects that the revisions planned at Kampala Conference in relation to the crime of aggression could produce in the dynamics of the relations between SC and ICC. Relevant for the purposes of this investigation is the introduction of art. 15 bis, adopted by the StICC review conference and relating to the conditions of prosecution for the crime of aggression[44]. In particular, par. 6 of the new provision provides that the Prosecutor, when he believes there are elements to proceed with an investigation into the crime of aggression, is required to ascertain first whether the SC has already expressed himself on the existence of an act of aggression by part of the State concerned and notify the situation of its attention to the UN Secretary General, attaching all the necessary information. Par. 7 then recognizes the possibility after 6 months from the notification and in the case of inertia of SC,

---

[44]Conference of revision of the StICC, Kampala 31 May-21 June 2010, Resolution RC/Res. 6, adopted at the 13th plenary meeting on 11 June 2010 by consensus.

the Prosecutor proceeds independently in the investigation of the Commission of a crime of aggression subject to authorization by the preliminary chamber and except of course the action of the Court by exercising its power of deferral. If the case of a referral of SC is excluded, the crime of aggression exactly like the other crimes under the ICC jurisdiction, cannot be prosecuted for events that occurred on the territory or committed by citizens of a State not part of StICC or of a State part that not accepted the changes occurred by the Kampala Conference. A series of coordination problems between ICC and SC can also arise on a substantial level. The introduction of art. 8 bis can place the ICC bodies in front of the difficulty of attributing any findings made by SC in this context to state acts of aggression which, by virtue of the new provision, can be the prerequisite for the repressive action of ICC.

The effect of attributing to SC a series of powers and prerogatives capable of affecting the ICC action is to accord a certain importance to the political decisions that the UN organ typically adopts towards the judicial activity of ICC. In other words, each of the powers here described in a more or less incisive way reserves to SC some prerogatives whose performance can produce a series of legal or material effects on the jurisdictional activity of ICC. The exercise of these powers can only be subject to the typical methods of adoption of decisions by SC and of course to the political dynamics that determine their choices. It then becomes essential for the purposes of this investigation to understand the different interactions that political and judicial bodies can have. In particular, placing this analysis in the perspective of ICC and StICC it is crucial to determine whether and to what extent this jurisdiction can make some form of union on the content of the political decisions made by SC towards it and in some way limit its effects.

4. Coordination problems of political and judicial bodies in the international legal system

The existence of a series of considerable difficulties in regulating possible interactions between political and judicial bodies is shared by any legal system and sphere of public law. The evolution of modern constitutional systems has always been marked by the constant search for delicate institutional balances that allow to reconcile two distinct and fundamental needs, i.e. a) preserve legislator's discretion in production of law and, b) guarantee judicial control over legitimacy and correctness of those chosen in the light of values and founding principles of the social community of reference. The problem of defining limits and preparing the consequent apparatus of controls on the exercise of a whole series of powers through which state officials determine the direction of public policies is also at the center of administrative law.

In state systems, the need to define the different spheres of influence and competence of the political and judicial bodies derives from a cardinal principle of modern legal systems, i.e. the separation of powers. The concrete implementation of this fundamental principle lives in a constant tension between the will of political orders to preserve their sphere of decision-making freedom and the action of judicial bodies which often mainly through their own interpretative activity adapt, integrate and in some cases modify or even remove the choices made by the executive and legislative bodies in light of the circumstances of the specific case or of what they believe to be the changed will of the social community of reference[45].

In principle, the political bodies guarantee a greater representativeness of the community of affiliates and for this reason they should be in the best position to determine community's interests. They may not be able to grasp the social changes that have occurred over time or may not enjoy the independence of judgment necessary to protect the rights of the subjects not represented by those who are temporarily in power. More generally, the executive and legislative bodies could somehow abuse the discretion of their decision-making power or simply not correctly interpret the meaning and exact scope of certain guarantees or fundamental rules of the system. On the other hand, no less problems arise from the idea of state or government judges where the power to identify the founding principles of the community is concentrated exclusively on the hands of the judicial organs. The delicate objective of each legal system is to guarantee the prerogatives of the bodies to which the task of determining the political orientations of the community of affiliates has been assigned but at the same time to prepare some forms of judicial control over the compatibility in the political choices made by those bodies with the basic rules of the order. In short, at the center of the relationship between politics and justice there is the eternal contrast between the importance of leaving the pursuit of collective interests to political discretion and the ascertaining and application of law to judges.

Some fundamental characteristics of the international legal system make it particularly complex despite the numerous attempts to do so[46], i.e. the transposition of models and categories typical of domestic law into international legal experience. It is all too obvious to note that the international system does not have properly legislative bodies or inevitably judges of the laws. The difficulty of attributing precise legislative, executive and judicial functions to the various subjects of the system makes the manifestation of a real separation of powers fatally elusive. Moreover, the particular conformation of the international legal system has a series of repercussions on the same representativeness of the political bodies and more generally on the democratic rate of the system[47].

---

[45]C. MÖLLERS, The three branches, Oxford University Press, Oxford, 2013. We will not deal with this investigation of the problem of the separation of internal powers of the ICC itself which raises a series of issues of no little importance. For some interesting insights on the theme see: R. RAAB, H. BEVERS, The international criminal court and the separation of powers, in International Organizations Law Review, 3(1), 2006, pp. 94ss.

[46]C.W. JENKS, Some constitutional problems of international organizations, in British Yearbook of International Law, 11, 1945, pp. 12ss. C. ROSS, Contribution of the United Nations: Analysis of structure and functions, ed. Rinehart, New York, 1950.

[47]It was the ICTY itself that recalled the absence of organs with strictly legislative functions: "(...) There is however no legislature in the technical sense of the term in the UN system and more generally in the world community. That is to say, there exists no corporate

Attempts to transpose models within the international system would lead, according to the most severe critics, to misleading analysis of the role of SC. Those seeking parallels between international legal experience and internal legal systems often conclude that the SC as a legislator lacks democratic legitimacy and as an almost judicial body should follow certain rule of law principles and be subject to judicial review[48]. According to these critical reconstructions, all consequences that would derive from wrong assumptions since the tasks assigned to SC, and more generally the role it plays in the international legal system, do not find precise correspondences in the typical functions of the political bodies of the internal legal systems. According to somewhat opposed conceptions, a process of constitutionalization of the international order not only found a fundamental moment in the ratification of UN Charter but would also have produced a series of extremely important regulatory repercussions in all the different areas of international law and towards all the actors who work in it, i.e. the SC[49].

---

organs formally unpowered to enact laws directly binding on international legal subjects (...)", ICTY, Prosecutor v. Tadić, decision on the defence motion for interlocutory appeal on jurisdiction, Appeals Chamber, IT-94-1-AR72, 2 October 1995, par. 43. The very concept of separation of powers perhaps does not lend itself to being used except with due caution, to the peculiar context of the international order. In a beautiful script of the late eighties, it was indeed observed that in a non-institutionalized order such as the international one there is no place for a judicial power. There is instead for a judicial function and this because even though carrying out the same type of work of their colleagues in domestic law, decision-making authority is not based on any institutional sovereign that is legally superior to the subjects of the dispute to be resolved. In the context of international criminal courts, at least in part that verticality typical of the exercise of the judiciary is sought, and the reference to some fundamental principles, typical of the internal legal systems such as the separation of powers, seems to make the professional deformation and intellectual myopia of the jurist trained in the cosmology of domestic law. All expressions used was referred to: O. SCHACHTER, International law in theory and practice. Developments in international law, ed. Springer, Berlin, 2001, pp. 208ss. M. IOVANE, L'influence de la multiplication des juridictions internationale sur l'application du droit international, in Recueil des cours, ed. Brill, Bruxelles, vol. 383, 2017, pp. 322ss.

[48]M. WOOD, Constitutionalization of international law. A skeptical voice, in K.H. KAIKOBAD, BOHLANDER, International law and power. Perspectives on legal order and justice. Essays in honor of Colin Warbrick, ed. Brill, Dordrecht, 2009, pp. 96ss. D. PEAT, Comparative reasoning in international courts and tribunals, Cambridge University Press, Cambridge, 2019, pp. 50ss. N. TSAGOURIAS, N.D. WHITE, Collective security. Theory law and practice, Cambridge University Press, Cambridge, 2013.

[49]B. FASSBENDER, The United Nations charter as constitution of the international community, in Columbia Journal of Transnational Law, 36, 1998, pp. 530ss. R. MACDONALD, The charter of the United Nations in constitutional perspective, in Australian Yearbook of International Law, 20, 1999, pp. 206ss. P.M. DUPUY, The constitutional dimension of the charter of the United Nations revisited, in Max Planck United Nations Yearbook, 1997, pp. 5ss. T. FRANCK, Is the UN Charter a constitution?, in J.A. FROWEIN, K. SCHARIOTH, I. WINKELMANN, R. WOLFRUM, Verhandeln für den Frieden. Liber amicorum Tono Eitel, C.H. Beck, Berlin, 2003, pp. 96ss. This last author identifies some features of the charter perpetuity, indelibleness, primacy and institutional

Particularly, one can imagine the existence of some constitutional limits to SC action and question the legitimacy of acts of a general and abstract nature incompatible with the poor representativeness of that body or assume that the International Court of Justice (ICJ) develop an international constitutional court role with the power to syndicate any political decision[50]. It can be objected that even if it is admitted that it can be attributed to the UN Charter the value of a world constitution as a regulatory instrument that contains some of the fundamental principles of the international legal order, it remains formally and first of all the treaty establishing a particular international organization and regulating the functioning of the organs part of that specific system.

These simple findings introduce some elements of complexity in the study of the relations between political and judicial bodies in the international legal experience. On a regulatory level, it is difficult to think of the power to reconstruct general rules applicable to the discipline of such relationships. When these bodies operate within the same organization, it is the rules of the organization often contained in the founding treaty of the same that govern the behavior and interactions of the bodies it has set up. These rules for coordinating the action of the subjects operating within a given system can of course be more or less precise. The variety of contents of these rules according to the different international organizations is at the origin of the wide heterogeneity of relations that can develop between political and jurisdictional bodies in the international legal system. The nature of these relationships can only depend on how it was decided to regulate those relationships within a given organization. The criteria for coordination between bodies and the limits and methods of any judicial control over political choices can for example be highly evolved and disciplined with a

---

autochthony, which would make it definitely to a constitution than to an ordinary contractual normative arrangement (pp. 102ss). C. EL SCHWÖBEL, Global constitutionalism in international legal perspective, Martinus Nijhoff Publishers, The Hague, 2011, A. BIANCHI, International law theories: An inquiry into different ways of thinking, Oxford University Press, Oxford, 2016. J. KLABBERS, A. WALLENDAHL, Research handbook on the law of international organizations, Edward Elgar Publishers, Cheltenham, 2011. C. DAU, Die völkerrechtliche Zulässigkeit von Selbstverteidigung gegen nicht-staatliche Aktueure, Nomos Verlag, Baden Baden, 2018. A. VON BOGDANDY, I. VENZKE, In whose name? A public law theory of international adjudication, op. cit.,

[50]A. PETERS, Global constitutionalism revisited, in International Legal Theory, 11, 2005, pp. 65ss, which is affirmed that: "(...) Constitutional arguments can inform critique directed at the lacking of representativeness of SC. They can confirm the existence of legal boundaries of that organ's inaction and suggest that ICJ develop its role as an international constitutional court reviewing the Security Council (...)". For further details see: J.G. VAN MULLIGEN, Global constitutionalism and the objective purport of the international legal order, in Leiden Journal of International Law, 24 (2), 2011. C. MAC AMHLAIGH, Harmonizing global constitutionalism., Cambridge University Press, Cambridge, 2016. A. O'DONOGHUE, Constitutionalism in global constitutionalism, Cambridge University Press, Cambridge, 2014.

considerable degree of precision or rather marked by a certain indeterminacy of the relevant rules and put more to practice the bodies involved under precise legal coordination rules[51].

Beyond the difficulty of identifying common models of interaction between political and judicial bodies within the different subsystems that make up the international one, a further problem is given by the fact that these coordination rules precisely because they are internal to a particular pact system they are not necessarily able to guarantee effective dialogue and above all, harmonious coordination with the other systems. On the one hand, it is necessary that these connection rules are interpreted and applied uniformly by the various bodies to which they are directed. On the other hand, it is essential that the external bodies, which usually operate in a separate and in turn autonomous system, respect or in any case adapt from time to time to coordination rules set up within a regulatory system that is foreign to them. In the case of divergent positions, the problem then arises of understanding whether and possibly who is entitled to express the last word to determine the correct interpretation and application of the relevant rules. It is necessary to establish, if necessary, the effects produced by the persistence of conflicting attitudes.

In the specific case covered by this investigation, it is necessary first of all to understand how the statutory rules aimed at relating ICC and SC must be interpreted. It will then be necessary to determine in the light of the interpretation these coordination rules whether and to what extent the jurisdictional body (the ICC) has the power to syndicate whether the political body (the SC) has operated within the limits and in accordance with these statutory rules. It is then a question of determining the possible legal consequences for the States, in the event that the two bodies take on conflicting positions.

Besides the possible existence of internal rules of a specific organization aimed at regulating any interactions with bodies belonging to other legal systems, there are also general coordination techniques specific to the international system. The latter should allow in substance to link the action of the various actors of the international legal system and to regulate in some way their interaction[52]. These techniques operate on a regulatory level and can therefore be useful to resolve or in any case avoid conflicts between provisions belonging to different legal

---

[51]The most immediate and illustrative comparison is that between EU legal system which sets up an articulated series of jurisdictional procedures and mechanisms for the control of the legitimacy of the acts of the political organs and UN within which it is difficult to reconstruct the limits of a possible judicial review of ICJ on political decisions. In this last particular context the material behaviors of the different actors seem to assume a preponderant role. For further details see: A. HAMONIC, Les relations entre l'Union europèenne et l'ONU dans le domaine de la gestion des crises, ed. Larcier, Bruxelles, 2018.

[52]It is sufficient here to underline the centrality of the problem to recall the work of special rapporteur Martti Koskenniemi on the subject of fragmentation. See in particular on the fragmentation of international law: Difficulties arising from the diversification and expansion of international law. Report of the study group of the International Law Commission, A/CN.4/L.682, 13 April 2006.

systems but do not offer criteria for coordination, supremacy or subordination of the action of the institutions involved. A clear example is art. 13 (3) (c) Vienna Convention on Law of Treaties (VCLT)[53] which reflects the customary rule of the systemic interpretation criterion and to which a crucial importance is attributed in order to connect the different legal systems that make up the international legal system[54]. Another coordination rule which, although contained within a specific treaty, has a general character is art. 103 of the UN. This standard indicates a prevalence (at least for states) of the standards produced within a given system over those belonging to all the other subsystems, by establishing the supremacy of the obligations for states deriving from their membership of the UN over other conventional obligations.

During the investigation, on the one hand we will try to reconstruct and determine the content of the particular statutory provisions governing the relations between ICC and SC and on the other to understand the role that general coordination techniques can play in resolving possible conflicts regulations that may arise in the interactions between the two bodies.

---

[53]See ex multis: I. BUGA, Modification of treaties by subsequent practice, Oxford University Press, Oxford, 2018. D. PEAT, Comparative reasoning in international courts and tribunals, Cambridge University Press, Cambridge, 2019. M. FITZMAURICE, O. ELIAS, P. MERKOURIS (eds), Treaty interpretation and the Vienna Convention on the Law of Treaties, 30 years on, Martinus Nijhoff, The Hague, 2010, pp. 9ss. G. NOUTE, Treaties and subsequent practice, Oxford University Press, Oxford, 2013, pp. 224ss. E. BJORGE, The evolutionary interpretation of treaties, Oxford University Press, Oxford, 2014. O. CORTEN, P. KLEIN, The Vienna Conventions on the law of treaties. A commentary, Oxford University Press, Oxford, 2011. O. DÖRR, Article 31. General rule of interpretation, in O. DÖRR, K. SCHMALENBACH (a cura di), Vienna Convention on the Law of Treaties. A commentary, Springer, Heidelberg-New York 2012, pp. 536ss. D. ROSENTRETER, Article 31 (3) c) of the Vienna convention on the law of treaties and the principle of systemic integration in international investment law and arbitration, ed. Nomos, Baden-Baden, 2015, pp. 217ss. M. SAMSO, High hopes, scant resources: a word of scepticism about the anti-fragmentation function of article 31(3)(c) of the Vienna Convention on the Law of Treaties, in Leiden Journal of International Law, 24, 2011, pp. 5ss. J.M. SOREL, V. BORÉ EVENO, Article 31. General rule of interpretation, in O. CORTEN, P. KLEIN, The Vienna Convention on the law of treaties. A commentary, Oxford University Press, Oxford, 2011, pp. 806ss.

[54]C. MCLACHLAN, The principle of systemic integration and article 31 (39 (c) of the Vienna Convention, in International & Comparative Law Quarterly, 54 (2), 2005, pp. 282ss. P. MERKOURIS, Article 31 (3) (C) VCLT and the principle of systems integration: Normative shadows in Platon's cave, ed. Brill, The Hague, 2015. A. RACHOVITSA, The principal of systemic integration in human rights, in International & Comparative Law Quarterly, 66 (3), 2017, pp. 560ss. G. ORELLANA ZABALZA, The principle of systemic integration. Towards coherent international legal order, Lit Verlag, Münster, 2012, pp. 236ss.

5. Models of interaction between political and judicial bodies: Prevalence, autonomy and limited control

Although inevitably roughly it is possible to try to trace the relationships between SC and ICC to different theoretical reference models that can be distinguished according to the different degree of autonomy recognized by the judicial and political body.

A first model that tends to limit the syndicate power of ICC can be reconstructed starting from an extensive concept of the function performed in this context by art. 103 of the UN Charter. Often this general mechanism of inter-systemic coordination instead of being used as a rule for the solution of regulatory conflicts between conflicting state obligations, has been invoked to sanction the inadmissibility of any claim of judicial control over the political decisions of SC. It is not possible to retrace the numerous interpretations that have been advanced on the content of art. 103, the scope of which appears in the light of application practice to be constantly evolving in recent decades[55]. What is important for an

---

[55]See in argument: J.M. THOUVENIN, Article 103, in J.P. COT, A. PELLET, M. FORTEAU, La charte des Nations Unies, ed. LGDJ, Paris, 2005, pp. 2134ss. C. TOMUSCHAT, International law as a coherent system. Unity or fragmentation?, in M.H. ARSANJANI, J.K. COGAN, R.D. SLOANE, S. WIESSNER, Looking to the future: Essays on international law in honor of W. Michael Reisman, ed. Brill, The Hague, 2011, pp. 338ss. S.R. RATNER, The thin justice of international law: A moral reckoning of the law of nations, Oxford University Press, Oxford, 2015. The primacy of the resolutions of SC on other international obligations has been guaranteed through reference to this provision on several occasions by CJRU. See the known decisions: T-306/01, Yusuf and Al Barakaat international Foundation v. Council and Commission of 21 September 2005, ECLI:EU:T:2005:331, II-03533. E. CANNIZZARO, A Machiavellian moment? The UN security council and the rule of law, in International Organization Law Review, 3, 2006, pp. 190ss. The European Court of Human Rights (ECtHR) has never directly applied art. 103 and has always effectively avoided expressing opinions on the scope of such rules with respect to the human rights obligations of the states party to the European Convention of Human Rights. The ECtHR has in some circumstances referred to the existence of art. 103 to affirm a sort of supremacy of the end of maintaining peace and security. As we can see in case Stichting Mothers of Srebrenica and others v. the Netherlands, application n. 65542/12 of 11 June 2013 and Mothers of Srebrenica v. The state of the Netherlands, 27 June 2017, C/09/295247/HA ZA 07-2973; and Behrami and Behrami v. France and Saramati v. France, Germany and Norway, application n. 71\412/01 and 78166/01 of 2 May 2007, par. 138. According to our opinion the ECtHR would naturally have had to resort to the criterion of effective control (to be interpreted as operational control) and ask which subject had possibly ordered not to remove unexploded cluster bombs: NATO, through the Com-KFOR and/or France, through its own national authorities? Such an operation would certainly not have been easy to carry out, because the scarce information available would not have allowed to easily establish whether the omissive conduct had been the result of decisions taken by the Com-KFOR, or had been caused by indications given to the French contingent by its own command national or, even, had arisen from a choice taken jointly

by the international and national command. It is superfluous to recall that, in the first case, the omissive conduct should have been attributed to NATO, in the second, to France and, in the third, to both subjects. It is good to specify that everything that can be disputed with the Court is the hasty definition of the mandate of KFOR and UNMIK in relation to demining activities, which led her to consider only UNMIK and not KFOR involved in the aforementioned activities; in any case, in light of the factual data as determined by the Grand Chamber, the attribution of the conduct of UNMIK is correctly determined. For further analysis see: G. VERDIRAME, Breaches of the European Convention on Human Rights resulting from the conduct of international organizations, in European Human Rights Law Review, 8, 2008, pp. 220ss. K.W. WATSON, Behrami v. France: constructive blue helmets protect KFOR nations from accountability, in Tulane Journal of International and Comparative Law, 16, 2007-2008, pp. 576ss. Also in this case, a "univocal" interpretation of the attribution of conduct prevails1682, which leads to attributing solely to the UN the responsibility for violations of international law committed during the operation. The Nuhanović case, however, contains an element of greater openness with respect to the Behrami and Saramati sentences: The Court, in fact, envisaged the possibility that, as part of a peace-keeping operation, under certain circumstances, the Dutch government could be held responsible for illegal conduct by acting in a position of "effective control" over UNPROFOR troops. In particular, the judges pointed out that "if it is established, it is a violation of the factual basis on which the attribution is based to the UN rests". The Court therefore acknowledged that the Netherlands could have "effective control" over the contingent and consequently respond internationally to its conduct, in the event that the troops had received orders from the Dutch government to contravene an order deriving from it from the chain of UN command (hypothesis of the cutting-across orders). For further analysis see: A. SARI, Jurisdiction and international responsibility in peace support operations the Behrami and Saramati cases, in Human Rights Law Review, 8, 2008, pp. 152ss. P. KLEIN, Responsabilitè pour les faits commins dans le cadre d'opèrations de paix et ètendue du pouvoir de contrôle de la cour europèenne des droits de l'homme: quelques considèrations critiques sur l'arrêt Behrami et Saramati, in Annuaire Français de Droit International, 53, 2007, pp. 44ss. P. LAGRANGE, Responsabilitè des Etats pour actes accomplis en application du Chapitre VII de la Charte des Nations Unies, in Revue Gènèrale de Droit International Public, 112, 2008, pp. 86ss. T. DANNENBAUM, Translating the standard of effective control into a system of effective accountability: How liability should be apportioned for violation of human rights by member state troop contingents serving as United Nations peace keeping, in Harvard International Law Journal, 51, 2010, pp. 115ss. P. KOUTRAKOS, The EU Common Security and Defence Policy, Oxford University Press, Oxford, 2013. F. NAERT, International law aspects of the EU's Security and Defence Policy, with a particular focus on the law of armed conflicts and human rights, Hart Publishing, Oxford & Oregon, Portland, 2010. P. EECKHOUT, The EU's Common Foreign and Security Policy after Lisbon: From pillar talk to constitutionalism, in A. BIONDI, P. EECKHOUT, S. RIPLEY, (eds.), EU Law after Lisbon, Oxford University Press, Oxford, New York, 2012, pp. 265-291. R.A. WESSEL, Division of international responsibility between the EU and its member States in the area of Foreign, Security and Defence Policy, in Amsterdam Law Forum, 3 (3), 2011, pp. 34-48. Ö.F. DIREK, Responsibility in peace support operations: Revisiting the proper test for attribution conduct and the meaning of the "effective control" Standard, in Netherlands International Law Review, 61, 2014, pp. 7ss. D. SAROOSHI (ed.), Remedies and responsibility for the actions of international organizations, Martinus Nijhoff Publishers,

analysis of the relationship between SC and ICC is the fact that in many cases art. 103 seems to have been invoked on an institutional level as expressing the superiority of the UN system or the supremacy of international security over any other purpose of the system. The concrete application of this conception would lead to recognizing to the SC a sort of unquestionable authority to impose the behaviors that it deems most appropriate for all subjects of the international

---

The Hague, 2014, pp. 444ss. H. KRIEGER, Addressing the accountability gap in peacekeeping. Law-making by domestic courts as a way to avoid UN reform?, in Netherlands International Law Review, 62, 2015, pp. 262ss. C. RYNGAERT, Apportioning responsibility between the UN and member states in UN peace-support operations: an inquiry into the application of the effective control standard after Behrami, in Israel Law Review, 45, 2012, pp. 152ss. N. VOULGARIS, Rethinking indirect responsibility: a study of article 17 of the Draft Articles on the Responsibility of International Organizations, in International Organizations Law Review, 11, 2014, pp. 8ss. D. WHITTLE, The intervention brigade, Monusco, and the application of international humanitarian law to United Nations forces, in Georgetown Journal of International Law, 6, 2014-2015, pp. 838ss. Internally the application of art. 103 as rules that establishes the prevalence of charter obligations of the UN was presented on more than one occasion, see Youssef Nada v. State secretariat for Economic affairs and federal department of economic Affairs, administrative appeal judgment of 14 November 2007, BGE 133 II 450, 1A 45/2007 and Association mothers of Srebrenica and others v. the United Nations, the state of the Netherlands, Netherlands Supreme Court of 13 April 2012, par. 4.3.6. For further analysis see: K. SCHMALENBACH, Preserving the gordian knot: UN legal accountability in the aftermath of Srebrenica, in Netherlands International Law Review, 62, 2015, pp. 313ss. J.J. PAUST, The U.N. is bound by human rights: understanding the full reach of human rights, remedies, and non immunity, in Harvard International Law Journal, 51, 2010, pp. 4-9. O. SPIJKERS, The immunity of the United Nations in relation to the genocide in Srebrenica in the eyes of a Dutch District Court, in Journal of International Peacekeeping, 13, 2009, pp. 197ss. THENQUET, International organizations in the Netherlands: immunity from the jurisdiction of the Dutch courts, in Netherlands International Law Review, 49, 2010, pp. 267ss. B.E. BROCKMAN-HAWE, Questioning the UN's immunity in the Dutch Courts: Unresolved issues in the Mothers of Srebrenica litigation, in Washington University Global Studies Law Review, 10, 2011, pp. 727ss. J. TAVERNIER, La responsabilité des Etats au regard de la Convention européenne des droits de l'homme pour la mise en oeuvre de résolutions adoptées dans la cadre du chapitre VII de la Charte des Nations Unies, in Revue Générale de Droit International Public, 117, 2013, pp. 102ss. R. PAVONI, Human rights and the immunities of foreign states and international organizations, in E. DE WET, J. VIDMAR, Hierarchy in international law: The place of human rights, Oxford University Press, Oxford, 2012, pp. 71ss. E. DE BRABANDERE, Immunity of international organizations in post-conflict international administrations, in International Organizations Law Review, 7, 2010, pp. 79ss. C. TOMUSCHAT, The European Court of Human Rights and the United Nations, in A. FØLLESDAL, B. PETERS, G. ULFSTEIN, Constituting Europe: The European Court of Human Rights in a national, European and global context, Cambridge University Press, Cambridge, 2013, pp. 334ss. C. ECKES, S. HOLLENBERG, Reconciling different legal spheres in theory and practice: Pluralism and constitutionalism in the cases of Al Jedda, Ahmed and Nada, in Maastricht Journal of European and Comparative Law, 20, 2013, pp. 218ss.

system, including any jurisdictional authorities called to apply SC decisions[56]. Art. 103 in other words can be the expression of a model which, although aimed at connecting different regulatory systems, would in fact guarantee a prevalence of the political discretion of SC as the bearer of the collective interests consecrated in the UN Charter on any form of judicial review. This perspective ends up subjecting the judicial function to the needs of peacekeeping.

A somewhat opposite conception which in some ways ends up eluding the need to connect the different systems together could leverage the mutual autonomy of the different legal subsystems to which the international order is articulated. Each body in the exercise of powers attributed to it by its founding treaty is always competent and free to interpret and apply the internal rules to the system in which it operates. In this context, the courts can substantially ignore the possible legal effects of their decisions against bodies external to their reference system.

In the well-known EU jurisprudence on targeted sanctions or individuals, the potential regulatory conflict between SC resolutions and fundamental rights was avoided precisely through the idea that the two systems, that of the EU and the international one, are separate and independent[57].

---

[56]C. CHINKIN, Jus cogens, article 103 of the UN charter and other hierarchical tecniques of conflict solution, in Finnish Yearbook of International Law, 17, 2006, pp. 64ss. R. KOLB, L'article 103 de la charte des Nations Unies, in Recueil des cours, ed. Brill, Bruxelles, vol. 365, 2013, pp. 250ss.

[57]It is not here of course possible to retrace all the problems raised by the recognition of an autonomy proper to the order of EU with respect to the international one among the many varied reasons and the nature of such autonomy. See: B. DE WITTE, European Union law: How autonomous is its legal order?, in Zeitscrhift für öffentiliches Recht, 65 (1), 2010, pp. 142ss. N. TSAGOURIAS, Conceptualizing the autonomy of the European Union, in R. COLLINS, N.D. WHITE, International organizations and the idea of autonomy, ed. Routledge, London, New York, 2011, pp. 340sss. J.W.C. VAN ROSSEM, The autonomy of EU law: more is less?, in A.R. WESSELS, S. BLOCKMANS, Between autonomy and dependence. The EU legal order under the influence of International organizations, ed. Springer, The Hague, 2013, pp. 14ss. Some considerations on the subject of the autonomy of the EU have been carried out in the light of the opinion n. 2/13 of the CJEU have been made on the accession agreement. (Opinion 2/13, Accession of the European Union to the European Convention for the Protection of Human Rights and Fundamental Freedoms, ECJ, 18 December 2014, ECLI:EU:C:2014:2454. For further details see: L. HALLESLOV STORGAARD, European Union law autonomy versus European fundamental rights protection. On opinion 2/13 on EU accession to the ECHR, in Human Rights Law Review, 15 (3), 2015, pp. 487ss. On the one hand, art. 53 does not oblige the States to guarantee a higher level of protection than that of the ECHR, on the other the same CFREU must guarantee the same level of protection of ECHR so that there is no conflict between the two provisions. Moreover, the CJEU has evoked the specificity of the Union's control system on respect for fundamental rights, in particular the principle of mutual trust in the areas of civil and criminal judicial cooperation, visa, asylum and immigration, namely the area of freedom, security and justice that obliges each member state to presume respect for fundamental rights by the other Member States and the absence of their jurisdictional

powers in the field of foreign and security policy. See also in case: C-168/13 PPU, *Jeremy F.* of 30 May 2013, ECLI:EU:C:2013:358, published in the electronic Reports of the cases. The CJEU affirmed that: "(...) The absence of the necessary provisions of the framework it must be that for the implementation of the objectives to a European Arrest Warrant (...)". In the same spirit see also: CJEU, C-399/11, Stefano Melloni of 26 February 2013, ECLI:EU:C:2013:107; C-396/11, Ministerul Public-Parchetul de pe lângă Curtea de Apel Constanţa v. Radu of 29 January 2013, ECLI:EU:C:2013:39, both of them published in the electronic Reports of the cases. F.M.W. BILLING, The right to silence in transnational criminal proceedings. Comparative law perspectives, ed. Springer, Berlin, 2016, pp. 323ss. C. JANSSENS, The principle of mutual recognition in European Union law, Oxford University Press, Oxford, 2013, pp. 208ss. F. KORENICA, The EU accession to the ECHR: Between Luxembourg's search for autonomy and Strasbourg's credibility on human rights protection, ed. Springer, Berlin, 2015, pp. 282ss. S. MORANO-FOADI, L. VICKERS (eds.), Fundamental Rights in the EU-A matter for two Courts, Oxford University Press, Oxford, 2015. T. LOCK, The future of EU accession to the ECHR after Opinion 2/13: Is it still possible and is it still desirable?, in Edinburgh School of Law Research Paper Series, 2015. F. PICOD, La Cour de justice a dit non à l'adhésion de l'Union européenne à la Convention EDH, in La Semaine Juridique, Édition Générale, 2015, pp. 230, 234. J.P. JACQUÉ, The accession of the European Union to the European Convention on Human Rights and Fundamental Freedoms, in Common Market Law Review, 48 (4), 2011, pp. 995, 1005. S. PEERS, The EU's Accession to the ECHR: The dream becomes a nightmare, in German Law Journal, 16, 2015, pp. 213, 222. E. SPAVENTA, A very fearful Court? The protection of fundamental rights in the European Union after Opinion 2/13, in Maastricht Journal of European and Comparative Law, 22, 2015, pp. 51ss. M. KUIJER, The accession of the European Union to the ECHR: A gift for ECHR's 60th anniversary or an unwelcome intruder at the party?, in Amsterdam Law Forum, 4 (3), 2011, pp. 17-32. C. LADENBURGER, Vers l'adhésion de l'Union européenne à la Convention européenne des droits de l'homme, in Revue Trimestrielle de Droit Européen, 47 (1), 2011, pp. 20-26. T. LOCK, The ECJ and the ECtHR: The future relationship between the two European Courts, in The Law and Practice of International Courts and Tribunals, 8, 2010, pp. 375-398. C. JANSSENS, The principle of mutual recognition in European Union law, op. cit., pp. 208ss. T. LOCK, The future of EU accession to the ECHR after Opinion 2/13: Is it still possible and is it still desirable?, in Edinburgh School of Law Research Paper Series, 2015. D. ASHIAGBOR, N. COUNTOURIS, I. LIANOS, The European Union after the Treaty of Lisbon, Cambridge University Press, Cambridge, 2012, pp. 109-135. N. O'MEARA, A more secure Europe of rights? The European Court of Human Rights, the Court of Justice of the European Union and EU Accession to the ECHR, in German Law Journal, 12, 2011, pp. 1813-1832. J. POLAKIEWICZ, EU law and the ECHR: Will the European Union's accession square the circle?, in European Human Rights Law Review, 6, 2013, pp. 592-605. A. POTTEAU, Quelle adhésion de l'Union Européenne à la CEDH pour quel niveau de protection des droits et de l'autonomie de l'ordre juridique de l'UE?, in Revue Générale Droit International Public, 115, 2011, pp. 77-111. A. TORRES PEREZ, Too many voices? The prior involvement of the Court of Justice of the European Union? in European Journal of Human Rights, 40, 2013, pp. 565-583. L. BESSELINK, M. CLAES, J.H. REESTMAN, A Constitutional moment: Acceding to the ECHR (or not), in European Constitutional Law Review, 11, 2015, pp. 2ss. D. HALBESTRAM, It's autonomy stupid. A modest defense of Opinion 2/13 on EU accession to the ECHR, and a way forward, in Michigan Law Paper, 105, 2015. L.H. HALLESLOV STORGAARD, EU law autonomy versus European

What interests us here is that this approach has allowed EU judges, in the particular area of individual sanctions, to proceed with the scrutiny of legitimacy of the enforcement measures adopted within their own system, without formally and directly questioning the lawfulness of the UN acts internationally[58]. An

fundamental rights protection-On Opinion 2/13 on EU accession to the ECHR, op. cit., pp. 485. J.P. JACQUÉ, CJUE-CEDH: 2-0, in Revue Trimestrielle de Droit Européen, 40 (4), 2014 pp. 823ss. C. KRENN, Autonomy and effectiveness as common concerns: A path to ECHR accession after Opinion 2/13, in German Law Journal, 16 (1), 2015, pp. 147ss. S. LAMBRECHT, The sting is in the Tail: CJEU Opinion 2/13 objects to draft agreement on accession of the EU to the European Convention on Human Rights, in European Human Rights Law Review, 15 (1), 2015, pp. 185ss. M. PETITE, The battle over Strasbourg: The protection of human rights across Europe has suffered a setback, thanks to the Court of Justice of the European Union, in Competition Law Insight, 2015, pp. 10ss. R.A. WESSEL, A. ŁAZOWSKI, When Caveats Turn into Locks: Opinion 2/13 on Accession of the European Union to the ECHR, in German Law Journal, 16, 2015, pp. 179ss. B. DE WITTE, Article 53, in S. PEERS et al. (eds.), The EU Charter of Fundamental Rights, A Commentary, Hart Publishing, Oxford & Oregon, Portland, 2014, pp. 1523-1538. J. MEYER (ed.), Charta der Grundrechte der Europäischen Union, ed. Nomos, Baden-Baden, 2014, pp. 813-826. J.P. JACQUÉ, La Cour de Justice de l'Union et l'application de la Charte dans les Etats membres: "Mehr Licht", in European Yearbook on Human Rights, 14, 2014 pp. 125-147). On the different conceptions of the same notion of autonomy see: J. D'ASPREMONT, The multifaceted concept of the autonomy of international organizations and international legal discourse, in R. COLLINS, N.D. WHITE, International organizaions and the idea of autonomy, ed. Routledge, London, New York, 2011, pp. 64ss. Among the notions identified in this last contribution we refer here to the institutional and non-political autonomy of the EU and within this first subdivision we clearly want to recall autonomy from the system of the UN and not from the international community in its together. For further details see: J. D'ASPREMONT, Epistemic forces in international law, Edward Elgar Publishers, Cheltenham, 2015, pp. 147ss. P. EECKROUT, M. LOPEZ-ESCUDERO, The European Union's external action in times of crisis, Bloomsbury Publishing, New York, 2016. M. CREMONA, A. THIES, R.A. WESSEL, The European Union and international dispute settlement, Bloomsbury Publishing, New York, 2017, pp. 8ss. I. GOVAERE, S. GARBEN, The interface between European Union and international law: Contemporary reflections, Bloomsbury Publishing, New York, 2019, pp. 19ss. A.S. BARROS, Governance as responsibility, Cambridge University Press, Cambridge, 2019. J. D'ASPREMONT, Epistemic forces in international law, op. cit., pp. 145ss. R. COLLINS, N.D. WHITE, International organizations and the idea of autonomy: Institutional independence in the international legal order, ed. Routledge, London & New York, 2011. M. ANDENAS, E. BJORGE, A farewell to fragmentation: Reassertion and convergence in international law, Cambridge University Press, Cambridge, 2015, pp. 324ss. E.U. PETERSMANN, Multilevel constitutionalism for multilevel governance of public goods: Methodology problems in international law, Bloomsbury Publishing, New York, 2017, pp. 338ss.

[58]CJEU, joined cases C-402/054 and C-415/05 P, Yassin Abdullah Kadi and Al Barakaat International Foundation v. Council and Commission of 3 September 2008, ECLI:EU: C:2008:461, I-6351, par. 326. Despite the difficulties of reconstructing a clear line of argument followed by the CJEU already in the first comments to the sentence it was mentioned the impression of discontinuity between the legal order of EU and international

obvious problem of this approach is that it does not resolve the conflict between the obligations of States deriving from their belonging to two different legal systems[59].

Within the SC and ICC relationship, a dualist or pluralist model practically grants the Court full power to interpret its statutory rules autonomously. This autonomy can also hang in the light of the references contained in the statute itself to SC powers, i.e. a union on the decisions made by the latter on the basis of the UN Charter. This approach could lead to the non-implementation of SC resolutions deemed contrary to the UN Charter. In other words, and more specifically, the fact that the statute itself recognizes a series of effects to the decisions taken on the basis of Chapter VII could give to ICC judges the power to determine whether requests from SC respect the limits of the exercise of those powers. For example, ICC could refuse to activate or deactivate its jurisdiction when it considers that SC has exceeded the limits of the powers provided for by Chapter VII or its action is not based on the assumptions provided for by art. 39 of the Charter[60].

Finally, one can imagine the existence of a model in some intermediate way in which the protection of bodies prerogatives involved is to a certain extent limited by the respective spheres of competence. The problem here is to trace the boundary of the different competences, that is, in practice to establish what is purely political and what can instead be judged. We can define this as a model of limited autonomy or if we look at the problem from the point of view of the Court we can speak of limited control.

This third approach may be inspired to some extent by that American legal construction known as political question theory. The basic idea of this conception is essentially that not all aspects of a dispute can be subject to a judicial solution. There would be some issues before which the judge must avoid invading the spaces reserved for the choices of the political bodies. In these cases, the purely political nature of the object of the judgment requires the judicial bodies to leave the field to the discretion of political power[61].

---

law that emerges from the sentence.

[59]K. LENAERTS, E. DE SMIJTER, The United Nations and the European Union. Living apart together, in E. SUY, K. WELLENS, International law. Theory and practice. Essays in honor of Eric Suy, Martinus Nijhoff Publishers, The Hague, Boston, London, 1998, pp. 454ss.

[60]D. WHITTLE, The limits of legality and the United Nations Security Council: Applying the extralegal measures model to chapter VII action, op. cit.

[61]In light of the reasoning of the American supreme court in the historic decision Marbury v. Madison (Supreme Court, 5 US (1 Cranch) 137 (1803)) prevent the judicial organs from invading the sphere of political discretion would be precisely the cardinal principle of the separation of powers. See, Marbury v. Madison, in reports of decision in Supreme Court, i.e. the traditionally ruling of the United States. On the theory of political question, see: T. FRANCK, Political question, judicial answers, Princeton University Press, Princeton, 1992. Even the constitutional courts and continental European legal systems have had to deal with the political question theory. The role assigned to the constitutional courts in

This doctrine could be rather assimilated to a model of prevalence. However, the political question theory does not always and necessarily imply the total inadmissibility of a judicial union on political decisions. Perhaps the most interesting aspect of this construction is the impact that it can have on the reach of the union rather than on its total negation. In practice, the scope of judicial review would be all the narrower as the political discretion granted for the particular decision is extended. Thus, while admitting in principle that any issue, including a political one, may be subject to a legality check, where the discretion granted to the political bodies is extremely wide, the judicial assessment could be limited to the formal aspects of the decision-making process or intervene only in the face of manifest abuse of power.

The limit to judicial control could therefore be given by the internal or external character of the system of the regulatory parameter on which the legitimacy of the action of the bodies involved is measured. To understand the relationship between SC and ICC, one could imagine that the judicial control over the action of SC stops at the proper statutory rules. The reference to the powers provided for in Chapter VII of the UN Charter would instead have a purely formal character and so would the forms of control over them, leaving entirely to that different system the determination of the substantial limits to the political discretion of the body responsible for peacekeeping. This model guarantees a certain freedom to SC in order to exercise the powers already recognized by the UN Charter and could limit the judicial control of ICC to those elements of the decision that are considered incompatible with the rules and principles of the Statute of Rome.

6. The role of SC in controlling the legitimacy of unilateral States' reactions to international crimes

In the interpretation that has prevailed in the last years, Chapter VII of the UN Charter no longer concerns only situations strictly related to the maintenance of peace, understood in its classical sense, of the absence of international conflicts, but is now offered more and more frequently as the basis for an organized collective reaction against violations of norms considered essential by the international community jointly understood. While in some cases this opening of the UN system constitutes the expression of an adaptation of the organization that matures within the same, so the organization itself actually operates on the basis of the statutory model reinterpreted in "extensive" way in light of the new regulatory context in which its action takes place (which can be justified and admitted within the limits allowed by an evolutionary interpretation

---

these systems is to assess whether the legislative choices are compatible with the parameters of constitution, a rather complex operation in the face of constitutional documents that identify more than anything else lists of fundamental rights to be protected and programmatic objectives. Even the principle of separation of powers can force the judge to escape from a union with respect to those aspects of the subject question that presuppose a certain discretion of the political bodies.

made in the light of the criteria recognized by the same general order) in the majority of cases, the activity of the organization, on the other hand, detaches itself from the original paradigm to assume connotations not foreseen by the Charter and are difficult to reconcile with the latter's dictation[62].

Such situations, if assessed within the context of an overall and unitary vision of the practice that simultaneously holds from the community of States, would testify to the assumption of UN and in particular of its body with more incisive powers, SC of new and external skills to the Charter to be connected to substantially unilateral activities of the States even if in principle aimed at the realization of fundamental interests that belong to the whole international society. The affirmation of these new competences is linked to the fact that States, when act or intend to act unilaterally to safeguard and guarantee the fundamental values of the international community, would attribute to UN and in particular to SC the task of endorsing the interventions that they intend to carry out, receiving a sort of approval and confirmation of the existence of a collective interest underlying the intervention itself. This is to allow the institutional deficit of the international community to be bridged at least in part, when the need arises to react to the injuries of essential collective interests that belong to all States and at the same time to provide a form of insurance against diversion risks and instrumentalization of the decentralized system to offenses. In this sense, the UN would have shown that it can operate according to two very different schemes, one statutory and one extra-statutory, which at least in terms of its concrete implementation must be seen in the context of decentralized reactions to the offense.

In this second model, which found its moment of main affirmation in the authorization resolutions adopted in the period from 1990 to 1995, SC intervention (which could manifest itself in very different material and procedural modalities) would not constitute a hypothesis of management and direct protection of erga omnes obligations but would rather carry out a sort of legitimacy check with respect to activities conducted unilaterally by the operating States, offering a further assessment in addition to that implemented by the States themselves. This determination would not be strictly indispensable, however, necessarily legitimate under international law, since SC does not have the competence and tools to operate assessments of this type with absolute reliability, since these are obviously legal judgments. In this sense, the role exercised by SC would have a purely procedural and non-substantial importance, since it could not, for the reasons set out above, guarantee alone the impartiality and correctness of the assessment carried out in the manner described.

---

[62]Compared to other widely known situations that see international organizations assume functions not foreseen by the related statutes on the basis of subsequent treaties concluded in formally autonomous contexts with respect to the same organizations, and which are intended to operate with respect to a circle of contracting states not necessarily coinciding with their membership. In the case indicated the novelty would be constituted by the fact that the conferment of extra-statuary powers would have on the basis no more than an agreement but by virtue of the same general international law.

The thesis summarily described has the merit of offering a joint letter of the practice of SC interventions and of those carried out unilaterally by the States. It does not seem that the activity devolves from the UN organs to protect the fundamental interests of the international community, despite the fact that the erga omnes obligations are certainly expanding completely, excludes that States can react unilaterally in defense of the values indicated at least in situations in which the Organization itself is unable to act. It is inevitable that States themselves can regain their prerogatives when the delegated system is unable to function. This solution is certainly confirmed in the persistence (if not even consolidation) of unilateral intervention models both in situations in which the multilateral system is completely paralyzed and in the hypotheses in which the latter is able to manage only some specific segments of the action to protect collective interests[63].

In this sense, the implementation of erga omnes obligations based on the current configuration of general international law would not at all rest exclusively on UN activity, but the activity of the latter would contribute to the decentralized interventions of the States acting on behalf of the international community. The practice revealed the existence of a far more complex situation than that generally highlighted by the majority of doctrine in which the collective security system far from prevailing on the unilateral management of the consequences of the violations of the most important values of the international community actually coexists with this model and is combined with it according to very diversified outlines and in which the division between organized activity and unilateral action can take on a wide range of configurations, favoring according to the most specific cases and contingencies either one or the other component.

The perspective indicated allows the central role of States to be recovered at a conceptual level as managers of the collective values belonging to the international community at first sight. Are the States themselves that, being holders of the collective rights corresponding to the erga omnes obligations,

---

[63]I. ÖSTERDAHL, The exception as the rule: Law making on force and human rights by the UN Security Council, in Journal of Conflict and Security Law, 10 (1), 2005, pp. 5ss. The author accepts the real logical and legal connection between SC activity and the decentralized action of States reverses the perspective in which the three relationships should be more correctly examined, mistakenly believing that it was the attitude of general international law on the subject of humanitarian intervention. On the contrary, while not denying that the two systems, the UN and international law are actually susceptible of influencing each other in the perspective we have accepted in the text, it is the evolution of the international orientation that has determined a new general international mode and in the powers that this attributes to States in the first instance for the protection of values and goods that belong to the international community as a whole. From this point of view SC practice on humanitarian interventions is rather a further proof confirming the formation in international law of a rule that eventually allows the use of force in the case of particularly large and significant humanitarian tragedies. Compliance with the limits set by the same general international law for the legitimacy of the intervention. See also in argument: C. BRÖLMANN, Y. RADI, Research handbook on the theory and practice of international law making, Edward Elgar Publishing, Cheltenham, 2016, pp. 186ss.

determine how management and protection can jointly delegate their implementation to international bodies. The existence of collective interests and values and the progressive emergence of a real international public order have taken place without the international community having institutions and bodies capable of implementing and managing these interests and values independently and on their own. Consequently, the protection of the latter can only be entrusted to the States acting as members of the international community and custodians of its interests.

The lack of an institutional structure capable of imposing itself on States means that the ascertainment of the illicit erga omnes and the reaction to it remains their prerogative. It is clear that in such a situation all States are damaged and are potentially enabled to react in the interest of the international community. This state of affairs is likely to produce highly detrimental effects when the offense has the characteristics of an international crime even when the imprimatur of SC is lacking. The main risk is that the reaction is not actually genuinely oriented towards the implementation of common values within the international community and that other objectives of a selfish nature accompany or end up absorbing the aims in a broad collective sense. The need arises to establish a check on the legitimacy of the reactions taken towards crimes. On the one hand, since the possibility recognized by States to react to the violation of fundamental erga omnes obligations must be linked to a requirement of the international community as a whole, it is necessary to prove the consent of the same to the intervention, that is to say, to obtain widespread approval by States to adopt coercive measures on behalf and in the interest of the community itself and to avoid pursuing not the common interests but the particular interests of the acting States. Secondly, it is necessary to verify that the methods of the reactions adopted are strictly functional to the restoration of the violated order and comply with the prescriptions established by general international law.

The legitimacy check that is currently achievable by SC in the manner described in the text, is not able to fully satisfy the requirements of legal certainty and impartiality which are the basis of its own affirmation in practice, i.e. this is the first reason of the logic that permeates the activity of this body and the same operating methods of the same. In recent years it is increasingly evident on the other hand how SC lends itself to be used by sstates and above all by those with greater power within it as a tool for achieving particularistic objectives. This situation has led to a very serious crisis of confidence towards multilateralism. It is essential to strengthen and better guarantee the system's adherence to compliance with international law: This aim almost naturally leads to questioning the possible role of ICJ in the matter of ascertaining the most serious and hateful violations of the fundamental rules of international law (in competition and/or as an alternative to SC).

Chapter 1
The Referral

1. SC power to activate the investigations of ICC Prosecutor: Art. 13 (b) of the Statute of Rome

The power to initiate the investigation of ICC Prosecutor is provided for by art. 13 b) that the SC may act on the basis of the powers conferred on it by Chapter VII of the UN Charter to report to the Prosecutor a situation in which it believes that one or more crimes have been committed among those envisaged by the Statute.

The main issues that emerged during the long process that led to the drafting of this provision are essentially three: The identification of the UN body which should have had the power to activate the Prosecutor's investigative activities, i.e. the legal basis for such prerogative and finally the content and more precisely the subject of the report submitted to the attention of ICC.

As regards the UN body that could possibly have given impetus to the action of the Court, it was initially thought to give to GA a power to authorize the prosecution following a report coming from the States. Art. 28 of this first draft of the Statute in fact provided that "no jurisdiction may be conferred upon the Court without the approval of the UN General Assembly"[64].

Several States noted that there was no legal basis in the UN Charter that could legitimize the exercise of such power under GA[65]. There were also those who denied in full the need for political control over the requests of the States to activation of the jurisdiction for the repression of international crimes[66]. The latter

---

[64]See the works of Committee on international criminal jurisdiction created by GA with the Resolution n. 489 (V), 5th Session, 12 December 1950. Draft Statute for an International Criminal Court, annex I. Report of the Committee UN doc. A/AC.48/4, 5 September 1951.

[65]See, Report of them 1953 Committee on international criminal jurisdiction, summary record of the seventeenth meeting, UN doc. A/AC.65/SR.17. See in particular the positions of France, Russia and Israel. The provision of an express approval of GA for the exercise of the jurisdiction, raised many perplexities among the representatives of the States and the idea was abandoned already in the following project of 1953. See in argument also: Y. LIANG, Notes on legal questions concerning the United Nations. The establishment of an international criminal jurisdiction. The second phase, in American Journal of International Law, 46 (2), 1953, pp. 640ss

[66]Report of the 1953 Committee on international criminal jurisdiction, Summary record of the seventeenth meeting, UN doc. A/AC.65/SR.17, p. 10.

position prevailed and forms of GA and SC control, over the conferral ICC jurisdiction by the States were effectively excluded.

In that same project, however, the hypothesis was put forward that political control could take place at a later stage in the beginning of the criminal action in order to arrest ICC's jurisdiction if this were necessary in the interests of the maintenance of peace[67]. To avoid the tortuosity and the probable delays that an approval by the Assembly of the request for activation of the States would imply from time to time, the idea that the Assembly body could intervene only in order to prevent criminal action was affirmed, within two years from the transfer of a case to ICC through its own explicit opposition[68]. In other words, the Assembly could have interrupted the judicial activity of the Court at a time after its beginning, by taking a position contrary to the exercise of jurisdiction rather than having to decide in any case whether or not to authorize the criminal action requested by the States[69]. It was therefore a forerunner version of what would later become the power of deferral.

When, in the nineties, the ILC began to deal with the creation of a permanent criminal court[70], another important hypothesis was proposed, i.e. the attribution of an autonomous power of activation of ICC to the prerogative of one of the two political UN bodies. In this regard, on the one hand, the composition and the voting system within the shareholders' meeting seemed to be able to constitute a more solid guarantee against improper complaints as well as against abuse of the veto[71]. On the other hand, emphasis was placed on the absence of a legal basis for any SC measures aimed at affecting the administration of international criminal justice. However, I was opposed to these arguments by the

---

[67]Report of the 1953 Committee on international criminal jurisdiction, UN doc. A/2638 (1954). For further analysis see in argument: L.S. WEXLER, The proposed permanent international criminal court. An appraisal, op. cit., pp. 667ss. M. CHERIF BASSIOUNI (ed.), International criminal law, vol. I: Sources, subjects and contents, Martinus Nijhoff Publishers, The Hague, 2013. L.N. SADAT, The Nuremberg paradox, in The American Journal of International Law, 58 (1), 2010, pp. 154ss.

[68]In this first project the ICC had the power to exercise jurisdiction autonomously only on the crime of genocide for the other crimes it was foreseen in the necessary reference of the cases by the States. For further details see: G. METTRAUX, International crimes: Law and practice genocide, Oxford University Press, Oxford, 2019.

[69]This change of perspective was proposed by the subcommittee (subcommittee) at the time in charge of the drafting of the statutes which advanced a different text centered on the idea precisely of a disapproval of GA to prevent ICC jurisdiction, UN doc. A/AC.65/L.7.

[70]For many years the debate on the subject remained somewhat suspended. Only following a definition of the acts qualifying as aggression, through the note Resolution n. 3314 of 1974. ILC has resumed dealing with the code of crimes against peace and the security of humanity. In 1990 then also the idea of establishing an international criminal jurisdiction returned to the agenda of codification with the eighth report of the special speaker Doudou Thiam.

[71]Eight report on the draft code on crimes against the peace and security of mankind by Mr. Doudoud Thiam, special rapporteur, in Yearbook of the International law Commission, vol. II, A/CN.4/SER.1/1990/Add.I (Part 1), 1990, p. 37.

fact that the seriousness of the crimes under ICC jurisdiction and in particular of the crime of aggression could not have implied an involvement of SC, in light of the role assigned to it by art. 24 of the UN Charter on the maintenance of international peace and security. At least for the hypothesis of the crime of aggression[72] there was therefore a tendency to recognize that the criminal action had to somehow depend on SC's prior assessment of the existence of such a situation pursuant to art. 39 of the UN Charter[73]. Furthermore, the same ILC work shows the belief that an intervention power could not instead be recognized to GA, as it does not have the necessary authority under the UN Charter to directly affect the rights of States against their will, especially in respect of issues of criminal jurisdiction[74].

To dispel the last doubts about the legal basis of an autonomous power of SC to activate ICC, the initiative which took place during these first debates aimed at establishing the ad hoc tribunals for the ex Yugoslavia and Rwanda. Those same courts in their first pronouncements, identified the legitimate foundation of SC power to establish them in Chapter VII of the UN Charter and

---

[72]For further details see also: E. WILMSHURST, (ed), International law and the classification of conflicts, Oxford University Press, Oxford, 2012. P. AKHAVAN, Reducing genocide to law: Definition, meaning and the ultimate crime, Cambridge University Press, Cambridge, 2012. N. BLOKKER, Outsourcing the use of force: Towards more Security Council control of authorized operations?, in M. WELLER (ed), The oxford handbook of the use of force in international law, Oxford University Press, Oxford, 2015. B. CHENG, Pre-emptive or similar type of self-defense in the territory of foreign states, in Chinese Journal of International Law, 13, 2014, pp. 4ss. O. CORTEN, The law against war: The prohibition on the use of force in contemporary international law, Hart Publishing, Oxford/Oregon & Portland, 2010. E. CREEGAN, Justified uses of force and the crime of aggression, in Journal of International Criminal Justice, 10, 2012, pp. 60ss. D.M. FERENCZ, Aggression in legal limbo: a gap in the law that needs closing, in Washington University Global Studies Law Review, 12, 2013, pp. 508ss. J.A. GREEN, Questioning the peremptory status of the prohibition of the use of force, in Michigan Journal of International Law, 32, 2011, pp. 216ss. P. GRZEBYK, Criminal responsibility for the crime of aggression, ed. Routledge, London & New York, 2013. V. KOUTROULIS, And yet it exists: In defence of the "equality of belligerents" principle, in Leiden Journal of International Law, 26, 2013. C. KRESS, The International Court of Justice and the "principle of non-use of force", in M. WELLER (ed), The oxford handbook of the use of force in international law, Oxford University Press, Oxford, 2015.

[73]In the Draft Statute of ILC of 1991 the only role reserved for SC concerned the crime of aggression. On this crime the ICC could have exercised its jurisdiction only after ascertaining the SC. See in argument: Draft code of crimes against the peace and security of mankind, in Yearbook of the International Law Commission, vol. II, UN doc. A/CN.4/436. Add. 1, 1991.

[74]Draft Statute of the international criminal Court with commentaries, in Yearbook of the International law Commission, 1994, vol. II, part two, p. 44. See also in argument: E. LA HAYE, The jurisdiction of the international criminal court: Controversies over the preconditions for exercising its jurisdiction, in Netherlands International Law Review, 46 (1), 1999, pp. 12ss.

precisely in art. 41[75].

The referral represents a sort of transposition, within the Statute of Rome, of a power that SC had in some way already exercised through the creation of ad hoc courts[76]. This eased the concerns expressed by some States about the need for a clear consensual basis for the exercise of these powers. The consensus of the States does not form part of the Statute to SC's power to intervene on its domestic jurisdiction. In fact it would have been directly attributable to the UN Charter and to the general acceptance of SC practice in the exercise of the envisaged powers of Chapter VII of the UN Charter, within which the creation of ad hoc courts and therefore more generally the power to initiate mechanisms of criminal expression at an international level is inscribed[77].

The subsequent debates highlight in many ways a shift of emphasis in the reactions of States to codification proposals. If the doubts about the legal basis of SC power to set up courts and therefore to direct criminal proceedings at an international level, were partly dispelled by the first case law of the ad hoc courts themselves. A series of hesitations and conflicts persisted regarding the political opportunity to recognize a general power of intervention of SC on the judicial action of a permanent tribunal created through a special international treaty. The criticisms of the recognition of such power by SC essentially concerned the possible effects on the autonomy of ICC and given the selectivity that SC could exercise in indicating the situations worthy of attention on the more general repercussions in terms of credibility of the whole system[78].

---

[75]ICTY, Prosecutor v. Tadić, Decision on the defence motion for interlocutory appeal on jurisdiction, Appeals chamber, IT-94-1-AR72, 2 October 1995, parr. 4, 32, 72 and ICTY, Prosecutor v. Kanyabashi, decision on the motion on jurisdiction, trial Chamber II, ICTR-98-44-T, 18 June 1997, parr. 14-16.

[76]In the commentary to art. 23 (action by SC) of the ICC Statute of 1994, the rest clearly speaks of this power to activate ICC: "(...) As an alternative to establishing ad hoc tribunals (...)" .Draft Statute of the international court with commentaries, in the Yearbook of the International law Commission, 1994, vol. II, part two, p. 44. The project of ILC is adopted following the work of working group created by the Commission itself. See Report of the Commission to GA on the work of its forty-sixth session, in Yearbook of the International Law Commission, vol. II, p. 20ss.

[77]SC confers on an international organization a jurisdictional power that could not directly execute but also already occurred through the institution of ad hoc tribunals can delegate to other organs without the need for further and new manifestations of consent by the States. See in argument: S. KIRSCH, Introduction to chapter VIII: The general framework, in N. WESSENDORF, B. SIMMA, D. ERASMUS KHAN, G. NOLTE, A. PAULUS, The charter of the United Nations. A commentary, Oxford University Press, Oxford, 2012, pp. 1264ss. D. SAROOSHI, The United Nations and the development of collective security, Oxford University Press, Oxford, 1999, pp. 20ss.

[78]The hypothesis of giving SC the power to activate the ICC jurisdiction for what is considered satisfactory by many. See for example the positions of Czech Republic (UN doc. A/C/49/SRF.21, p. 10), Spain (UN doc. A/C.6/49/SR.19, p. 6), Chile (UN doc A/C.6/49/SR.21, p. 6) has not in fact found the states unanimous. As the project of the statute was the subject of examination in the sixth Commission, several delegates, despite

A role of the Council in the administration of international criminal justice, however, was considered by many parties to be strictly necessary precisely to ensure greater legitimacy for the action of the Court. A purely pact regime that did not include an intervention of SC, in fact, in the view of several members of ILC, would have had the not insignificant limit of resting on the political agenda of individual States rather than on the collective decision of SC[79]. In other words, instead of basing the system of criminal repression of the most important international crimes on the sole consent of States interested in being part of it, it was preferred to guarantee through the action of SC a potentially universal scope to ICC jurisdiction, precisely because of the fundamental purpose pursued through its institution[80].

Furthermore, always in light of the legitimacy requirements of the system, the creation of ICC had among its objectives, the overcoming of the numerous criticisms that the special character and ex post facto intervention of the ad hoc courts had raised the need to limit the as much as possible the use of these mechanisms. For this reason, it was ultimately preferred to link the role already recognized to SC in the field of international criminal justice to a permanent tribunal whose stability would have guaranteed greater autonomy and independence of judicial action[81]. Moreover, in more practical terms, allowing SC

---

their varied positions, expressed their concerns about the content of art. 23 some have generally insisted on the dangers posed to the independence of ICC (Bahren (UN doc. A/C.6/49/SR.17, p. 4); Japan (UN doc. A/C.6/49/SR.18, p. 8); Israel (A doc. A/C.6/49/SR.20, p. 6); Algeria (A doc. A/C.6/49/SR.20, p .17)); on the criticism that the power of referral places as a limit to the free will of States to accept the jurisdiction of an international court (Australia (A doc. A/C.6/49/SR.17, p. 14); Egypt (UN doc. A/C.6/49/SR.20, page 11), others have highlighted the obvious and unacceptable disparity that is thus introduced between the States (whether they are part or not of the Statute) with the privilege granted to SC Member States and, in particular, of those with veto power (Guinea (UN doc. A/C.6/49/SR.17, p. 9)); Venezuela (UN doc. A/C.6/49/SR.19, pp. 12-13). Naturally the selectivity that the SC can exercise in determining the situations to report to ICC has aroused the greatest criticisms and concerns: The purely political reasons that could have characterized the cases submitted to ICC. See in argument: K. AINLEY, The international criminal court on trial, in Cambridge Review of International Affairs, 23 (3), 2011, pp. 320ss. R. MENON, The conceit of humanitarian intervention, Oxford University Press, Oxford, 2016. H. JO, B. SIMMONS, Can the International Criminal Court defer atrocity?, in International Organization, 70 (3), 2016, pp. 446ss. C. ROYER, The Bête Noire and the Noble Lie: The International Criminal Court and politics, in Criminal Law & Philosophy, 13 (2), 2019, pp. 230ss.

[79]Report of the ad hoc Committee on the establishment of an international criminal court, General Assembly official records. Fifteen session, supplement n. 22, UN doc. A/50/22, 1995, p. 27, par. 121.

[80]The high number of ratifications envisaged for the entry into force of the Statute tempered the further complexity related to the different cost basis on which SC action is based with respect to ICC. See, draft Statute of the international criminal court with commentaries, in Yearbook of the International Law Commission, 1994, vol. II, part two, p. 44.

[81]This emerges clearly from the positions expressed in the sixth Commission by some

to apply to a permanent court for the repression of the most serious international crimes would have avoided incurring the costs and potential obstacles of a political nature that the establishment of special courts may from time to time arise[82].

During the preparatory Commission's works, in the years immediately preceding the Rome Conference, some new proposals had emerged that deserve to be recalled here. An advance from France intended to sanction the need that even in the event of ICC activation by SC, the request was accompanied by all supporting material available, thus imposing on SC procedural obligations similar to those already provided for the States[83]. However, this paragraph then disappeared from the final text. The relationship of 2004 agreement has somehow remedied these shortcomings. The only element of the agreement aimed at specifying the interaction between ICC and SC in case of exercise of referral power provides that SG must transmit immediately the decision of SC to the "Prosecutor to gather with documents and other materials that may be pertinent to the decision of the Council (...)" (art. 17 (1)[84].

The second proposal presented elements of greatest interest. Also within the Preparatory Commission, the hypothesis which was not confirmed in the definitive text of the Statute that SC could activate ICC jurisdiction based on Chapter VI of the UN Charter was elaborated[85]. The SC would therefore have been entitled to submit to the permanent Court even those situations which did not yet pose a threat to international peace and security. The concerns relating to a compression of the free will of States, previously expressed by numerous delegations on the referral power of ex Chapter VII, could only increase in the face of an extension of this prerogative also in relation to the conciliatory activity of SC. At the Rome Conference, despite persistent and sometimes rather severe criticism from some delegations[86], most States finally accepted the idea that the

---

States. See in particular the statements of the US representative and the Hungarian representative. UN Press release, GA/L3011, 31 October 1996.

[82]The establishment of ICC has not prevented the establishment of other international or mixed criminal courts and does not exclude the possibility that SC decides to resort to the creation of ad hoc tribunals, a hypothesis further advanced also for the situation in Syria.

[83]Art. 14 (2) of the Statute.

[84]D. SAROOSHI, The United Nations and the development of collective security, op. cit.

[85]Report of the Preparatory Committee on the establishment of an international criminal court, General Assembly official records, fifty-first session supplement n. 22, UN doc. A/51/22, 1996, vol. I, par. 134.

[86]United Nations diplomatic conference of plenitpotentiaries on the establishment of an international criminal court, Rome, 15 June-17 July 1998, official records vol. II, UN doc. A/Conf.183/3. According to the Italian delegate: "(...) The power to refer is now unnecessary. SC set up ad hoc tribunals because no judicial mechanism then existed to try the extraordinary crimes committed in the former Yugoslavia and in Rwanda. Now, the ICC exist and States Parties would have the right given to it is predicated on two assumptions. First, that Council's referral would be more binding on the Court than other referrals, this would clearly be an attempt to influence justice. Second it would imply that

exercise of the referral was expressly limited in the Statute to the powers provided for in Chapter VII[87].

On the other hand, it would be difficult to find any basis in referral power in the provisions of Chapter VI. In particular, it must be excluded that the activation of the jurisdictional action of an international criminal court (whose task is the repression of crimes committed by individuals) can be framed among the judicial regulations aimed at the peaceful resolution of (interstate) disputes governed by art. 33 of the UN Charter[88]. That the exercise of criminal jurisdiction is not part of the measures directly addressed to the States is a question that has also arisen in terms of the legitimacy of the creation of international criminal courts on the basis of Chapter VII of the Charter[89], and was then overcome by a general acceptance of the practice implemented by SC.

On the other hand, it would be difficult to find any basis in referral power in the provisions of Chapter VI. In particular, it must be excluded that the activation of the judicial action of an international criminal court (whose task is the repression of crimes committed by individuals) can be framed among the judicial regulations aimed at the peaceful resolution of (interstate) disputes governed by art. 33 of the UN Charter. That the exercise of criminal jurisdiction is not one of the measures directly addressed to the States is a question that has also arisen in terms of the legitimacy of the creation of international criminal courts on the basis of Chapter VII of the UN Charter, and was then overcome by a general acceptance of the practice implemented by SC.

A final and fundamental element of the power envisaged by art. 13 b) of the Statute which plays a central role in order to determine the compatibility of a certain practice of SC with the Statute of Rome, concerns the subject of the referral. Art. 13 b) provides that SC refers to situations in which one or more crimes committed by ICC's jurisdiction have been committed. The choice of the crime situation has been at the center of an articulated confrontation between the States and cannot certainly be considered random[90]. The word "situation" not only

---

some members of the Council do not plan to accede to ICC. They will not accept the obligations imposed by the Statute, but want the privilege to refer cases to it. This too is unacceptable (..)". See also in argument M. BERGSMO, Occasional remarks on certain state concerns about the jurisdictional reach of the international criminal court and their possible implications for the relationship between the Court and the Security Council, in Nordic Journal of International Law, 69 (1), 2000, pp. 94ss.

[87]Only Brazil hoped for an extension of the possibility of activating ICC on the base of Chapter VI of the UN Charter. See UN diplomatic conference of plenipotentiaries on the establishment of an international criminal court, Rome, 15 June-17 July 1998 official records, vol. II, UN doc. A/Conf. 183/3 (vol. II), p. 209.

[88]F. BAETENES, Legitimacy of unseen actors in international adjudication, op. cit.,

[89]D. WHITTLE, The limits of legality and the United Nations Security Council: Applying the extralegal measures model to chapter VII action, op. cit.

[90]N. WHITE, R. CRYER, The ICC and the Security Council. An uncomfortable relationship, in J. DORIA, H.P. GASSER, M. CHERIF BASSIOUNI, The legal regime of the international criminal court. Essays in honor of professor Igor Blishchenko. In memory

takes up the terminology of UN Charter (the expression is used for example in art. 40) but its use has a specific purpose. It aims to limit the impact of SC power on discretion of the Prosecutor and in particular on the autonomy of the latter in carrying out the investigations and in formulating his own accusations against the accused[91].

The notion of "situation" was preferred to other initial proposals that rather recalled the concepts of case or matter[92]. ILC had indeed oriented itself at least initially towards the latter term (art.23 (1)) stating however that the expression matter means a situation to which Chapter VII of the UN Charter applies[93]. The record seems to indicate that at least within the ILC the concepts "situation" and "matter" were considered interchangeable. From the positions expressed on the point by the States, however, it emerges that the choice between one and the other term was precisely linked to the degree of specificity that was to characterize the object of the referral. The States that expressed a preference for the term situation considered the word matter still excessively specific in order not to harm the independence of ICC[94]. While it may not be easy to grasp the

---

of professor Igor Pavlovich Blishchenko (1930-2000), Martinus Nijhoff Publishers, Leiden, 2009, pp. 462ss. P. KRISCH, D. ROBINSON, Referral by states parties, in A. CASSESE, P. GAETA, J.R.W.D. JONES, The Rome statute o0f the international criminal court, Oxford University Press, Oxford, 2001, pp. 623ss. G.M. LENTNER, The United Nations Security Council and the International Criminal Court. The referral mechanism in theory and practice, Edward Elgar Publishers, Cheltenham, 2018, pp. 1644ss. A. ORAKHELASHVILI, Collective security, Oxford University Press, Oxford, 2011, pp. 340ss. R. CRYER, D. ROBINSON, S. VASILIEV, An introduction to international criminal law and procedure, Cambridge University Press, Cambridge, 2019, pp. 152ss. R. BELLELLI, International criminal justice: Law and practice from the Rome statute to its review, ed. Routledge, London & New York, 2016, pp. 40ss.

[91]Report of the Preparatory Committee on the establishment of an international criminal court, General Assembly official records, fifty-first session supplement n. 332 UN Doc. A/51/22, 1996, vol. I, pp. 132-136.

[92]Also this last term was finally discarded as it was still considered excessively specific with respect to the more general situation. See in argument: S. YEE, The international criminal court and the Security Council, in S.K. LEE, The International criminal court: The making of the Rome statute. Issues, negotiations, results, Martinus Nijhoff Publishers, The Hague, 1999, pp. 150ss.

[93]The word matter already seemed, according to various States, to safeguard the independence of ICC. See in argument: Draft Statute of the international criminal Court with commentaries, in Yearbook of the International Law Commission, 1994, vol. II, par. 2, comment of art. 23 of the project. For further analysis see: B.F. MCPHERSON, Building an international criminal court for the 21st century, in Connecticut Journal of International Law, 13, 1998, pp. 54ss. C. ÇAKMAK, A brief history of international criminal law and International Criminal Court, ed. Springer, Berlin, 2017, pp. 161ss.

[94]United Nations diplomatic conference of plenipotentiaries on the establishment of an international criminal court, Rome 15 June-17 July 1998, official records, vol. III, art. 10, par. 1, Report of the preparatory committee on the establishment of an international criminal court. Addendum, part one, A/CONF.183/2/add. 1, p. 167.

difference between these two notions, what certainly seemed established was that SC "would not normally refer to the Court a case in the sense of an allegation against named individuals"[95],would thus be preserved "the independence and autonomy of the Court in the exercise of its investigative, prosecutorial and judicial functions"[96].

The shared idea seemed essentially to be that a recognition by SC of the power to report individual suspects of the crime Commission would have greatly limited Prosecutor's freedom to investigate the prosecution and put de facto the repressive tool at the mercy of SC. In this regard, there are those who have pointed out that it would be precisely having reconnected the referral power to generic situations, leaving the Prosecutor the task of identifying possible defendants to make the entire system compliant "à la sèparation des pouvoirs politique et judiciare"[97]. However, the definition of the term "situation" raises few interpretative problems that have already emerged in part in the relevant practice, which will be taken up in the next pages.

2. Practices regarding the exercise of referral power

2.1. The situation in Darfur

To date, SC has activated ICC jurisdiction on two occasions. The first concerns crimes committed in Darfur, in western Sudan. The Resolution 1593 of 31 March 2005 with which the situation was referred to ICC[98], followed an instance of the Commission of inquiry into crimes committed in Darfur[99], in

---

[95]Draft Statute for an international criminal court with commentaries, in Yearbook of the International Law Commission, 1994, vol. II, part two, p. 44.

[96]Report of the ad hoc Committee on the establishment of an international criminal court. General Assembly official reports. Fiftieth session, supplement n. 22, UN doc. A/50/22, 1995, parr. 120-121.

[97]L. CONDORELLI, L. VILLALPANDO, Les Nations Unies et les juridictions penales internationales, in J.P. COT, M. FORTEAU, A. PELLET, La charte des Nations Unies commentaire article par article, op. cit., pp. 228ss. These same authors do not exclude the possibility that the situation identified from SC concerns some political or military leaders. Many, on the other hand, insist on the fact that the term situation was chosen precisely to prevent the SC from deciding on individual cases and negatively affecting the autonomy, independence and discretion of the prosecutor. See also in argument: V. GOWLLAND-DEBBAS, The role of the Securtiy Council in the new international criminal court from a systemic perspective, in L. BOISSON DE CHAZOURNES, V. GOWLLAND-DEBBAS, The international legal system in quest of equity and universality. L'ordre juridique international, un système en quête d'èquitè et d'universalitè: liber amicorum Georges Abi-Saab. Melange Abi-Saab, op. cit., pp. 634ss.

[98] Resolution 1593 (2005) of 31 March 2005 with which the case was referred to ICC, it was adopted with 11 votes in favor and 4 abstentions (including China and United States, as well as Algeria and Brazil) on the basis of a proposal from the United Kingdom.

[99]The Commission of inquiry for Darfur was created by the General Secretary following the Resolution SC 1564 (2004) of 18 September 2003. In the Commission's report, it is estimated that there are about 70,000 victims of numerous war crimes and against

which SC was recommended to "immediately refer the situation of Darfur to ICC"[100]. The legal basis for the Resolution is Chapter VII of the UN Charter on the assumption that the situation in Sudan "continues to constitute a threat to international peace and security"[101].

Despite the Resolution does not expressly mention art. 13 b) StICC and this lack has been the subject of some criticisms[102], the language used in the first paragraph in which SC decides to refer the situation in Darfur since 1 July 2002 to ICC Prosecutor, clearly refers to the only provision which allows SC to initiate Prosecutor's investigations. The referral contains a particularly controversial and devoid of a specific basis in the Statute, limitation of ICC's activity, since in the sixth paragraph of the device it has the exclusive jurisdiction of the sending status, for all alleged acts or omissions arising out of or related to operations in Sudan established or authorized by the Council or the African Union. In other words, the conferral of jurisdiction to ICC is excluded with regard to a certain category of people, i.e. the personnel of States is not part of the statute that participates in operations for the maintenance or restoration of peace.

It was not easy to reach an agreement on this first activation of ICC by SC due above all to US attitude towards the jurisdiction of the Court[103]. In addition

humanity. Sudan has been the scene of coups several times. The last one was by the president Hassan Al-Bashir that took place in 1989 leading to a strong tension between the north of the country, mainly between Muslims and the indigenous that inhabit in the southern part. In particular, the unfair redistribution of the oil resources found in this area of the country and the accentuated islamization of the country were at the origin of the revolts of the liberation movements and the harsh government repression that followed.

[100]Report of the international Commission of inquiry on Darfur to the UN Security Council, UN doc. S/2005/60, 25 January 2005, parr. 571-572.

[101]Preamble of Resolution, parr. 5 and 6.

[102]A. CIAMPI, L. CONDORELLI, Comments on the security council referral of the situation in Darfur to the ICC, in Journal of International Criminal Justice, 3 (3), 2005, pp. 592ss. M. KAMTO, L'affaire Al Bashir et les relations de l'Afrique avec la cour pènale internationalke, in Liber amicorum Raymond Ranjeva. L'Afrique et le droit international: Variations sur l'organisation international. Africa and international law. Reflections on the international organizations, ed. Pedone, Paris, 2013, pp. 150ss. O.Y., ELAGAB, Indicting the Sudanese president by the ICC: Resolution 1593 revisited, in International Journal of Human Rights, 13 (5), 2009, pp. 658ss. E. DE WET, Referrals to the International Criminal Court under chapter VII of the United Nations Charter and the immunity of foreign state officials, in ASIL Unbound, 112, 2018, pp. 36ss. G. WERLE, F. JESSBERGER, Principles of international criminal law, op. cit., M.E. FOUTER, J. SCHMIDT, N.D. WHITE, Security and international law, Bloomsbury Publishing, New York, 2016, pp. 106ss. K.H. NATHANIÉL, La Cour Pènale Internationale (CPI) à l'èpreuve des poursuites en Afrique, in Afrique et Dèveloppement, 41 (2), 2016, pp. 134ss.

[103]The reasons for this hostility in particular in relation to the protection that must be guaranteed to personnel on mission, can be found in J.R. BOLTON, The risks and weaknesses of the international criminal court from America's perspective, in Law and Contemporary Problems, 64 (1), 2001, pp. 168ss. See also in argument. W.W. BURKE-WHITE, A community of courts. Toward a system of international criminal law

to the exemption that is granted to personnel engaged in peacekeeping operations, the Resolution is characterized by two other problematic elements. The explicit exclusion of financial support from UN and a singular reference to some bilateral agreements concluded in cooperation with ICC pursuant to art. 98 (2)[104]. These particular aspects of the Resolution are the result of a delicate political compromise which has been painstakingly achieved precisely to avoid the US veto. At the time of the vote, the latter abstained, not failing to emphasize the preference for the establishment of an ad hoc Court and, more generally, recalling their long standing and firm objections and concerns regarding the Court[105]. US continue to question the entire system created through the Treaty of Rome, as it would not guarantee "sufficient protection from the possibility of politicized prosecutions"[106].

Beyond this general concern, the central element of US criticism concerns rather the possibility that ICC exercises its jurisdiction over citizens of States not part of the Statute. This can occur, in fact both in the hypothesis of a referral of SC and in the case in which the crimes are committed on the territory of a State Party to the Statute. According to the American delegate: "Non-parties have no obligations in connection with that treaty"[107] and the exercise of Court jurisdiction over its citizens even in SC referral would be unacceptable[108].

From the critical positions expressed by the other States, concerns of a completely different nature arise precisely from the particular exemption provided for in the Resolution. Apart from the general complaint that the de facto legitimate Resolution makes "use of double standard (...) and a two-track justice"[109], several

---

enforcement, in Michigan Journal of International Law, 24 (2), 2002, pp. 5ss. M. MANDANI, Responsibility to protect or right to punish?, in Journal of Intervention and State Building, 4 (1), 2010, pp. 56ss.

[104]M. MANDANI, Responsibility to protect or right to punish?, op. cit.,

[105]The American delegate refers in particular to the creation of a hybrid tribunal in Africa, see, UN doc. S/PV.51538, 31 March 2005, p. 3.

[106]UN doc. S/PV.51538, 31 March 2005, p. 3.

[107]UN doc. S/PV.51538, 31 March 2005, p. 3.

[108]For the same reason, the Resolution recognizes the existence of the agreements stipulated on the basis of art. 98, par. 2 that the United States has concluded with numerous States to avoid the delivery to ICC of its own citizens, in the hypothesis in which such a request is made by the Court. See in argument: UN doc. S/PV.5158, 31 March 2005, p. 3. On this attitude of opposition to ICC action by US, to which some reference has already been made, we can see that China then assumed a position perhaps even more guaranteed of the sovereign prerogatives and the will of the State involved by the possible court action. On the one hand, it called for a solution that would see the Sudanese judicial system as a protagonist, possibly through technical assistance and monitoring by UN, and on the other hand it opposed the idea of a referral that did not also rely on the consent of the government itself. Sudanese emphasizing more generally the fear that the activation of ICC could produce negative effects on the peace process, UN doc. S/PV.51538, 31 March 2005, p. 5.

[109]See the position of Algeria, p. 5.The Algerian delegate also expressed his disappointment at the fact that SC has not paid the slightest attention to a proposal for intervention in Darfur coming from the African Union. More generally, the refusal of the other members of the

States seem to consider the guarantee of an exclusive jurisdiction of the State of citizenship for a given category of individuals, i.e. a legal exception that is inconsistent with international law[110]. The exclusion of citizens of some States from ICC jurisdiction, essentially "within the letters and spirit of the Rome Statute"[111], since in fact "circumvent the jurisdiction of the Court"[112] submitting thus the "ICC independence into the political and diplomatic vagaries of SC"[113]. In short, according to many States, SC Resolution raises several legal problems, as it limits the judicial action of the ICC contrary to the Statute and affects its autonomy with respect to SC action[114]. According to these criticisms art. 13 b) StICC would not accept the hypothesis that SC reports a situation to the Prosecutor by excluding certain categories or groups of individuals from the investigation.

The provision of the exclusive jurisdiction of the sending State also has a series of effects on national prosecutions. Although these aspects of the decision are not directly relevant for the purposes of this investigation, as non concern the judicial action of ICC, it seems however pertinent to underline the attitude of open opposition of some States towards the effects potentially produced on their own jurisdictional bodies by the exemption under exam. In fact, at least two States, France and Denmark have expressly stated that they wish to preserve their jurisdiction for the Commission of international crimes on the basis of the principle of universal jurisdiction or in the name of other criteria that may justify their legitimate exercise (victim's nationality)[115].

Through their oppositions, these States point out that this part of the device would in any case be the object if this was necessary for independent interpretation by the internal courts and that this interpretative activity of the national courts could not fail to take into account the other international obligations of the State and the other relevant criteria for the division of criminal jurisdiction in the event of an international crime Commission[116].

In essence, France and Denmark claim the possibility that their criminal courts will not follow up on the exemption provided by SC if they consider this measure incompatible with other rules relevant for the determination of their jurisdiction. What can be observed here is that a similar speech but on the point of course we will have to return, it could be done for ICC judges if they consider the requests coming from SC in contrast with the statutory rules relating to the

---

Council to adopt an African approach is the only one that could have led to peace and reconciliation.

[110]See the position of Brazil, p. 11. The States that voted in favor of the Resolution have also expressed their own regret for the planned exception. See also the positions of United Kingdom and Argentine, pp. 7 and 10ss.

[111]UN doc. S/PV.51538, 31 March 2005 p. 8, (Argentine)

[112]UN doc. S/PV.51538, 31 March 2005 p.9 (Tanzania)

[113]UN doc. S/PV.51538, 31 March 2005, p. 6 (Philippines)

[114]UN doc. S/PV.51538, 31 March 2005, p. 8 (France).

[115]UN doc. S/PV.51538, 31 March 2005, p. 6 (Denmark)

[116]UN doc. S/PV.51538, 31 March 2005, p. 8 (France)

exercise of jurisdiction.

2.2 The situation in Libya

The second case of referral power by SC concerns the situation in Libya. In the context of the so-called Arab springs of 2011 and harsh repression against opponents of the Gaddafi's regime, the UN High Commissioner had expressly called for an investigation by the ICC Prosecutor into the crimes committed in that country[117]. At the same time, many western States, the organization of the Islamic conference, the Arab league and the African union asked the international community to intervene and stop the widespread violence perpetrated by the regime. Thus through the Resolution n.1970 of 26 February 2011, SC has adopted a series of measures aimed at stopping violence against the civilian population and subjecting a situation created on the territory of a State not part of the Statute to ICC jurisdiction.

The legal basis for SC action is once again Chapter VII of the UN Charter. The Resolution also in this hypothesis, does not expressly mention art. 13 b) of the Statute[118]. However, it appears to the latter even more clearly attributable to the case of Darfur. Paragraphs 4 to 8 of the Resolution relating to ICC jurisdiction are placed under a title that leaves no room for uncertainty, i.e. ICC referral[119].

An important aspect of the Libyan case lies in the close link or better in the possible coexistence and compatibility, which SC implicitly recognizes with its own action in this context between the criminal repression of serious international crimes and military intervention. Through the subsequent Resolution n.1973 of 17 March 2011, SC also authorized the use of force to protect victims of the violent repression waged by the Gaddafi government. For the first time, in other words, the activation of ICC's criminal jurisdiction is accompanied by and overlaps with a military action authorized by UN. The choice made by SC seems to indicate that in some circumstances the measures involving the use of force and the instruments aimed at the prosecution of criminal proceedings can work together and contribute together for the restoration of peace[120]. The exercise of

---

[117]Navy Pillay, UN High Commissioner of Human Rights, to the fifteenth special session of the human rights Council, situation of human rights in the Libyan Arab Jamahiriya, 25 February 2011.

[118]M. MANDANI, Responsibility to protect or right to punish?, op. cit.,

[119]M. MANDANI, Responsibility to protect or right to punish?, op. cit.,

[120]C. STAHN, Libya, the international criminal court and complementarity, in Journal of International Criminal Justice, 10 (2), 2012, pp. 327ss. M.H. ZAWATI, The International Criminal Court and complementarity, in Journal of International Law and International Relations, 12, 2016, pp. 208-228. L.E. CARTER, The future of the International Criminal Court: Complementarity as a strength or a weakness?, in Washington University Global Studies Law Review, 12, 2013, pp. 454ss. D. ROBINSON, The mysterious mysteriousness of complementarity, in Criminal Law Forum, 21, 2010, pp. 6ss. C. STAHN, One step forward, two steps back? Second thoughts on a “sentence-based” theory of complementarity, in Harvard International Law Journal, 53, 2012, pp. 183-196. A. DAZA

jurisdiction by ICC may in some cases be combined with the use of force without at least in light of the political assessment made by SC, i.e. in the present case hampering the achievement of peace and international security[121].

The unanimity with which the Resolution was adopted may perhaps be an indication of a promising and renewed support for the penal system created through the Statute of Rome of 1998. The favorable vote was also expressed by countries, such as United States, Russia and China who not only are not part of the Statute but have always assumed skeptical attitudes if not open opposition to ICC and its work. Unlike the previous Resolution on Darfur, where there were eleven votes in favor and almost every delegation had for different reasons, expressed many doubts about some parts of the device, one could at first sight read the unanimity and the lack of protests by the representatives of the States as an acceptance of a well-established practice, that of guaranteeing an exemption from ICC jurisdiction (and from any other jurisdiction other than that of the sending State) for personnel engaged in missions abroad of nationalities not part of the StICC. On this second occasion, convinced of the importance of an intervention to stop the violence committed in Libya, most of the SC Member States did not detect any particular critical issues regarding the renewed prediction that: "(...) Nationals, current or former officials or personnel form a State outside the Libyan Arab Jamahiriya which is not subject to the exclusively jurisdiction of that State for all alleged acts or omissions arising out of or related to reparations in the Libyan Arab Jamahiriya established or authorized by the Council, unless

---

GONZÁLEZ, El principio de complementariedad en el derecho penal internacional, ed. Universidad Catòlica de Colombia, Bogotà, D.C, 2015. D. SASCHA, D. BACHMANN, L. EDA NWIBO, Pull and push- Implementing the complementarity principle of the Rome Statute of the ICC within the AU: Opportunities and challenges, in Brooklyn Journal of International Law, 43, 2018, pp. 464ss.

[121]A. BIRDSALL, The responsibility to protect and the ICC: A problematic relationship?, in Criminal Law Forum, 26 (1), 2015, pp. 26ss. M.S. ELLIS, Y. DOUTRIAUX, T.W. RYBACK, Justice and diplomacy: Resolving contradictions in diplomatic practice and international humanitarian and international humanitarian law, Cambridge University Press, Cambridge, 2018, pp. 102ss. S. GROVER, The responsibility to protect: Perspectives on the concept's meaning proper application and value, ed. Routledge, London & New York, 2018, pp. 101ss. J. RALPH, The international Criminal Court, in A.J. BELLAMY, T. DUNNE, The oxford handbook of the responsibility to protect, Oxford University Press, Oxford, 2016. By virtue of the numerous evidence collected against the defendants, the prosecutor decided about three months after the referral of the SC to ask the pre-trial chamber for the issue of an arrest warrant against Gaddafi, his second-born son and his brother-in-law and then head of intelligence services. A few days after the request of the prosecutor was accepted by the preliminary chamber which issued the three arrest warrants (ICC, Decision on the prosecutor's applicationn poursuant to article 58 as to Muammar Mohammed Abu Minyar Gaddafi, saif Al-Islam Gaddafi and Abdullah Al-Senussi, Pore trial chamber I, ICC-01/112-01/11-1, Warrant of arrest for Muammar Mohammed Abu Minyar Gaddafi, ICC-01/11-01/11-2; warrant of arrest fror Saif Al-Islam Gaddafi, ICC-01/11-01/11-03; Warrant of arrest fro Abdullah Al-Senussi, ICC-01/11-01/11-4, 27 June 2011).

such exclusive jurisdiction has been expressly waived by the State" (par. 6 of disposal)[122]. Only the Brazilian delegate, while explaining the reasons for his favorable vote in light of the gravity of the situation in Libya and the urgent need for the Council to send a strong, unified message has not given up expressing "strong reservation concerning paragraph 6" and the conviction that this practice of SC is not useful "to advancing the cause of justice and accountability" and more generally to strengthen the role of ICC on the international scene[123].

An interesting aspect of the reference to ICC of the situation in Libya concerns the forecast of a temporal datum aimed at limiting Prosecutor's investigations. The situation is referred only to crimes committed after 15 February 2011. It is not possible to find the reasons for this choice in the positions expressed by the States within SC. However, many have noted the interest of several western States so that their relations (in particular on the practice of so-called extraordinary deliveries) with Libya and the political and economic support offered to the Gaddafi regime until that date were not the subject of investigation by the Prosecutor[124]. As far as the choice can be criticized from a political point of view, this type of limitation ratione temporis of the situation open to investigations does not seem to be expressly precluded by any rule of the Statute.

The Libyan referral has another peculiarity that could and in principle raise some legal problems. The preamble of the Resolution in fact contains a qualification of the crimes committed in Libya con extensive and systematic attacks against the civilian population which according to SC "may amount to crimes against humanity"[125]. In the dispositive part, Statute's own language is used with reference to a general situation. At first glance it would therefore seem to be excluded at least in the present case that the activation of SC is intended to limit Prosecutor's investigations to some of the crimes that on the basis of art. 5 StICC fall within the ICC jurisdiction. In general, the possibility that SC qualifies some conduct as falling within a certain category of crime, or brings to the attention of the Prosecutor only a few criminal cases deserves our attention and will be investigated.

3. The "missed" referrals

3.1. The situation in Syria

In May 2014, after 3 years from the beginning of the violent armed conflict that still opposes the Syrian government to various insurrectional

---

122D. SAROOSHI, The United Nations and the development of collective security, op. cit.
123UN doc. S/PV-6491, p. 7
124See in argument: M. KERSTEN, Between justice and politics. The ICC's intervention in Libya, in C. DE VOS, S. KENDALL, C. STAHN, Contested justice. The politics and practice of international criminal court interventions, Cambridge University Press, Cambridge, 2015, pp. 462ss. P. CLARK, Distant justice: The impact of the International Criminal Court on African politics, Cambridge University Press, Cambridge, 2018.
125C. DEPREZ, L'applicabilitè des droits humains à l'action de la Cour pènale internationale, ed. Larcier, Bruxelles, 2016.

movements (and to the proclaimed Islamic State) and after a series of resolutions aimed at quickly implementing a dismantling program of the chemical weapons present in Syria[126], some permanent SC Member States have tried unsuccessfully to obtain the adoption of a resolution that reported to ICC the crimes committed in that country by the Syrian government and pro-government authorities and rebel groups starting from March 2011[127]. The motion for a resolution from France was presented as an appeal to human conscience and the exercise of veto power stigmatized as proof that some have learned from history and more generally as an act against justice[128]. China and the Russian Federation opposed this resolution while 13 votes in favor and none abstained[129]. US for the first time expressed an intense and passionate trust in ICC's activity aimed at suppressing the violence of the Syrian government. The other SC Member States, noted that in order to guarantee ICC independence and maintain the integrity of the Statute, the Prosecutor would eventually open preliminary investigations into the crimes committed by both parties. And this, moreover, was what was foreseen in the French proposal itself. The repressive action would in fact have concerned the criminal conduct perpetrated by Syrian authorities, pro-government militias and all the non-armed groups involved in the conflict. In other words, the proposal aimed to suppress crimes committed by all sides of the conflict without any distinction between government forces and opponents.

However, the draft resolution under examination also contains in the device the indication that "nationals current or former officials or personnel from a State outside the Syrian republic which is not a party to ICC Rome Statute shall be subject to the exclusive jurisdiction of that State for all alleged acts or

[126]See in particular Resolution n.2118 of 27 September 2013. Indeed, this Resolution already referred to the need to end impunity for the crimes committed in Syria and contained a first hint of the possibility of calling the ICC into question.

[127]Project of Resolution of 22 May 2014, S/2014/348.

[128]S/PV.7180, 22 May 2014, p. 4. For further details see: N. RONZITTI, Coercitive diplomacy sanctions and international law, Martinus Nijhoff Publishers, The Hague, 2016, pp. 234ss. G. WERLE, A. ZIMMERMANN, The International criminal Court in turbulent times, ed. Springer, Berlin, 2019. S. GROVER, The responsibility to protect: Perspectives on the concept's meaning, proper application and value, op. cit.,

[129]The Russian delegate insisted on the political use of ICC by US that on the one hand invoke the action but on the other impose the exemption of its citizens from the exercise of that jurisdiction. In the opinion of the Russian Federation, United States and United Kingdom (despite being the latter part of the Statute) they move with an arbitrary and selective approach that prevented ICC from investigating what happened in Iraq in 2003. As State not part of the Statute, China merely reiterated its reservations on the activation of ICC, considering in particular that any appeal to ICC should be conducted on the basis of respect for the state of sovereignty and the principle of complementarity. In a language not far from that used by US on previous occasions, the statements of the Chinese delegate are instead aimed at reaffirming the supremacy of the principle of state sovereignty in criminal matters. A sovereignty that is effectively protected by the consensual basis of the treaty of Rome and by the principle of complementarity which should guarantee the priority of national jurisdictions over that of ICC, even for States.

omissions arising out of or related to the Syrian Republic, established or authorized by the Council, unless such exclusive jurisdiction has been expressly waived by the State"[130].

Some States have criticized the choice to renew this practice. Argentina, for example, has decided not to be among the promoter States of the initiative, feeling the need to preserve the integrity of the Statute which would require formulating activation requests in the appropriate terms so as not to undermine the legal foundations of the Rome Statute or Court's validity and effectiveness[131].

Basically, some of the techniques already mentioned in the comparisons of a practice that, in the opinion of many States would conflict with the lethargy of the statutory provisions and compromise the legitimacy and effectiveness of the entire pact system, re-emerge here. In other words, it would be a power to amend the Statute of Rome and the SC cannot exercise. Even more interesting is the thesis supported by some States that this method of exercising the power of referral as contrary to the Statute, however, could not have any effect on the jurisdictional activity of ICC. In fact, since the Court is ultimately the judge of its own jurisdiction[132], when SC acts outside the statutory limits, court bodies would not be required to follow up on its requests[133].

A further element of interest is the provision of a time limit aimed at limiting the investigation activity. We refer to the serious violations of human rights and humanitarian law perpetrated in the course of the ongoing conflict in the Syrian Arab Republic since March 2011[134]. In this as well as in the precedent case relating to Libya the time limit set by SC does not seem to have aroused particular critical attitudes by States.

Finally, despite their support for the resolution, neither United States nor United Kingdom have expressed their opinion on another interesting element advanced during the debate always by the French and which has met with the approval of numerous States4[135], i.e. the idea to agree to the use of the right of

---

[130]Par. 7 of the disposal.

[131]UN doc. S/PV.7180, 22 May 2014, pp. 10ss.

[132]UN doc. S/PV.7180, 22 May 2014, pp. 10ss.

[133]Even the Chad, with more nuanced tones and indeed, to say the truth stating that these exemptions are in some cases justified (without however specifying to cases it refers), regrets that the draft Resolution, like those on Darfur and Libya, provides for the discretionary treatment of a category of nationals with respect to the same crime. In more general terms, the States that voted in favor of the Resolution argued that the ICC intervention could help restore stability in the country and contribute to the cessation of the most serious violations of humanitarian law. China and Russian Federations recalling the Libyan precedent, believed that the referral would only lead to an escalation of the conflict and would not be of any help to the restoration of peace and the pursuit of justice.

[134]UN doc. S/2014/348, 22 May 2014, parr. 1 and 2.

[135]See for example among the other SC Member States the positions of Rwanda, Jordan, Luxembourg, Chile, Australia. The Luxembourg delegate speaks explicitly of a abuse of the right of veto and how it affects the Securities Council's credibility and effectiveness, condemning it to inaction in the face of impunity. Lithuania, does not express itself on the

veto in the event that the SC finds itself intervening on issues related to the repression of genocidal crimes, war crimes or against humanity[136]. In practice, an attempt was made to suggest the idea that in the areas of SC intervention on the jurisdictional activity of ICC and in the exercise of the referral and deferral powers, the permanent members refrain from using their power to veto. The possibility of a consensus forming on this proposal among the permanent members is strictly political in nature, since such a limit to the exercise of the veto power has no legal basis or possible regulatory holds in the UN Charter.

3.2. The Islamic State (ISIS)

On 27 May 2015 SC discussed the possibility of reporting crimes committed by ISIS to ICC. Once again the initiative was taken by the French government and supported by several States[137]. The internal debate in SC in this case highlights the uncertainty of States with respect to the exact delimitation of the situation which may be the subject of the referral power. In a particularly complex context, such as that which characterizes the action to combat the Islamic State, the problem of establishing to what extent the SC circumscribe in ratione personae Prosecutor's investigative activity.

Most States have requested an activation of ICC jurisdiction for crimes committed by the Islamic State in Syria and Iraq[138]. Others have used more controversial expressions. The Argentine delegate referred to some "cases"[139], thus giving the impression that SC cannot only report single episodes of violence but perhaps also the suspected individuals. France always in the context of the violence perpetrated in Syria and Iraq instead it spoke of the need to deal with a series of matters concerning the "(...) perpetrators of war crimes and against humanity (...) in particular the Daesh terrorists (...)"[140]. In all these requests the idea that the referral of the SC could limit the jurisdictional action of the ICC to

---

possibility of a voluntary renunciation of the permanent members to the use of the veto power in situations like the Syrian one but underlines that the veto exercised from China and the Russian Federation is a stand on the wrong side of justice and accountability, a stand on the wrong side of humanity, see S/PV.7180, 22 May 2014, p. 10.

[136]See the previous proposal by President Hollande, opening of the 68th UN General Assembly of 24 September 2013. According to some, however, this proposal represents a credible and interesting solution to avoid insoluble conflicts between ICC and SC in exercising the powers that the Statute has attributed to the latter.

[137]Concept note for the Security Council open debate on the victims of attacks and abuses on ethnic or religious grounds in the Middle East, Annex to the letter dated 12 March 2015 from the chargè d'affaires, i.e. of the permanent mission of France to UN addressed to the Secretary General, 27 March 2015.

[138]S/PV-7419, 27 March 2015, see the positions expressed by the delegates of Bulgaria (p. 44), Slovenia (p. 60) and Croatia (p.68). Belgium (p.55) and Luxembourg (p. 65) as other States require the exercise of the power of referrals by SC with respect to the crimes committed in Syria and instead wish Iraq to join StICC.

[139]S/PV-7419, 27 March 2015, p. 78.

[140]S/PV-7419, 27 March 2015, p. 8.

the crimes committed by some specific groups of individuals in the present case ISIS. Solution that other states have clearly opposed. Hungary, for example, stressed that "such investigations should be conducted into all perpetrators not only Daesh (...)"[141]. To date, the ICC Prosecutor has simply clarified the reasons why its power of action is limited in the present case. First, the crimes in question were committed in Iraq and Syria, two States not part of the Statute. For this reason, ICC "has no territorial jurisdiction over crimes committed on their soil"[142]. Unless of course it is SC who reports the situation to the Prosecutor. Regarding ICC's ratione personae jurisdiction, Prosecutor said that the possibility of undertaking investigations without a referral from SC appears limited. In fact, although it has emerged that many of the components of the Islamic State are of nationality of States that are part of StICC (they mention in particular, Tunisia, Jordan, France, United Kingdom, Belgium, the Netherlands, Germany and Australia), the office of Prosecutor recalled that ICC's task is to prosecute the major perpetrators of international crimes under its jurisdiction. In light of the information available, it is particularly emphasized that ISIS is a military and political organization primarily led by nations of Syria and Iraq. In light of these considerations in the absence of a referral of SC, Prosecutor has highlighted that the possibility of activating one's action in the present case depends on the will of the two States which are not parties to the Statute, which can always pursuant to art. 12 (3) accept ICC jurisdiction[143].

Beyond Prosecutor's statements, aimed more than anything else to stimulate an intervention of SC, the question that remains controversial today and that is highlighted by the case in question, concerns the possibility for SC to delimit the investigations of the Prosecutor to a specific group of individuals. In short, the uncertainties once again concern the object of the referral and the extent of SC power to define its contours.

4. Legal problems between SC and ICC in the exercise of referral power

4.1. The meaning of the term "situation" and the ICC jurisdiction

The analysis of the preparatory work and the SC practice has already highlighted the importance of the definition of the term "situation" in order to delimit the subject of the referral. This notion presents elements of evanescence and indeterminacy which make the defining work particularly complex[144]. The

---

[141]S/PV-7419, 27 March 2015, p. 38.

[142]C. SOLER, The global prosecution of core crimes under international law, ed. Asser Press, The Hague, 2019.

[143]Statement of the Prosecutor of the international criminal court, Fatou Bensouda on the alleged crimes committed by ISIS, 8 April 2015.

[144]One can also recall the debate on the use of this term and the difficulty of distinguishing this notion from the controversy in artt. 12, 34 and 36 of the UN Charter.

expression is in fact deliberately broad and the statutory data does not help to understand how and to what extent it can be circumscribed and specified.

The only element contained in art. 13 StICC which in some way qualifies the notion in question is the circumstance that within the situation being reported, one or more crimes have been committed among those on which ICC can exercise its jurisdiction[145].

Indeed all the elements characterizing the situation subject to referral (not only the material ones) must fall within the jurisdiction of the Court so that it can exercise its jurisdiction over the violence reported by SC. In other words, once decided to activate the ICC jurisdiction, three SC must live within the parameters of the Rome Statute with respect to such matters as jurisdiction[146]. In the same way, Prosecutor's investigative action, even when it starts from a SC request, will have to comply with the statutory parameters. To put it in the words of court judges, through the exercise of referral power, SC "accepted that the investigation into the said situation, as well as any prosecution arising therefrom, will take place in accordance with the statutory framework provided for in the Statute (...)"[147].

So the Prosecutor who has the latest decision regarding the request to open the investigations (art. 53, (1))[148], will assess at least prima facie whether within the situation reported by SC there have actually been crimes committed by ICC and if the subject of the referral complies with the other jurisdictional criteria laid down by StICC[149]. In the light of this assessment, it will decide whether and within what limits to proceed with the reported situation. It is advisable to try to determine to what extent the possible interventions on the competence of ICC, possibly envisaged within the report coming from SC, can actually affect the

---

[145]This implies that the reporting of SC may relate to a situation in which even a single crime subject to ICC jurisdiction has been committed. In this case the subject of the referral is not the specific criminal conduct but remains the most general context within which the SC assumes what it has materialized. See in argument: F. BERMAN, The relationship between the international criminal Court and the Security Council, in H.A.M. VON HEBEL, J.G. LAMMERS, J. SCHUKKING, Reflections on the international criminal court: Essays in honor of Adriaan Bos, T.M.C. Asser press, The Hague, 1999, pp. 175ss.

[146]M. CHERIF BASSIOUNI, The legislative history of the International Criminal Court: Introduction, analysis and integrated text. Volume I, ed. Brill/Martinus Nijhoff Publishers, New York, 2005, pp. 151ss. W.A. SCHABAS, The international criminal court. A commentary to the Rome statute, Oxford University Press, Oxford, 2010, pp. 302ss. W.A. SCHABAS, G. PECORELLA, Article 13, in O. TRIFFTERER, K. AMBOS, The Rome statute of the international criminal court. A commentary, C.H.Beck-Hart-Nomos, München, Oxford, Baden-Baden, 2016, pp. 702ss. O. QUIRICO, International criminal responsibility. Antinomies, ed. Routledge, London & New York, 2019.

[147]ICC, Prosecutor v. Omar Hassan Ahmad Al Bashir, decision on the prosecution's application for a warrant of arrest against Omar Hassan Ahmad Al Bashir, pre-trial Chamber I, ICC-02/05-01/09-3, 4 March 2009, par. 45.

[148]W.A. SCHABAS, The international criminal court. A commentary to the Rome statute, op. cit.,

[149]H. OLASOLO, The triggering procedure of the International Criminal court, Martinus Nijhoff Publishers, Leiden, Boston, 2005, pp. 122ss.

personal, territorial, temporal and material context of the investigation activity.

4.1.1. The competence ratione personae

It does not apply to the referral of SC art. 12 (2) b) StICC which identifies as one of the two conditions for the exercise of ICC jurisdiction, the fact that the accused is a citizen of a State party of StICC. The Prosecutor therefore within the situation reported by SC will be able to conduct its own investigative activity against any individual, regardless of the state of citizenship of the same.

However, StICC is limited to ICC's ratione personae jurisdiction despite the French proposal to include forms of criminal liability for legal entities within it[150]. Art. 25 (1) establishes in an extremely clear way that ICC "shall have jurisdiction over natural persons"[151]. Obviously this limit cannot be overcome even when the activation request comes from SC. Another impassable limit is expressed by art. 26 StICC in light of which the ICC cannot exercise its jurisdiction "over any person who was under the age of eighteen at the time of the alleged commission of a crime"[152].

A different and more complex question is whether the report may concern an individual, suspected of having committed one or more of the crimes of ICC jurisdiction. Some authors, who also underlined the importance of choosing the term "situation" in guaranteeing an effective separation of powers within the ICC system do not exclude that the SC may consider a criminal action necessary against for example a political or military leader. The admissibility of such a hypothesis derives from the fact that the impunity of such a subject may in itself represent a threat to international peace and security[153].

Indeed, one of the few elements of certainty that can be deduced from an analysis of the meaning that States have intended to attribute to the term "situation" concerns precisely the impossibility of including individual notifications in this notion[154]. The preparatory work clearly reveals that the choice of the word "situation" was dictated precisely by the need to prevent the from reporting individual cases to the Prosecutor, adding to the notitia criminis its own indication of the author or suspected perpetrators of criminal conduct. This

---

[150]United Nations diplomatic conference of plenipotentiaries on the establishment of an international criminal court, Rome, 15 June-17 July 1998, official records, vol. II). Proposal submitted by France, UN doc. A/CONF.183/C.1/L.3, Art. 23, parr. 5 and 6 and UN doc. A/CONF.183/C.1/WGGP/L.5.

[151]O. QUIRICO, International criminal responsibility. Antinomies, op. cit.,

[152]O. QUIRICO, International criminal responsibility. Antinomies, op. cit.,

[153] SC according to this position, could report to the Prosecutor a situation in which one or more crimes were committed: "Even by one single individual". See in argument: L. CONDORELLI, L. VILLALPANDO, Referral and deferral by the Security Council, in A. CASSESE, P. GAETA, J.R.W.D. JONES, The Rome statute of the international criminal court. A commentary, Oxford University Press, Oxford, 2002, pp. 634ss.

[154]F. BERMAN, The relationship between the international criminal Court and the Security Council, in H.A.M. VON HEBEL, J.G. LAMMERS, J. SCHUKKING, Reflections on the international criminal court: Essays in honor of Adriaan Bos, op. cit., pp. 174ss.

solution was as a direct consequence the reduction of the risks of a political use of the criminal instrument and to guarantee some form of separation between political and judicial power[155]. ICC said that criminal proceedings before the Court begin with a situation and end with a concrete case, when one or more suspects have been identified for the purpose of prosecution[156]. In essence, a criminal context should be reported to the Court, within which it will then be up to its bodies to identify the individuals responsible for the individual illegal conduct. As repeatedly mentioned by the ICC judges, the situation covered by the referral should in any case be defined in its territorial, temporal and possible personal parameters[157]. It would therefore seem that SC as well as the States Parties that address the Prosecutor must not only identify the geographical areas and the time span of the situations within which it considers what crimes subject to jurisdiction have been committed, but can also indicate the group (s) of individuals it considers responsible for these serious violations[158].

---

[155]All judicial systems are inspired by this objective of independence of the return, as the interesting report of the European Commission for Democracy through Law (Commission of Venice). European standards on the independence of the judicial system reminds us Part II. The public Prosecutor, adopted by the Commission of Venice at its 85th plenary Session (Venice, 17-18 December 2010), pp. 6ss. According to some reconstructions, the power to refer individual cases would also be contrary to SC powers deriving from Chapter VII of the UN Charter. Article 39 would allow SC to deal only with situations of emergency for international peace and not with individual cases. Also the measures provided for in articles 41 and 42 would be characterized by a certain width which would lead to the exclusion of the reporting of a specific case among those that can be adopted for the purpose of maintaining peace and international security. See in argument: D. SAROOSHI, The peace and justice: Paradox. The international criminal court and the UN Security Council, in D. MCGOLDRICK, P. ROWE, E. DONNELLY (ed. by), The Permanent International Criminal Court. Legal and policy issues, Hart Publishing, Oxford & Portland, Oregon, 2004.

[156]ICC, Decision pursuant to article 125 of the Rome Statute on the authorization of an investigation into the situation in the Republic of Kenya, pre-trial Chamber II, ICC.01-09/09-19-Corr., 31 March 2010, par. 41.

[157]ICC, Prosecutor v. Lubanga, Decision concerning pre-trial Chamber decision of 10 February 2006 and the incorporation of documents into the record of the case against Mr. Thomas Lubanga Dyilo. Pre-trial chamber I, ICC-01/04-01/06-8-Corr, 24 February 2006, par. 21. Prosecutor v. Katanga, decision on the evidence and information provided by the prosecution of issuance of a warrant of arrest for Germain Katanga. Pre-trial Chamber I, ICC-01/04-01/07-4, 5 November 2007, par. 9. Prosecutor v. Bemba, decision on Prosecutor's application for a warrant of arrest against Jean-Pierre Bemba Gombo. Pre-trial Chamber III, ICC-01/05-01/08-14-tENG, 10 June 2008, par. 16. See also in argument: W.A. SCHABAS, The international criminal court. A commentary to the Rome statute, op. cit., pp. 374ss.

[158]Unlike an ICC Chamber stated that the referral would not be limited to crimes "committed by certain persons or crimes committed before or after a given date, as long as crimes are committed within the context of the situation of crisis that triggered court jurisdiction of investigations and prosecution can be initiated". See, Prosecutor v. Mbarushimana, Decision on the defence challenge to the jurisdiction of the court, pre-trial

Against this thesis we often tend to highlight how the term "situation" was chosen also to avoid the so-called one sided referrals hypothesis. We try to recall reasons of judicial policy, linked to the inopportunity of a political selection of the party responsible for the violence in contexts of conflict. In support of this argument, there would still be the need to guarantee in some way an effective separation of powers, the independence of the judicial bodies in identifying those responsible for crimes and the principle of equality of individuals before the law[159].

The criticism and the argument of the one-sided referral appears decisive if the report comes from a state party and is done in order to repress the crimes committed by a part of the conflict and guarantee forms of impunity for those possibly perpetrated by the forces in power[160]. Even a partisan choice made by SC aimed at protecting the general interest of the collectivity of States in the maintenance of peace, however, can pose many problems from a political point of view and for this reason it concerns the independence that should be guaranteed to exercise the judicial function. On the other hand, even in the past experiences of the courts for the former Yugoslavia and Rwanda the SC has been careful not to indicate the crimes committed by one or some of the parties to the conflict as the only object of criminal repression. The jurisdiction of those courts was limited only from a temporal, territorial and material point of view[161].

It is clear that the hermeneutical difficulties posed by the definition of the term "situation" force the impartiality of judicial action and its autonomy with respect to the action of political bodies rather than the interpretation of the relevant provisions[162].

---

chamber I, ICC-01/04-01/10-451, 26 October 2011, par. 27. The attitude of the judges to the possible delimitation of the situation appears different, however, when SC activates the jurisdiction. No critical findings have been made, for example on the expected time limit in the Libyan case.

159 It is interesting to recall some reflections made in the doctrine that basically the selectivity exercised from SC in referring certain situations: "Is in some sense more transparent than the rather opaque determination by the Prosecutor". See in argument: W.A. SCHABAS, Selecting situations and cases, in C. STAHN, The law and practice of the international criminal court, Oxford University Press, Oxford, 2015, pp. 375ss.

160 P. GAETA, Is the practice of self-referrals a sound start from the ICC?, in Journal of International Criminal Justice, 2 (4), 2004, pp. 952ss.

161 It may be recalled that these courts have dealt only with the individuals most responsible for the crimes subject to jurisdiction. However, it has never been thought to draw a distinction based on the nationality or belonging of the individual to a particular group. There was no lack of accusations of impartiality with regard to the activity of these tribunals, much has been written about it, so you can see some general reflections in P. AKHAVAN, The rise and fall and rise of international criminal justice, in Journal of International Criminal Justice, 11 (3), 2013, pp. 528ss.

162 Among the principles that are usually put in place there is of course also that of equality of individuals before the law. Although guiding the interpreter, this principle can hardly be decisive since it is intentionally compressed by the same Statute through its own with the conferral of referral and deferral powers to SC. See in argument: V. GOWLLAND-

If we look at the internal legal systems, the autonomy of judicial action or in a broad sense the separation of powers, is not considered in itself incompatible with the attribution of a certain role to the executive bodies in determining the people against whom start a criminal case. A comparative analysis of the relationships between executive bodies and prosecutors in internal systems shows the variety of forms that the practice of separation of powers principle can take. Here we limit ourselves to remembering due to the impossibility of delving into the complexity of the theme that despite the heterogeneity of the formulas chosen by the different legal systems, forms of political orientation of the investigative activities of prosecutors are almost always provided.

Discretion in the orientation of repressive policies should in principle concern categories of crime rather than people. It does not seem that the legitimacy of a choice of criminal policy aimed at making the repressive action prioritize compared to other criminal conduct, on the illicit behaviors perpetrated by a particular criminal organization and therefore by specific groups of individuals, can absolutely be excluded. Internally, there has been no lack of political guidelines aimed at directing the attention of repressive action to certain terrorist groups or particular criminal organizations, to those of the mafia type. These are political choices aimed at repressing the crimes that arouse greater social alarm in the community or rather in the perspective more closely linked to SC action that threaten the international order's stability.

The priority eventually indicated by the political bodies does not imply an exclusivity of the repressive action with respect to those particular groups of individuals. In other words, the possibility that SC identifies a sort of precedence to be accorded in the course of investigations to the crimes committed by some criminal groups does not seem to affect the principle, confirmed in some way by the experiences of the ad hoc courts and considered central to guarantee the impartiality of the judicial body for which a referring body cannot limit the jurisdictional parameters of a situation to one side of the conflict[163].

Ultimately, the political direction expressed by SC does not prevent the Prosecutor from investigating and prosecuting international crimes committed by other parties involved in the conflict on the territory subject to referral. For example, in the face of a report by SC relating to the crimes committed by the Islamic State in Iraq or in Syria it can be argued that the investigations should in

---

DEBBAS, The relationship between the Security Council and the projected ICC, in Journal of Armed Conflict, 3 (1), 1997, pp. 115ss.

[163]R. RASTAN, Situation and case. Defining the parameters, in C. STAHN, M. EL ZEIDY, The international criminal court and complementarity, Cambridge University Press, Cambridge, 2011, pp. 432ss. Y. DERMOTT, The Ashgate research companion to international criminal law: Critical perspectives, ed. Routledge, London & New York, 2016. R. CRYER, D. ROBINSON, S. VASILIEV, An introduction to international criminal law and procedure, op. cit., pp. 422ss. A. SKANDER GALAND, United Nations Security Council referrals to the International Criminal Court: Legal nature, effects and limits, ed. Brill, The Hague, 2018, pp. 206ss.

principle focus on those particular criminal conduct without however excluding that the Prosecutor if a need emerges during the course of the investigative activities then ask for authorization to open investigations into crimes committed on those territories by other parts of the conflict. Moreover, it is precisely this latter possibility that has induced SC to include within its reports the exemption from the jurisdiction of the Court to be able to citizens of States not part of StICC who participate in peacekeeping missions.

As far as they indicate on the same problem the possible delimitation of ICC competence ratione personae, the practice referred to the exemptions from ICC jurisdiction some categories of individuals must be kept distinct from the hypothesis just examined. In doctrine many investigations tend to treat the report and in some way its opposite, the exemption of a particular group of individuals from ICC jurisdiction, in a joint manner inevitably reaching the same result, that is that the referral of SC can be made only without conditions as to the personal scope of prosecutions[164].

The opposition of StICC to the practice that emerged in the resolutions relating to Darfur and Libya is in general connected once again to the preference given to the term "situation" over that of "cases"[165]. It is common to recall, as an element of practice in support of this thesis, the Ugandan case. It is often highlighted, as in the Ugandan government's self-referral for crimes committed on its territory by the Lord's Resistance Army, the ICC Prosecutor replied that "the scope of the referral encompasses all crimes committed in northern Uganda in the context of the ongoing conflict involving LRA (...)"[166].

In short, in the face of a report concerning the crimes committed by a particular group of individuals, it is underlined how the Prosecutor proceeds against all the crimes committed in the broader context of armed conflict in which that particular group was involved. This hypothesis is similar to the one just considered in relation to the Islamic State and would ultimately demonstrate that "no (...) exception ratione personae could be effective (...)"[167].

---

[164]W.A. SCHABAS, The international criminal court. A commentary to the Rome statute, op. cit., pp. 374ss.

[165]W.A. SCHABAS, G. PECORELLA, Article 13, in O. TRIFFTERER, K. AMBOS, The Rome statute of the international criminal court. A commentary of the international criminal court. A commentary, op. cit., pp. 700ss. S.A. WILLIAM, W.A. SCHABAS, Article 13, in O. TRIFFTERER, Commentary on the Rome statute, observer's notes, article by article, Oxford, Baden-Baden, München, 2008, pp. 572ss. D. RUIZ VERDUZCO, The relationship between the ICC and the United Nations Security Council, op. cit., pp. 36ss.

[166]See decision to convene a status conference on the investigation in the situation in Uganda in relation to the application of article 53, ICC-02/04-01/05, 2 December 2005, par. 5. D. RUIZ VERDUZCO, The relationship between the ICC and the United Nations Security Council, op. cit., pp. 36.

[167]W.A. SCHABAS, G. PECORELLA, Article 13, in O. TRIFFTERER, K. AMBOS, The Rome statute of the international criminal court. A commentary of the international criminal court. A commentary, op. cit., pp. 700ss. While denying that the exemptions can be part of the referral draws a parallelism with the Ugandan case. C. CRYER, Sudan,

Although the idea of impossibility of applying personal limits to ICC jurisdiction through the referral is generally shared the forms of exemption arranged to protect certain categories of individuals do not seem to fall within the scope of application of art. 13 b). If the purpose of the "trigger" mechanisms is to activate the action of the Prosecutor with respect to situations in which one or more crimes have been committed, it is not clear how the exclusion from ICC jurisdiction of some categories of individuals could represent a notitia crimins, thus constitute the object or part of the referral object. In light of the letter of art. 13 b), what the SC (or a State Party) signals to the Prosecutor is nothing but a context of violence where crimes have been committed[168].

In the next chapter we will try to see if and in what way those exemptions or other limitations of the action of the bodies of ICC can be rather an expression of the power of SC to suspend the jurisdictional activity of ICC provided by art. 16 StICC[169].

4.1.2. (Follows) Competence ratione personae and immunity rules

A final question concerning ICC's ratione personae competence, which is also extremely complex, concerns the relationship between SC's exercise of referral power and the customary rules on personal immunity. What we are interested in examining is whether the resolutions through which SC signals a situation of widespread violence to ICC organs can produce effects on immunities enjoyed by the highest offices of States not part of the Statute, possibly affected by the repressive action.

The problem arose in relation to the arrest warrant issued against the Sudanese President Al Bashir is particularly controversial to the point of having produced a decidedly fluctuating ICC jurisprudence. It should be made clear immediately that this jurisprudence largely concerns the (alleged) violation of the obligations of cooperation with the ICC of the States Parties of StICC and will be taken up for those purposes in chapter three. In many of the decisions under consideration, the denial by the judges of the Sudanese President's personal immunity essentially has the effect of avoiding the application of art. 98 (1) StICC[170]. What concerns us now concerns only the possible effects of SC

---

resolution 1593 and international criminal justice, in Leiden Journal of International Law, 2006, 19, pp. 212ss.

[168]D.J. SCHEFFER, Staying the course with the international criminal court, in Cornell International Law Journal, 35 (1), 2001-2002, pp. 90ss. W.A. SCHABAS, N. BERNAZ, Routledge handbook of international criminal law, ed. Routledge, London & New York, 2010. O. BEKOU, The International Criminal Court, ed. Routlege, London & New York, 2017.

[169]O. BEKOU, The International Criminal Court, op. cit.,

[170]In the light of this provision the ICC in the field of assistance and judicial cooperation, cannot require a State Party to act in a way incompatible with international obligations regarding immunity that it has towards a third State, unless ICC has not obtained from the

resolutions on the exercise of ICC jurisdiction ratione personae and not on the obligations of States to cooperate with ICC.

In one of the first ICC decisions, Al Bashir's personal immunity was denied on the basis of the existence of a customary rule in the light of which there would be an exception to the immunity of heads of State when the crime Commission proceeding international proceedings against him is conducted by an international tribunal[171]. No particular effect on personal immunities was in principle directly attributed to the fact that ICC's action is grounded in a SC decision. Beyond the existence of the exception recognized by the pre-trial Chamber, this solution has the advantage of somehow detaching the problem of personal immunity from that of the scope of SC referral.

In more recent decisions, however, the removal of the immunity of the Sudanese President is directly descended from SC Resolution n.1593 (2005)[172]. However, the arguments put forward by the Court chambers in support of this conclusion were different. At first the judges considered that through the Resolution, SC "implicitly waived the immunities guaranteed to Omar Al Bashir under international law and attached to his position as a head of State (...)"[173]. This

---

latter the waiver to invoke the immunities of its organs.

[171]ICC, Prosecutor v. Omar Hassan Ahmad Al Bashir, decision pursuant to article 87 (7) of the Rome Statute on the failure by the Republic of Malawi to comply with the cooperation requests issued by the Court with respect to the arrest and surrender of Omar Hassan Ahmad Al Bashir, pre-trial Chamber I, 12 December 2011, par. 43. Customary international law creates an exception to head of State immunity when international courts seek an arrest for the commission of international crimes. ICC has adopted ICTY jurisprudence (see in particular, Prosecutor v. Milošević, decision on preliminary motions, 8 November 2001, par. 28) and of the Special Court for Sierra Leone (SCSL) (Prosecutor v. Charles Taylor, decision on immunity from jurisdiction, Appeals Chamber 31 May 2004, parr. 50-54. There is a winter who has criticized the SCSL latest decision: The exception would not only apply to international courts but would be general. See in particular: J. WOUTERS, The judgment in the arrest warrant case: Some critical remarks, in Leiden Journal of International Law, 16 (2), 2003, pp. 259ss. See also ILC, Draft code of crimes against the peace and security of mankind, in Yearbook of the International Law Commission, 1006, article 7. A. CASSESE, International criminal law, Oxford University Press, Oxford, 2008, pp. 312ss. P. GAETA, Official capacity and immunities, in A. CASSESE, P. GAETA, J.R.W.D. JONES, The Rome statute of the international criminal court. A commentary, Oxford University Press, Oxford, 2002. D. AKANDE, International law immunities and the international criminal court, in American Journal of International Law, 98 (3), 2004, pp. 416ss. B. KRZAN, Prosecuting international crimes, ed. Brill, Martinus Nijhoff Publishers, The Hague, Bruxelles, 2016.

[172]C. STAHN, The law and practice of the International Criminal Court, Oxford University Press, Oxford, 2015. G. SLUITER, H. FRIMAN, S. LINTON, International criminal procedure: Principles and rules, Oxford University Press, Oxford, 2013.

[173]ICC, Decision on the cooperation of the Democratic Republic of the Congo regarding Omar Al Bashir's arrest and surrender to the court, pre-trial chamber II, ICC-02/05-01/09-195, 9 April 2014, par. 29. See also in argument: E. DE WET, The implications of president Al-bashir's visit to South Africa for international and domestic law, in Journal of

implicit removal would be the result of cooperation obligations imposed on Sudan by the Resolution, aimed at eliminating any impediment to the proceedings before the Court, including immunities lifting[174]. This solution is not particularly convincing. It is not clear why a SC decision aimed at removing (explicitly or implicitly) the immunities of the Sudanese bodies should amount to a waiver by the State concerned, which could only be expressed by the subjects legitimated to express the consent of it (the Sudanese government, however, it has constantly called for the immunity of President Al Bashir). It is not clear on what basis from the SC resolution such an implicit removal of the personal immunities of individuals-organs of the Sudanese State should be deduced[175]. Not only is there no textual element supporting this interpretation, but issues relating to the immunities of the Sudanese bodies have never been discussed in SC in the debates prior to the adoption of the decision.

Also because of these inconsistencies in July of 2017 the ICC judges further revised their approach. No implicit or explicit waiver would be in ICC's opinion necessary to bring down the immunity of Al Bashir. More simply, when the SC decides to use ICC for the repression of international crimes under ICC jurisdiction the interactions between Sudan and the Court with respect to Court's exercise of jurisdiction in the situation in Darfur are regulated by the Statute. In other words, all the statutory provisions would apply to Sudan, as if it were a state party to the Statute. Art. 27 (2) makes "inapplicable any immunity on the ground of official capacity belonging to Sudan that could otherwise exist under

International Criminal Justice, 13 (5), 2005, pp. 1050ss. W.A. SCHABAS, The international criminal court. A commentary to the Rome statute, op. cit., pp. 604ss. G. METTRAUX, J. DFUGARD, M. DU PLESSIS, Heads of state immunities, international crimes and president Bashir's visit to South Africa, in International Criminal Law Review, 18 (4), 2018. C.C. JALLOH, K.M. CLARKE, V.O. NMEHIELLE, The African court of justice and human and peoples' rights in context: Development and challenges, Cambridge University Press, Cambridge, 2019, pp. 730ss. G. METTRAUX, International crimes: Law and crimes, genocide, op. cit., pp. 128ss. N. DYANI-MHANGO, South Africa's dilemma: Immunity laws, international obligations and the visit by Sudan's President Omar al Bashir, in Washington International Law Journal, 26 (3), 2017, pp. 544ss.

[174]ICC, Decision on the cooperation of the Democratic Republic of the Congo regarding Omar Al Bashir's arrest and surrender to the court, Pre-trial Chamber II, ICC-02/05-01/09-195, 9 April 2014. The judges argue that the resolution would be meaningless if interpreted differently. The criterion of useful effect in practice would require not to deprive the referral of its purpose of pursuing crimes necessarily committed by state organs. We are talking about the personal immunities enjoyed by the highest state authorities. Excluding the head of state and government and perhaps the foreign ministry, the ICC would remain fully free to prosecute all other individuals-organs suspected of committing the crimes.

[175]Has anyone wondered why the resolution of SC implicitly removed the personal immunities of Sudanese individuals-organs when it explicitly provided forcing Sudan to assist ICC? The renunciation of immunity by the State must always be explicit and emerges from the works of ILC, Third report on the immunity of state official's from foreign criminal jurisdiction, Special rapporteur Kolodkin, UN doc. A/CN.4/646, 24 May 2011, parr. 39-42.

international law"[176].

The latter solution appears correct only to the extent that and in this part of the discussion the statutory rules applicable to the third State are those related to the exercise of ICC jurisdiction, i.e. in practice the substantive and procedural rules governing the operation of ICC in the exercise of the criminal action. On this point we return in the chapter dedicated to the subject, which cannot instead be made for the cooperation obligations that concern the relations between ICC and the States and are expressly governed by the Statute in order to distinguish the position of the been part of those not part of the treaty.

In other words, the cooperation with ICC does not concern the competence and exercise of ICC jurisdiction, but a different area, so to speak, of the external relations of ICC governed by specific statutory rules and above all by any agreements concluded between ICC and third States. The exercise of ICC jurisdiction instead in whatever way it is activated has a single set of operating rules that are necessarily applied in their entirety by the ICC bodies, regardless of the particular mechanism on which the jurisdiction rests. These rules include art. 27 which provides for the irrelevance of the official qualification for the exercise of ICC jurisdiction[177].

---

[176]ICC, Decision under article 87 (7) of the Rome Statute on the non-compliance by South Africa with the request by the Court for the arrest and surrender of Omar Al Bashir, Pre-trial chamber II, ICC-02/05-01/09, 6 July 2017, par. 91. Solution which is not accepted from O. TRIFFTERER, C. BURCHARD, Article 27, in O. TRIFFTERER, K. AMBOS, The Rome statute of the international criminal court. A commentary of the international criminal court. A commentary, C.H.Beck-Hart-Nomos, München, Oxford, Baden-Baden, 2016, pp. 1054ss. But it was acceptable from P. AKANDE, The legal nature of Security Council referrals, in Journal of International Criminal Justice, 7 (2), 2009, pp. 342ss: "Sudan is to be treated as bound by the Statute and as if it were a party to it". Moreover, this solution does not seem so distant from that expressed when the arrest warrant was issued against it Al Bashir. The Pre-trial Chamber made use of the following arguments: The scope of the treaty put an "end to the impunity for the perpetrators of the most serious crimes of concern to the international community"; Art. 27 StICC, which is: "Applicable to all persons without distinction based on official capacity (...) capacity as Head of State or government (...) shall in no case exempt a person from criminal responsibility". Art. 21 StICC which has recourse to customary law only when there are gaps in the statutes. And in finis, the fact that SC when it refers to ICC also accepts the regulatory framework established by the Statute. See also in argument: ICC, Prosecutor v. Omar Hassan Ahmad Al Bashir, Decision on the prosecution's application for a warrant of arrest against Omar Hassan Ahmad Al Bashir, Pre-trial chamber I., ICC-02/05-01/09-3, 4 March 2009, parr. 42-45. The Pre-trial Chamber had not in this case clarified and developed the consequences of SC Resolution on immunity rules. This decision was criticized in its arguments and not in the result achieved, by those who consider the solution based on the idea that art. 27, par. 2 corresponds to customary law. See, P. GAETA, Does president Al Bashir enjoy immunity from arrest?, in Journal of International Criminal Justice, 7 (2), 2009, pp. 324ss. A. SKANDER GALAND, United Nations Security Council referrals to the International Criminal Court: Legal nature effects and limits, op. cit.,

[177]O. BEKOU, The International Criminal Court, op. cit.,

4.1.3. The ratione temporis competence

The only time limit provided for ICC jurisdiction is contained in art. 11 StICC. This provision guaranteeing the principle of non-retroactivity of the criminal law does not seem to leave room for referrals to SC relating to situations prior to 2 July 2002. The rule is extremely clear in stating that the ICC has jurisdiction only with respect to crimes committed after the entry into force of this Statute. Moreover, the limit is confirmed by another statutory provision which looks at the defendant's guarantees. Art. 24 (1) which makes explicit the principle of non-retroactivity states that no individual shall be criminally responsible for conduct prior to the entry into force of the Statute. In light of these principles, the ICC should limit its investigative activity within situations that are the subject of reporting to crimes committed in a period subsequent to the entry into force of the Statute[178].

The second paragraph of art. 11 is addressed instead to the States that ratified the Statute on 1st July 2002. In this case the competence of ICC will be limited to the crimes committed since the entry into force of the Statute for that particular State Party. Here one might then ask whether SC could extend ICC's jurisdiction also in relation to crimes committed on the territory of that State on a date prior to the entry into force of the Statute for that State but in any case subsequent to 1st July 2002. It seems that the question is affirmative. It is not clear why, and the Statute does not offer arguments to support the existence of such a limit, the SC can impose the ICC jurisdiction towards States not part of the Statute. SC cannot activate the ICC jurisdiction towards a State for crimes committed on its territory in the period when it was not yet part of the Statute, that is, for crimes committed from 1st July 2002 until the date of entry into force of the treaty for that State.

It is more problematic to establish whether the SC can also set a time limit for the situation being reported, that is, a date beyond which it is not possible to proceed with the investigation. This is particularly relevant for those situations, which are the subject of referrals concerning crimes committed on the territory of States not part of the Statute. As for the States Parties, in fact, the Prosecutor will always have the opportunity to act on his motu even beyond the time limit set by SC.

In general, it can be observed that if the situation of violence reported by SC has already ended and the subject of referral are the crimes committed in a

---

[178]According to some analyzes, the Statute could be interpreted in the sense of non-application of art. 11 in case of SC referral. The time limit would therefore not be used for events that occurred before the establishment of ICC or the ratification of the Statute by the State concerned as long as it is of course (in observance of the principle of non-retroactivity) conduct that can already be prosecuted in the light of customary law, see L. CONDORELLI, L. VILLALPANDO, Can the Security Council extend the ICC's jurisdiction, in A. CASSESE, P. GAETA, J.R.W.D. JONES, The Rome statute of the international criminal court. A commentary, Oxford University Press, Oxford, 2002, pp. 582ss.

certain period of time already past, it is decidedly less worrying and problematic than the hypothesis of the opposition of a time limit in relation to ongoing violence. In the latter case, the decision of SC can be particularly arbitrary, affecting a repressive action in full swing and against existing criminal conduct[179].

Apart from the different implications that depending on the contexts may have a time limit affixed to the situation subject to referral, this hypothesis has not yet occurred in practice and at the moment it seems difficult to offer a definitive answer to the question. Especially since another question closely related to the one under consideration is not resolved by the Statute. The possibility for SC to withdraw its referral.

On these aspects, we can limit ourselves to observing how the Statute indeed provides only one means for SC to temporally limit the exercise of ICC jurisdiction. This is the suspensive power recognized by art. 16. It can therefore be argued that the possibility for the political body to arrest through repeated annual renewals lies in that particular and pregnant power. The judicial activity of the Court once activated proceed for the binaries of the statutory rules and the discretion of the judicial organs. In this regard, one cannot underestimate the fact that in light of art. 53 (1) c)[180], the Prosecutor may believe that the interests of justice are better guaranteed through an extension of investigative activities and this choice could of course be influenced and conditioned by the positions expressed by SC and also perhaps by the fact that the situation from this reported was limited to a specific period of time.

4.4.1. The ratione loci competence

The other condition foreseen by art 12(2) StICC does not apply to SC referral, i.e. the fact that the crime was committed on the territory of a State Party (let. A). SC may report to the Prosecutor in situations which crimes have been committed within the territory of States not part of the Statute[181]. And it is very likely that as it has already done in Darfur and Libya cases, it uses this power precisely towards third States.

One question that could be asked concerns the hypothesis that SC decides to report the Commission of crimes committed on a certain portion of the territory of a State. Art. 12 relating to conditions of jurisdiction exercise in Prosecutor's motu or in referral action by a State, limits itself to establishing a ICC competence in the territory of a State Party. The rule does not refer to crimes that have occurred throughout the State, nor does it exclude that the situation subject to referral

---

[179]This admissibility is given according to the author from the fact that ICC jurisdiction has no other basis than the referral of SC and the limits imposed by the latter if compatible with the Statute, must comply.

[180]W.A. SCHABAS, The international criminal court. A commentary to the Rome statute, op. cit.,

[181]S. BOURGON, Jurisdiction ratione loci, in A. CASSESE, P. GAETA, J.R.W.D. JONES, The Rome statute of the international criminal court. A commentary, Oxford University Press, Oxford, 2002, pp. 560ss.

directs the Prosecutor's investigations towards a specific geographical area within a State. The latter hypothesis has already occurred in relation to Darfur. Resolution n.1593 (2005) on the one hand states that the situation in Sudan constitutes a threat to peace but on the other reports to the Prosecutor the crimes committed in a particular region, Darfur precisely. Also among the reports from States Parties, a referral aimed at limiting the territorial competence of ICC was addressed to the Prosecutor in relation to northern Uganda. What may be interesting to note here is that the non-correspondence of the latter geographical area with a specific administrative region can pose many problems of territorial delimitation of the investigative activity of Prosecutor[182].

To avoid the occurrence of this circumstance of the territory subject to reporting, the spatial boundaries of the situation subject to the repressive action of ICC should have the greatest possible degree of precision and therefore correspond to an easily identifiable geographical area.

4.1.5. The ratione materiae competence

The ICC can only deal with crimes under Statute, listed in art. 5 and disciplined in articles 6, 7 and 8. The referral of SC it cannot in any way impose on the Prosecutor to investigate conduct that is not subject to ICC jurisdiction. This limit, however, is the only one expressly sanctioned by the same art. 13 b) StICC[183].

In relation to the crime of aggression as already mentioned and as it will be better said, the ICC can exercise its jurisdiction only starting from 17 July 2018 and against the States that have ratified the relative amendments to the Statute. I can here also briefly recall the attempts made during the drafting of the Statute to include ratione materiae in ICC jurisdiction, some particularly serious international crimes and already contained within specific international treaties. For several reasons, including the fact that several States Party to Rome Statute have not ratified some of those agreements, this hypothesis was eventually ruled out[184].

Once ICC jurisdiction has been activated for crimes committed in a specific territory, ICC will be able to exercise its jurisdiction over all the crimes envisaged in art. 5 StICC (except of the moment of the crime of aggression). The material parameter is perhaps the only one that cannot be delimited or conditioned in any way by the SC decision. This was furthermore confirmed by ICC itself, according to which "a referral cannot limit the Prosecutor to investigate only

---

[182]W.A. SCHABAS, An introduction to the international criminal court, Cambridge University Press, Cambridge, 2017, pp. 144ss.

[183]O. BEKOU, The International Criminal Court, op. cit.,

[184]H. OLASOLO, The triggering procedure of the international criminal court, op. cit., The mentioned article refers to these crimes 20 e) of the project of ILC Statute (1994) are listed in the annex at the same title: Crimes pursuant to treaties. See, Draft Statute for an international criminal court, in Yearbook of International Law Commission, 1994, vol. II, part two, pp. 67ss.

certain crimes (...)"[185].

However, it cannot be excluded that the SC qualifies some conduct in the ICC activation resolution as falling within a particular category of crimes. In the case of Libyan referral, the preamble of Resolution n.1970 (2011) refers specifically to the widespread and systematic attacks currently taking place in the Libyan Arab Jamahiriya against the civilian population "which according to SC" may amount to crimes against humanity. SC qualification is not contained in the dispositive part of the Resolution and does not seem indeed aimed at circumscribing the criminal action of ICC to some criminal conduct. Moreover, in one of the numerous reports on the situation in Libya, the same office of Prosecutor had found whereas the subject of investigation would have foreseen by the Statute and in particular in the present case the crimes against humanity and war crimes[186]. Beyond the specific Libyan case, the classification of the crime or the crimes committed, possibly contained in the decision, it will not be binding on the judicial bodies, which will always be able to frame the conduct and relevant criminals in a case other than that indicated by the SC.

4.2. Referral and principle of complementarity

The exercise of the SC referral power also produces some limited effects on the application of the complementarity principle. These effects are not expressly regulated by the Statute. Among the statutory provisions, it is possible to grasp some indications of a partially more limited impact of the principle of complementarity in the hypotheses of activation of ICC jurisdiction by the SC.

The idea that there may be repercussions on the principle of complementarity in the event of the exercise of referral power has some origin in the presumption that the SC when deciding to contact ICC has already made its own appreciation of the actual capacity and will of the State involved in prosecuting those responsible for international crimes[187]. Indeed, the political or judicial incapacity of the State could indeed be the basis of the action of ex Chapter VII. The inaction of state courts which should exercise jurisdiction could

[185]Prosecutor v. Mharushimana, Decision on the defence challenge to the jurisdiction of the court, (ICC-01/04/01/10-451), Pre-trial chamber I, 26 October 2011, par. 27.

[186]Office of the Prosecutor, Third report of the prosecutor of the international criminal court to the Security Council. Pursuant ot UNSCR 1970 (2011), 16 May 2012, par. 54.

[187]H.D. OHLIN, Peace, security and prosecutorial discretion, in C. STAHN, G. SLUITER, The emerging practice of the international criminal court, op. cit., pp. 193ss. There are also those who supported this hypothesis in the light of more general reasons linked to the supremacy of the obligations deriving from SC decisions on other international obligations (articles 25 and 103 of the Charter). See also in argument: D.N. NSEREKO, The ICC and complementarity in practice, in Leiden Journal of International Law, 26 (2), 2013, pp. 432ss. This naturally has a basis with regard to States that are part or not of the Rome Statute, they cannot claim their own sovereign power to prosecute perpetrators or not cooperate with the ICC if the SC requires the activation of ICC. Those provisions do not prevent ICC from making an assessment of the condition of unable or unwilling of the State concerned.

constitute one of the elements in the light of which the SC believes that the situation in that country represents a threat to international peace and security. On the other hand and in more general terms, if the principle of complementarity represents the maximum guarantee offered by the Statute to the sovereignty of States[188], one could imagine and maintain that this protection ceases to operate when there is an intervention of SC[189].

Indeed, the impact of a report from SC on the application of the principle of complementarity appears limited. It does not apply in substance to the case of exercise of referral power by SC, art. 18 StICC and the preliminary procedure provided therein for the purpose of the declaration of admissibility of the case[190]. The exercise of the referral power of SC affects only some preliminary guarantees of dialogue between the Prosecutor and the State concerned and in practice excludes the possibility for the latter to ask the Prosecutor before the start of investigations to transfer the competence to national authorities.

The Prosecutor is not obliged to notify the State concerned of its decision to open the investigations. A guarantee provided to allow the State involved to demonstrate its ability to prosecute those responsible and therefore have the case declared inadmissible. In the event of an action of the Prosecutor or referral of a State Party, in front of an instance of the State concerned, the Prosecutor may on the contrary decide to remit the case directly to the national authorities or ask the pre-trial to deny this transfer of jurisdiction (art.18 (2))[191]. If, on the other hand, the referral comes from SC, the request from the State is necessarily and directly subject to scrutiny by the Court[192]. This sort of circumvention of the role normally

---

[188]According to some reconstructions, the principle of complementarity as governed by the Statute would indeed be too deferential with respect to state sovereignty for certain critical findings. A. CASSESE, The statute of the international criminal court: Some preliminary reflections, in European Journal of International Law, 10 (1), 1999, pp. 24ss. It is interesting to note here that the ad hoc courts were given precedence over national jurisdictions. In that different context, any conflict of jurisdiction between international and domestic courts: "Have been addressed at the political rather than judicial level (...)". See in argument: W.A. SCHABAS, The rise and fall of complementarity, in C. STAHN, M. EL ZEIDY, The international criminal court and complementarity, Cambridge University Press, Cambridge, 2014, pp. 152ss.

[189]G.P. FLETCHER, J.D. OHLIN, The ICC-Two courts in one?, in Journal of International Criminal Justice, 4, 2006, pp. 432ss. These authors do not go so far as to state that the principle of complementarity does not apply to referral cases of SC. They stress, however, that the cases reported by SC "are placed on a separate track, with greater weight given to the legal determination made by the Council under its law-making authority, and supplanting the regular procedures of ICC as a traditional criminal court operating under rules of admissibility (...)".

[190]O. BEKOU, The International Criminal Court, op. cit.,

[191]W.A. SCHABAS, The international criminal court. A commentary to the Rome statute, op. cit.,

[192]D.N. NSEREKO, Article 18, in O. TRIFFTERER, K. AMBOS, The Rome statute of the international criminal court. A commentary of the international criminal court. A commentary, C.H.Beck-Hart-Nomos, München, Oxford, Baden-Baden, 2016, pp. 836ss.

played by the Prosecutor in this preliminary phase stems precisely from the idea that before reporting a situation to ICC, the SC has already made its own assessment "at least to which the referral belongs"[193]. In light of art. 19 (3), however the Prosecutor may also in the case of SC referral ask the ICC to rule on any question relating to the admissibility of the case and ICC jurisdiction and then submit its assessments on the application of the complementarity principle[194].

The intricate regulatory framework prepared by the Statute of Rome seems to be aimed in some way at compressing the role of the Prosecutor but does not exclude the possibility that the ICC bodies and the Prosecutor itself reach a different conclusion on the assumptions of complementarity, respect to that implying (or even explicitly) expressed from SC through the exercise of referral power[195]. Also from this point of view, a conflict situation between SC and ICC can be imagined which could express divergent positions on the ability or the will of the State concerned to repress the crimes under ICC jurisdiction.

---

[193]F. LATTANZI, Concurrent jurisdictions between primacy and complementarity, in R. BELELLI, International criminal justice. Law and practice from the Rome statute to its review, Ashgate Publishing, Farnham, 2010, pp. 202ss.

[194]According to this positions very negative was: J.D. OHLIN, Peace, security and prosecutorial discretion, in C. STAHN, G. SLUITER, The emerging practice of the international criminal court, op. cit., pp. 193ss. Indeed, the latter argues that the discretion granted to the prosecutor and the ICC in general: "is simply inconsistent with the basic principles of international law". In essence, according to the fifth approach when the SC establishes the need for a jurisdictional intervention for the maintenance of international peace and security: "The Prosecutor cannot substitute his discretion for the discretion of SC in such situations" (p. 207).

[195]In this sense see: J. HOLMES, Complementarity: National courts versus the ICC, in A. CASSESE, P. GAETA, J.R.W.D. JONES, The Rome statute of the international criminal court. A commentary, Oxford University Press, Oxford, 2002, pp. 684ss. N. WHITE, R. CRYER, The ICC and the Security Council. An uncomfortable relationship, in J. DORIA, H.P. GASSER, M. CHERIF BASSIOUNI, The legal regime of the international criminal court. Essays in honor of professor Igor Blishchenko. In memory of professor Igor Pavlovich Blishchenko (1930-2000), op. cit., pp. 464ss. F. GIOIA, The International Criminal Court and national jurisdictions, ed. Routledge, London & New York, 2016. L. GROVER, Interpreting crimes in the Rome statute of the International Criminal Court, Cambridge University Press, Cambridge, 2014, pp. 114ss. P. DASKALOPOULOU-LIVADA, The principle of complementarity and Security Council referrals, in F. GIOIA, M. POLITI, The international criminal court and national jurisdictions, ed. Routledge, Aldershot, 2008, pp. 60sss. M.H. ARSANJANI, The Rome statute of the international criminal court, in American Journal of International Law, 93, 1999, pp. 28ss. It may be recalled here that following the notification received by the Sudanese authorities regarding the creation of a special Court for the crimes committed in Darfur, the Office of the Prosecutor reiterated that before deciding to open an investigation it is always obliged to assess the admissibility of the case also in light of the principle of complementarity. See, Registration in a record of proceedings of statement by Luis Moreno-Ocampo, fourth session of the Assembly of States Parties, 28 November 2005.

5. UN financial responsibility in the event of the referral being exercised by SC

SC's exercise of the power to activate ICC can have financial consequences for the UN. Art. 115, StICC provides that ICC and States Parties Assembly expenses are to be borne by the contributions of the same States part of StICC lett. a) and through other funds provided by UN lett. b), subject to approval on GA. This second hypothesis or the functioning of GA is necessary in relation to the expenses incurred due to referrals by the Council[196].

It would be an interesting reconstruction of one of the numerous and tangible indices of the fact that "ICC is really two Courts in one" when it operates at the request of States or on the initiative of the Prosecutor, it is the Assembly of the States part of the StICC. The latter becomes in all respects an organ that operates against the UN under the political control of SC and with the financial support guaranteed by GA[197].

The question of financing ICC's activity was immediately considered crucial for the creation of the new institution and for its correct and effective functioning[198]. On the other hand, the choices that the Prosecutor makes regarding the opening of the investigation activity itself or in order to initiate a proceeding against individuals are often dictated by the financial resources of their office and take into account the ICC workload as a whole and the ability to source it. In short, from the beginning it was clear that the future of ICC, and in particular the quantity of cases it would be able to deal with, would also depend on the economic and financial resources available to it. For this reason and bearing in mind the possibility that some of the economically more powerful States did not become part of StICC, most States argued that ICC should have been fully funded by UN[199].

---

[196]O. BEKOU, The International Criminal Court, op. cit.,

[197]G.P. FLETCHER, J.D. OHLIN, The ICC-Two courts in one?, op. cit., pp. 429ss.

[198]Moreover, from the beginning the difficulty of predicting the actual annual expenses of ICC, since they may depend on the quantity of conflicts that arise annually in the various areas of the world. See in argument: G. WITSCHELL, Financial regulations and rules of the court, in Fordham International Law Journal, 25, 2002, pp. 668ss. T.S. WARRICK, Organization of the international criminal court. Administrative financial issues, in Denver Journal of International Law & Policy, 25, 1997, pp. 334ss.

[199]See, preliminary report of the Security Council, UN doc. A/AC.244/L.2, 20 March 1995, in particular parr. 244-249. This of course would have made ICC "more representative and accessible to all UN Member States regardless of their financial, circumstances, and thus more global in its orientation and possible intervention". See in general for an interesting analysis of the logic of an economic nature that guides the behavior of the States towards ICC and the effects of these attitudes on the action of ICC. For further analysis see also: S. KENDALL, Modifying global justice. Economics of accountability at the international criminal court, in Journal of International Criminal Justice, 13 (1), 2015, pp. 113ss. J. HOHMANN, D. JOYCE, International law's objects, Oxford University Press, Oxford, 2019, pp. 372ss. P. CAPPS, H. PALMER OLSEN, Legal authority beyond the state,

Already in the preparatory works for the Rome Conference the hypotheses emerged which were then somehow contemplated in the text of art. 115[200], on which, however, it was not possible to find an agreement between the States[201]. In particular, it was a question of establishing whether the funds should come from the States Parties to StICC or from UN, or jointly from the States Parties and UN[202]. The latter option was preferred thanks to a compromise solution proposed by Japan. The possibility that the costs were incurred only by the UN proved to be in fact impractical. Unlike the courts for the former Yugoslavia and Rwanda, subsidiary SC bodies, therefore financially supported by the mandatory contributions of all UN Member States, the ICC because it was established through an international agreement, it could only be funded in the first place and to a greater extent than the States Parties to that particular covenant system.

What is most relevant here, however, is the last sentence of the provision according to which if the SC decides to use the ICC to prosecute those responsible for the Commission of international crimes in some part of the world, the UN must bear the costs resulting from this activation of ICC. The rationale of the provision dwells in the idea that when the SC uses ICC for peacekeeping purposes, under UN it must (shall) bear the costs of such employment[203].

As seen, the possibility that the expenses are incurred at least in part of the UN is subject to the same art. 115, to the approval of the financing by the GA. The irrelevance of this specification contained in the provision is given by the fact that the UN Charter establishes GA competence in organization's expenses (art.17 of UN Charter)[204]. It is obvious that StICC States Parties cannot, through this treaty, modify the procedures relating to UN expenses or in any case intervene on the prerogatives of GA in the matter, or in any other way amend the UN Charter. In these terms and more simply it is not possible through an international treaty

---

Cambridge University Press, Cambridge, 2018.

[200]United Nations diplomatic conference of plenitpotentiaries on the establishment of an international criminal court, Rome, 15 June-17 July 1998, Official records, vol. III, UN doc. A/CONF.183/C.1/SR.40, parr. 12-16.

[201]See the different positions expressed by the delegates of the states, UN doc. A/CON.183/C.1/SR.18.

[202]See art. 104 of the project of the articles presented by the preparatory committee, which included the three distinct hypotheses mentioned and underlined in notes regarding the third option which "in the case of referral by the Security Council, the relevant expense of the Court should be borne by the United Nations". Furthermore, in this last case, a UN loan was envisaged for the first phase of ICC activity, see: UN doc. A/CONF.183/2/Add.1, p. 160.

[203]However, during the initial phase, the expenses of the court shall be borne by the UN subject to the approval of the GA of the UN.

[204]M. HALFF, D. TOLBERT, R. VILLACIS, Article 115. Funds of the court and of the Assembly of states parties, in O. TRIFFTERER, K. AMBOS, The Rome statute of the international criminal court. A commentary, C.H.Beck-Hart-Nomos, München, Oxford, Baden-Baden, 2016.

to impose obligations on an international organization without the consent of the latter.

In practice it has not succeeded as much as they had wished[205], to define an obligation of UN economic support through the 3004 agreement. The latter in fact limits itself to providing that the conditions under which the UN undertake to finance ICC activity "shall be subject to separate arrangements"[206].

This means that any UN decision to financially support ICC's business is left to future agreements between the two organizations. Ultimately, the material support of UN will depend from time to time on the will expressed by the majority of States within GA.

Although the provision seems to indicate the existence of an obligation, the need for an authorization of expenses by GA reflects the fact that obviously the financing is not automatic. It will depend on the will of an organ, i.e the GA external to the system created by StICC. In this sense, art. 115 seems to express more than anything else "the general sentiment" according to which "if SC refers to court matters, the UN should pay the expenses"[207].

In other words, the provisions of art. 115 can only be interpreted as a sort of indication of principle that only materializes if the necessary consensus is reached within the GA. This consent in light of art. 13 of the 2004 report agreement will have to be sanctioned from time to time and made explicit through a further agreement between the two organizations.

Finally, it should be highlighted that art. 115 does not of course exclude that the UN may bear the costs of ICC even in cases other than activation by the SC. In other words, if on the one hand the UN are not formally obliged to bear ICC's expenses in case of activation by SC, on the other hand it is possible that the ICC will obtain financial support from UN even outside of that particular

---

[205]C.P.R. ROMANO, T. INGADOTTIR, The financing of the international criminal court, in C. ROMANO, A. NOLLKAEMPER, J. KLEFFNER, Internationalized criminal courts and tribunals. Sierra Leone, East Timor and Cambogia, Oxford University Press, Oxford, 2004. ICC discussion paper 2, the project on international courts and tribunals, June 2000, pp. 47. C. CRYER, H. FRIMAN, D. ROBINSON, E. WILMSHURST, An introduction to international criminal law and procedure, Cambridge University Press, Cambridge, 2014, pp. 200ss.

[206]See the first due paragraphs of art. 13: "Financial matters 1. The UN and the Court agree that the conditions under which any funds may be provided to the Court by a decision of the GA of the UN pursuant to article 115 of the Stature shall be subject to separate arrangements. The registrar shall inform the Assembly of the making of such arrangements. 2.The UN and the Court further agree that the costs and expenses resulting from cooperation or the provision of services pursuant to the present agreement shall be subject to separate arrangements between the UN and the Court. The registrar shall inform the assembly of the making of such arrangements (...)".

[207]M.H. ARSANJANI, Financing, in A. CASSESE, P. GAETA, J.R.W.D. JONES, The Rome statute of the international criminal court. A commentary, Oxford University Press, Oxford, 2002, pp. 325ss.

hypothesis[208].

5.1. Practices regarding UN financial support in case of exercise by the SC of referral power

We have already seen how art. 115, lett. b) StICC suggests the need for financial support from the UN in the event that the SC activates ICC jurisdiction. It was also observed that the relationship agreement of 2004, not resolving the ambiguities of that provision, limited itself to providing for the possibility of concluding from time to time specific agreements between ICC and UN in order to establish the extent of the economic support of the latter to ICC activity.

SC practice on this matter does not seem to reflect the underlying rationale of art. 115 StICC, nor does materialize the possibility provided by the relationship agreement to conclude specific agreements between the two institutions. In both cases of exercise of the referral power it was chosen to expressly exclude a financial liability of UN. Let Resolution n. 1593 of 2005 relating to Darfur case and n.1970 of 2011 on the situation of Libya. The latter clearly stipulate that none of the expenses incurred in connection with the referral, including expenses related to investigations or prosecutions in connection with that referral shall be borne by UN and such costs shall be borne by the parties to the Rome Statue and those States that wish to contribute voluntarily[209].

As already noted, this opening of the device relating to any costs borne by UN is another of its conditions for the adoption of Resolution n.1593 (2005). The American representative at the UN made clear on the occasion of the referral decision, that any attempt to question the principle that the expenses of the ICC's activities are borne by the States Parties of StICC could result in the withdrawal of the financial support of US to UN or to other international organizations[210].

In a latter circumstance, as indeed during the Resolution n.1970 (2011), no particular oppositions emerged from the other Member States on this specific aspect of the device. Although the criticisms of the States have focused on other elements of the Resolution, it has already been underlined how the financial resources have a decisive influence on ICC activity. In this regard, it is sufficient to recall one of the reports submitted to SC by the same office of the Prosecutor in the course of investigations into the crimes committed in Libya. The document noted first that the crimes committed by all parties of the conflict would be investigated and prosecuted (the NATO mission had just ended and some criticisms had been raised for a disproportionate use of force and the possibility of the Commission of war crimes). However, the possibility of continuing the examination of these delicate issues could only depend on the funds available to

---

[208]Just as States Parties can voluntarily finance the ICC by virtue of art. 116 StICC.

[209]Resolution 1970 (2011), par. 8 and n.1593 (2005), par. 7.

[210]Press release, Security Council, Security Council refers situation in Darfur, Sudan to prosecutor of international court, IUN doc. SAC/8351, 31 March 2005, pp. 3-4 "any effort to retrench on that principle by the UN or other organizations to which the US contributed could result in its withholding funding or taking other action in response (...)".

the office to conduct the Libya investigation[211].

The fears expressed in 2011 seem to find confirmation in the words spoken a few years later from Prosecutor Bensouda, in one of the numerous reports to SC on the situation in Libya. In the document, after dramatically highlighting the serious general worsening of the Libyan situation and despite having in fact renounced pursuing any crimes committed by NATO, Prosecutor Bensouda found that "an unfortunate reality, however, remains the combined effect of instability and lack of resources has severely undermined my office's investigative efforts"[212].

Lastly, it is also interesting to recall the proposed activation of ICC jurisdiction contained in the Resolution relating to the situation of Syria. Although the vetoes of China and the Russian Federation have prevented the adoption of this Resolution, it is important to highlight here that SC's practice of excluding any economic contribution of the UN from SC to the jurisdictional activity of ICC in the event exercise the referral seems to be moving towards consolidation[213].

Also in that case, it had been prepared an exemption of UN from any type of expense, in a language identical to the two previous resolutions. This time, some arguments have been put forward by the Argentine delegate, who stressed that this part of the device "is not in accordance with the Rome Statute and the relationship agreement" and more generally, the decision taken by SC regarding expenses "is blantantly unfair"[214].

---

[211]Office of the Prosecutor, Second report of the Prosecutor of the international criminal court to the UN Security Council pursuant to UNSCR 1970 (2011), 2 November 2011, par. 53: "Allegations have been made against all parties to the conflict regarding the disproportionate use of force that could constitute a war crime in accordance with article 8 (2) b of the Rome Statute. The office will continue to examine these maters as well and welcomes submission of any information or evidence that would facilitate investigation of allegations of the sproportionate use of force by any party to the conflict. It is not yet determined whether the office's investigation into allegations of war crimes will move forward in this or the coming period, depending on the funds available to the force to conduct the Libya investigation". See also part. 55 where on the possible Commission of war crimes by NATO forces, reference is made to the work of the International Commission of Inquiry. The question of the effects of the limited financial resources on the activity of ICC, on the other hand, had already been highlighted for time, see Office of the Prosecutor, prosecutorial strategy 2009-2012, 1st February 2010.

[212]Statement to the United Nations Security Council on the situation on Libya pursuant to UNSCR 1970 (2011), Mrs Fatou Bensouda, Prosecutor of the international criminal court, Eight report of the Prosecutor of the international criminal court to the UN Security Council pursuant to UNSCR 1970 (2011), 13 November 2014.

[213]SC, Proposal of resolution, UN doc. SA/2014/348, par. 8. For further details see: R. HIGGINS, P. WEBB, D. AKANDE, Oppenheim's international law: United Nations, Oxford University Press, Oxford, 2017. A. ZIMMERMANN, M. SENER, Chemical weapons and the International Criminal Court, in American Journal of International Law, 108 (3), 2014, pp. 438ss.

[214]UN Doc. S/PV.7180, p. 11.

5.2. The impossibility of imposing a financial responsibility on UN through StICC and related obligations deriving from the relationship agreement

The most thorny problems that emerged from the financial liability practice of UN in the case of the exercise of referral power concern the relationships between SC and GS and therefore transcend the scope of this investigation. SC, in fact through these resolutions, intervenes in a matter that should be the responsibility of GA[215].

Some considerations can also be made on some problematic aspects of the relationship between UN and ICC in this particular area. The compromise reached between those who wanted an ICC financed entirely by UN and those who demanded a total exclusion of economic burdens for the latter led to a standard that was not unambiguous. As already mentioned the ambiguity of art. 115 b) originates from the fact that this provision could not have been the legal basis of a UN obligation to financially support ICC.

On the other hand, through the relationship agreement UN could have consecrated their commitment to bear all the expenses of ICC, at least in cases where the judicial activity had been induced by a request of SC. As seen, however, this did not happen. The agreement is rather limited to postponing the matter to future separate arrangements between the two organizations.

In general terms, it can perhaps be recognized that the revision of a generic financing obligation for ICC's judicial activity would also have entailed a series of practical problems. Expenditure decisions cannot fail to take into account the actual and variable financial needs of the two organizations, as well as for what matters most here, the workload that is expected for ICC, in light of the frequency with which the SC decides to resort to the judicial activity of ICC. These economic and financial assessments can only be made through a specific and concrete estimate, annual or in any case periodic, of the resources available to UN at the costs to be incurred for ICC. For this purpose, the idea of referring to specific and timely agreements in the matter contained in the relationship agreement may seem more reasonable than a general financing obligation set up within the StICC. Certainly less reasonable is the practice put in place up to now from SC, aimed in fact at hindering any collaboration on this aspect between the two organizations.

The practice examined however seems to suggest that if necessary to activate ICC jurisdiction, States Parties to the Statute willing to accept and bear

---

[215]The latter aspect was also highlighted by the Argentine representative during the session of the SC concerning the situation in Syria and the possibility of a new activation of ICC. See, UN Doc, S/PV.7180, p.11: "The Council cannot assume powers that it does not possess, such as that of deciding the funding of the referral. Under the UN Charter that is within the General Assembly's jurisdiction". In the same orientation see the opinion of representative Brazil, UN doc. S/PV.107, p. 23.

the costs of the lack of financial support of UN. This does not mean that the resolutions of SC aimed at excluding any financial burden for UN, as well as affecting the prerogatives of GA, effectively prevent the start of any negotiation on the expenses between ICC and UN. The obligations assumed through the relationship agreement would instead require the parties to try at least to find an agreement from time to time on the modalities and conditions of a possible financial support of one in favor of the other (art.13 (2)) of the 2004 agreement[216].

[216]The resolutions in the part where they exclude the financial support of UN would essentially be: "At odds not only with the decision to refer, but also with the duty of good faith negotiations". For further details see: A. CIAMPI, L. CONDORELLI, Comments on the Security Council referral of the situation in Darfur to the ICC, op. cit., pp. 594ss.

Chapter 2
The Deferral

1. Security Council power to suspend ICC's judicial activity: Art. 16 StICC

StICC recognizes SC's power to temporarily suspend ICC jurisdictional activity. Its raison d'etre is found in the need to prevent the criminal repression of international crimes from hindering the achievement of stable and lasting peace. The very existence of the power of deferral can therefore be considered a tangible manifestation of the difficulty of reconciling peace and justice. More precisely, the suspension power attributed to SC expresses the fact that these fundamental values and purposes of international law can in some cases conflict with each other and cannot be pursued jointly.

In the course of armed conflict or post-conflict transitions, the immediate and undoubted purpose of SC is to come to an end the hostilities or to re-establish a situation of normal and peaceful coexistence. In such contexts, the criminal repression of those responsible for the crimes and the satisfaction of the victims and their family members can be considered secondary or better extendable, with respect to the need to restore peace and security, stop the ongoing violence or avoid its repetition. It can therefore be more generally stated that the possibility that SC intervenes to attest ICC judicial action also represents an explicit recognition of the non-absolute character of the value of international criminal justice[217]. StICC admits in high words the need that in some cases the administration of criminal justice at an international level can give way to political initiatives aimed at protecting the legal good of maintaining international peace and security. To this aim, art. 16 in practice grants a sort of prevalence, albeit temporary, over the assessment of individual responsibility for the Commission of international crimes under ICC jurisdiction.

As has already been mentioned in part when referring to referral power, the need to provide for a power to suspend ICC by GA or other UN bodies had been felt both in the early debates[218]. Although the existence of this suspension

[217]L. CONDORELLI, L. VILLALPANDO, Relationship of the court with the United Nations, in A. CASSESE, P. GAETA, J.R.W.D. JONES, The Rome statute of the international criminal court. A commentary, op. cit., pp. 628ss. A. ABBAS, The competence of the Security Council to terminate the jurisdiction of the international criminal court, in Texas International Law Journal, 4, 2005, pp. 272ss.

[218]In particular, one can find in those first meetings a proposal aimed at attributing to GA

power has been proposed even before the activation one, the possibility that SC arrest the judicial activity of ICC has nevertheless raised more legal policy problems than the power to activate its action. And this for the obvious reason that there is a contrast here between the activity of the two bodies and not as in the case of the referral, a coincidence of purposes and interests.

The results achieved at the of Rome Conference on the nature and scope of this particular power show various critical issues and, for many, the achievement of compromise solutions dictated by the need to find a difficult balance between peacekeeping and justice needs. There are two elements that most characterized the debates that took place during the works that led to the drafting of this provision. The first concerns the very way in which the judicial activity of ICC would have been interrupted or otherwise limited by SC action. In particular, it was a question of deciding whether the use of the criminal instrument should be automatically precluded by the mere circumstance that SC was already dealing with the situation subject to potential investigations or instead foreseeing and on the basis of which assumptions, the need for an explicit and formal request for suspension by the political body. The second crucial aspect concerns the temporal element or the possibility of setting a limit to the duration of the suspension and the possibility of renewing and extending it by SC.

As regards the first point, it should be remembered that despite the persistent problems and the inevitable criticisms that the exercise of the power of deferral still provokes the arrest of the criminal action, it was originally conceived in a much more incisive form than it currently holds[219]. Still in the draft Statute of 1994 drawn up by ILC, in fact, the ICC could in no case have intervened on issues with which SC was dealing in the exercise of the powers attributed to it by Chapter VII of the UN Charter. In other words, the blocking of ICC judicial activity did not require a prior and explicit political decision, the impossibility of ICC action being rather conceived as a direct and automatic consequence of the need not to interfere with the ongoing action of SC. Art. 23 (3) of the project of the Statute provided that ICC could not deal with any case "being dealt with the SC" unless the latter had decided otherwise[220].

In this first hypothesis-considered the inevitable consequence of the primacy recognized in SC by art. 12 of UN Charter of the primary responsibility attributed to it under art. 24 regarding peacekeeping[221], it would therefore have

---

or to other UN organs, the exercise of a particular power, potentially necessary for the purpose of the maintenance of peace "to stop the presentation or prosecution of a particular case before the Court". See, Committee on international criminal jurisdiction, summary record of the eighteenth meeting, UN doc. A/AC.65/SR.18, p. 15.

[219]See revised report of the working group on a draft Statute for international criminal court, A/CN.4/l.490 and Add. 1, in Yearbook of the International Law Commission, 1993, vol. 2, pp. 109ss.

[220]Report of the international law Commission on the work of its forty-sixth session, UN doc. A/49/10, 2 May-22 July 1994, art. 23, par. 3.

[221]Draft Statute for an international criminal court with commentaries, in Yearbook of the International Law Commission, 1994, vol. II, part two, art. 23, pp. 45ss. See also art. 12,

been sufficient for any matter to be dealt with SC to prevent ICC judicial activity. And this potentially for an indefinite time. The SC, through the introduction of prolonged sanctioning regimes[222], could have prevented ICC judicial activity for at least in theory the unlimited period. In fact, sometimes rather long times are known, in which a situation of conflict, even if only potential, can remain on the agenda of SC and how complicated it can be to establish the moment when a given situation is no longer on the agenda[223].

As noted by some representatives of States, the UN Charter and in particular the aforementioned art. 12 does not grant a similar priority to SC action compared to ICC judicial activity, but only to GA. In light of the relevant ICC jurisprudence without this being considered as an obstacle to the tasks assigned to SC[224]. A similar speech could therefore have been made for ICC.

In order to remedy the critical remarks made against the solution just outlined during the works of the second half of the nineties, two different proposals were therefore made. The first-although aimed at limiting the effects of art. 23 (3) through the important clarification that the SC had to be actively engaged in resolving the situation of threat to peace, the basic idea of the project took up substance[225]. The second decidedly more innovative proposal proposed

---

par. 1 of the Charter.

[222]The sanctions adopted in the 1990s against Iraq are certainly included in this category. Moreover in the period of the cold war in which SC was not able to adopt decisions because of the known practice of the crossed vetoes, different situations were found constantly in the agenda of SC, without however that they could be assumed concrete misuse of intervention.

[223]Report of the ad hoc Committee on the establishment of an international criminal court, Official records-Fiftieth session, supplement n. 22, UN doc. A/50/22, 1995, par. 120. Some state representatives argued that this approach merely reflected the nature and scope of the SC's prerogatives in maintaining international peace and security. However, this initial hypothesis was also the subject of numerous reservations, once again concentrated on the excessive limits and obstacles that the ICC's judicial activity would have encountered. See for example the position of New Zealand in sixth Commission, UN General Assembly, 1st November 1995, p. 2, which is affirmed that: "(...) It would be shameful if the large and powerful, with permanent privileges on SC, were able to prevent the criminal Court from dealing with a situation by simply claiming that they were already of the matter (...)".

[224]Report of the ad hoc Committee on the establishment of an international criminal court, General Assembly official records-Fiftieth session, supplement n. 22, UN doc. A/50/22, 1995, parr. 124-125. See in particular, ICJ, Case of diplomatic and consular personal of the American Embassy in Tehran v. United States v. Iran, sentence of 24 May 1980, in ICJ Reports 1980, pp. 21 and Nicaragua v. United States, sentence of 26 November 1948, in ICJ Reports 1984, pp. 434ss.

[225]Preparatory Commission Draft Statute, article 10 (7), option 2, par. 2. For further details see: R. SCHVERCH, The International Criminal Court at the mercy of powerful states. An assessment of the neo-colonialism claim made by African stakeholders, ed. Springer, Berlin, 2017, pp. 224ss. S. BABAIAN, The International Criminal Court. An international criminal world court? Jurisdiction and cooperation mechanisms of the Rome statute and its practical implementation, ed. Springer, Berlin, 2018, pp. 23ss.

by Singapore was destined to obtain some success and become the starting point of the debate within the Rome Conference[226].

While retaining SC power to stop ICC's activity, the well-known Singapore compromise has completely overturned the prospect emerged from the project. It is no longer possible for SC to obstruct the jurisdictional activity of ICC simply by dealing with a specific situation. It is necessary to adopt a resolution expressly aimed at suspending the ICC action, otherwise always possible. The new proposal imposes in practice the assent (or at least the abstention) of the permanent members to prevent the Prosecutor or the ICC judges from continuing to exercise their investigative powers or continue the ongoing proceedings. The possible exercise of veto power in this case plays a positive role, i.e. that the investigations or proceedings could continue. Singapore's proposal provided that "no investigation or prosecution may be commenced or proceeded with under this Statute where the SC has acting under Chapter VII of the UN Charter given a direction to that effect (...)"[227].

On the basis of this text, the final compromise solution contained in art. 16 of the Rome Statute. Not without two important changes that must also be recalled for the importance that they will assume during the course of this investigation. With the first, due to a proposal from Costa Rica, the generic and imprecise term direction was created to describe the initiative undertaken by SC, with the provision of a real formal request and specific decision. The second proposal from Canada, on the other hand, was aimed at setting a time limit of 12 renewable months for the suspension request[228].

In relation to this second element, the other aspect emerges, i.e the object of a broad comparison between the States mentioned above. Quite a few delegations had insisted that the possibility of resorting to the deferral be somewhat limited. It was in particular but not only the Latin American states that

---

[226]The proposal of Singapore back in session of August of 1996 of preparatory committee, A/AC.249/WP.51, See non paper WG.3/N.16, 8 August 1997.

[227]J. MARC DE LA SABLIÉRE, Le Conseil de sècuritè des Nations Unies, ed. Larcier, Bruxelles, 2018.

[228]The reversal of perspective described and the two proposed changes have won the support of most States. Opponents were not lacking. The United States still did not appreciate a provision that did not adequately guarantee SC's power of control over ICC. Among the permanent members of SC worried in different ways and of losing a power of dominion over the activity of ICC, the soil carried out by the United Kingdom was decisive, which first and at least initially, in an isolated manner, supported the Canadian variant to the compromise proposed by Singapore. For further details see: A. MOKHTAR, The fine art of arm-twisting. The US resolution 1422 and security council deferral power under the Rome statute, in International Criminal Law Review, 3 (4), 2003, pp. 305ss. C.K. HALL, The first two sessions of the UN preparatory committee on the establishment of an international criminal court, in American Journal of International Law, 91 (1), 1997, pp. 1822ss. H.P. KAULK, Towards a permanent international criminal court, in Human Rights Law Journal, 7, 1997, pp. 172ss. G. VON GLAHN, J.L. TAULBEE, Law among nations: An introduction to public international law, ed. Routledge, London & New York, 2015.

asked that this tool could be used by SC only once, without the possibility of renewal[229]. Italy itself supported the idea that the power of deferral should not only be confined to a specific period of time but also characterized by a limited possibility of renew[230].

These positions were evidently driven by the fear that the SC through the repetition of suspension requests could in fact paralyze ICC's activity for an indefinite time. According to some of the criticisms often addressed to the provision in question, the absence of a limit to the renewal and therefore the fact that the SC not only suspend but also definitively lend ICC action produces a dangerous dependence of the judicial body on the political one. If these concerns appear to be well founded in principle, the need to formulate a further request for suspension requires SC to reconsider the situation in which it believes that ICC criminal action is an obstacle to peace. The adoption of a new resolution on the basis of Chapter VII of the UN Charter will be necessary with the possibility from time to time that the exercise of the veto power by one of the permanent members allows ICC to start or resume its work[231].

Despite the important adjustments introduced during the negotiations, art. 16 represents the most controversial and problematic tool of the relationship between the eminently political role of SC and the necessary independence of ICC. Many of these criticalities emerge in particular from how the power of deferral was understood and put into practice by SC, rather than from its formulation which, although not without elements of uncertainty and ambiguity[232], appears to be the result of a complex, but all in all balanced between opposing needs.

Finally, it is interesting to remember that the arrangement has been the

---

[229] UN diplomatic Conference of plenipotentiaries on the establishment of an international criminal court, official records, vol. II, 15 June-17 July 1998, Summary record of the plenary meetings and of the meetings of the committee of the whole, A/CONF.183/C.1/SR.1, pp. 207.

[230]W.A. SCHABAS, The international criminal court, op. cit., pp. 422ss. K. ELABY, The role of the Security Council, op. cit., pp. 45ss.

[231]An exercise of deferral power renewed periodically in order to permanently block the action of ICC as much as possible would be "difficult to judge and support in the eyes of the international community (...)". S. BOURGON, Ratione temporis, in A. CASSESE, P. GAETA, J.R.W.D. JONES, The Rome statute of the international criminal court. A commentary, Oxford University Press, Oxford, 2002, pp. 564ss.

[232]Just think to give an example to the silence of the Statute on the effects of the suspension of a proceeding with respect to the collection of evidence against the suspects or the preservation of those already collected. On this point we will return, but we can recall an interesting proposal from the Belgian government aimed at allowing the Prosecutor to preserve the evidence gathered during the suspension period. See, United Nations diplomatic conference of plenipotentiaries on the establishment of an international criminal court, Official records, vol. II, 15 June-17 July 1998, summary records of the plenary meetings and of the meetings off the committee of the whole, A/CONF.183/C.1/SR.1, pp. 97ss.

subject of some modification proposals in the last drafts[233]. These requests show a certain dissatisfaction at least by some States, towards the prerogative recognized to SC through art. 16 or at least of the practice relating to its exercise.

2. Practices in the exercise of the deferral

2.1. Resolutions n.1422 (2002) and 1487 (2003): The exemption of ICC jurisdiction for personnel of States not part of the Statute engaged in operations established or authorized by the UN

After just over ten days from the entry into force of the Statute and even before the ICC became fully operational, the SC adopted one of the most controversial resolutions among those adopted in the exercise of powers recognized by the Treaty of Rome. It refers to Resolution n.1422 of 12 July 2002

---

[233]Towards the end of 2009, South Africa proposed to the Assembly of states to discuss an amendment to art. 16 with the aim of introducing two new paragraphs. On the one hand it was intended to foresee that the state competent to exercise jurisdiction over the situation subject to ICC's attention could formally ask the SC to cancel the power of suspension. On the other hand, in the event that the SC had not taken a decision on the matter within 6 months of the request from the state concerned, it could have submitted the same question to the GA (Proposal for amendment by South Africa to the statute, C. N851.2009. TREATIES-10, 30 November 2009). A year later, in view of the review conference of the statue of Kampala, the African Union promoted a similar request: the case of inaction of the SC following a request for suspension, the GA could exercise its own autonomous power of deferral African Union executive Council, 16th ordinary session, report on the ministerial meeting on the Rome statute, 25-29 January 2010 (EC.CL/568 (XVI) Annex 1). The document states that this power would be used: "in conformity with UN General Assembly Resolution 377 (V)1950 known as Uniting for peace resolution. It emerges from these proposals all the dissatisfaction of the African states on the use of the SC of this very delicate instrument and the attempt to at least partially transfer some possibility of intervention to the GA. The proposal was not taken into consideration at the revision conference of the statute of Kampala in 2010. In 2013, the possibility to amend to the art. 16, however, is once again the subject of discussion. The Assembly of the states has commissioned the working group on amendments to continue to deal with the amendment proposals and in particular those: "submitting following the decision by the extraordinary summit of the Afircan Union held on 12 October 2013" (See, Mandates of the Assembly of states parties fro the intersessional period, ICC-ASP/12/Res.8, Annex I, 27 November 2013, par. 12 (A)). This last decision provides for the establishment of an executive committee, composed of five members of the different regions of the African continent charged with discussing with the SC of the UN a series of questions relating to the relationships between the SC itself and the ICC. Among the issues expressly object of this comparison stand out the proposals to stop the international penal action in the cases of Kenya and Sudan and more generally the modalities of exercise of such power by the SC (Extraordinary session of the Assembly of the African Union, 12 October 2012, Addis Abeba, Ext/Assembly (AU/Dec.1-2 (Oct. 2013)-Ect/Assembly/AU/decl.1-4 (Oct.,2013), decisions and declaration, op. 4).

through which expressly referring to art. 16 StICC and acting on the basis of Chapter VII of the UN Charter[234], SC asked the ICC to refrain from 1st July 2002 for a period of 12 months from investigations or proceedings involving current or former officials or personnel form a contributing State not part to the Rome Statute over acts or omissions relating to UN established or authorized operation. Obviously, all this except SC does not decide otherwise[235]. Not only did the second paragraph of the same Resolution show "the intention to renew the request" under the same conditions every day in July and as long as it was deemed necessary. And the following year, the SC approved an act of similar content, the Resolution n.1487 of 12 July 2003[236].

The two decisions are the result of strong US opposition to the even more remote[237] eventuality that the ICC exercises its jurisdiction over American citizens engaged in peacekeeping operations. In both cases the SC has expressly stated that it acts consistently with the provisions of article 16 of the Rome Statute. The same United States that drafted the proposal of the Resolution n.1422 (2002) underlined that they had sought to work within the provisions of that Statute[238].

While the latter decision was taken unanimously, its renewal, through the Resolution n.1387 (2003)[239], was marked by the abstention of France, Germany and Syria. Despite the still large majority that characterized the adoption of these resolutions, the positions taken by the States testify numerous and all but secondary, perplexities and oppositions towards this method of exercising the

---

[234]D. WHITTLE, The limits of legality and the United Nations Security Council: Applying the extralegal measures model to chapter VII action, op. cit.

[235]SC, Resolution 1522 (2002) of 12 July 2002, par. 1.

[236]SC, Resolution 1487 (2003) of 12 June 2003.

[237]It is difficult to imagine that the crimes falling under the jurisdiction of the ICC due to their seriousness and above all to the elements of systematic and necessary planning that characterize them are committed in the context of a peacekeeping operation authorized or established by the UN. Furthermore the principle of complementarity and the numerous statutes of forces agreements (SOFAs concluded between the states already guarantee in most cases, a priority to the jurisdiction of the states that participate in peacekeeping missions. These aspects as well as the possibility of concluding the agreements envisaged from article 98, par 2 StICC, they are sorted out by almost all the states as elements that would have had to induce the United States not to perceive the jurisdiction of the ICC as a threat (UN, doc. S/PV.4568 and UN doc. S/PV.4568 (Resuption 1). The General Secretary himself considered the adoption of a completely useless resolution to be seen: UN doc. S/PV. 4772, pp. 2-3. M. ZWANENBURG, The statute for an international criminal court and the United States: Peacekeepers under fire?, in European Journal of International Law, 10, 1999, pp. 131ss. M. O'BRIAN, Prosecutorial discretion and obstacle to prosecution of United Nations peacekeepers by the international criminal court. The big fish/small fish debate and the gravity threshold, in Journal of International Criminal Justice, 10 (3), 2012, pp. 526ss.

[238]UN doc. S/PV.4568, p. 10. G.M. LENTNER, The United Nations Security Council and the International Criminal Court. The referral mechanism in theory and practice, op. cit.,

[239]G.M. LENTNER, The United Nations Security Council and the International Criminal Court. The referral mechanism in theory and practice, op. cit.,

power of deferral. The decisions seem to pose a series of compatibility problems both with the UN Charter and in particular with the assumptions of SC action of ex Chapter VIII and with the ICC Statute especially with the requirements and conditions for exercise of the power provided for by art. 16[240].

According to various criticisms it would be difficult in these cases to frame the basis of the action of SC in Chapter VII of the UN Charter. Canada, for example, in one of the numerous debates that led to the adoption of Resolution n.1422 (2002) noted that "in the absence of any apparent threat to international peace SC passed the Chapter VII of the draft Resolution on ICC of the kind currently circulating world (…) ultra vires"[241]. In a similar way Lichtenstein invoking chapter VII without having established what the threat or violation of peace is, this would therefore seem to imply according to the delegate of that state, the unacceptable consequence that the ICC constitutes such a threat.

It is indeed quite easy to understand what the threat to international peace and security is at the basis of these resolutions. A clue can be found in the last and ambiguous paragraph of the preamble to the two decisions, which certifies that it is in the interests of international peace and security to facilitate Member States ability to contribute to operations established or authorized by the UN Security Council. This statement seems to suggest that the threat to peace stems from the failure to recognize an exemption from ICC jurisdiction for peacekeeping personnel or personnel authorized by the UN. Without this recognition, the ability of States to contribute to peacekeeping operations would be compromised in practice. However, it should be noted that following this interpretative line, the

---

[240]O. BEKOU, The International Criminal Court, op. cit.,

[241]UN doc. S/POV.4568, 10 July 2002, pp. 3ss. The Jordanian representative also asks rhetorically what the threat to peace in this situation may be and speaks expressly of SC ultra vires action (UN doc. S / PC.4568, p. 16). According to New Zealand even if the unlikely event that some members of the peacekeeping force commit an international crime under ICC jurisdiction and the State of citizenship does not want or cannot pursue them."Could not in any event be said to constitute a threat to international peace and security" (ivi, p. 5). Also for Guinea "in the absence of a situation threatening or breaching international peace and security, would we question the vires in the purported use of Chapter VII, in this case to thing article 39 of the Charter and Chapter VII", UN doc. S/PV. 4568 (Resumption 1), 10 July 2002, p. 7. That there is no threat to peace, violation of peace or aggression is also clearly stated by Germany: "Chapter VII requires the existence of a threat to the peace, a breach of the peace or an act of aggression-none of which in our view, is present in this case" (ivi, p. 9). It uses a more cultured language that seems to go in the same direction, even the United Kingdom when it claims to share "the concern that actions of the Council should remain within the scope of its powers. Article 39 of the Charter is relevant in this respect" (ivi, p. 16). Also on the occasion of the renewal of Resolution n.1422 (2002) the representative of Trinidad and Tobago emphasized that: "Any continuous renewal on an annual basis, without establishing the necessary Chapter VII situation contemplated by the drafters of the Statute, would be incompatible with the objective of the Statute (...) contrary to the UN Charter" (UN Doc. S/PV., 4772, p. 15). G.M. LENTNER, The United Nations Security Council and the International Criminal Court. The referral mechanism in theory and practice, op. cit.,

threat to peace would arise only in the event that individuals of nationality of States not part of the Statute are potential targets of the Court's action.

Beyond the doubts raised in relation to the assessment of the conditions laid down by art. 39 of the UN Charter, to which we will return here emerges the political concession that the SC Member States had to the United States. If the Resolution n.1422 (2002) had not been adopted, the latter threatened to withdraw their support for the mission of the UN in Bosnia Herzegovina (UINMIBH) or not to authorize its renewal[242]. The US position is quite clear and expresses the need for that State to ensure (...) nature jurisdiction over personnel and officials involved in UN peacekeeping and in coalition of the willing operations[243]. To demonstrate the importance of the condition imposed by the United States on the same day as the adoption of Resolution n.1422, the SC also approved Resolution n.1423 (2002) aimed at extending the mandate of the UNMIBH mission[244]. Moreover, in a broader perspective, it is interesting to remember that in May of the same year the United States had withdrawn the signature previously affixed to the Rome Statute, explaining that they no longer felt bound to respect the purpose and object of that treaty[245].

---

[242]It is interesting to mention the fact that French was willing to support the United Kingdom proposal "allowing for the orderly withdrawal of UNMIBH and its replacement (...) by the EU Police Mission", S/PV. 4568, 19 July 2002, p. 12.

[243]These are the words of John Negroponte, US delegate at the time of the veto affixed to the Resolution of 2002 which provided for the extension of the mandate of the peacekeeping mission in Bosnia Herzegovina. See: UN Doc. S/PV.4563 of 30 June 2002, pp. 2-3. It is worth reporting at least one more passage of the rather explicit statements made by the United States representative on that occasion: "the United States wants to participate in international peacekeeping but the United States a major guarantor of peace and security around the globe and founding UN member, does note and will not accept ICC jurisdiction over the peacekeepers that it contributes to operations established and authorized by the UN". Moreover, the American soldiers in 2002 did not risk any proceedings before ICC, since they were engaged in States not part of the Statute or in any case in territories under the ICC jurisdiction. See the Charter of the coalition for an ICC. See also the letter from the president to the speaker of the case as well as of the president pro tempore of the Senate, in Weekly compilation of presidential document, n. 39, 1243, 29 July 2002. For further details see also: S. ZAPPALÁ, The reaction of the US to the entry into force of the ICC statute: Comments on UN SC Resolution (2002) and article 98 agreements, in Journal of International Criminal Justice, 1 (1), 2003, pp. 115ss. C. STAHN, The ambiguities of Security Council Resolution 1422, in European Journal of International Law, 14 (3), 2003, pp. 87ss.

[244]G.M. LENTNER, The United Nations Security Council and the International Criminal Court. The referral mechanism in theory and practice, op. cit.,

[245]The contents of John Bolton's letter to the Secretary-General should also be reported to UN. "Dear Mr. Secretary-General: This is to inform you, in connection with the Rome Statute of ICC adopted on 17 July 1998, that the United States does not intend to become a party to the treaty. Accordingly, the United States has no legal obligations arising from its signature on 31 December 2000. The United States requests that its intention not to become a party, as expressed in this letter, be reflected in the depositary lists of the Statute

Identical reasons are the basis for the following renewal of the exemption from jurisdiction. Also during the adoption of Resolution n.1487 (2003) the United States underlined the fundamental role that peacekeeping operations play in the action of SC and the importance therefore of allowing States to participate in it[246].

As anticipated, in addition to the criticisms relating to the existence of conditions for the exercise of powers provided for in Chapter VII of the UN Charter, further and even more perplexities have emerged on the compatibility of these decisions with the Rome Statute and in particular with the provision relating to the exercise of suspension power, i.e. art. 16. Almost all States used the words of the Jordanian representative that there is a misapplication of article 16 and a contravention of the Rome Statute here[247]. The objections raised focus on the general abstract and predetermined nature of the exemption provided for by the Resolution and the intention to annually renew its effects. According to these criticisms, the power of deferral should be exercised on the occasion of a particular fact or a series of specific and urgent concrete events. It should be dealt with situations where the opening or continuation of an investigation or proceeding can concretely and not only in the abstract harm the effectiveness of SC action and more generally the needs of peacekeeping[248].

---

relating to this treaty".

[246]UN Doc. S/PV.4722, 12 June 2003, p. 23. To further clarify the ratio of the particular limitation placed on the ICC jurisdictional activity, the US representative stressed that because "it is not always easy to recruit contributors" it is important that States do not add "concern about ICC jurisdiction to the difficulty of participating". In this second decision, there is no specific and contextual need to renew a particular peacekeeping mission even if the underlying reasons as stated in these references are identical.

[247]As mentioned, many states have expressed themselves in a similar way. For example, Costa Rican argued that the motion for a resolution: "is completely without foundation because article 16 of the Rome statute involved by the proposal's advocates, refers to an entirely different situation", UN Doc. S/PV. 4568, p. 14. On the occasion of the public debate on resolution 1422 (2002), the Colombian representative noted that a resolution of the Council: "cannot inteprет the man dates of the statute above and beyond their content, or contradict the purpose of their provisions" (S/PV.4568 (Resumption 1, p. 6). According to Samoa the same project of resolution; "will (…) undermine the purpose and meaning of the Rome statute" as well as being: "unnecessary" and incompatibile fon art. 16. According to the Argentine delegate, the proposed resolution from United States: "might lead to a distortion of the spirit and a departure form the letter of a key provision of the Rome statute" (ibidem, p. 13). The representative of the EU, on the other hand, confines himself to an obvious statement of principle which, however, seems to imply a possible violation of the statute. The Danish Loj, affirmes that: "article 16 should be involked only in conformity with the statute" (UN Doc. S/PV.4568, p. 8)

[248]Although these criticisms were mostly raised in terms of compatibility with the arr. 16 of the bylaws, also the assumption of the exercise of the powers provided by art. 39 of he charter of the UN seems at least in origin, to have been conceived as involving elements of concreteness and actuality of the threat. The elements of specificity and concreteness that characterize the situation at the origin of the request to suspend the ICC's jurisdictional

On the compatibility of Resolution n.1422 (2002) with the letter and spirit of art. 16, the statements made by numerous state representatives, according to which the true purpose and meaning of art. 16 "is to enable SC to judge each case on the basis of its particular circumstances"[249] and for this reason "there is clearly no ground for a determination in advance and then in perpetuity"[250]. In this same direction, the Swiss delegate noted that art. 16 must be applied on a case-by case basis otherwise it is like believing that ICC is in itself an obstacle to peace[251]. On this latter aspect, some States have noted more generally the absurdity of perceiving the activity of ICC almost by nature in conflict with the creation or authorization of peacekeeping operations[252].

---

activity seem therefore to have a double value: they can also take on importance for an assessment regarding the correct exercise of the powers of the SC ex chapter VII of the charter of the UN: in addition to doctrinal positions aimed at supporting the actuality and concreteness that should characterize the assumptions of the action of the SC pursuant to art. 39 of the charter, some states have highlighted this element. See the words expressed by the New Zealand representative according to which: “consistent with the mandate of the chapter VII, the Council should act to reach solutions in specific cases taking into account of the full range of facts in each situation. Such facts will inevitably vary from case to case and from mission to mission” S/PV.4568, p. 6.

[249]O. BEKOU, The International Criminal Court, op. cit.,

[250]Guinea, UN Doc. S/PPV.4568 (Resumption 1, p. 7). According to Guinea, the decision of SC would be both in the light of the chapter VII and from art. 16, "plainly ultra vires". See the identical position expressed by the Lichtenstein, see: UN Doc. S / PV.4568, p. 20. Mexico also believes that the action of the SCX that does not respect the spirit and the letter of a treaty must be considered in contrast with the charter of the UN and international law. The words expressed by the representative of New Zealand in expressing the fear that: “the use of the specific procure laid down in article 16 in a generic resolution not in response to a particular factual situation and with the intention to renew it on an annual basis, was inconsistent with both the terms and the purpose of that provision”, UN Doc. S/PV.4568, p. 5.

[251]The Canadian representative argues that the history of the negotiations: “makes cclear that recourse to article 16 is on a case-by-case only, where a particular situation-for example the dynamic of a apce negotiation-warrants a 12 months deferral”. In the same mode Germany whihs is referrede in the possibilities clearlu provided for in article 16, UN Doc. S/PV.4568 (Resumption 1, p. 9) and Brazil: “strongly discourage proposals with respect to article 16, whose provisions are applicable only on a case-by-case basis” UN Doc. S/PV.4568, p. 22.

[252]See the position of Fiji, UN Doc. S/PV.4568 (Resuption 1), 10 July 2002, p. 2: “it is inconceivable that one stands to threaten the other” and of Malesia: “the objectives of the ICC and peacekeeping operations do not contradict each other, and the existence of one shoulòd not preclude the other”. According to argentina, peace and justice: “should not and cannot appear to be in contraddiction or collision”. In this direction also the words of the delegate of Lichtenstein seem to say that maintaining peace and justice are "complementary concepts" and cannot be understood as "mutually exclusive", in other words there cannot be a choice: “between onr or the other”, S/PV.4569, p. 20; also for Brazil peace and justice “are not conflicting objectives” and in the same orientation see also: Venezuela, which affirmed that: “entirely complementary”.

At the time of the renewal of the exemption from jurisdiction (2003), many States again highlighted the difficulty of reconciling the Resolution with what is provided to from art. 16 which according to the EU representative: "Cannot be interpreted as permitting the automatic renewal of that Resolution without taking into account the specific condition under which such a request is being made"[253]. Even the Secretary General at the beginning of the debate stated in a harsh warning to SC that art. 16 "was not intended to cover such a sweeping request but only a more specific one relating to a particular situation"[254].

During these meetings, however, few States have supported the US position. On the occasion of the adoption of Resolution n.1422 (2002), India (State not part of the Statute) declared itself against to accept an outside authority purporting to sit in judgment towards its troops[255]. At the time of the renewal of the exemption United Kingdom limited itself to affirming that the two resolutions are consistent with article 16 of the ICC Statute[256] and in the same way, Spain stressed that the statutory provision is mentioned in the Resolution adopted today in accordance with the Statute and for this reason only the extension decided by SC does not affect the integrity of the Statute[257].

As seen, however, beyond the latter positions, the interpretation of art. 16 proposed by SC aimed at extending its applicative scope in most States at odds with both the letter, the purpose and the object of the Rome Statute and the UN Charter. In more general terms, during the various sessions that preceded the adoption of the two resolutions, a considerable number of States contested the existence of a SC power to modify the content of the Rome Statute. Just to give an example, Brazil recalled that SC "cannot after international agreements that have been duly negotiated and freely entered into by States Parties" for the simple fact that this body "is not vested with treaty-making and treaty-reviewing

---

[253]UN doc. S/PV.4722, 12 June 2003, p. 9. According to Brazil the dispositions of the statute and in paricular arrt. 16: "were never intended to give place to ad aeternam defferrals of the court's jurisdiction" (UN Doc. S/PV.4568, p. 22); also for Switzerland: "generalized preventive usage of article 16 would be contrary to the treaty". Mexico in the same orientation affirmes that: "that such a suspension might become unlimited" (p. 26)

[254]UN Doc. S/PV.4772, p. 2

[255]For the peremptoriness of the affirmations, it is worthwhile here to report a broader except of the intervent of the Indian delegate, which is affirmed that: "As representatives of the largest in the world democracy with an independent judiciary whose contribution to the jurisprudence of the rights of the individual is likely to have few equals, we find it difficult to accept an outside authority purporting to sit in judgment upon actions of our troops. Quite part from the exemplary discipline and commitment to the case of peace displayed by them, we see them as answerable for their behavior to authorities within the established hierarchy of command and to our own established institutions, not to those whose jurisdiction we do not recognize", UN Doc. S/PV.4568, p. 14.

[256]UN Doc. S/PV.4772, p. 23.

[257]G.M. LENTNER, The United Nations Security Council and the International Criminal Court. The referral mechanism in theory and practice, op. cit.,

powers"[258].

Precisely because of the numerous critical issues that emerged and the tough opposition expressed by the States, the practice of the annual renewal of these resolutions has been interrupted. The SC has also, through some resolutions that will be analyzed, sought to protect in other ways the categories of individuals subject to suspension requests.

2.2. Other resolutions with suspensive effects of the ICC's jurisdictional activity

The stern blame by the UN Secretary-General on the practice of SC for precluding ICC's action against certain categories of individuals has not gone unheeded[259]. Thus the annual Resolution that guaranteed immunity to military and

---

[258]See the declarations of the Brazilian representative in UN Doc. S/PV.4568, 10 July 2002, p. 22. See also the position of islands Fiji, which is declared that: "SC's functions and powers, including those set out in Chapter VII, do not include amending treaties", UN Doc. S/PV.4568 (Resumption 1), 10 July 2002, p. 2. Also Canada has observed that "the Council has not been empowered to rewrite treaties" and the resolution "would undermine the treaty-making process". See, UN Doc. S/PV.4568, 120 July 2002, p. 3. Iran stated that "the Council is not authorized to interpret or amend treaties". In this sense also Ireland (ivi, p. 18), New Zealand (ivi, pp. 5-6) and South Africa (ivi, p. 6). France also sustained that "cannot accept modification by means of a SC Resolution of a provision of a treaty" (ivi, p. 11) and also Mexico observed that "would be damaged if we allow the Council to set the negative precedent of using its resolutions to amend treaties" (ivi, p. 26). According to Guinea (UN Doc. S/PV-.4568 (Resumption 1, p. 5). Colombia stated that "the need to adopt positions compatible with the Statute" and the fact of Resolution of SC adopted according to Chapter VII of the UN Charter "cannot ignore the content of the provisions of the Rome Statute" (ivi, pp. 5-6). Also Malesia affirmed that "it is vitally important for the Council not to take a decision that would have the effect of changing or amending the terms of an international treaty" (ivi, p. 8). Also Syria affirmed that "SC does not have the right to take decision under Chapter VII to amend an international treaty that has entered into force" (ivi, p. 10). For the performance of the affirmations, it is worthwhile here to report to broader excerpt of the intervention of the Indian delegate: "(...) To say the very least, restricted the legitimate limits of the role and responsibility entrusted to the Council under the Charter" UN Doc. S/PV.4772, pp. 5-6. See also: S. KIM, Maintaining the independence of the International Criminal Court: The legal and procedural implications of an article 16 deferral request, in Agenda Internacional, 29, 2019, pp. 177ss.

[259]Some words of the general secretary on the suspension exercised from SC have already been recalled. More generally, the Secretary-General had hoped that the exemption would not become an annual routine, fearing that in this way "the Council wished to claim absolute and permanent immunity for people serving it in the operations that established and authorizes". This practice according to Secretary General "would undermine not only the authority of ICC but also of the Council and the legitimacy of UN peacekeeping", UN Doc. SW/PV.4772, p.3. It is also worth recalling here that in addition to the protests of numerous States aimed at countering the practice of SC, irrefutable evidence of torture committed by some US soldiers within the Abu Ghraiv and Guantanamo prisons emerged. These last facts could only weaken the position of the United States as stated they would have liked the suspension to be renewed annually.

civilian personnel engaged in established or authorized operations from UN was no longer repeated. SC practice has taken on partly different forms as just mentioned and also emerges from the criticisms raised by some even more problematic States[260].

The resolutions just analyzed are the only ones that explicitly refer to art. 16 of the Statute. There are, however, other resolutions which, while producing suspensive effects on ICC jurisdictional activity, seem more difficult to trace back to the deferral power envisaged by the Statute. One of these decisions was taken in order to authorize a peacekeeping mission and the other two, already under investigation, are an expression of the SC's power to activate ICC jurisdiction. In relation to the latter, however, it is necessary to refer to the opening of the discussion regarding many of the critical positions expressed by the States on the exemptions provided by SC.

As just mentioned, some of the effects that the decisions in question produce can be assimilated to those following the exercise of the power of deferral since, albeit in a slightly different way compared to the two decisions just analyzed, they are aimed in fact at suspending the exercise of ICC jurisdiction, at least towards certain categories of individuals. Moreover, the relevant peers of the operative part of the decisions in question in this section represent a clear continuation of the two resolutions set out in the previous paragraph. Here too, in fact, forms of exemption from ICC jurisdiction are provided for citizens of non-Member States of the Statute engaged in operations authorized or established by UN. In short, these decisions seem to respond to a ratio common to that of the resolutions just examined and which were expressly adopted on the basis of art. 16 of the Statute.

The decisions that will be recalled in the next pages are therefore the Resolution n.1497 (2003) which authorized the intervention of a multinational force in Liberia and ordered the sending of a stabilization force of UN and the already analyzed resolutions that activated ICC jurisdiction regarding the situations of Darfur ((1593) (2005)) and Libya ((1970 (2011))[261].

Resolution n.1497 (2003) relating to the mission in Liberia and n.1593 (2005) on the situation in Darfur have prepared a particular form of permanent exemption from ICC jurisdiction and all jurisdictions other than those of their sending status for "current or former officials or personnel" of States not part to the Rome Statute. Immunity from jurisdiction is aimed at covering "all alleged acts or omissions arising out of or related to operations"[262] established or authorized by SC (or the African Union, at least as regards Darfur) in Liberia and Sudan respectively. In other words, and more simply, these resolutions of SC provide for the exercise of exclusive jurisdiction over their personnel of the status

---

[260] A. ABBAS, The competence of the Security Council to terminate the jurisdiction of the international criminal court, op. cit., pp. 267ss.

[261] G.M. LENTNER, The United Nations Security Council and the International Criminal Court. The referral mechanism in theory and practice, op. cit.,

[262] O. QUIRICO, International criminal responsibility. Antinomies, op. cit.,

of dispatch of the quotas engaged in UN operations. The exclusive jurisdiction of the supplier State in the generic terms used in resolutions, implies that also the citizens of States Parties to the Statute, over which ICC could normally exercise its jurisdiction pursuant to art. 12 (2) b), would enjoy the exemption provided by SC decision, if they were "acting as officials or personnel" of the sending State not part of the Statute[263]. Not long after this decision, however, Liberia became part of the Treaty of Rome. The Resolution therefore has in this case the effect of limiting the scope of the other ICC competence (art. 12 (2) a)) as not being able to exercise its jurisdiction over any crime committed on the territory of a State Party.

The Resolution n.1980 (2011) has slightly different content from the previous two. The first two decisions protect, as we have just seen, state personnel who contribute by sending their own officers to missions created or authorized by the UN for the maintenance of peace. The Resolution on the situation in Libya, on the other hand, does not refer to the personnel of a contributing State but protects more generally from the jurisdiction of ICC and the other national jurisdictions of any State that is not part of the Rome Statute, provided that the action or the release of these individuals is linked to the armed intervention. The protection here would therefore not only cover individuals who have an organic relationship with the sending State, but soldiers belonging to private military companies. The latter even if not sent by the States engaged in operation authorized by the SC, would enjoy the privilege of the exclusive jurisdiction of their status of nationality does not form part of the Statute, in the event that their activity is considered in any case connected to the military mission of UN.

The exemptions provided by SC in these three hypotheses with respect to the suspension contemplated by the two resolutions analyzed in the previous paragraph have the advantage of establishing case by case, at the time of authorization of the intervention of the multinational force (Liberia) or activation of ICC jurisdiction (Sudan and Libya), the blockade of the latter. It therefore does not have the characteristics of abstractness and generality of the previous requests for suspension of SC. The absence of a time limit to the dispensation provided for by the resolutions poses many problems. Moreover, the exemption does not concern only ICC but also all national jurisdictions. Ultimately, by not providing alternatives to the jurisdiction of the sending or citizenship State, it does not guarantee the criminal repression of the crimes under ICC jurisdiction in the event that such State cannot or do not want to prosecute those responsible.

2.2.1. Resolution n.1497 (2003) and the mission authorized by UN in Liberia

At the time of the adoption of Resolution n.1497 (2003) on 1st August 2003 through which the SC authorized the intervention of a multinational force in

---

[263]S.A.G. TALMON, Security Council treaty action, in Revue Hellenique de Droit International, 62, 2009, pp. 10ss.

Liberia, three States: Germany, France and Mexico, motivated their abstention contesting the general scope of the exemptions provided in the Resolution aimed at limiting both the jurisdiction of ICC and that of the national courts as well as sanctioning discriminatory treatment against peacekeepers from countries that are members of the Rome Statute of ICC[264]. The States that abstained from voting have identified a general problem of consistency of SC action with respect to its declared intention of spearheading the movement of reject impunity in all its forms. More specifically, immunity from jurisdiction achieved through Resolution would limit ICC jurisdiction in an incompatible manner with the Statute of Rome and would run counter to international obligations States on the repression of international crimes.

The Resolution under consideration was adopted on the basis of Chapter VII of the UN Charter[265]. However, it not only does not contain any reference to art. 16 StICC but neither is it formulated contrary to the previous decisions and the provisions of the same statutory provision, in terms of a request addressed to ICC bodies. The Resolution also says nothing about the duration of the arrest of

---

[264]UN Doc. S/PV.4803, p. 4 (see the declarations of Germany). Moreover, if such exemptions for state personnel not part of the Statute become a constant and generalized practice, negative effects of not insignificant effects on the willingness of States part of the Statute to participate in peacekeeping missions could occur, precisely because of the discriminatory treatment that would be reserved for its own soldiers. The abstention of Germany, France and Mexico is not solely linked to the compliantness of the Resolution to the Statute of Rome. The scope of these decisions is in fact extremely general and the priority granted to the sending status is more extensive than usually provided by the Status of Force Agreements (SOFAs). These agreements generally do not recognize an exclusive but only primary jurisdiction of the sending State except in the case of crimes that are not punishable in light of the domestic law in the territorial State. The SOFAs are also obvious only for the States that subscribe them. The Resolution essentially surpasses these aspects. From another imposes an always exclusive jurisdiction of the sending status. On the other hand, it operates in relation to all UN Member States regardless of any agreements in courses between States on the subject. In practice Resolution n.1497 (2003) by imposing the exclusive jurisdiction of the State of dispatch, also precludes the competence of other national courts possibly legitimized for penal repression by virtue of the traditional connecting criteria expressed in the principles of passive nationality and universal jurisdiction and in the absence of eventual agreements of re-opening of jurisdiction on the armed forces. For this reason, the three States that opted for the extension noted the incompatibility of this form of immunity not only with international law but also with its own criminal legislation (Doc. S/PV. 4803, pp. 2-3). Germany noted that the inability to prosecute some individuals for crimes committed in Liberia against German citizens "is not in agreement with international and German law" (ibid., P. 4) and France stated that jurisdictional immunity decreed with the Resolution is not compatible with "the provisions of the Rome Statute of the international criminal court, the norms of french law or the principles of international law" (ivi, p. 7). For further analysis see also: F. TANNER, Addressing the perils of peace operations. Toward a global peacekeeping system, in Global Governance, 16 (2), 2010, pp. 212ss.

[265]D. WHITTLE, The limits of legality and the United Nations Security Council: Applying the extralegal measures model to chapter VII action, op. cit.

the judicial activity. The suspension of ICC judicial action against those categories of individuals is not expressly limited to the 12 months provided for by art. 16 StICC to which the previous decisions instead referred.

2.2.2. Suspensive effects in the exercise of referral power: Resolutions n.1593 (2005) and n.1970 (2011)

Resolution n.1593 (2005) through which, as seen by SC for the first time, ICC jurisdiction provides, in a manner similar to the Resolution just examined, the exclusive jurisdiction of the sending status for all alleged acts or omissions arising out of or related to operations in Sudan established or authorized by the Council or the African Union.

Compared to the Resolution on Liberia, art. 16 is in this case referred to in the preamble of the Resolution. Paragraph 6 which provides for the exclusive jurisdiction of the status of dispatch of the personnel participating in the missions of UN, seems to be the only part of the device possibly attributable to that standard. Apart from the general reference contained in the preamble, however, during the debate that led to the adoption of the Resolution, no State has made the slightest reference to the expected power of art. 16 StICC. That part of the preamble therefore seems to represent a simple and formal information of SC that remains free at any time to suspend jurisdiction over investigations or proceedings relating to a situation which it has brought to the attention of the Prosecutor[266].

Some States have pointed out by linking the limiting measure of ICC jurisdiction to the exercise of referral power by SC that "it would be a contradiction to mention, in the very text of a referral by the Council to ICC, measures that limit the jurisdictional activity of the Court"[267]. This last consideration seems to somehow deny the possibility of a contextual exercise of the power to activate the jurisdiction of ICC for a given situation and suspend its repressive action against some individuals.

Similar reasoning can be made for Resolution n.1970 of 2011. Also in this case the preamble contains a reference to the power provided by art. 16 StICC, except then providing for the exemption from ICC jurisdiction for citizens, organs and personnel of States not part of the Statute under that part of the Resolution expressly entitled: ICC referral. Resolution n.1970 (2011) was adopted unanimously in a context of general sharing and support for an intervention that was aimed at least in the wishes of SDC members to end the violence against civilians of the Gaddafi regime. The activation of ICC has aroused some enthusiasm among many States and as already pointed out, in this case there are not many critical positions[268]. Beyond the intervention in Libya and the consent

---

[266]It is not expressed in these terms, but certainly in the sense that the reference to art. 16 is not sufficient to identify in that provision the legal basis of the decision. D. AKANDE, The effect of Security Council resolutions and domestic proceedings on state obligations to cooperate with the ICC, in Journal of International Criminal Justice, 12, 2012, pp. 310ss.

[267]UN Doc. S/PV.5158, p. 11.

[268]See the position of Brazil, UN Doc. S/PV.6491, p. 7.

expressed towards the exercise of the referral, the absence of the nourished and sometimes vehement criticisms that had accompanied the previous resolutions could be interpreted as a partial acceptance by the States of a SC practice aimed at limiting the jurisdictional activity of ICC towards some categories of individuals.

3. Missed deferrals

3.1. The cases of Darfur and Libya

SC has on some occasions been the subject of explicit requests for political expressions from some States and international organizations aimed at obtaining a suspension of the judicial activities of ICC. However, these instances did not reach the necessary consensus among the Member States of SC.

Perhaps an indication of an uncertain support for SC's choice to activate Prosecutor's investigations, some States have supported or in any case proposed the possibility of an arrest of the ICC's judicial action in both Darfur and Libya. As regards the first situation, the entire proceeding against the Sudanese President Omar Al-Bashir was characterized by a strong and prolonged contestation by the African Union[269]. A hostility that has also accompanied the prosecution proceedings initiated by the Prosecutor, in relation to the crimes committed in Kenya. Also as a result of the negative results of the requests for suspension relating to both cases, the contrast between the African Union and the ICC action has intensified over time and is at the origin of the almost total absence of cooperation with the ICC by the African States for the capture of the Sudanese President Al-Bashir[270].

On several occasions and this is what is now interesting to underline, the African Union has tried to obtain a Resolution of SC aimed at suspending the judicial activity of ICC in relation to the situation in Darfur[271]. In particular, the African States that requested the arrest of the proceeding against Al-Bashir argued

[269]Indeed, other regional organizations, such as the Arab League, the non-aligned state movement and the organization of the Islamic Conference, have also expressed their opposition to the arrest of Al-Bashir. See in argument: UN Doc. S/2009/117, identical letters dated on 25 February 2008 from the representatives of Cuba, Oman, Senegal and Uganda addressed to the UN Secretary General and the SC president.

[270]On this point we will return, but we can recall that it is in this general context of mutual distrust that the African Union has come to propose the establishment of a penal chamber with jurisdiction over the repression of international crimes within the African Court of justice and human rights. See: Draft protocol on amendments to the protocol on the Stature of the African Court of justice and human rights, revisions up to Tuesday 15th May 2012, Exp/Min/IV/Rev. 7.

[271]J. FALLIGANT, The prosecution of Sudanese president Al Bashir: Why a security Council deferral would harm the legitimacy of the international criminal court, in Wisconsin International Law Journal, 27, 2010, pp. 748ss. O. BEKOU, D. BIRKETT, Cooperation and the International Criminal Court: Perspectives from theory and practice, ed. Brill, Bruxelles, 2016.

that "the potential destabilizing effects" of the arrest warrant issued by the Court could not be ignored. In other words, according to these critical positions, the repressive action in a context such as the Sudanese "could seriously undermine the ongoing efforts aimed at facilitating the early Resolution of the conflict in Darfur and the promotion of long-lasting peace and reconciliation in Sudan[272]. In short, the aims of international criminal justice would be in this specific situation in contrast with the main and fundamental purpose of the UN Charter and the international community, i.e. the maintenance of peace and collective security[273].

Although the possibility of a referral has never really been discussed within SC it is worth mentioning that when (already in 2011), western States began to doubt that the intervention in Libya would be concluded quickly and without too many complications, both the United Kingdom and the France sketched the hypothesis of dropping the criminal case against Gaddafi in exchange for his voluntary dismissal. As well as in the other debates relating to a possible exercise of the deferral, the strongly political connotations of the instrument created through art. 16 StICC[274].

3.2. The Kenya case

The African Union proposed in 2013 the adoption of a Resolution aimed at interrupting ICC's judicial activity towards the president of Kenya, Uhuru Muigai Kenyatta and its vice president, William Samoei Ruto[275]. Both are accused of committing crimes against humanity in the aftermath of the elections in Kenya in December 2007[276]. This need recently re-emerged in the public debate following the new elections of 2017 which saw the reaffirmation of President Kenyatta but also hundreds of died in protests following the announcement of the election results. The request for deferral, not approved due to the abstention of eight Member States and despite the absence of opposing votes, was based on the assumption that the attacks occurred in Kenya in September 2013 (in particular

[272]UN Doc. S/2009/117 identical letters dated 25 February 2008 from the representatives of Cuba, Oman, Senegal and Uganda to the United Nations addressed to the Secretary general and the President of the Security Council.

[273]It is interesting to note that even an important American think tank in recent years has repeatedly called for SC to use its power under art. 16 StICC and suspend for a year the jurisdictional activity of ICC on the situation in Darfur, so as to favor the continuation of peace talks and not to worsen constantly the humanitarian situation. See: International crisis report n. 211, 27 January 2013.

[274]O. BEKOU, The International Criminal Court, op. cit.,

[275]UN Doc. S/2013/660 of 15 November 2013. For further analysis see: A. FOLLESDALL, G. ULFSTEIN, The judicialization of international law: A mixed blessing?, Oxford University Press, Oxford, 2018.

[276]Prosecutor then decided not to continue the investigations against the Kenyan president, given the lack of evidence and the impossibility of finding them. This however "without prejudice to the possibility of bringing a new case should additional evidence become available". Notice of withdrawal of the charges against Uhuru Muigai Kenyatta, ICC-01/09-02/11-983, 5 December 2014.

the shooting at the Westgate Mall of Nairobi) required the presence of a stable government capable of acting and actively responding to the looming terrorist threat[277].

The basis therefore in Chapter VII of the proposal of Resolution aimed at suspending the activity of ICC, would have been identified in the need not to compromise the ability of the most malt exponents of the Kenyan government to maintain peace and security in a region exposed to constant risk of attacks. To take up the words used by the representative of the African Union during the debate in SC, President Kenyatta and his vice Ruto "ought to be given support" in the fight against terrorism and for the achievement of stability in his country. The African delegate did not then renounce to express a general distrust towards ICC, a consequence of an attitude considered not strictly impartial by ICC. The fear that President's Kennyata political activity is distracted by a body whose track record on African matters has not exactly been the kind that inspires confidence is underlined[278]. Rwanda also contested the different use of art. 16 by SC when the interests of the western powers are at stake and said that the prerogative recognized in that provision "was never meant to be used by an African State or any of the developing countries" but was rather conceived "as an additional tool for the big powers to protect themselves"[279]. The Russian federation also supported the motion for a resolution on the deferral against Kenya by supporting in a broader perspective that its application would ultimately enhance the authority of the system of international justice among African countries. The exercise of deferral power in this particular situation would also demonstrate that

---

[277]You can also see the reasons for the request for deferral given by the States that voted in favor of the Resolution proposal. UN Doc. S/PV.7060.

[278]According to some reconstructions, instead the ICC action would have had a series of positive effects in terms of deterrence from the commission of crimes in the future and more generally in having brought to the attention of the international community the violence perpetrated in the country. See in argument: C.L. SHIRAM, S. BROWN, Kenya in the shadow of the ICC: Complementarity, gravity and impact, in International Criminal Law Review, 12, 2012, pp. 220ss. The confidence of African States against ICC could be further undermined by the decisions taken on the admissibility of the case which would be in the light of various critical analyzes, influenced decisively by political evaluations: C. BRIGHTON, Unwillingness: Addressing the political pitfalls inherent in the complementarity regime of the international criminal court, in International Criminal Law Review, 2012, pp. 630ss. O.C. IMOEDEMHE, The complementarity regime of the ICC: National implementation, ed. Springer, Berlin, 2016. Still in a more general perspective of relations between the African States, SC and ICC jurisdictional activity, even though the failure to adopt this Resolution has led to a series of strong recriminations and protests by numerous States in the African continent. The latter underline the continuing mistrust that western States have towards African political representatives and their ability to resolve complex situations that concern the maintenance of peace and the fight against impunity for the commission of international crimes. In particular, African States express their disappointment with the way in which SC has so far interpreted the powers attributed to it by StICC in particular to request the suspension of investigations and proceedings.

[279]O. QUIRICO, International criminal responsibility. Antinomies, op. cit.,

system's maturity and readiness to address complex and ambiguous situations responsively. China also in favor of the Resolution limited itself to noting that the request of African States "is reasonable and well founded on the basis of the purposes and principles of the UN Charter"[280].

By contrast, several States have observed that pursuing the suit in ICC against the President and deputy president of Kenya does not in itself create a threat to regional or indeed international peace and security[281]. To justify their abstention, many delegates have therefore highlighted that the reference contained in art. 16, Chapter VII of the UN Charter "means that SC must assume the existence of a threat to peace due to the very fact of the proceedings under way in ICC"[282]. As most clearly pointed out for United Kingdom, the question we are dealing with is in practice "whether or not continuing with ICC proceedings constitutes in itself a threat to international peace and security"[283].

---

[280]O. QUIRICO, International criminal responsibility. Antinomies, op. cit.,

[281]These are the words of the representative of Luxembourg. See also the similar positions taken by United Kingdom (p. 67) and Australia (p. 9). Even France (p. 7) and Guatemala (p. 21) have argued through less explicit statements but that go substantially in the same direction, the inapplicability of art. 16 in the present case. The same position also emerges from the letter, sent by numerous non-governmental organizations to the foreign ministries of the African States pertaining to the Statute and directed in fact to have the request for suspension reconsidered. See Gabon, Nigeria, South Africa: Reconsider support for deferral of ICC Kenya investigation civil society to the ministers of foreign affairs of the African States parties on the UN Security Council. In the subsequent letter of 21 November 2013 addressed to the Assembly of States part of the Statute, the representative of the African Union clearly stated in response to the positions expressed by the States that did not support the deferral. The failure to use the power to suspend ICC jurisdiction by SC and the contrast of the ongoing proceedings with the principle of complementarity, would be the demonstration that ICC "(...) is no longer a Court for all but only to deal with Africans in the most rigid way". Once again the idea for which the African Union "strongly believe in African solutions to African problems". See in particular the statement of Hon. Frederick Ruhindi, Deputy Attorney General/Minister of state for justice and constitutional affairs of the Republic of Uganda on behalf of the African Union at the 12th Assembly of States Parties to the Rome Statute of the international criminal court, 21 November 2013. In this regard, it is interesting to recall that in 2015 Kenya was the promoter of a proposal for amendment of the preamble of the Statute "in order to ensure that the principle of complementarity sufficiently recognizes regional criminal judicial mechanisms". The road taken by the African States seems to be that of creating regional mechanisms of penal repression for the serious international crimes committed within the continent. See in argument: Report of the working group on amendments, fourteenth session, ICC-ASP/14/34, 18-26 November 2015, par. 18.

[282]UN Doc. S/PV.7060, 15 November 2013, pp. 3-4 (Luxembourg). For further analysis see: L. SIEVERS, S. DAWS, The procedure of the United Nations Security Council, Oxford University Press, Oxford, 2014.

[283]Also Australia underlines that the decision to suspend ICC action "should be taken only in exceptional circumstances when the proceedings themselves threaten international peace and security and alternative options have been exhausted" (p. 9). The Argentine delegate also noted that SC has the duty "to interpret strictly whether the trial posed a threat to

These positions, in addition to highlighting the exceptional nature of the use of power of deferral, highlight an issue of no small importance that will have to be addressed in the course of this investigation. It is a question of whether actually how these States support both the repressive action of ICC to have to pose a threat to peace or rather the ongoing investigations and proceedings are only some of the elements of potential obstacle to the stability of international relations, but they do not constitute necessarily and in itself the condition of ex art. 39 of the UN Charter of the SC action.

3.3. The Uganda case

The activation of ICC on the situation in Uganda, as already mentioned, is based on a request from the same State on whose territory the crimes were committed[284]. In late 2003, President Museveni asked the ICC Prosecutor to investigate the crimes committed by the Lord's resistance army, a rebel group led by Joseph Kony[285]. Museveni had in 2006 announced the plans to grant Kony and the other leaders of the rebel movement an amnesty in the event of their participation in peace talks and the cessation of terrorist attacks. At the end of that same year, a presidential statement of SC still called for (also following the interruption of a case between the parties, resulting in a series of violence against

---

international peace and security". See: UN Doc. SC/11176, Security Council resolution seeking deferral of Kenyan leaders, trial fairs to win adoption with 7 voting in favor, 8 abstaining, 15 November 2015, 7060th meeting.

[284]Indeed, the power of self referring to ICC by a State is not contemplated by the statutes but would be the result of a creative interpretation of art. 14 StICC. W.A. SCHABAS, Complementarity in practice: Creative solutions or a trap fro the court?, in F. GIOIA, M. POLITI, The international criminal court and national jurisdictions, ed. Routledge, Aldershot, 2008, pp. 32ss. M. EL ZEIDY, The Ugandan government triggers the first test of complementarity principle: An assessment of the first state's party referral to ICC, in International Criminal Law Review, 5, 2005, pp. 100ss.

[285]The Ugandan letter addressed to ICC is dated on 16 December 2003. The office of the Prosecutor (president of Uganda Resistance Army in Northern and Western Uganda also emerges from ICC) decision to convene a state Conference on the application of article 43, par.3, p. 68. Following a subsequent request to do so by the Prosecutor, the preliminary chamber issued a series of arrest warrants, initially withheld against the same Joseph Kony, of Vincent Otti, Okot Odhiambo, Dominic Ongwen and Raska Oykwiya for crimes against humanity and war. See, warrant of arrest for Joseph Kony issued on 8th July 2005 as amended on 27th September 2005, pre-trial chamber II, ICC-02/04-01/05-53, 28 September 2005 and the Prosecutor v. Joseph Kony, Vincent Otti, Raska Lukwiya, Okot Odhiambo and Dominic Ongwen, situation in Uganda. Decision on the Prosecutor's application for unsealing of the warrants of arrest, pre-trial chamber II, ICC-02/04-01/05-52, 13 October 2005. For further analysis see: A. USACKA, Building the international criminal Court, in Global Business & Development Law Journal, 23 (2), 2011, pp. 228ss. K. PESCHKE, The ICC investigation into the conflict in norther Uganda: beyond the dichotomy of peace versus justice, in B.S. BROWN, Research handbook on international criminal court, op. cit., The interesting reconstruction of the facts shows how the possibility of obtaining an interruption of the ICC activity has influenced the various negotiations between the parties.

the civilian population) UN Member States to take action to end the conflict, but also "to ensure that those responsible for serious violations of human rights and international humanitarian law are brought to justice"[286].

President Musevani has in 2008 put forward the hypothesis that ICC ceded jurisdiction to national courts. This is due to a series of reconciliation agreements between the two conflicting parties aimed precisely at restoring the jurisdiction of the internal courts of their crimes[287]. What interests us here is that despite the fact that no motion for a Resolution has been discussed, the Ugandan government seems to have considered in the course of the negotiations the possibility of SC[288] claiming an exercise of the power of deferral.

---

[286]Security Council presidential statement demands release of women and children by Lord's Resistance Army, expeditious conclusion of the peace process, 16 November 2006, Doc. SC 8860.

[287]See: Agreement on accountability and reconciliation between the government of the Republic of Uganda and the Lord's Resistance Army Movement, Juba, Sudan, 29 June 2007, parr. 4.1, 4.2, 6.1. and 6.2. See also the Annex of 19 February 2008 establishing a "special division of the High Court of Uganda" for the crimes committed during the conflict. One of the main effects of the arrest warrants issued by ICC was certainly to make both sides of the conflict recognize the importance of ascertaining responsibility for the crimes committed. See in argument: O. OTIM, M. WIERDA, Justice at Juba: International obligations and local demands in Northern Uganda, in N. WADDELL, P. CLARK, Courting conflict? Justice, peace and the ICC in Africa, Oxford University Press, Oxford, 2008, pp. 23ss. L. MOFFETT, Justice for victims before the International Criminal Court, ed. Routledge, London & New York, 2014. J. MCKNIGHT, Accountability in Northern Uganda: Understanding the conflict, the parties and the false dichotomies in international criminal law and transitional justice, op. cit., pp. 194ss. M. KERSTEN, Justice in conflict. The effects of the international criminal court's interventions on ending wars and building peace, Oxford University Press, Oxford, 2016. P.S. WEGNER, The International Criminal Court in ongoing infra-state conflicts: Navigating the peace-justice divide, Cambridge University Press, Cambridge, 2015. D.N. SHARP, Re-thinking transitional justice for the 21st century, Cambridge University Press, Cambridge, 2018, pp. 54ss. After two years of negotiations (see Juba Talks, 2006-2008), Joseph Koni refused to sign the agreements. In the light of these events ICC judges in 2009 considered that national jurisdictions would not effectively prosecute the perpetrators of the violence and therefore declared the eligibility of the case. See: The Prosecutor v. Joseph Kony, Vincent Otti, Okot Odhiambo, Dominic Ongwen decision on the admissibility of the case under article 19 (1) of the statute, pre-trial chamber II, ICC-02/04-01705, 10 March 2009. At present the defendants, Dominic Ongwen was handed over to the ICC. One has died, Raska Lukwyia, and the other three are still at large.

[288]See in argument: K.P. APUULI, The ICC's possible deferral of the LRA case to Uganda, in Journal of International Criminal Justice, 6 (4), 2008, pp. 802ss. S. RANGANATHAN, Strategically created treaty conflicts and the politics of international law, Cambridge University Press, Cambridge, 2014. L. GISSEL, The International Criminal Court and peace processes in Africa: Judicialising peace, ed. Routledge, London & New York, 2018. K. MILLS, International responses to mass atrocities. Responsibility to protect, prosecture and palliate, University of Pennsylvania Press, Pennsylvania, 2015. See also the Report of SC Association, 11 April 2008, n. 1, Uganda, LRA. The possible exercise of the deferral

This case therefore seems to show how ICC can be used by national governments as a political tool of pressure or repression against the adverse faction[289]. The Ugandan government de facto reported the crimes committed by the rebels to ICC, naturally offering its full cooperation. Once learned that ICC would deal with the crimes committed by all parties involved in the conflict and fearing some negative repercussions resulting from this attitude of the Prosecutor[290], the government then used the negotiating tool with the rebels as well as the possibility to ask for the interruption of investigations through the action of SC which is the most viable way of obtaining a declaration of inadmissibility of cases following the establishment of internal mechanisms for ascertaining individual responsibilities in the name of applying the complementarity principle.

All this supports the idea that the claim that SC suspends the criminal action is also included among the political tools available to the parties involved. The opportunity to respond to these requests for suspension must of course be assessed on a case-by-case basis with a view to restoring peace but it is clear that if SC were to bend requests dictated solely by the need to protect from ICC jurisdiction the militants of a part of the conflict would risk corroding the credibility of ICC action and the independence of the same with respect to the political contingencies and opportunisms of some ruling classes.

4. Legal problems in the matter of deferral or in any case relating to the suspension of ICC jurisdictional activity between ICC and Security Council

4.1. Conditions for exercising the power of deferral

4.1.1. The temporary nature of suspension

It has already emerged through the analysis of the debates that led to the

appears indeed very unlikely for at least two reasons. On the one hand the gravity and the quantity of the crimes committed by the rebels (which also involved several States bordering on Uganda) and on the other the scarce probability that the suspension of a single year of ICC activity leads to the conclusion of an agreement for a stable and lasting peace.

[289]See: S.M.H. NOUWEN, G. WERNER, Doing justice to the political: The international criminal court in Uganda and Sudan, in European Journal of International Law, 21 (4), 2010, pp. 942ss. W.A. SCHABAS, Complementarity in practice: Creative solutions or a trap for the court?, op. cit., pp. 37ss.

[290]It should be remembered that after having initially favorably accepted the questionable terms of an activation limited to only one of the parties in conflict (the Lord's Resistance Army), the Prosecutor then established that "the scope of the referral encompasses all crimes committed in Northern Uganda in the context of the ongoing conflict involving LRA". ICC, Press release, President of Uganda refers situation concerning the Lord's Resistance Army (LRA) to the ICC, ICC-20040129, 29 January 2004. It is equally appropriate to recall, however, that at least until now the Prosecutor has dealt exclusively with the crimes committed by the rebels.

drafting of art. 16, the importance assumed by the temporal element in order to limit in some way the invasiveness on the exercise of the criminal action of the power of deferral attributed to SC. The request of SC can be directed to suspend the activity of ICC only for a period of 12 months, at the end of which it is necessary to adopt a new resolution and to submit a further request to ICC for renewal purposes. We have already mentioned the rejection of numerous proposals aimed at placing a further limit on SC power, through the provision of the possibility of carrying out a single request for suspension, without any extensions. The need for an explicit renewal at the end of the 12 months, however, requires SC to re-verify that the prosecution represents an obstacle to maintaining peace and of course the adoption of a further decision which obviously requires the absence of vetoes[291].

Resolutions n.1422 (2002) and 1487 (2003) which actually provide for a 12 month duration of the suspension and comply with art. 16, however, present a critical element. In point 2 of the device it is stated as already mentioned "the intention to renew the request (...) under the same conditions each 1 July for further 12 month periods for as long as may be necessary (...)"[292].

If from a formal point of view the suspension requested for a period of 12 months is compatible with the letter of art. 16 StICC, the manifest intention to ask for an annual renewal seems to somehow ignore the need for a new and concrete appreciation of SC regarding the fact that ICC's action is effectively hampering the restoration of peace. Such an assessment should take into account any changes that have occurred in the conflictual context on which the action of ICC would affect. This part of the device seems instead to suggest that SC has made an ex ante evaluation in relation to the renewal opportunity and therefore ends up colliding with the ratio itself the provision[293].

---

[291]N. WHITE, R. CRYER, The ICC and the Security Council. An uncomfortable relationship, in J. DORIA, H.P. GASSER, M. CHERIF BASSIOUNI, The legal regime of the international criminal court. Essays in honor of professor Igor Blishchenko. In memory of professor Igor Pavlovich Blishchenko (1930-2000), op. cit., pp. 466ss, which is affirmed that "must consider the matter afresh a year after the earlier resolution". In the same orientation see also: J. ELIAS, A. QUAST, The relationship between the security council and the international criminal court in the light of resolution 1422 (2002), in Non-State Actors and International law, 3 (2-3), 2003, pp. 170ss.

[292]W.A. SCHABAS, Complementarity in practice: Creative solutions or a trap for the court?, op. cit.,

[293]N. JAIN, A separate law for peacekeepers: The clash between the security council and the international criminal court, in European Journal of International law, 16 (2), 2005, pp. 248ss. According to other reconstructions, the time limit would be rather circumvented by both the obligation of the Council to put the issue on its agenda and the factual pressure on its member to renew the deal. See also in argument: C. STAHN, The ambiguities of Security Council Resolution 1422, op. cit., pp. 92ss. For the political pressures see also: R. CRYER, H. FRIMAN, D. ROBINSON, E. WILMSHURST, An introduction to international criminal law and procedure, op. cit., pp. 139ss. It is not clear why the annual renewal intention: "implies that the resolution be automatically prolonged, unless the

The other resolutions with suspensive effects (the two referrals and the authorization to the mission in Liberia) do not provide for the time limit of 12 months at all. A problem of compatibility with the Statute of Rome certainly arises in the hypothesis in which the arrest of ICC jurisdiction is expressly arranged by SC for a period longer than 12 months. In the absence of a time limit, however, SC decisions must be interpreted in accordance with the Statute of Rome and the limited suspension, therefore at the annual time frame established by art. 16[294]. Ultimately, and as far as it can be assumed that in these specific cases the intention of SC was to obtain a permanent exemption from the jurisdiction of ICC for a period exceeding 12 months, the resolutions that provide for the exclusive jurisdiction of the status of dispatch on personnel engaged in peacekeeping operations while not providing for the time limit required by articles 16 for the purposes of the suspension do not directly conflict with this statutory condition, leaving open the possibility for the ICC bodies to interpret its content in accordance with the Statute of Rome[295].

4.1.2. The specific nature of the suspension request

A further and fundamental element that characterizes the exercise of the power envisaged by art. 16 StICC resides in the specific nature of the request coming from SC. The emphasis placed by many States on the need for a case-by-case assessment of situations that can be removed from SC for the jurisdiction of ICC has already been widely highlighted. Moreover, in doctrine, moreover, the need for SC in asking for suspension to take into consideration the current activity of the Court, and particularly the case pending before it, was stressed[296].

---

prohibition is lifted". A. MOKHTAR, The fine art of arm-twisting. The US resolution 1422 and security council deferral power under the Rome statute, op. cit., pp. 316ss. It is shared however the idea that "the intention to renew the request for as long as may be necessary does not (...) make the deferral a permanent one since the SC (...) is not a position to bound it as it will be composed by the time the renewal comes up for reconsideration (...)". A. ZIMMERMANN, "Acting under chapter VII (...)": Resolution 1422 and possible limits of the powers of the Security council, in J.A. FROWEIN, K. SCHARIOTH, I. WINKELMANN, R. WOLFRUM, Verbandeln für den Frieden. Liber amicorum Tono Eite, ed. Springer, Berlin, 2003, pp. 270ss.

[294]O. BEKOU, The International Criminal Court, op. cit.,

[295]G.M. LENTNER, The United Nations Security Council and the International Criminal Court. The referral mechanism in theory and practice, op. cit.,

[296]L. CONDORELLI, L. VILLALPANDO, Referral and deferral by the Security Council, in A. CASSESE, P. GAETA, J.R.W.D. JONES, The Rome statute of the international criminal court. A commentary, op. cit., pp. 648ss. C. STAHN, The ambiguities of Security Council Resolution 1422, op. cit., R. LAVALLE, A vicious storm in a teacup: The action by the United Nations Security Council to narrow the jurisdiction of the International Criminal Court, in Criminal Law Forum, 14 (2), 2003, pp. 212ss: "article 16 was indeed meant to apply in concrete situations where the Council is acting under Chapter VII and ICC is investigating or prosecuting, or could be poised to investigate or prosecute, individuals suspected of committing crimes arising within that situation (...)". M. ARCARI, De l'action parajudiciaire du Conseil de Sècuritè, in M. ARCARI, L. BALMOND, La

This latter interpretation can put the exercise of the power of deferral under tension with the autonomy of ICC, since it leaves open the possibility of a suspension aimed at a specific procedure. This solution seems supported by the same letter of art. 16. The provision refers to the suspension of an investigation or prosecution that cannot be commenced or proceeded respectively. Art. 16 basically regulates the possibility of an intervention of SC aimed at suspending a proceeding in progress against one or more individuals or at preventing the start of an investigation in relation to some crimes already committed[297].

The object and purpose of the deferral, moreover, also confirm the correctness of this interpretative solution. The hypothesis envisaged by art. 16 is that the exercise of ICC jurisdiction constitutes an obstacle to reaching a political solution to the ongoing conflict, which more generally implies the risk of an exacerbation of the crisis situation. In this perspective, it is the individual investigation or the specific procedure that represents an impediment to maintaining peace. Investigative activities or judicial investigations relating to criminal events that have already taken place or are in progress constitute the potential object of the deferral as they are potentially impeding the re-establishment of a peaceful coexistence between the parties to the conflict.

The wording of the provision and its rationale therefore seem to preclude the possibility of generic and abstract suspensions that are not arranged in relation to a specific ongoing procedure or investigative activities relating to particular criminal conduct[298]. From this point of view, therefore, a problem of compatibility

sècuritè entre lègalitè et dèfies à la lègalitè, ed. Giuffrè, Milano, 2008, pp. 106ss. C. CHERNOR JALLOH, I. BANTEKAS, The International Criminal Court in Africa, Cambrdige University Press, Cambridge, 2017, pp. 198ss.

[297]O. BEKOU, The International Criminal Court, op. cit.,

[298]C. FRITSCHE, Security Council resolution 1422: Peacekeeping and the international criminal court, in J.A. FROWEIN, K. SCHARIOTH, I. WINKELMANN, R. WOLFRUM, Verbandeln für den Frieden. Liber amicorum Tono Eite, ed. Springer, Berlin, 2003, pp. 116, which is stated that “it was assumed that suspension of ICC investigations or prosecutions by SC would be limited to particular cases, not to the entire class of individuals”. D. SAROOSHI, The peace and justice: Paradox. The international criminal court and the UN Security Council, in D. MCGOLDRICK, P. ROWE, E. DONNELLY (ed. by), The Permanent International Criminal Court. Legal and policy issues, op. cit., pp. 119ss, which is affirmed that “the language of article 16 cannot bee stretched to provide a basis for a blanket-that it is non-specific, exemption to Court's jurisdiction (...)”. However, preliminary examinations potentially undertaken by the prosecutor are excluded from the possible suspension. See also in argument: H. EL AMINE, Article 16, in J. FERNANDEZ, X. PACREAU, Statut de Rome de la cour pènale internationale-Commentaire article par article, ed. Pedone, Paris, 2012, pp. 676ss. These activities include in the light of art. 15, parr. 2 and 6 StICC, the search for information in the States or organs of UN or receive written testimonies. SC cannot intervene on these activities, but it can still prevent as foreseen by art. 16 the start of investigation. The position of those who maintain that the SC is not shared “may only step in at the earliest once an investigation has been commenced”, according to A. ZIMMERMANN, "Acting under chapter VII (...)": Resolution n.1422 and possible limits of the powers of the Security Council, op. cit.,

with the Statute developed here by SC[299]. As already seen in the previous pages, Resolutions n.1422 (2002) and 1487 (2003) do not concern any ongoing investigation or proceeding, since still no situation had been brought to the attention of the Prosecutor, nor had even potential investigations been activated in relation to certain criminal events. On the contrary, these decisions sanction in the abstract and absolute the incompatibility between peacekeeping operations and international criminal repression. They have a general scope and are intended to produce their effects in a large number of possible cases only. They essentially exempt certain categories of individuals from ICC jurisdiction for the actions they will carry out in the context of any peacekeeping mission established or authorized by the UN.

Art. 16, as mentioned also refers to the hypothesis of the arrest of an investigation activity but these, however only possible, can be suspended from SC in relation to violence already committed, not only potential. Ultimately this practice appears to be in contrast with art. 16 StICC. In light of the numerous and extremely explicit oppositions of the States and the cessation by SC itself of these forms of suspension of ICC judicial action, it seems difficult to support the formation of a subsequent practice which by virtue of art. 31 (3) b) of VCLT[300] demonstrates the existence of an agreement between the States Parties to the Statute regarding the meaning to be attributed to art. 16. In essence, it cannot be argued that this practice supports an extensive interpretation of art. 16 StICC aimed at admitting that the request for suspension of CS does not present certain characteristics of concreteness and specificity[301].

4.1.3. The basis in Chapter VIII of the UN Charter of the suspension request

The call made of art. 16 of Chapter VII of the UN Charter transfers, at least in part, the assessment on the legitimacy of the request for suspension of SC on a regulatory parameter external to the Rome Statute. On this point and in particular on the possibility that ICC exercises judicial control over the conditions and limits of SC decision in the light of Chapter VII, we will therefore have to go back further. It is now necessary to highlight some problematic aspects relating to this additional requirement set by the Statute for the purposes of the exercise of deferral.

A first relevant question concerns the need or not that the SC makes explicit the connection between the suspension request addressed to ICC organs

---

[299]A.J. BELLAMY, P. WILLIAMS, Peace operations and global order, ed. Routledge, London, New York, 2014.

[300]I. BUGA, Modification of treaties by subsequent practice, op. cit., D. PEAT, Comparative reasoning in international courts and tribunals, op. cit., M. FITZMAURICE, O. ELIAS, P. MERKOURIS (eds), Treaty interpretation and the Vienna Convention on the Law of Treaties, 30 years on, op. cit., pp. 9ss. G. NOUTE, Treaties and subsequent practice, op. cit., pp. 224ss. E. BJORGE, The evolutionary interpretation of treaties, op. cit.,

[301]O. BEKOU, The International Criminal Court, op. cit.,

and the need to restore peace. In other words, it is a question of understanding whether art. 16 implicitly requires an obligation to state reasons on the part of SC regarding the decision to suspend ICC action. Some authors claim that the requirement of a foundation of Chapter VII of the decision to suspend an investigation or proceeding suggests that SC has to justify the request as a measure serving the maintenance or restoration of international peace and security[302].

Other observers have pointed out that in these cases it would indeed be the particular area of SC intervention, the administration of international criminal justice to impose an obligation to motivate the request for suspension as a corollary of the principle of legality and expression of a duty of the public powers to guarantee the public interest in the transparency of court proceedings. The problem of transparency and more specifically of the motivation of SC decisions is evidently internal to UN Charter[303]. Here we can limit ourselves to observing, however, that if from a substantial point of view the reference to Chapter VII of Charter contained in art. 16 clearly presupposes a link between the arrest of the action of ICC and the need to maintain peace and security from a formal point of view, the statutory provision does not provide for SC to explain the reasons for the request and clarify the link between the existing threat and the need to stop judicial activity[304]. The literal data and in truth the same practice of SC do not seem to presuppose the existence of this obligation to motivate the requests for suspension.

Another crucial question concerns the nature of the threat to peace which it owes in light of art. 16 the basis of SC decision to suspend the action of ICC. As already noted, the exercise of referral power also has its basis in a Resolution adopted on the basis of Chapter VII of the UN Charter. The provision of this requirement within art. 13 b) StICC does not raise particular problems. In the event that SC decides to report a specific situation to ICC, it is rather easy to connect the alleged International Crime Commission within the situation referred

---

[302]K. BLOME, N. MARKARD, Contested collisions: Successful conditions management. The example of article 16 of the Rome Statute, in Leiden Journal of International Law, 29 (2), 2016, pp. 572ss. A. CIAMPI, The proceedings against president Al Bashir and the prospects of their suspension under article 16 ICC Statute, in Journal of International Criminal Justice, 6 (5), 2008, where the author merely notes that any operation of the deferral by SC, in a situation previously reported, should be dictated by a substantial change in the circumstances in order to require intervention to protect peace and security. However, it is not possible to find in these contributions an implicit reference to the need for SC to justify its choice.

[303]See in argument: A. TZANAKOPOULOS, Transparency in the Security Council, in A. BIANCHI, A. PETERS, Transparency in international law, Cambridge University Press, Cambridge, 2013, pp. 368ss. And for more specific considerations on some evolutions in the working methods of SC occurred in the nineties. See: M.C. WOOD, Security Council working methods and procedure. Recent developments, op. cit., pp. 150ss.

[304]D. WHITTLE, The limits of legality and the United Nations Security Council: Applying the extralegal measures model to chapter VII action, op. cit.

to in the referral to the assumptions of art. 39 of the UN Charter[305]. It is the commission of those crimes itself that poses a threat to international peace and security.

In the hypothesis of exercising the power of deferral, however, it may not be so simple to identify a connection between the existence of a threat to peace and the need to stop the prosecution. In this regard, part of the doctrine believes that the SC must expressly establish and affirm that the launch of a specific investigation or the continuation of a specific procedure represent a threat to peace[306]. In other words, some observers perceive in ICC activity the threat to peace which the SC would end through suspension. However, the extent of the reference to Chapter VIII of the Charter, contained in art. 16 StICC seems rather to admit the possibility that the request of SC is based on a larger factual or political background[307]. In this different perspective, therefore, the repressive action of ICC would not in itself constitute the presupposition of SC action but only removal is necessary in some way. It can perhaps be read in this sense as far as the difference is subtle the choice not to recall the traditional acting under Chapter VII a formula typically used by SC and recalled by art. 13 b) for the exercise of referral power but rather to establish the somewhat more generic need for the request to be contained in a Resolution adopted under Chapter VII[308].

The problem of a possible absence of the assumptions underlying the powers provided for in Chapter VII arose clearly in Resolutions n.1422 (2002) and 1487 (2003)[309].

Even if we want to identify the reasons for the suspension in the effects produced by the potential action of ICC on the ability to contribute to the UN peacekeeping missions, it is not clear how this could represent a threat to international peace and security.

In very general terms, it can be noted that the inaction of SC due to the political impossibility of intervening in certain conflictual contexts is certainly not an exceptional event and has never been framed in itself as a threat to peace[310].

---

[305]O. BEKOU, The International Criminal Court, op. cit.,

[306]A. CASSESE, The statute of the international criminal court: Some preliminary reflections, op. cit., pp. 164ss., which is affirmed that: "Explicitly decides that continuation of his investigation or prosecution may amount to a threat to the peace (...)". According to our opinion it seems plausible to believe that SC can request the suspension only if it determines that the action of the Prosecutor could cause a serious political crisis in international relations or the destabilization of a certain political situation, thus endangering international peace and security.

[307]L. CONDORELLI, L. VILLALPANDO, Referral and deferral by the Security Council, in A. CASSESE, P. GAETA, J.R.W.D. JONES, The Rome statute of the international criminal court. A commentary, op. cit., pp. 648ss.

[308]D. WHITTLE, The limits of legality and the United Nations Security Council: Applying the extralegal measures model to chapter VII action, op. cit.

[309]A.J. BELLAMY, P. WILLIAMS, Peace operations and global order, op. cit.,

[310]C. FRITSCHE, Security Council Resolution n.1422: Peacekeeping and the international criminal court, in J.A. FROWEIN, K. SCHARIOTH, I. WINKELMANN, R. WOLFRUM,

The reasoning in these terms, however, would lead to the conclusion that any obstacle to the ability of States to provide personnel for UN peacekeeping operations represents a threat to peace. Further threats to peace could therefore also be represented by the existence of other criteria of criminal jurisdiction in favor of national ones including, for example, the principle of universal criminal jurisdiction.

Furthermore, as observed by many parties and not only by the representatives of the States, the assessment made from SC would be difficult to comply with Chapter VII of the Charter due to the fact that it was made ex ante and in abstracto and in relation to each and every investigation and prosecution (...) related to all future UN established or authorized missions[311]. Once again we enter a field that transcends at least for the moment the present investigation as it regards the limits to the discretion of SC in ascertaining the existence of a threat to peace. It is interesting, however, to observe how the element of concreteness that characterizes art. 16 StICC, analyzed in the previous paragraph and the very concreteness that at least according to most of the doctrinal investigations should characterize the ascertainment of the existence of a threat to peace appear not really distinct issues from each other[312]. As broad as the notion of threat to peace is, it can perhaps be assumed that if the request for suspension must relate to specific ongoing proceedings or potential investigations with respect to past episodes of violence or the assumption of SC action should be based on a current and specific threat and more generally on a need for peacekeeping that risks being compromised by that specific repressive action of ICC whose suspension is being requested.

In the Resolution that authorized the mission of Liberia and in the two cases of referrals, the threat to peace is, as said, clearly attributable to the particular contexts of conflict in which SC has decided to intervene. However,

---

Verbandeln für den Frieden. Liber amicorum Tono Eite, ed. Springer, Berlin, 2003, pp. 114ss.

[311]A. ZIMMERMANN, "Acting under chapter VII (...)": Resolution 1422 and possible limits of the powers of the Security Council, op. cit., pp. 266ss. C. STAHN, The ambiguities of Security Council Resolution 1422, op. cit., pp. 86ss. R. LAVALLE, A vicious storm in a teacup: The action by the UN Security Council to narrow the jurisdiction of the International Criminal Court, op. cit., pp. 212ss. N. WHITE, R. CRYER, The ICC and the Security Council. An uncomfortable relationship, in J. DORIA, H.P. GASSER, M. CHERIF BASSIOUNI, The legal regime of the international criminal court. Essays in honor of professor Igor Blishchenko. In memory of professor Igor Pavlovich Blishchenko (1930-2000), op. cit., pp. 468ss. According to other reconstructions, Resolutions n.1422 (2002) takes up the requirements for the exercise of powers provided by Chapter VII since the measure was expressly adopted for the purpose of maintaining the peace and in particular to allow States to participate in UN missions. J. ELIAS, A. QUAST, The relationship between the security council and the international criminal court in the light of resolution 1422 (2002), op. cit., pp. 172ss.

[312]R. LAVALLE, A vicious storm in a teacup: The action by the UN Security Council to narrow the jurisdiction of the International Criminal Court, op. cit., pp. 212ss.

and for the same reasons just explained, it does not seem easy in the absence of relevant factual elements and in light of the wider contexts on which the SC action affects these cases, recognizing an obstacle to maintaining peace in the event of a ICC judicial action aimed at the particular categories of individuals against whom the exemption is prepared[313].

4.1.4. A procedural requirement: The request not to continue the investigation or the procedure provided for by art. 17 (2) of the relationship agreement

As noted in the introductory Chapter, the 2004 Report Agreement should have clarified many of the controversial elements of the provisions governing the relationship between ICC and SC. The agreement between the two organizations has an extremely general character. As stated above, it establishes some important principles of cooperation and mutual respect but it does not help to understand how the complex rules of interaction that this investigation aims to analyze should be interpreted and applied in practice.

Within the agreement, however, there is art. 17 aimed at regulating some specific reciprocal obligations between the two institutions in the three main areas of SC intervention on the judicial action of ICC, i.e. referral, deferral and judicial cooperation. Par. 2 of art. 17, relating to the power to suspend, establishes that SC's request to terminate an investigation or proceeding shall immediately be transmitted by the Secretary General to the president of the Court and the Prosecutor. In other words, the request for suspension must be formalized in some way and then sent to the president of ICC and the Prosecutor.

This procedural obligation could take on some significance. In particular, the absence of the required formality can favor interpretations of SC Resolutions aimed at excluding that the latter intended to exercise the power provided for by art. 16[314]. In the face of, for example, a resolution with an ambiguous content, failure to comply with this procedural requirement envisaged by the agreement can contribute with other elements to excluding that SC action is attributable to the power envisaged by art. 16.

The Resolutions relating to the situations in Darfur and Libya that triggered ICC jurisdiction were sent to the President and Prosecutor. However both letters of the Secretary General contain an explicit reference to art. 17 (1) of

---

[313]S. ZAPPALÁ, Are some peacekeepers better than others? UN Security Council resolution 1497 (2003) and the ICC, in Journal of International Criminal Justice, 1 (3), 2003, pp. 674ss. In the same orientation see also: A. CIAMPI, L. CONDORELLI, Comments on the security council referral of the situation in Darfur to the ICC, op. cit., pp. 594ss.

[314]A.S. KNOTTNERUS, The Security Council and the international criminal court: The unsolved puzzle of article 16, in Netherlands International Law Review, 61 (2), 2014, pp. 198ss.

the liaison agreement between UN and ICC[315]. This provision specifically relates to the referral power and provides for the obligation for the secretary to transmit the referral power, the decision and all the relevant materials to ICC Prosecutor. No reference is made to paragraph 2 of that same provision. Moreover, the parts of the device aimed at producing suspensive effects on ICC jurisdictional activity contained in Resolutions n.1593 (2005) and 1970 (2011) are not formulated in terms of a SC request addressed to ICC bodies. Further, indicative is the fact that the Resolution n. 1497 (2003) that authorized the mission in Liberia has not been the subject of any notification to ICC, despite the exemptions provided for. It could be argued that the limitations on the exercise of ICC jurisdiction contained in the devices of such decisions were not considered by SC to be an expression of the exercise of the particular power recognized by art. 16 StICC.

4.2. Relationship between activation and suspension in ICC jurisdictional activity

The analysis conducted in relation to the exercise of the referral power has highlighted the crucial relevance of the meaning to be attributed to the term “situation” in order to determine whether SC can limit the investigation of the Prosecutor's activity. Depending on how that notion is interpreted, in particular as regards the possible limitation or extension of ICC jurisdiction, a series of suspensive effects on the judicial action could be envisaged, not so dissimilar from those potentially produced by the exercise of power deferral required by art. 16 StICC. More precisely, if it is believed that SC can somehow circumscribe Prosecutor's action, the referral tool may also end up performing suspensive functions with respect to ICC action, typical of the tool governed by art. 16 StICC. The admissibility of an activation of the investigations that provides for the exemption from the jurisdiction of some categories of individuals, would in practice have the effect of at least partially precluding the repressive action of ICC for various reasons already explained in the previous chapter. The exemptions provided by SC Resolutions do not seem compatible with the fundamental characteristics of the exercise of referral power.

However, all this does not seem to exclude that the two powers of activation and suspension of the judicial action can be exercised simultaneously by SC. Some authors have indeed denied this hypothesis by drawing a parallel between the referral power provided by art. 13 b) StICC and the establishment of ad hoc courts. The statutes of these international criminal jurisdictions in effect "do not recognize any power of the Council to prevent or stop the tribunals from investigating or prosecuting specific individuals"[316]. Once the jurisdiction of an

---

[315]See also the letter of Secretary General Kofi Annan to Prosecutor Moreno-Ocampo of 1st April 2005, annexed in decision assigning the situation in Darfur, Sudan to the pre-trial Chamber, Office of the Prosecutor, 21 April 2005 and the letter of Secretary General Ban Ki-Moon to Prosecutor Moreno-Ocampa dated 1st March 2001.

[316]M. BERGSMO, J. PEJIC, Article 16, in O. TRIFFTERER, Commentary on the Rome statute, observer's notes, article by article, Oxford, Baden-Baden, München, 2008, pp.

international tribunal was activated, it would therefore no longer be possible for SC to stop its action.

As much as one can criticize, the particular formulation of art. 16, that is the power of deferral is not by chance the subject of the most heated debates during the preparatory work that has no precedent in the history of relations between SC and the international criminal courts established by it[317] and therefore cannot find a useful term in those experiences for comparison. Not only does such a pre-eminence of political power over judicial power find no correspondence or analogy in the relations that SC has with any other international jurisdiction including ICJ[318].

In a different perspective art. 16 should however be interpreted in symmetry with the language used in article 13. In practice and for the same reasons already amply highlighted in the previous Chapter, SC would have the power to suspend situations (as required by art.13 b)) but it could not instead intervene in specific cases. If this were not the case, the power to select the targets of the Court's investigations and prosecutions would be recognized in practice[319]. As seen the literal data and the ratio of the provision, however, do not seem to limit the power of SC to suspend a particular proceeding or a particular investigation activity with respect to only some of the crimes committed or against certain individuals within the wider situation referred to ICC. It can therefore be imagined, for example, that SC asks the ICC bodies to suspend within a wider situation which it remits to them only a specific proceeding in progress against a head of State. In the same way, SC could prevent the launching of gaps in investigations relating to particular criminal conduct set in motion in the wider context of a referral armed conflict. Ultimately the particular power contained in art. 16 StICC does not seem to exclude that SC limits ICC jurisdictional activity, even in the case in which the activation of the judicial bodies originated from a request to that effect by SC.

The delicacy and pervasive potential inherent in the exercise of this power is completely evident. It allows SC to compress ICC's criminal prosecution

---

604ss. M. BERGSMO, J. PEJIC, D. ZHU, Article 16, in O. TRIFFTERER, K. AMBOS, The Rome statute of the international criminal court. A commentary, C.H.Beck-Hart-Nomos, München, Oxford, Baden-Baden, 2016, pp. 774ss.

[317]A. ZIMMERMANN, The creation of a permanent international criminal court, in Max Planck Yearbook of United Nations Law, 2, 1998, pp. 236ss.

[318]According to M. BERGSMO, J. PEJIC, Article 16, in O. TRIFFTERER, Commentary on the Rome Statute, observer's notes, article by article, op. cit., pp. 600ss, "is also unprecedent in terms of the legal relationship it establishes between SC and a judicial body. Neither ICJ in its work nor national courts dealing with crimes arising from situations on SC's agenda under Chapter VII, are under an express obligation to defer proceedings upon a request by the Council (...)".

[319]A. CIAMPI, The proceedings against president Al Bashir and the prospects of their suspension under article 16 ICC Statute, op. cit., pp. 889ss. Shortly after the author acknowledges the possible suspension of the proceedings against Al Bashir but only how "part of a wider decision to defer the situation of Darfur".

and limit it even only in relation to some specific situations such as the case of the procedure undertaken against a head of State. It is for the good to keep in mind the political costs of the explicit recognition made by SC in relation to the fact that ICC judicial activity in the repression of international crimes represents an obstacle to the maintenance of international peace and security[320]. Beyond the political implications resulting from the suspension requests, which may in any case limit the use of this instrument, it is then necessary to take into due consideration the conditions set by the Statute for the exercise of this particular power by SC. It is precisely these limits analyzed in the previous pages that mitigate the repercussions of the deferral on the independence and autonomy of ICC and try to somehow reconcile the demands of peace with those of justice.

4.3. Some problems regarding the preservation of justice interests in the event criminal action's suspension

Finally, it is necessary to mention some problematic issues which, although not yet emerged in practice, may arise in cases of suspension of the ICC's activities following a request by SC. We refer in particular to the consequences of the deferral on the preservation of the evidence collected on the danger of the defendants' escape on the protection of witnesses and on the very possibility of being able to hear them[321]. More concretely, to give just a few examples, it is not clear whether, following the deferral, a defendant must be released in full freedom with the risk that it will no longer be possible to capture him when the procedure is reactivated. In the same way it is necessary to understand what should be done of those tests that expose themselves to a possible deterioration and that if not collected in a timely manner can become unusable for the purposes of the process.

No statutory provision deals with disciplining in case of suspension of the proceeding by SC, Prosecutor's powers and ICC to guarantee the integrity of the suspended proceeding and the effectiveness of its continuation. A regulation of these aspects would certainly have been desirable.

Indeed problems similar to those just mentioned emerge when a State raises a question of inadmissibility with respect to a specific case. In these hypotheses, the Prosecutor is forced to suspend its investigations for a certain period and wait for an ICC decision. The latter, however, may authorize the Prosecutor himself to hear the witnesses, to adopt a series of conservative measures relating to the evidence already collected or to order precautionary measures against individuals for whom an arrest warrant has already been

---

[320]M. BERGSMO, J. PEJIC, Article 16, in O. TRIFFTERER, Commentary on the Rome statute, observer's notes, article by article, op. cit., pp. 604ss.

[321]D. RUIZ VERDUZCO, The relationship between the ICC and the United Nations Security Council, op. cit., pp. 60ss. H. EL AMINE, Article 16, in J. FERNANDEZ, X. PACREAU, Statut de Rome de la cour pènale internationale-Commentaire article par article, op. cit., pp. 676ss.

requested (art. 19 (8))[322]. Moreover, at least as regards the protection of witnesses and the collection of evidence, a legal basis for Prosecutor's powers can be found in the same Statute of Rome. In fact, among the prerogatives of that office listed in art. 54 StICC, the last letter f) also provides for the possibility of adopting the necessary measures "to ensure the confidentiality of information, the protection of any person or the preservation of evidence"[323]. Moreover, according to some reconstructions even in the absence of art. 54 f) just referred to "all three powers listed must have been considered inherent insofar as they are essential to the functioning of an independent office of the Prosecutor"[324]. The legitimate adoption by ICC bodies of provisional measures useful to guarantee the future initiation of a proceeding or the continuation of the suspended measures could then be justified in the light of the theory of implicit powers and the need, therefore, that ICC also exercises those powers not expressly provided for by the Statute that allow it to perform its functions[325]. It may perhaps be considered that the measures indicated in the provision are not exhausted but the Prosecutor may in any case adopt similar measures, if it deems them essential for a correct administration of justice and for a greater protection of the independence and autonomy of ICC. These assessments must be made by ICC bodies in light of the Statute and the needs related to the exercise of the judicial function regardless of any requests in this area by SC, whose only prerogative is to preclude the start or continuation of a investigation or an ongoing proceeding.

---

[322]O. BEKOU, The International Criminal Court, op. cit.,

[323]The relevance of this provision even in the hypothesis of the deferral being exercised by the SC is underlined by F. DARQUES-LANE, C. MADEC, S. GODART, Article 54, in J. FERNANDEZ, X. PACREAU, Statut de Rome de la cour pènale internationale-Commentaire article par article, ed. Pedone, Paris, 2012, pp. 1256ss. F. FOKA TAFFO, Le pouvoir discretionnaire du procureur de la cour pènale internationale, Nomos Verlag, Baden-Baden, 2018. Moreover, the ICC has extended the applicability of this provision also to the trial phase despite the placement of the provision within the statute that would make it applicable only to the investigation phase. See in this case: Prosecutor v. Lubanga, reasons for oral decision lifting the stay of proceedings, trial Chamber, ICC-01/04-01-06. 23 January 2009, par. 39. W.A. SCHABAS, The international criminal court. A commentary to the Rome statute, op. cit., pp. 858ss.

[324]M. BERGSMO, P. KRUGER, O. BEKOU, Article 54, in O. TRIFFTERER, K. AMBOS, The Rome statute of the international criminal court. A commentary, B.C. Beck, Hart, Nomos, München, Oxford, Baden-Baden, 2016, pp. 1392ss.

[325]J. ALBERT, J.B. MERLIN, L'avenir de la justice pènale internationale, ed. Larcier, Bruxelles, 2018.

Chapter 3
Interactions between ICC and SC on cooperation and mutual legal assistance

1. Security Council role in States' cooperation and mutual legal assistance to ICC

The effectiveness of the ICC's action, like that of any other judicial body, depends on the effectiveness of the tools it has available to arrest the persons subject to trial and even before to obtain the evidence useful for the purposes of the investigations. However, ICC is not equipped with its own coercive tools and can therefore only rely on other subjects to be able to fully perform its functions. In practice, the effectiveness of ICC action is largely dependent on the ability and willingness of States Parties to the Statute to comply with the obligations undertaken in order to arrest and hand over the accused and to assist the Prosecutor in the collection of evidentiary material, for example, carrying out searches and seizures[326]. Moreover, the importance that the obligations of cooperation assumed by the States have in ICC activity is even more evident if one thinks that the latter operating in a complementary regime can hardly obtain the state assistance as deemed incapable or unwilling to pursue those responsible for the crimes.

The centrality of states cooperation for the effective functioning of the judicial activity and for the correct administration of justice had already emerged in the practice of the international courts for ICTY and International Criminal Tribunal for Rwanda (ICTR)[327]. It should be noted from the outset, however, that

---

[326]A. CASSESE, On the current trends towards criminal prosecution and punishment of breaches of international humanitarian law, in European Journal of International Law, 9, 1998, pp. 20ss. That the cooperation of States is fundamental for the effective functioning of ICC is well known and constantly reaffirmed in all relevant reading, the words of the head of the German representation in Rome who recounts the progressive awareness acquired during the negotiations. "The Court is totally dependent, on full, effective and timely cooperation in particular from States Parties (...)". H.P. KAUL, The ICC and international criminal cooperation. Key aspects and fundamental necessities, in F. GIOIA, M. POLITI, The international criminal court and national jurisdictions, ed. Routledge, Aldershot, 2008, pp. 86ss.

[327]ICTY: "(...) It is self-evident that the international tribunal in order to bring to trial persons living under the jurisdiction of sovereign States not being endowed with enforcement agents of its own, must rely on the cooperation of States (...)". See: The Prosecutor v. Blaškić, decision on the objection of the Republic of Croatia to the issuance

the different legal basis of the founding act of ICC, compared to the experiences of the ad hoc tribunals, greatly affects the cooperation obligations of the States. SC Resolutions that set up the ad hoc tribunals in fact laid down cooperation obligations for all UN Member States[328] and the same States of those jurisdictions then contained provisions aimed at sanctioning the mandatory nature of legal assistance[329]. ICC Statute, on the other hand, as an international treaty, obviously cannot impose cooperation obligations on States that are not parties to the agreement.

The relevant provisions are contained in the ninth chapter of the Statute where the possible requests for assistance that the ICC can address to the States and the cooperation obligations of the latter towards it are governed[330].

The fundamental rule for the execution of the decisions and measures ordered by the Prosecutor and the judges is the general obligation of cooperation

---

of subpoena duces teum, appeals chamber, IT-95-14-AR 1209 bis, 29 July 1997, par. 17.

[328]The Resolutions instituting the courts provide in their own device that: "All States shall cooperate fully with the international tribunal and its organs" (UN Resolution 827 (1993) and 955 (1994). This element already emerged in the report of the general secretary to whom is attached the Statute of the tribunal for the former Yugoslavia where it was clearly stated that the fact that the Court was instituted through a SC Resolution adopted on the basis of Chapter VII of the Charter "means that all States would be under an obligation to cooperate with the international tribunal and to assist it in all stages of the proceedings to ensure compliance with requests for assistance in gathering evidence, hearing witnesses suspects and experts, identification and location of persons and the service of documents". Report of the Secretary-General pursuant to paragraph 2 of Security Council Resolution 808 (1993), UN Doc. S725704 (1993), parr. 125-126. Some reflections on the differences in cooperation between ICC and the ad hoc tribunals arising from the different legal basis can be found in B. SWART, G. SLUITER, The ICC and international criminal co-operation, in H.A.M. VON HEBEL, J.G. LAMMERS, J. SCHUKKING, Reflections on the international criminal court: Essays in honor of Adrian Bos, T.M.C. Asser Press, The Hague, 1999, pp. 902ss.

[329]The statutes themselves then establish an obligation of cooperation and judicial assistance: Article 28 ICTY and 29 ICTR.

[330]At the Rome Conference and even before during the Preparatory Committee's work not all States were of the view that it was necessary to provide for real legal obligations regarding cooperation. The letter of articles 98 (1) and 93 (1) confirms the position taken by the majority in the sense of guaranteeing full cooperation with ICC. In general the whole part 9 of the Statute is oriented in the sense of considerably limiting the causes of justification that the States Parties can advance to refuse cooperation with ICC. See in argument: P. MOCHOCHOKO, International cooperation and judicial assistance, in S.K. LEE, The international criminal court. The making of the Rome statute. Issues, negotiations, results, Martinus Nijhoff Publishers, The Hague, 1999, pp. 306ss. The author chaired the working group on international cooperation and judicial assistance, which the Committee of the whole assigned the preparation of part 9 to the Rome Conference and the analysis therefore offers a detailed reconstruction of the legislative history of some aspects relating to the obligations of the States in the matter of cooperation and in particular of the possible legitimate causes of refusal of assistance and delivery of the individuals that many States would have liked to insert in the statutes.

provided for by art. 86 StICC[331]. In light of this provision, States Parties must cooperate fully with the Court in its investigation and prosecution. This general obligation to cooperate is followed by more specific provisions aimed at substantiating its content and for what interests us most here to predict what will happen if a State does not comply with the requests coming from ICC.

In particular as regards the States Parties to the Treaty of Rome, art. 87 of the Statute provides on several occasions, the possibility that ICC will address to these some requests for cooperation. Despite the use of the undemanding request term, it must be considered that the requests addressed to the States Parties coming from ICC bodies have in light of the general obligation of cooperation foreseen by art. 86, binding nature. The possible instances addressed to the States by ICC in fact do nothing but implement the general obligation of cooperation and the more specific ones provided for by art. 89 (1), for the purposes of arrest and surrender of the accused and by art. 93 (1) for other forms of assistance aimed at collecting evidence[332].

As regards third countries, art. 87 (5) a) of the Statute states that ICC: "May invite many States not party to this Statute to provide assistance (...) on the basis of an ad hoc arrangement, an agreement with such State or any other appropriate basis"[333]. The analysis of the preparatory works of art. 87 (5) highlights an interesting change of perspective between the first proposal of the working group[334] which later merged into the ILC project and the definitive text of the Statute, which instead reflects the moves from the report of the Preparatory Commission of 1996[335]. The project of the Commission framed the relationship between ICC and third States on cooperation from the latter's point of view. It was expected in art. 56 that States not part of the Statute could assist ICC "on the basis of comity, a unilateral declaration, an ad hoc arrangement or other agreement with the Court"[336]. The proposal of the Preparatory Committee leaves the task of undertaking and seeking to conclude cooperation agreements with third States directly to ICC and not to the voluntary initiative of the States, providing in the text of the then art. 86 (4) a) in a perspective similar to the one ultimately adopted

331W.A. SCHABAS, The international criminal court. A commentary to the Rome statute, op. cit.,

332O. BEKOU, The International Criminal Court, op. cit.,

333J. ALBERT, J.B. MERLIN, L'avenir de la justice pènale internationale, op. cit.,

334Report of the working group on a draft Statute for an international criminal court, UN Doc. A/CN.4/L.491/Rev.2/Add.3, 18 July 1994. for further analysis see: S. NTUBE NGANE., The position of witnesses before the International Criminal Court, ed. Brill, Bruxelles, 2015. J.A. SWEENEY, The elusive right to truth in transitional human rights jurisprudence, in International & Comparative Law Quarterly, 67 (2), 2018, pp. 359ss.

335Art. 56, Draft statute for an international criminal court, in Yearbook of the International Law Commission, 1994, vol. II, Part. Two.

336Report of the International law Commission on the work of its forty-sixth session, UN Doc. A/49/10, 2 May-22 July 1994, pp. 130ss. See in argument: R. DUBBLER, M. KALYK, Crimes against humanity in the 21st century: Law, practice and threats to international peace and security, ed. Brill, Bruxelles, 2018, pp. 222ss.

that ICC "may (call on) (invite) any State not party to this Statute to provide assistance under this part on the basis of (comity) an ad hoc arrangement, an agreement with such State (or any other appropriate basis)"[337].

ICC may only invite non-party States of the Statute to collaborate with ICC through the conclusion of a general or ad hoc agreement, or any other appropriate basis[338]. It should be noted here that a third State that has accepted ICC jurisdiction through the unilateral declaration provided for by art. 12 (3) StICC, "shall cooperate with the Court any delay or exception in accordance with part 9"[339]. For these States, the rules on cooperation and mutual legal assistance provided by StICC for the States Parties apply.

In order to grasp the role of SC in this particularly delicate area, it is necessary to reconstruct the ways in which the ICC of its requests for assistance and cooperation addressed to States. The practical nature of the Rome Statute places the States Parties and the third parties on necessarily distinct levels. As mentioned, ICC cannot coercively impose any obligation on States (whether they are part or not of the Statute). For this reason, the problems concerning the non-execution of the requests and decisions of ICC and the related role of SC are in part similar. In other words, to States that do not intend to cooperate whether they are part or not of the Statute, ICC can only respect the commitments undertaken but cannot impose respect for them. A similar task can instead be carried out by SC (and at least to some extent, from the Assembly of States Parties) confirming the centrality assumed by this UN body for the functioning of international criminal justice also within the system created through the Rome Treaty.

In the event of non-compliance by States Parties with the assistance obligations, therefore art. 87 (7) provides that ICC can ascertain the failure to comply with the obligation to cooperate and report the matter to the Assembly of States Parties or if the situation in question is the consequence of a SC referral, contact the latter. In essence, in light of the Rome Statute, ICC ascertains the violation of an international obligation to cooperate with it by a State Party of the Statute, and reports this situation to SC in the event that it was the latter activate its jurisdiction[340].

As regards the lack of assistance and cooperation of third States, or the

---

[337]R. DUBBLER, M. KALYK, Crimes against humanity in the 21st century: Law, practice and threats to international peace and security, op. cit.,

[338]It is interesting to note that commenting on a first draft of this provision, the International Law Commission has indeed recalled the interest of all the States of the international community in the repression of international crimes and has therefore been concerned to stress that: "Even those States which are not parties to the Statute are encouraged to cooperate with and to provide assistance to the Court". See: Draft Statute for an international criminal court with commentaries, in Yearbook of the International Law Commission, 1994, vol. II, Part Two, pp. 66.

[339]R. DUBBLER, M. KALYK, Crimes against humanity in the 21st century: Law, practice and threats to international peace and security, op. cit.,

[340]W.A. SCHABAS, The international criminal court. A commentary to the Rome statute, op. cit.,

failure to fulfill an obligation assumed with the ICC through an agreement or a unilateral declaration, art. 87 (5) b) once again provides that ICC can inform the Assembly of States Parties or SC always in the event that the referral was made by the latter[341]. In both cases, in light of the provision in question, the third country must have previously concluded a cooperation agreement with ICC so that ICC can notify the political bodies of the lack of assistance. As anticipated, the consequences of non-cooperation are not very different from those foreseen for the States Parties of the Statute. It is clear that even third States that have committed themselves to cooperating with ICC could fail to fulfill their obligations towards ICC. The Statute does nothing but regulate in an identical way the effects of a similar breach, that assumed in the matter of cooperation through a pact or unilateral commitment of the States[342].

It can therefore be observed that the same power to ascertain the non-cooperation of States that ICTY has recognized as inherent in its jurisdictional function[343], is now explicitly attributed to ICC by art. 87, par. 5 and 7 StICC[344]. It should also be stressed that in making the decision regarding the reference to the Assembly of States Parties or to SC relating to the lack of cooperation, ICC enjoys wide discretion. Judges will be able to consider whether, even when faced with a breach of care obligations, the reporting of such failure is appropriate in light of the specific circumstances of the case it is dealing with[345]. In particular, ICC will have to assess whether the reference to the political bodies about the failure to comply with the cooperation obligations would promote the functions of the Court and assist a fair trial including the protection of the rights of the accused, the integrity of the proceedings or the wider interests of justice.

The Statute also does not deal with regulating the consequences of the

---

[341]W.A. SCHABAS, The international criminal court. A commentary to the Rome statute, op. cit.,

[342]The fact that the communication of ICC to SC regarding non-cooperation can only be made in cases of exercise of the power of referral is the result of an attitude of general opposition by numerous States to any political intervention by SC on the jurisdictional activity of the Court. We have tried to limit the SC's intervention space to cases in which ICC jurisdictional action was actually the latter activated. For further details see: K. MISKOWIAK, The international criminal court: Consent, complementarity and cooperation, ed. Djøef, Copenhagen, 2000, pp. 172ss. F. BENEDETTI, K. BONNEAU, J. WASHBURN, Negotiating the International Criminal Court: New York to Rome, 1994-1998, op. cit.,

[343]ICTY, The Prosecutor v. Blaškić, decision on the objection of the Republic of Croatia to the issuance of subponea duces teum, Appeals chamber, IT-95-14-A-AR 108 bis, 29 July 1997, par. 33: "The international tribunal is endowed with the inherent power to make a judicial finding concerning a State's failure to observe the provisions of the stature or the rules".

[344]O. BEKOU, The International Criminal Court, op. cit.,

[345]ICC, Prosecutor v. Kenyatta, Decision on prosecution's application for a finding of non-compliance under article 87 (7) of the Statute, Trial Chamber V (b), ICC-01/09-02/11, 3 December 2014, par. 39.

communication that is made to SC by ICC. Moreover, the Rome Treaty could not have imposed or foreseen what conduct an organ outside the ICC system should have followed following an assessment of non-cooperation made by the ICC itself. In other words, the decision on non-compliance with the cooperation obligations does not affect the autonomy and political discretion of the action of SC. In this regard, the same ICTY had observed that the assessment by States must not include any recommendations or suggestions as to the course of action the SC may wish to take as a consequence of that finding[346].

In both hypotheses that the State concerned is part or not of the Stature, SC naturally maintains its discretionary power and may thus decide not to intervene or to forcefully enforce compliance with the obligations of cooperation. It may act, for example, by using the powers attributed to it by Chapter VII of the UN Charter and possibly reach the adoption of sanctioning measures against the defaulting States. It is perhaps superfluous to add that even if there has not been a prior referral pursuant to art. 13 b) and in the absence therefore of an explicit notification of default by the ICC, SC could always intervene to ask the States (part or not of the Statute) to cooperate with the international tribunal. In other words, nothing excludes that the SC autonomously decides to intervene where it believes that failure to cooperate with ICC may create a situation likely to jeopardize international peace and security. This therefore regardless of whether it has been specifically informed by ICC about the non-compliance of the obligations of assistance with ICC by the States concerned.

Precisely because of a discipline that leaves a wide margin of discretion to the subjects potentially involved in the cooperation (in particular, of course of SC and third States) it is important to note that the whole chapter nine of the Statute is based on dialogue and consultation between the different actors. Thus, for example, the ICC asks the States to cooperate and communicates any breaches to the Assembly of the States Parties or to SC. States in the event of delays or impediments in the execution of a request must consult ICC to resolve the matter (art. 97) and other examples of this nature could be made regarding the necessary dialogue between States, ICC and SC in the execution phase of ICC requests[347].

As a result of the ICC's assessment of non-cooperation, the cooperation it sends to SC and the Assembly can therefore have various consequences. We have just mentioned the discretion of SC in deciding whether or not to take coercive measures. It can be remembered even though it is not directly relevant for the purposes of this investigation, that even the Assembly of States Parties

---

[346]ICC, Prosecutor v. Blaškić, Judgment on the request of the Republic of Croatia for review of the decision of trial Chamber II of 18 July 1997, Appeals Chamber, 29 October 1997, par. 36.

[347]Dialogue that can often turn into a sort of bargaining between ICCs and has been with a bargaining power that can vary considerably depending on the context as well highlighted by S.D. ROPER, L.A. BARRIA, State co-operation and international criminal court bargaining influence in the arrest and the surrender of suspects, in Leiden Journal of International Law, 21 (2), 2008, pp. 458ss.

must simply "consider the question relating to non-cooperation" (art. 112 (2) f))[348]. It is therefore not clear from the letter by art. 87 if necessary what measures the Assembly can take against the defaulting or third party that has not respected the cooperation agreement. The possibility could be envisaged that the Assembly proposes the adoption of countermeasures by the same States Parties in reaction to the violation of the covenant obligation.

It is interesting to note that at least according to some reconstructions the exercise of the referral power by SC would automatically imply a general obligation of cooperation with ICC for all States. In other words, in the event that ICC jurisdiction is set in motion by SC, one could assume the existence of a general obligation of cooperation also for States not part of the Statute. However, no statutory provision allows this conclusion to be drawn. Furthermore, despite the universal vocation of ICC and its centrality in the repression of international crimes, it seems difficult to support the existence of a customary rule that imposes on all States an obligation to execute requests from an international tribunal created through an international treaty. It could be argued to the contrary but on this point it will be returned that assistance obligations for States that are not part of the Statute exist only in the event that a decision of SC (that of activating ICC or other subsequent) expressly provides for them[349].

Finally, the general obligation of cooperation set out in art. 86 is, as already mentioned, taken up again concerning the arrest and surrender of an individual suspected, accused or held responsible for the Commission of a crime among those of the ICC's jurisdiction (art. 89)[350]. Even in this more specific area, SC intervention may be decisive or more precisely the obligations for the States deriving from the Resolutions adopted by it may be relevant. In particular art. 98 StICC places some limitations on ICC's power to claim the surrender of individuals suspected of the Commission of crimes under its jurisdiction against a State Party. These limits are linked to the customary and pact-related obligations on immunities that are incumbent on States.

Art. 98 was introduced only at the Rome Conference and was not the subject of particular debates and comparisons between the representatives of States[351]. This provision, however, raises many interpretative problems due to the

---

348O. BEKOU, The International Criminal Court, op. cit.,

349The words of the ICC President seem to go in this direction. Sang Hyun Song: Statement of President Song, 2012 Open debate on peace and justice, UNSC 6849th meeting, 17 October 2012, UN Doc. S/PV6849 Resumption 1, pp. 5ss. "If ICC is to effectively deal with situation referred by the Council under Chapter VII, it needs to be able to count on the full and continuing cooperation of all UN members, whether they are parties to the Rome Statute or not it would be very helpful if SC could underline this obligation of full cooperation, without which it is very difficult for ICC to discard the mandate the Council has given it (...)".

350The term person is generally used in the Statute to indicate suspects, defendants and offenders.

351W.A. SCHABAS, The international criminal court, op. cit., pp. 1038ss. Among the possible reasons at the basis of the failure to sign does not at least initially appear the rules

complex relationship it has with another rule of the Statute, art. 27 (2) which establishes the principle of the irrelevance of the quality of State organ for the exercise of ICC jurisdiction[352]. What is particularly relevant here is the fact that in light of art. 98 (1), ICC cannot ask States to "act consistently with its obligations under international law with respect to the State or diplomatic immunity of a person or property of a third State"[353] unless ICC has first obtained a waiver of the third State to take advantage of immunity. Through this generic reference to the international obligations of States, art. 98 (1) therefore ascertains a certain relevance to the customary immunity rules, as a possible obstacle to the requests for cooperation of ICC[354]. The relevance of art. 98 (1) as a possible impediment to the arrest and surrender of certain individuals to the international tribunal, it clearly emerges in practice regarding the Sudanese situation and will be the subject of some analysis and reflections in the following pages.

2. Practices in matters of cooperation and mutual legal assistance

2.1. The Darfur case

The type of mechanism by which the ICC is activated can significantly affect the degree of cooperation accorded to the organs of ICC by States. In the hypotheses of the so-called self-referral, for example, it is reasonable to expect an active collaboration of the local government that has reported the Commission of crimes on its territory and probably a certain availability to assist the ICC territory and probably a certain willingness to assist the other States Parties to the

---

concerning the immunity of the organs. The discussion focused instead on the potential conflicting obligations that could derive from the relationship between the obligations of delivery of the accused and the rules on extradition. See in argument: Report of the ad hoc Committee on the establishment of an international criminal court, General Assembly Official Records-Fifteen sessions, supplement n. 22, UN Doc. A/50/22, 1995, par. 218.

[352]This has been recognized by ICC itself. Decision pursuant to article 87 (7) of the Rome Statute on the failure by the Republic of Malawi to comply with the cooperation requests issued by the Court with respect to the arrest and surrender of Omar Hassan Ahmad Al Bashir, pre-trial Chamber I, ICC-02/05-01/09-139, 12 December 2011, par. 37. "There is an inherent tension between articles 27 (29 and 98 (1) of the Statute (...))". For further analysis see: J. D. VAN DER VYVER, The Al Bashir debacle, in African Human Rights Law Journal, 15 (2), 2015. Y. TAN, The identification of customary rules in International Criminal Court, in Utrecht Journal of International and European Law, 34 (2), 2018, pp. 96ss.

[353]W.A. SCHABAS, The international criminal court, op. cit.,

[354]It is not important here to examine the content of customary international law on immunity. However, it should be emphasized that many delegations considered it unnecessary to include a provision on immunity for international crimes. According to this last perspective, in fact, customary international law would have evolved and consolidated today in the sense of excluding immunity for the crimes envisaged by the statutes, particularly if an international Court is to exercise jurisdiction.

Statute[355]. The exercise of the referral power by SC may instead lead to a contrast between the national authorities and the requests of an international ICC whose action is imposed externally. Even the States Parties of the Stature who for any reason opposed the decision taken by SC may not be particularly cooperative with respect to the requests of the ICC bodies. The SC may not have the necessary political will to force States to comply with cooperation obligations if there is no full support for the action of the international tribunal within it. Some of these reasons may explain why both situations reported by SC to the ICC have encountered numerous obstacles in the field of cooperation and mutual legal assistance.

The Darfur case is certainly the most interesting and highlights all the difficulties that ICC can meet in obtaining the cooperation of States and in trusting if necessary in the active collaboration of SC. Moreover, the conflicts that emerged during the adoption of Resolution n.1593 (2005) and the absence of a widespread and shared political will with respect to the involvement of ICC were already little encouraging signs of what would then have been the effective support of SC to ICC action in the Sudanese context[356].

Indeed, at the time of the activation of ICC jurisdiction SC imposed some obligations of cooperation aimed at giving effect to ICC action. Through Resolution n.1593 (2005), SC has in fact decided that the Sudanese government and all parties to the conflict in Darfur shall cooperate fully with and provide any necessary assistance to the Court and the Prosecutor. As for the other States not part of the Statutes, however, SC was concerned first of all that States not party to the Rome Statute have no obligation under it and then limited itself to soliciting ("urges") their cooperation. In other words, while for those involved in the conflict, Resolution n.1593 expressly provided for an obligation of full cooperation, the other States not part of the Statute were simply encouraged to assist ICC action. The need to clarify this distinction has been supported by the United States within the SC have stressed that the ability of some States to cooperate with the ICC investigation will be restricted in connection with applicable domestic law. In particular, the US representative noted that the deep concern about the Court that would emerge from its internal regulations can only represent a limit to the ability of the United States to cooperate with the ICC[357].

Despite the obligations imposed by SC, the Sudanese authorities contested the ICC activation from the beginning from the Khartoum government declared that it would not cooperate with the ICC bodies. The attitude of opposition and non-cooperation with ICC then intensified following the arrest

---

355P. GAETA, Is the practice of "self-referrals" a sound start for the ICC?, op. cit., pp. 950ss.

356G. SLUITER, Obtaining cooperation from Sudan-Where is the law?, in Journal of International Criminal Justice, 6, 2008, pp. 874ss. The author affirms that already at the time of the first arrest warrants, that the support that could have been expected from SC in this affair would have been little to nothing.

357See in particular the position expressed from the United States within SC, UN Doc. S/PV.5158, p. 4.

warrants issued against some local political and military leaders. At present, all the suspects of the Commission of crimes in Darfur are at liberty despite the various arrest warrants issued by ICC, the ICC's pronouncements about Sudan's violation of its cooperation obligations and the consequent reports to SC[358]. The vicissitudes of the Sudanese President Omar Al-Bashir are also quite well known in the chronicles despite the two arrest warrants issued against him by ICC in 2009[359] and 2010[360]. In light of the second mandate, however, Al Bashir is not accused only of the Commission on crimes against humanity and war crimes but must also answer for the accusation of genocide.

The failure of Sudan and of several other African States to capture Al Bashir also part of the Rome Statute was justified on the basis of the immunity enjoyed by the Sudanese President[361]. One of the reasons put forward by States that on several occasions, in particular during the meetings of the Common Market for Eastern and Southern Africa (COMESA), hosted the Sudanese President Al Bashir is in fact the need to respect the privileges and immunities of heads of State in line with the established principle of international law[362].

In this regard, it is interesting to note that the African Union has repeatedly called for the adoption of what it considers to be some necessary amendments to the Rome Statute in particular its article 27[363]. The African Union

---

[358]ICC, Prosecutor v. Ahmad Harun and Ali Kushayb, Decision informing the United Nations Security Council about the lack of cooperation by the Republic of the Sudan, pre-trial chamber I, ICC-02/05-01/07-57, 25 May 2010. Prosecutor v. Omar Hassan Ahmad Al Bashir, Decision on the Prosecutor's request for a finding of non-compliance against the Republic of the Sudan, ICC-02/05-01/09-227, pre trial chamber II, 9 March 2015. Prosecutor v. Abdel Raheem Muhammad Hussein, Decision on the prosecutor's request for a finding of non-compliance against the Republic of the Sudan, pre-trial chamber II, ICC-02/05-91/12-33, 26 June 2015. Prosecutor v. Abdallah Banda, Decision on the prosecution's request for a finding of non-compliance, trial chamber IV, ICC-02/05-03/09-641, 19 November 2015.

[359]ICC, Prosecutor v. Omar Hassan Ahmad Al Bashir, Decision on the prosecution's application for a warrant of arrest against Omar Hassan Abhmad Al Bashir, pre-trial chamber I, ICC-02/05-01/09-3, 4 March 2009.

[360]ICC, Prosecutor v. Omar Hassan Ahmad Al Bashir, Second warrant of arrest for Omar Hassan Ahmad Al Bashir, pre-trial chamber I, ICC-02-05/01-09, 12 July 2010.

[361]Among the states visited by Al-Bashir in recent years: Egypt, Libya, Saudi Arabia, Kenya, Qatar, Chad, Malawi, Iran, Eritrea, Ethiopia, China, Iran, Djibouti and South Africa. Among these: South Africa, Kenya, Djibouti, Chad and Malawi were part of the statute.

[362]See the arguments of Malawi to report in Prosecutor v. Omar Hassan Al Bashir, Decision pursuant to article 87 (7) of the Rome Statute of the failure by the Republic of Malawi to comply with the cooperation requests issued by the Court with respect to the arrest and surrender of Omar Hassan Ahmad Al Bashir, pre trial chamber I, ICC-02/05-01/09-139, 12 December 2011.

[363]Statement by the Hon. Frederick Ruhinddi, Deputy Attorney General/Minister of state for justice and constitutional affairs of the Republic of Uganda on behalf of the African Union at the 12th Assembly of states parties to the Rome statute of the International

itself, also because of the failure to take into consideration ICC on the Sudanese case, it asked the Member States of the Organization not to collaborate. This last request would be based on the provisions of article 98 of the Rome Statute of the ICC relating to immunities[364].

The African States against which ICC has ascertained the violation of the obligations of cooperation have therefore repeatedly called for the need to comply with the obligations deriving from them from participation in the African Union[365]. In particular, these States believe they must comply with the decision taken by the Union pursuant to which non serving AU Head of State or government (...) shall be required to appear before any international court or tribunal during their term of office[366].

The arguments put forward by the African Union and the States concerned therefore seem to suggest that the obligation to respect the immunity of foreign heads of State derives from the same rules as the Statute, in particular, art. 98 (1) which safeguards compliance with customary immunity rules and the participation of those States in an international organization, the African Union precisely with the consequent obligation to respect the binding decisions made by it.

Specifically, ICC has had at least two occasions to ascertain the violation of Sudan cooperation obligations and to report the situation of SC. On 25 May 2010, in fact, a Court Chamber asked SC to take the necessary measures against Sudan, following the failure to cooperate in relation to the arrest warrants issued against Ahmad Muhammad Harun and Ali Muhammad All Abd-Al-Rahman[367]. The ICC then (on 9 March 2015) again asked SC to take the measures it deems necessary to counter Sudan's failure to cooperate during the several years since the arrest warrant, which has been chased towards President Al Bashir. The judges of the Court in this case recalled the obligations deriving for Sudan from Resolution n.1593 (2005) in particular the obligation of full cooperation imposed in that circumstance by SC. The pre-Chamber ruling underlines how the principle that a treaty obliges only States Parties to it may be altered by SC which may be

Criminal Court, op. cit.

[364]African Union, Decision on the meeting of African States parties to the Rome statute of the ICC, Thirteenth ordinary session, 3 July 2009, Assembly/AU/13/13 (XIII), par. 10.

[365]You can once again see the positions of Malawi, reported in the ICC, Prosecutor v. Omar Hassan Al Bashir, Decision pursuant to article 87 (7) of the Rome Statute on the failure by the Republic of Malawi to comply with the cooperation requests issued by the Court with respect to the arrest and surrender of Omar Hassan Ahmad Al Bashir, ICC-02/05-01/09-139, 12 December 2011.

[366]African Union, Extraordinary session of the Assembly of the African Union, Decision on Africa's relationship with the International Criminal Court (ICC), 12 October 2013, par. 10.

[367]ICC, Pre-trial chamber I, The prosecutor v. Ahmad Muhamamd Harun ("Ahmad Harun") and Ali Muhammad Ali Abd-Al-Rahman ("Ali Kushayb"), Decision informing the United Nations Security Council about the lack of cooperation by the Republic of the Sudan, ICC-02/05-01/07, 25 May 2010.

means of a Resolution adopted under Chapter VII of the UN Charter, create an obligation to cooperate with the Court on those UN Member States which are not parties to the Statute. In these cases, the judges still observe the obligation to cooperate stems directly from the UN Charter and not by the Rome Statute[368].

As anticipated, in addition to ascertaining the violations of the assistance obligations made by Sudan, against which the SC Resolution directly imposed cooperation obligations over the years, the ICC also had to note the non-cooperation of some other African States which are part of the Statute and in which President Al Bashir went for official visits. Despite requests for arrest from ICC, these States did not proceed to the arrest of the Sudanese president and their lack of cooperation has been the subject of some pronouncements by ICC. The opposition of these States to cooperation with ICC as mentioned has mainly leveraged art. 98 (1) StICC. In particular, the comparison between African States and ICC chambers highlights divergent interpretations on the compatibility of the requests for delivery of defendants advanced by the ICC with the international rules on immunity of organs and consequently with that specific statutory provision.

The arguments proposed by ICC chambers in order to affirm the irrelevance of art. 98 (1) were different. Following the Democratic Republic of Congo's failure to arrest Al Bashir, for example, ICC stated that through Resolution n.1593 (2005), SC implicitly waived the immunities granted to Omar Al Bashir under international law and attached to his position as a Head of State[369]. This implicit waiver would be the result of both the activation of ICC jurisdiction towards Sudan and the cooperation obligations imposed on Sudan by the SC Resolution aimed at eliminating any impediment to the proceedings before the Court, including the lifting of immunities.

Another ICC Chamber has taken a different position which recalls general international law instead. In ascertaining the violation of the cooperation obligations of Chad and Malawi, the ICC retraced the jurisprudence of the international criminal courts and of ICJ itself in particular the well-known sentence on the arrest warrant[370] and came to the conclusion that the principle in

---

[368]ICC, The Prosecutor v. Omar Hassan Ahmad Albashir, Decision on the Prosecutor's request for a finding of non-compliance against the Republic of the Sudan, pre-trial Chamber II, ICC-02/05-01/09, 9 March 2015, par. 13.

[369]ICC, Decision on the cooperation of the Democratic Republic of the Congo regarding Omar Al Bashir's arrest and surrender to the Court, ICC-02/05-01/09-195, pre-trial chamber II, 9 April 2004, par. 29. For further details see: F. HALDEMANN, T. UNGER, The United Nations principles to combat impunity: A commentary, Oxford University Press, Oxford, 2018.

[370]International Court of Justice, arrest warrant of 11 April 2000 (Republic Democratic of Congo v. Belgium), sentence of 14 February 2002, in ICJ Reports 2002, par. 60. ICJ clarified that the limit indicated would not prevent from dealing with: "Si elle l'estome nècessaire ou souhaitable". This flexibility in the application of the non ultra petita principle has assumed very broad outlines in the judgment of oil platforms, Iran v. United States of 6 November 2003, in ICJ Reports, 2003, par. 161, in the part of the device in

international law is that immunity of either former by an international court[371]. In this different perspective, the impossibility of invoking the immunity of Al Bashir would not derive from SC Resolution but from customary international law.

However, ICC has returned to support the argument that the loss of immunity of the Sudanese president is instead the effect of the SC Resolution. According to this different reconstruction, the SC acting on the basis of Chapter VII has implicitly lifted the immunities of Omar Al-bashir. In this further and different circumstance, the ICC judges also assessed the effects for the Democratic Republic of Congo of the obligations deriving from the African Union decision. ICC noted in particular that the obligations deriving from participation in the regional organization are not in contrast only with those deriving from StICC, but also and above all with the same Resolution n.1593 (2005) of SC. The judges reiterated, once again that through full cooperation required from Sudan, SC was meant to eliminate any impediment to the proceedings before the Court and consequences under articles 25 and 103 of the UN Charter, the Democratic Republic of Congo would be obliged to give priority to the obligations arising from SC Resolution over any other international obligation. During 2016, these latter considerations were taken up and confirmed by ICC in reporting the violations committed by Djibouti and Uganda[372] to the Assembly of States Parties

---

which ICJ acknowledged without Iran requesting in its submissions this assessment that the United States had violated the international rules concerning the use of force. In this regard Buergenthal, Higgins and Kooijmans, respectively, see par. 3 and par. 9. For further details see: M.A. BECKER, The dispute that wasn't there. Judgments in the nuclear disarmament cases at the ICJ, in Cambridge International Law Journal, 6, 2017, pp. 4ss. S. DAS, A. NARGAS, Mapping the Jadhav dispute at the world court. Evaluating India and Pakistan's arguments, in California Western International Law Journal, 48 (1), 2018, pp. 40ss. A. ZIMMERMANN, C. TOMUSCHAT, K. OELLERS-FRAHM, C.J. TAMS, M. KASHGAR, D. DIEHL, The statute of the International Court of Justice. A commentary, Oxford University Press, Oxford, 2019, pp. 1418ss.

[371]ICC, Corrigendum to the decision pursuant to article 87 (7) of the Rome Statute on the failure by the Republic of Malawi to comply with the cooperation requests issued by the Court with respect to the arrest and surrender of Omar Hassan Ahmad Al Bashir, pre-trial chamber I, ICC-02/05-01/09-139-Corr, 13 December 2011, par. 36 and Decision pursuant to article 87 (7) of the Rome Statute on the refusal of the Republic of Chad to comply with the cooperation requests issued by the Court with respect to the arrest and surrender of Omar Hassan Ahmad Al Bashir, pre-trial chamber I, ICC-02/05-01/09-140-tENG, 13 December 2011. According to Chad, ICC then found on other occasions the lack of cooperation. See for example: Decision on the non-compliance of the Republic of Chad with the cooperation requests issued by the Court regarding the arrest and surrender of Omar Hassan Ahmad Al-Bashir, pre-trial chamber I, ICC-02/05-01/09, 26 March 2013.

[372]ICC, Decision on the non-compliance by the Republic of Djibouti with the request to arrest and surrender Omar Al-Bashir to the Court and referring the matter to the UN Security Council and the Assembly of the State Parties to the Rome Statute, pre-trial chamber II, ICC-02/05-01/09-266, 11 July 2016 and Decision on the non-compliance by the Republic of Uganda with the request to arrest and surrender Omar Al-Bashir to the court and referring the matter to the UN Security Council and the Assembly of State Parties

and SC.

Finally, in July of 2017 while deciding not to report South Africa to the Assembly of States Parties and of SC in light of the particular circumstances of the case, ICC ascertained the violation of the cooperation obligations also by this State. In the latter ruling, however, it is stated that no waiver, implicit or explicit, would be in ICC's opinion necessary to bring down the immunity of Al Bashir. More simply, when SC decides to use ICC for the repression of international crimes under ICC jurisdiction, the interactions between Sudan and the Court with respect to latter exercise of jurisdiction in the situation in Darfur are regulated by the Statute. The other terms would apply to Sudan as if it were a State Party to the Statute, all statutory provisions including art. 27 (2), thus making inapplicable any immunity on the ground of official capacity belonging to Sudan that would otherwise exist under international law[373].

The idea is that when the situation in Sudan is reported by the SC to the ICC, the StICC applies to that state, making the immunity rules irrelevant to the Sudanese bodies which cannot therefore be in turn opposed to the ICC from any other state that requires assistance.

Also due the inertia of SC, Al Bashir has continued to move through numerous not part States of StICC. In fact, the investigations of the violations of the obligations of cooperation just reported and if the case of South Africa are excluded, reported by ICC to SC, have not produced any practical consequence. In this regard, the Prosecutor has observed in a series of reports to SC relating to

---

to the Rome Statute, pre-trial chamber II, IC-02/05-01/09-267, 11 July 2016.

[373]ICC, Decision under article 87 (7) of the Rome Statute on the non-compliance by South Africa with the request by the Court for the arrest and surrender of Omar Al-Bashir, pre-trial chamber II, ICC-02/05-01/09, 6 July 2017, par. 91. See also in argument: Minority opinion of judge Marc Perring de Brichambaut, (ICC-02/05-01/09-302-Anx) according to which it would not be possible to interpret SC Resolution, to reach a definitive conclusion of the question (in particular, pp. 36-45). Previously, the Chamber was more clearly oriented towards the thesis of implicit renunciation. In June of 2015, in fact Al Bashir was for a few days stopped in Johannesburg where he was just in the occasion of a summit of African Union. Despite the arrest warrant issued by the local authorities, the Sudanese president was launched an escape route from the military airport of Pretoria. With urgency during those confused days of detention of Al Bashir, the II preliminary Chamber of ICC had had the opportunity to reiterate that: "The immunities granted to Omar Al Bashir under international law and attached to his position as a Head of State have been implicitly waived by the UN Security Council of Resolution n.1593 (2005) referring the situation in Darfur, Sudan to the Prosecutor of the Court, and that the Republic of South African cannot invoke any other decision, including that of the African Union, providing for any obligation to the contrary (...)". See, pre-trial chamber II, Decision following the prosecutor's request for an order further clarifying that the Republic of South Africa is under the obligation to immediately arrest and surrender Omar Al Bashir, ICC-02/05-01/09-242, 13 June 2015, par. 9. Moreover, the Supreme Court of South Africa also condemned the behavior of the government for failing to comply with the internal rules implementing the statute of Rome. See: The minister of justice and constitutional development v. the southern African litigation centre (867/15 (2016) ZASCA 17 (15 March 2016)).

the application of Resolution n.1593 (2005) that if one wishes to attribute some sense to the referrals experienced by SC the UN Member States which are also part of the StICC must face consequences for serious and inexcusable violations of their duties to cooperate with the Court and to honor the Council's Resolutions[374]. As the ICC reminded SC on more than one occasion, however, if there is not follow up action on the part of UNSC, any referral by the Council to ICC under Chapter VII of the UN Charter would never achieve its ultimate goal, namely to put an end to impunity[375]. To date, SC has not deemed it necessary to take any measures to follow up on the reports received from ICC regarding the non-execution by the States Parties of the requests of ICC[376].

2.2. The Libya case

Even in the Libyan case, cooperation problems concern a State that is not part of StICC and whose situation has been reported to ICC through a SC Resolution adopted on the basis of Chapter VII of the UN Charter. Resolution n.1970 (2011) provided in the part relating to the referral and with the same words used in the previous Sudanese that the Libyan authorities provided full cooperation to ICC and Prosecutor. SC has invited all other States to cooperate including those not part of the Statute, stressing however and once again how the latter have no obligation under it. As already seen at the time of the unanimous adoption of this Resolution, several criticisms were addressed to the exemption from ICC jurisdiction of some categories of individuals. On the other hand, there were no particular debates about the obligations of cooperation towards the international tribunal of States not part of the Statute.

To date, Libya has not yet followed up on three different requests for

---

[374]The Office of the Prosecutor, twenty-first Report of the Prosecutor of the International Criminal Court to the UN Security Council pursuant to UNSCR 1593 (2005), 29 June 2015, par. 34.

[375]ICC, Decision on the Prosecutor's request for a finding of non-compliance against the Republic of the Sudan, pre-trial Chamber II, ICC-02/05-01/09-227, 9 March 2015.

[376]The SC has indeed never even explicitly condemned the attitude of non-cooperation held by Sudan, as already critically observed a few years after the activation of ICC. For further details see: E. STOVER, V. PESKIN, A. KOENIG, Hiding in plain sight: The pursuit of war criminals from Nuremberg to the war on terror, in University of California Press, California, 2016. R. PIERIK, W. ERNER, Cosmopolitanism in context. Perspectives from international law and political theory, Cambridge University Press, Cambridge, 2010, pp. 206ss. K.A. RODMAN, Justice as a dialogue between law and politics: Embedding the International criminal Court within conflict management and peace-building, in Journal of International Criminal Justice, 12 (3), 2014, pp. 442ss. V. PESKIN, The international criminal court, the Security Council and the politics of impunity in Darfur, in Genocide Studies and Prevention: An International Journal, 4 (3), 2009, pp. 316ss: "(...) analysis of the numerous resolutions and statements the Security Council has adopted on Sudan, prior to June 2008 statement no formal criticism or explicit acknowledgment of Sudan's non-compliance. The Security Council's reluctance to confront Sudan for its non-cooperation with ICC bears a parallel to their Council's reticence to take action against Serbia in the 1990s for failing to cooperate with the ICTY (...)".

cooperation by ICC. Firstly it was not handed over to the organs of ICC Al-Islam Gaddafi[377]. Libya, on the other hand, has repeatedly tried, but without success, to have international criminal proceedings against the latter declared inadmissible[378]. Secondly, ICC asked the Libyan government to forward the original copies of the documents that were stolen by the Libyan authorities to the defendant's previous lawyer during a visit to his client in Zintan to the defensive college of Al Islam Gaddafi. ICC also called for the destruction of any reproduction of those documents[379]. Both of these requests have not been met. Finally, ICC had asked the Libyan authorities to allow the defensive college at Al Senussi to visit their client[380]. An agreement to this effect, of which ICC had partly proposed the content has never been reached[381]. Al Senussi was declared later inadmissible by ICC, thus also eliminating Libya's assistance obligations[382].

ICC ascertained Libya's non-compliance (on 10 December 2014) with its cooperation obligations in relation to the first two requests made to it. The situation was reported to SC. The obligation to cooperate deriving from Resolution n.1970 (2011) has never been questioned by Libya, which however claims its ability and willingness to prosecute those responsible for the crimes[383]. SC, although urged by the judges of the pre-Chamber to enforce the requests coming from ICC, limited itself to reiterating the existence of cooperation obligations deriving from Resolution n.1970 (2011) without however taking new measures against the Libyan authorities to make them effective. SC has in fact

---

[377]ICC, Decision on Libya's submission regarding the arrest of Saif Al-Islam Gaddafi, pre-trial Chamber I, ICC-01/11-01/11-7, 7 March 2012.

[378]ICC, Decision on the postponement of the execution of the request for surrender of Saif Al-Islam Gaddafi pursuant to article 95 of the Rome Statute, pre-trial Chamber I, ICC-01/11-01/11-163, 2 June 2012. ICC has instead declared inadmissible the case. Prosecutor v. Saif Al Islam Gaddafi and Abdullah Al-Senussi, Decision on the admissibility of the case against Saif Al-Islam Gaddaffi, pre-trial Chamber I, ICC-01/11-01/11, 31 May 2013.

[379]ICC, Decision on the "urgent defence request", pre-trial Chamber I, ICC-01/11-01/11-291, 1st March 2013.

[380]ICC, Decision on the "urgent application on behalf of Abdullah Al-Senussi for pre-trial chamber to order the Libyan authorities to comply with their obligations and the orders of the ICC". Pre-trial Chamber I, ICC-01/11-01/11-269, 6 February 2013.

[381]ICC, Decision concerning a privileged visit to Abbdullah Al-Senussi by his defence, pre-trial Chamber I, ICC-01/11-01/11-456, 26 September 2013.

[382]ICC, Decision on the admissibility of the case against Abdullahh Al-Senussi, 11 October 2013, ICC-01/11-01/11-466-Red. 9; Appeals Chamber, judgment on the appeal of Mr Abdullah Al-Senussi against the decision of pre-trial Chamber I of 11 October 2013 entitled: "Decision on the admissibility of the case against Abdullah Al-Senussi", pre trial Chamber I, 24 July 2014, ICC-01711-01/11-565.

[383]In May of 2014, the appeals Chamber confirmed the pre-Chamber decision and rejected the Libyan request to declare the case inadmissible, in this case denying that the investigations conducted in the African country concerned the same conduct of the proceedings before ICC. See: Judgment on the appeal of Libya against the decision of pre-trial Chamber of 31 May 2013 entitled: Decision on the admissibility of the case against Saif Al-Islam Gaddafi, Appeals Chamber, ICC-017111-01/11-547-red., 21 May 2014.

limited itself to some generic references aimed at affirming the importance of Libya government cooperation with ICC and Prosecutor[384]. Urged again by ICC through Resolution n.2213 (2015) of 27 March 2015, SC then further invited the Libyan government to cooperate fully with and provide any necessary assistance to ICC and the Prosecutor as required by Resolution n.1970 (2011)[385].

Urged again by ICC through Resolution n.2213 (2015) of 27 March 2015, SC then further invited the Libyan government to cooperate fully with and provide any necessary assistance to ICC and the Prosecutor as required by Resolution n.1970 (2011).

SC Member States also reiterated during a meeting in 2015 with Prosecutor Bensouda the crucial importance that the cooperation of the Libyan authorities with ICC is to combat impunity for the crimes that have been committed and continue to be committed in Libya[386]. However, it may be noted that while US representative limited himself to encouraging cooperation the Libyan authorities other States insisted that Libya must comply with the judges decision on this key issue[387]. The meeting saw the participation of the same Libyan permanent representative whose presence according to some States must be seen as a testament to Libya's determination to maintain a positive dialogue with the Court[388].

Libya stressed the importance of the meetings between Prosecutor and ICC and the Libyan judicial and governmental authorities and reaffirmed their commitment to cooperate with ICC and respect the decisions of international judges. Specifically, apart from the commitments formally made on this occasion too, the Libyan government has once again confirmed its intention[389] to exercise its jurisdiction over cases pending in the name of the principle of complementarity.

2.3. Security Council referalls and art. 98 (2) StICC

Another element of relevant practice in terms of cooperation between States and ICC regards the agreements concluded by some States on the basis of art. 98 (2) StICC. In particular, as is known, the United States has concluded a series of so-called immunity bilateral agreements with a considerable number of States many of which are part of StICC. These agreements provide in practice that American citizens cannot be surrendered or transferred by any means to ICC for

[384]See the preamble of Resolution n.2174 (2014) of 27 August 2014 and Resolution n.2095 (2013).

[385]W.A. SCHABAS, The international criminal court. A commentary to the Rome statute, op. cit.,

[386]See the position of United Kingdom in UN Doc. S/PV.74421, 12 May 2015, p. 7. But also the similar words expressed by the representatives of Jordan, United States, Spain, France, the Bolivarian Republic of Venezuela, Chile and Lithuania.

[387]These are the words of the French delegate, ivi, p. 8.

[388]These are the words of New Zealand delegate, ivi, p. 8.

[389]These are the words of Libya delegate, ivi, p. 8.

any purpose by the authorities of the contracting States, unless there is the consent of the United States themselves. The conclusion of these bilateral agreements is aimed in practice at preventing ICC from requiring States that have signed them to surrender US citizens. In light of art. 98 (2) in fact ICC cannot proceed with a delivery request that requires a State Party to act contrary to its obligations deriving from international agreements with third States by virtue of which the consent for a sending State in required to surrender in person in the presence of these agreements, ICC can request the delivery of a third-country national to a State Party only if it has first managed to obtain the cooperation of the sending State for the giving of consent for the surrender. In this case an assent to the surrender of its citizens by the United States.

What may be relevant for the purpose of this investigation is the fact that a reference to the existence of such agreements is contained in Resolution n.1593 (2005)[390]. In particular at the request of the United States[391], the preamble of that Resolution takes note of the existence of agreements referred to in article 98 (2) of the Rome Statute. The reference to those agreements which had already been the subject of numerous criticisms was also contested within SC[392]. Argentine, for example, expressly wanted to affirm its opposition to any agreement aimed at excluding ICC jurisdiction towards citizens of any State, because that would affect the basis for such jurisdiction and thwart the letter and the spirit of the Rome Statute[393]. Denmark, on the other hand, underlined the purely factual nature of this reference to the agreements concluded pursuant to art. 98 (2) and the fact that that recall cannot in any way impose(s) on the integrity of the Rome Statute[394],while the Brazilian delegation it had some difficulty accepting a reference that not only does not favor the fight against impunity but also stresses a provision whose application has been a highly controversial issue[395].

They are on the other hand despite SC decision does not contain references to the agreements concluded by the United States or more generally to art. 98 (2) some positions taken by the States on the occasion of the already analyzed Resolution n.1422 (2002). It is the first to have guaranteed a sort of immunity from ICC jurisdiction for states personnel not part of the Statute that participates in the maintenance operations of peace. In particular, the Canadian representative, after having bitterly criticized the double standard of jurisdiction

---

[390]W.A. SCHABAS, The international criminal court. A commentary to the Rome statute, op. cit.,

[391]UN Doc. SP.V/5154, p. 4.

[392]See the Resolution adopted from European Parliament relating ICC of 26 September 2002, P5_TA(2002)0449 and the separate opinion expressed by the European Commission, Effective functioning of the international criminal court undermined by bilateral agreements as proposed by the U.S. See also from the Amnesty international, international criminal Court: US efforts to obtain impunity for genocide crimes against humanity and war crimes.

[393]UN Doc. S/PV/5158, p. 8.

[394]UN Doc. S/PV/5158, p. 6.

[395]UN Doc. S/PV/5158, p. 11.

created by that Resolution, observed that the United States can freely negotiate bilateral agreements with the host States of the peacekeeping missions and that this rationale would be consistent with article 98 of the Rome Statute[396]. Numerous other States have in that circumstance hypothesized the use of the agreements protected by art. 98 (2) as a possible solution to obtain the same effects that Resolution n.1422 (2002) proposed to pursue the exemption from ICC jurisdiction of citizens of States not part of the Statute engaged in peacekeeping missions.

Beyond the conflicting positions expressed by the States regarding the conclusion of these agreements, the recognition of the existence of the same by SC seems to have more of a political value and perhaps represent a support for that particular practice. As pointed out by others, however, from a more strictly legal point of view, by the mere recognition of the existence of these bilateral agreements contained in the preamble of SC decision no validation of their merit or approval may be inferred. Furthermore and consequently the reference made by SC to those agreements does not seem to be able to represent a limit to the power of ICC organs to make requests for delivery towards the States Parties to StICC.

3. Legal problems in the relationship between Security Council and ICC in matters of cooperation and mutual legal assistance

Before addressing some of the most relevant legal issues among those concerning the relations between ICC and SC in the field of cooperation and mutual legal assistance, it is advisable to make a preliminary general consideration useful for framing the problems that arise in the relations between the two organizations in this particular area.

As has already emerged in the previous pages in the field of cooperation, a decisive role is played by States, whether they are part or not of the Statute[397]. As far as this investigation is concerned with investigating the interactions between ICC and SC, therefore, the rules on cooperation and mutual legal assistance govern relations that no longer strictly or in any case exclusively concern these two institutions. In other words, in determining the content of the obligations of cooperation incumbent on States it is not enough to analyze the rules contained in Rome Statute and any requests made by ICC but is also necessary and inevitably to take into consideration the effects on those obligations of the decisions taken by SC. The triangular nature, so to speak, of the dynamics

[396]UN Doc. S/PV.4568, p. 4

[397]As emerged from the analysis of the relevant provisions, however, a role of particular importance for the States Parties can emerge not only in that they were directly interested and obliged to guarantee full cooperation with ICC, but also and above all as members of the Assembly of States Parties. See for further analysis: B. BROOMHALL, International justice and the international criminal court: Between sovereignty and the rule of law, Oxford University Press, Oxford, 2003, pp. 162ss.

of relationship that characterizes this particular area complicates the analysis of the statutory rules and of the relevant SC decisions, forcing the interpreter to consider every question in the perspective of the various subjects potentially involved, not only ICC and the political body but also States that are part of the Statute and third States.

3.1. The effects of exercising referral power on cooperation and mutual legal assistance obligations

Turning now more specifically to legal issues raised by the practice concerning the relationship between SC action and cooperation of States with ICC, a first problem concerns the possible effects on the legal assistance obligations of States that derive from the exercise by SC of the referral power.

In the absence of statutory provisions aimed at regulating the legal consequences of the referral in this particular area, it is in fact necessary to ask whether the exercise of this prerogative by SC automatically implies a general obligation of cooperation for all UN Member States. In other words, one of the effects of ICC activation that finds its foundation in a SC Resolution could be considered to oblige all UN Member States to follow up on requests for collaboration from ICC bodies. As argued in doctrine, the foundation of Chapter VII of the UN Charter the referral power would have the effect of rendering the provisions of the Statute on cooperation obligations for all UN Member States regardless of whether or not they are parties to the Statute[398]. The basis of these obligations would evidently be identified in the UN Charter as an effect of SC Resolution and certainly not of the provisions of the Rome Statute whose recipients remain the States Parties to the treaty.

Otherwise it could be argued that the assistance obligations of States that are not part of the Statute should be made explicit in the decision by which SC reports a specific situation to ICC. If SC does not foresee these obligations, it can be assumed that third countries are not required to cooperate with ICC. In practice, therefore, the cooperation obligations envisaged by the Rome Treaty would always and only be relevant for the contracting States[399].

---

[398]B. SWART, Arrest and surrender, in A. CASSESE, P. GAETA, J.R.W.D. JONES, The Rome statute of the international criminal court. A commentary, Oxford University Press, Oxford, 2002, pp. 1678ss. A. CIAMPI, The proceedings against president Al Bashir and the prospects of their suspension under article 16 ICC Statute, op. cit., pp. 1616ss, which is affirmed that: "When the Security Council has referred a case to the Court (...) the distinction between States Parties and not States loses significance". In other words, the exercise of referral by SC would not only have the effect of extending the jurisdiction of ICC towards States not part of the Statute but "also involves the obligations of full cooperation with the Court in view of allowing it to fulfill its functions". See also in argument: J. WENQI, On co-operation by states not party to the international criminal court, in International Review of the Red Cross, 88, 2006, pp. 92ss.

[399]G. SLUITER, Obtaining cooperation from Sudan-Where is the law?, op. cit., pp. 878ss. D. RUIZ VERDUZCO, The relationship between the ICC and the United Nations Security Council, op. cit., pp. 42ss.

Finally, an intermediate position can be to expect that an obligation of full cooperation arises automatically without the need for the decision of SC expressly providing for it only towards the State or States not part of the Statute directly affected by the referral of SC.

In addition to the absence of indications expressed in the Statute, it does not seem that the issue has been the subject of particular attention in the works that led to the drafting of the Rome Treaty. It is significant, however, that in this regard the Commission of international law has limited itself to observing that all States as members of the international community have an interest in the suppression of international crimes and that therefore States not party to the Statute are also encouraged to cooperate with ICC[400]. A rather cautious language that could lead to presume in the beginning the absence of real legal obligations for States not part of the Statute even if they are directly affected by an exercise of the referral power by SC.

Some important indications for dealing with the issue come from the practice of SC. In its decisions to activate ICC jurisdiction relating to situations in Darfur and Libya, SC considered it necessary to specify the cooperation obligations incumbent on third States, making a distinction according to whether these States are part of the ongoing conflict[401]. While for the former it has laid down an obligation of full cooperation, SC has instead simply hoped for a collaboration of third States not involved in hostilities, explicitly reminding them that the latter States have no obligations towards ICC in principle.

This choice has been the subject of some criticism. A decision that had imposed on all States of the international community to guarantee full collaboration with ICC bodies would certainly have strengthened the action of ICC by attesting the existence of a shared political will to repress the crimes committed in those territories consequent to the choice of SC to activate international criminal jurisdiction[402].

From a strictly legal point of view, the content of these Resolutions suggests, however, in the opinion of SC, the exercise of referral power does not have the automatic consequence that all States are bound by the obligations of cooperation and mutual legal assistance provided for by the Rome Treaty. This is evident from the fact that as just said against third States not involved in the violence in Darfur and Libya, SC limited itself to soliciting collaborative behavior

---

[400]Report of the Preparatory Committee on the establishment of an international criminal court, Addendum, Draft statute for the international criminal court, UN Doc. A/CONF.183/2/Add.1, p. 31.

[401]M. KAMTO, L'affaire Al Bashir et les relations de l'Afrique avec la cour pènale internationale, in L'Afrique et le droit international: variations sur l'organisation internationale. Liber amicorum en l'honneur de Raymond Ranjeva, op. cit., pp. 167ss.

[402]C. HEYDER, The UN Security Council's referral of the crimes in Darfur to the international criminal court in light of US opposition to the court: Implications for the international criminal court's functions and status, in Berkeley Journal of International Law, 24 (2), 2006, pp. 654ss.

with ICC.

The fact that the cooperation obligations of the parties involved in the conflict and of the States on whose territory the crimes were committed were also expressly sanctioned in the activation decisions of ICC jurisdiction could suggest that even for these subjects particularly affected by the referral of SC service obligations with ICC are not a direct and automatic effect of the exercise of that particular power. This seems to emerge once again from the specification made by SC about the fact that in the beginning and therefore without prejudice to the provisions of the Resolution, third countries have no obligations to cooperate with ICC.

It can therefore be argued that SC's exercise of referral power does not in itself affect those cooperation obligations of States which remain those defined by the Rome Treaty including the distinction that the pact nature of the Statute necessarily implies between party and not States.

This interpretation of SC of the rest seems to agree better also with the letter of art. 87 (5) b) StICC[403]. As already mentioned, these rules provide that when ICC jurisdiction is activated through the exercise of referral power, ICC can inform SC of the non-cooperation of States not part of the Statute, provided that these States have concluded a cooperation agreement with ICC. If the editors of the Statute had intended the referral as a tool which was automatically associated with the effect of imposing on the basis of the UN Charter an obligation to cooperate towards all States not part of the Statute, it is not seen for which reason the Statute then ordered that for ICC to notify SC of its assessment relating to the non-cooperation of States not part of the treaty, the latter must have previously made some formal cooperation commitment with ICC. The third State following the thesis that the referral would automatically give rise to the obligations of cooperation should already be obliged to assist ICC as a result of the exercise by SC of the power to activate ICC without some need to have previously committed to this end.

The difficulty of reconciling an automatic obligation of cooperation deriving from the referral of SC with the letter of art. 87 led several authors to consider that part of the provision completely irrelevant. It would have no meaning that the third party affected by SC report has assumed an obligation to cooperate with ICC[404]. It may perhaps be more simply to consider also in the name of the principle of the useful effect which requires as far as possible to recognize all the elements of the provision that art. 87 (5) b) and in particular ICC power to inform SC in case of violation of the cooperation obligations also applies in the event that these obligations derive from a Resolution of the same SC and therefore not as direct effect of the exercise of referral power. To the obligations potentially deriving from the commitments undertaken by the third State, therefore, a further

[403]O. BEKOU, The International Criminal Court, op. cit.,

[404]See those reconstructions that tend to qualify the reference to ad hoc agreements and other forms of agreement referred to in art. 87, par. 5 StICC refers to ICC States for the purposes of regulating the cooperation obligations of the third States.

hypothesis must be added, not foreseen by the provision, namely that the obligation of cooperation derives from a SC decision. This is to avoid the absurd result that SC cannot notify the violation of an obligation imposed on the third State by itself.

As seen in the analysis of the relevant practice, ICC did not hesitate to inform SC of Sudan non-compliance with its cooperation obligations. And despite this, Sudan, a State not part of the Statute, has not concluded any agreement with ICC. The first preliminary Chamber, however, did not justify this power to inform SC as a consequence of the fact that the Darfur case had been submitted as a consequence of the fact that it had been subject to ICC jurisdiction through the exercise of referral power. The judges rather recalled the obligations for the States to implement SC Resolutions deriving by art. 25 of the UN Charter and in particular evidently to carry out the part of Resolution n.1593 (2005) relating to cooperation and mutual assistance towards ICC[405].

3.2. The meaning of "full cooperation" foreseen in ICC jurisdiction activation Resolutions

A further aspect on which it is necessary to focus attention concerns the content of cooperation obligations that SC can impose on States. It is therefore appropriate to first investigate the extent of the mutual legal assistance obligations that have so far been imposed by SC towards the States Parties or not of the Statute.

As seen in the referrals relating to the Darfur and Libya crises, SC has used similar terms regarding the scope and content of cooperation obligations of the actors involved. In particular, as far as the Resolutions of activation of ICC jurisdiction are concerned, the government of Sudan the other parties involved in the conflict in Darfur and the Libyan authorities shall cooperate fully with and provide any necessary assistance to the Court and the Prosecutor. The ICC therefore requires the recipients of the relevant parts of the device to cooperate fully with it.

In the absence of further indications obtainable from the decisions of SC, it may not be easy to reconstruct the exact meaning, scope and content of this general obligation of full cooperation. It is basically a matter of understanding what the legal obligations incumbent on the recipients of these parts of SC Resolution device are.

It could in principle be assumed that a generic obligation of full cooperation implies the fulfillment by the subjects to whom the decision is addressed of any request coming from ICC bodies. It should be noted that such a wide result obligation by virtue of which any request of ICC should be performed by the subjects to which it is addressed is not imposed even towards the States

[405]ICC, The Prosecutor v. Ahmad Muhammad Harun ("Ahjmad Harun") and Ali Muhammad Ali Abd-Al-Rahman ("Ali Kushayb"), Decision informing the UN Security Council about the lack of cooperation by the Republic of the Sudan, pre-trial chamber I, ICC-02/05-01/07, 25 May 2010, pp. 6ss.

Parties of the Statute for which they operate as best you will see a series of guarantees of no small importance aimed at containing and limiting the scope of cooperation obligations[406]. In the case relating to Darfur, moreover, ICC Prosecutor noted that ICC imposed on Sudan any cooperation duties required in the discharge of the Court's mandate[407]. This statement suggests that the content of the SC's request for full cooperation addressed to Sudan should be presumed to correspond to the rules governing ICC action in this area.

More generally, it seems correct to assume that SC Resolutions aimed at affecting the action of ICC should be interpreted if possible in accordance with the Rome Statute. In these cases, however, nothing can be adduced to counter this presumption of conformity since SC itself seems to refer to the general obligation established by the Treaty establishing SC. The expression used by SC follows in fact as we may remember, art. 86 StICC which states that States Parties shall in accordance with the provisions of this Statute, cooperate fully with the Court in its investigation and prosecution of crimes.

From a partially different perspective, it can be noted that SC power exercised through those parts of the device was in practice to extend the application of the statutory provisions on cooperation and mutual legal assistance to States not bound by the Rome Treaty[408]. Indeed, SC decision constitutes the

---

[406]There are those who have rightly pointed out that as much as one may be tempted to consider the obligation of full cooperation as an obligation of result "in the sense that every request of assistance must be executed". The Statute foresees indeed and in part we will see "a number of grounds for justifying refusal of cooperation". See in argument: G. SLUITER, Obtaining cooperation from Sudan-Where is the law?, op. cit., pp. 878ss.

[407]ICC, The Prosecutor v. Omar Hassan Ahmad Al Bashir transcript, Open session, pre-trial Chamber II, ICC-02/05-01/09-T-2-ENG, 7 April 2017, pp. 70ss.

[408]However, it is worth noting that as far as this is not directly relevant for the purposes of the present investigation, for the States that are not part of the Rome Treaty, a series of problems could emerge in relation to some specific obligations foreseen by the statutory provisions. These are obligations that require States to adapt their internal regulations to allow the execution of assistance obligations. We refer in particular to art. 88 StICC, which provides that the States "shall ensure that there are procedures available under their national law for all of the forms of cooperation which are specified under this part". It is evident that the States not part of StICC, not being in principle obliged to adopt internal procedures aimed at guaranteeing the effectiveness of the forms of cooperation envisaged by the statutory provisions, may not be able to respond to requests from ICC. The impossibility for States to oppose their own internal law as justification for failure to comply with an international obligation would in such cases arise state responsibility (ILC, Draft articles on responsibility of States for internationally wrongful acts,with commentaries, in Yearbook of the International Law Commission, 2001, vol. II, Part Two, art. 32 and the advisory opinion Permanent Court of International Justice, Treatment of Polish nationals and other persons of polish origin or speech in the Danzig territory, Series A/B, n. 44, 4 February 1932, pp. 24). In fact, however, and beyond the possible consequences in terms of international responsibility, the cooperation obligations imposed by SC would need to be disregarded by the internal organs of the state, unable due to the shortcomings of the relevant internal legislation to implement them.

legal basis for the requests for cooperation made by ICC to States that have not assumed obligations to assist ICC. If, on the other hand, a request for full cooperation of SC had the States Parties of the Statute as recipients, the Resolution would obviously have the mere effect of strengthening the binding nature of already existing obligations in light of the Rome Treaty.

3.3. Other hypotheses of impact of SC decisions on the scope of the statutory obligations

The hypothesis that SC asks one or more States for full cooperation with ICC does not pose many problems for ICC bodies. As just seen beyond the fact that the State concerned is part of the Statute or not, a SC decision that recalls the formula of full cooperation would only refer to the regulatory framework outlined by the Rome Treaty.

However, it is also possible to envisage the possibility that SC requests States to conduct conduct not expressly provided for in the statutory provisions or in any case not clearly attributable to a specific obligation of cooperation governed by the Treaty. These may be direct obligations, as appropriate, to favoring and strengthening but also possibly compressing the mutual legal assistance of States with respect to SC action[409].

First of all, it can be assumed that SC imposes on States a series of cooperation obligations which, although not expressly foreseen by the Rome Treaty, do not directly conflict with the statutory provisions. Similarly to what has been seen for the obligation of full cooperation, a presumption of conformity deriving from the more general principle of systemic interpretation can also be considered in this case (art. 31, (3) c) VCLT)[410]. In other words, ICC bodies must assume that SC intended to act in accordance with the legal framework on cooperation set out in the Statute. The judges will try in practice to reconstruct the content of SC decisions in a manner consistent with their founding treaty. In this way, however, SC Resolutions could favor certain interpretations of the relevant statutory rules. This in particular for those provisions which have gaps or whose interpretation leaves a certain margin of discretion. An example of this could come from art. 93 (1) l) StICC, a regulation of closure of the pact system in the matter of cooperation, which requires States in general terms, to guarantee any other type of assistance (...) with a view to facilitating the investigation and prosecution of crimes within the jurisdiction of the Court. It can be assumed that ICC bodies

---

[409]Some of the first comments on the rules on cooperation and judicial assistance seem to go in this direction where it was observed that art. 13 b) StICC: "Recognizes the power of the Security Council under Chapter VII of the UN Charter to transform the ICC's jurisdiction into a universal one, and nothing prevents the Security Council, while acting under this Chapter, from strengthening the cooperation regime by way of a specific Resolution to this extent". See in argument: H.P. KAUL, C. KRESS, Jurisdiction and cooperation in the statute of the international criminal court. Principles and compromise, in Yearbook of International Humanitarian Law, 2, 1999, pp. 172ss.

[410]O. BEKOU, The International Criminal Court, op. cit.,

deem a particular request for assistance addressed by SC to States to be compliant with the Statute and attributable to one of these other forms of cooperation, even if the specific obligation imposed by SC is not expressly governed by the Rome Statute, but is nevertheless aimed at facilitating investigations and in general ICC action.

However, one could also imagine, and the hypothesis is evidently more problematic, that SC sets up a series of cooperation obligations towards States that go beyond what is required by the Statute to the point of compressing some forms of protection of the interests of been recognized by the Statute itself. In other words, it could be verified that through some SC decisions intends in some way to modify the scope of some assistance and cooperation obligations foreseen by the Rome Treaty and to limit the scope of some guarantees prepared in favor of the States.

It does not seem to be noted here that this occurs following or in the context of SC exercise of the power of referrals or in different hypotheses or with respect to situations reported by a State Party or in cases of action proper to the Prosecutor[411]. SC in fact remains as is obviously free to impose on States the cooperation obligations that it deems necessary regardless of the fact that the proceedings in question have found their own basis in the exercise of the referral power. What is interesting in this hypothesis is that those obligations do not correspond to the dictates of the Rome Treaty and therefore to the legal framework within which ICC organs are called to move.

Also the fact that the obligations contained in SC Resolution are addressed to States Parties or not of the Statute does not assume particular importance from the perspective of ICC. Once again, the problem here lies in the fact that the SC asks States to behave towards ICC that ICC bodies could not, in the light of their own treaty establishing. This is regardless of whether the obligations imposed by SC concern States part of the Stature (already required to cooperate with ICC) or States not part of the Statute (whose obligation of cooperation derives directly from SC decision).

For greater clarity and to try to give more concreteness to the issue that is being tried to highlight, a series of provisions can be recalled to protect certain prerogatives of States whose scope could at least in theory be limited by a SC Resolution. It is possible to mention art. 93 (4) which allows States Parties to

---

[411]The only difference according to the letter of the Statute is that in these last two hypotheses the ICC will not be able to inform SC of the failed cooperation of the State. Likewise, this change cannot be made if the third State has not previously undertaken a collaboration commitment with ICC. The absence of this possibility of communication between ICC and SC, whose ratio is difficult to understand, however, following an investigation by ICC concerning the lack of cooperation of the State Party or the third State (to which SC has imposed to cooperate), SC automatically decides to intervene to force those subjects to collaborate with ICC. In general, SC power to impose certain behaviors on States is not circumscribed by StICC or, as a consequence, to the findings of ICC, nor is it related to the prior exercise of the activation power provided for by art. 13 b) StICC.

oppose the request for the delivery of certain documents in the name of national security needs. Then think of art. 94 (1) which allows the State to postpone the delivery of some documents in order to guarantee the efficacy and correct conduct of an investigation or of an ongoing procedure other than that covered by ICC jurisdiction. Or you can remember that in the light of art. 93 (3), the State to which a request for cooperation is addressed could oppose ICC an existing fundamental legal principle of general application which prevents the execution of the assistance measure requested by ICC.

Although these are hypotheses of school, in these cases one can imagine an intervention of SC aimed at limiting the scope of these guarantees for the States prepared by the Statute. In other words, SC could, for example, request a State to deliver documents whose secrecy is considered by that State to be fundamental to guarantee national security by circumventing the limit established by art. 94 (4) or impose the immediate delivery of evidentiary material useful for the purposes of other proceedings in progress before the internal courts, ignoring the statutory guarantee provided by the aforementioned art. 94 (1)[412].

In reality, faced with ICC requests, the States continue to benefit from the guarantees provided by the Statute and will therefore be able to oppose those requests with the excuses just described. SC decisions do not alter the discipline of relations between ICC and the States which remains regulated by the Rome Statute. The Resolutions and obligations of cooperation and mutual legal assistance imposed by these States also do not bind ICC bodies[413], whose requests for assistance must be adopted in accordance with their founding treaty and in compliance with the protection it provides for States on which the latter must be able to rely in order to possibly oppose those requests. ICC bodies therefore cannot leverage SC Resolutions to circumvent the limits placed on their jurisdiction over States. It is the stretch of Rome that guides and possibly also limits ICC action. On the other hand, the Statute expressly regulates the hypotheses in which ICC can base on a Resolution of the SC intervention powers with respect to situations in which otherwise it would not be entitled to intervene. The referral of SC is the most emblematic case. Apart from these hypotheses, it must be assumed that ICC does not lay the foundation for an intervention capacity that goes beyond the limits set by the Statute on SC decisions.

3.4. The effects of Security Council Resolutions on the application of art. 98 (1) StICC

Art. 27 (2) StICC provides, as already mentioned, that immunities "which may attach to the official capacity of a person, whether under national or

---

[412]O. BEKOU, The International Criminal Court, op. cit.,

[413]D. AKANDE, The effect of Security Council resolutions and domestic proceedings on state obligations to cooperate with the ICC, op. cit., pp. 300ss. G.H. OOSTHUIZEN, Some preliminary remarks on the relationship between the envisaged international criminal court and the UN Security Council, in Netherlands International Law Review, 46 (3), 1999, pp. 314ss.

international law, shall not bar the Court from exercising its jurisdiction over such a person"[414]. The irrelevance of the official qualification of the individuals suspected of the Commission of crimes under ICC jurisdiction, sanctioned through this work provision is obvious for the organs of the States Parties to the Statute. As already noted during the first chapter, also against the bodies of States that are not part of the Statute, but on whose territory a situation of widespread violence reported by SC to ICC is taking place, it is applied art. 27[415]. It has been said that following SC's exercise of referral power, the rules relating to the exercise of jurisdiction inevitably remain those contained in the Rome Treaty regardless of the place where the crimes were committed or the fact that those who are suspected of the crimes themselves are citizens of a third State or not.

However, the question we intend to address here concerns another aspect. It is a question of determining the legitimacy or otherwise of certain requests for arrest and surrender of third-party bodies put forward by ICC against the States Parties of StICC[416].

In light of art. 98 (1) in particular ICC cannot ask States to behave contrary to their international immunity obligations. More precisely, by virtue of this provision, before asking a State Party for the arrest or surrender of an organ of a third State, ICC should make sure that the latter has expressly waived the immunity of its organs or that in any case such immunity may be considered to have failed under international law[417].

A first question subject to conflicting interpretations concerns the determination of the third State to which art. 98 (1) is not entirely clear, whether you are dealing with a State not part of the Statute or any State also part of it, different from the one to which ICC director is addressed.

Those who supported the thesis that the third State would be any State other than the one to which the request is directed, however, has come to affirm the impossibility for States Parties to invoke in their mutual relations the rules on immunity against of delivery requests by ICC. In these reconstructions it is argued that the third party State of the Treaty has already renounced to make use of the

---

[414]G.H. OOSTHUIZEN, Some preliminary remarks on the relationship between the envisaged international criminal court and the UN Security Council, op. cit.,

[415]W.A. SCHABAS, The international criminal court. A commentary to the Rome statute, op. cit.,

[416]For further analysis see: D. JACOBS, The frog that wanted to be an ox: The ICC's approach on immunities and cooperation, in C. STAHN, The law and practice of the international criminal court, Oxford University Press, Oxford, 2015, pp. 282ss.

[417]The numerous and delicate problems related to the possible conflicts between the ICC action and the international rules on immunity have emerged only in the final phase of the Rome Conference. Precisely because of the complexity of the theme, it was decided to leave a generic reference to the general international law, without specifying the content of the relevant rules. This also helps to prevent future developments in customary law in this area. See in argument: C. KRESS, The international criminal court and immunities under international law of states not party top the court's statute, in M. BERGSMO, L. YAN, State sovereignty and international criminal law, ed. TOAEP, Beijing, 2012, pp. 232ss.

rules on immunity in proceedings before ICC precisely by virtue of art. 17 StICC[418]. Otherwise, we would be faced with the paradoxical situation in which ICC would otherwise face the paradoxical situation in which ICC should always obtain a waiver of the immunity of a part, probably a reluctant State both to deliver its own organ and to renounce the immunity, in order to obtain the arrest and surrender of an organ of the former from another State. If so, it is evident that the effects and scope of art. 27 would be almost canceled.

Precisely in the light of the arguments briefly illustrated here, the first hypothesis, that a third State is to be understood as a State not part of the Statute then appears more convincing and in line with the overall legal framework outlined by the Rome Treaty. On the one hand, this solution does not conflict art. 98 with art. 27 StICC[419]. If art. 98 concerns relations with States not part of the Statute there is no problem of understanding what relevance should be attributed to art. 27. On the other hand, and more generally, the thesis that a third State must be understood as a State not part of the Treaty does not end up precisely in resolving the conflict with art. 98, to attribute to art. 27 a scope that transcends the exercise of jurisdiction by affecting this rule on relations between States in matters of cooperation.

The question is therefore whether and when ICC bodies can ask the States Parties to arrest and surrender an organ of a State that is not part of the Statute. In other words, the question arises as to whether the fact that ICC can exercise its jurisdiction over the Sudanese President Al Bashir. This also means that States Parties are required to arrest and surrender the accused to ICC at the request of the latter or if instead the immunity obligations imposed on States Parties to the Treaty should preclude ICC bodies from the power to formulate such applications.

As in part emerged from the analysis of the relevant practice, the major conflicts between African and ICC States regarding cooperation have focused precisely on the interpretation of art. 98 (1), and on the choice between the options just illustrated. As seen, ICC has always demanded the arrest and surrender of Al Bashir from the States. It has already been highlighted, however, that the thesis which excludes the effects of art. 98 (1) leveraging on customary international immunity law[420] a different solution has been replaced over time which attributes

---

[418]W.A. SCHABAS, The international criminal court. A commentary to the Rome statute, op. cit.,

[419]O. BEKOU, The International Criminal Court, op. cit.,

[420]Moreover, the possible customary nature of the irrelevance of the official qualification for the proceedings before the international courts concerns the possible exercise of jurisdiction by ICC, but does not seem to be able to produce effects on the scope of art. 98, par. 2 and on the possibility therefore that a State arrests and delivers to ICC an organ of a third State. In other words, the arrest and surrender are acts of the State that can break the privileges accorded to some organs of foreign States must be kept distinct from the subsequent eventuality that the jurisdiction of an international court exercises over those individuals. See in argument for further analysis: D. TLADI, The international criminal court and the duty to arrest and surrender. The case of Omar Al-Bashir in South Africa, in

a decisive role to the effects produced by Resolution n.1593(2005) of SC. One of the effects of the Resolution would be to remove any immunity of the bodies of the States concerned by the SC referral.

According to some reconstructions this removal would be the result of an interpretation of Resolution n.1593 (2005) which takes into account the purpose and object of the decision itself. The activation of ICC by SC would in fact be aimed at bringing to justice the perpetrators of the ongoing crimes in Darfur[421]. To this end, it is argued that the foundation of Chapter VII of SC action would have the effect of making the ICC Statute applicable to Sudan, placing it in a situation analogous to that of a State Party[422]. It should then be concluded that if Sudan cannot invoke the immunity of President Al Bashir then States Parties cannot invoke article 98 (1) as a ground to delay or refusal the execution of the Court's request fro assistance and surrender.

On the contrary, according to a different view, the refusal to surrender the Sudanese president opposed to ICC by some States Parties of the Statute would be from this point of view fully legitimate. In fact, SC Resolution would not exempt ICC from compliance with art. 98 (1) and the need to obtain the waiver of Sudan's immunity in order to request a State Party to arrest and surrender Al Bashir. The referral of SC would only be a mechanism provided by StICC to activate ICC jurisdiction, which "does not and cannot turn a State not Party to the Statute into a State Party"[423]. In other words, the attribution to ICC jurisdiction over a given situation "does not imply that national judicial authorities are permitted to do whatever an international Court asked them to do" and this above all "if that Court has been established by virtue of a Treaty, like ICC and therefore its authority derives from an instrument based upon consent"[424].

In fact and as already noted, SC referral, far from making Sudan part of the Rome Statute, has the effect of activating ICC's jurisdiction over a specific situation in which international crimes have been committed. Furthermore, on the one hand, art. 27 justifies the exercise of ICC jurisdiction despite the immunity of the Sudanese president. On the other, Sudan cannot invoke the immunity of Al bashir to oppose the requests directly addressed to it by ICC organs not because

---

Zeitschrift für Internationale Strafgerichtsdogmatik, 10, 2015, pp. 498ss.

[421]N. BOSCHIERO, The ICC judicial finding on non-cooperation against the DRC and no immunity for Al-Bashir based on UNSC Resolution 1593, in Journal of International Criminal Justice, 13, 2015, pp. 654ss.

[422]N. BOSCHIERO, The ICC judicial finding on non-cooperation against DRC and no immunity for Al-Bashir based on UNSC Resolution 1593, op. cit., pp. 645ss, which the author stated that: "(...) As Resolution n.1593 has not intented to established a cooperation legal framework (applicable to Sudan all other States) different from that resulting from the ICC's Statute, it seems self-evident that SC intended simply to exercise its Chapter VII powers by relying on a pre-established legal system, applying the essential features of ICC and ICC Statute (...)".

[423]O. BEKOU, The International Criminal Court, op. cit.,

[424]N. BOSCHIERO, The ICC judicial finding on non-cooperation against DRC and no immunity for Al-Bashir based on UNSC Resolution 1593, op. cit.,

of an obligation deriving from the Statute and not even as a direct and automatic consequence of the referral due to the effect of the obligation of cooperation put in Sudan by SC through the Resolution n.1593 (2005).

As for the States Parties, as mentioned above, the request for arrest or surrender of the Sudanese President can be made by ICC only if does not conflict with the other international obligations of those States towards Sudan or if the latter has renounced immunity. As has been pointed out elsewhere, it is difficult to believe that this renunciation took place or that you know an implicit effect of SC Resolutions. However, it remains to be understood and this is the bone of contention whether SC Resolution may have undermined the immunity obligations of States towards Sudan.

In this regard, it could be argued that the obligation of full cooperation established by SC towards Sudan also implies an obligation for all the UN Member States to deny immunity to the organs of that State, if the recognition of immunity constitutes an obstacle to cooperation between Sudan and ICC. No part of the device seems to support this conclusion in a certain way. Neither through the positions expressed by States during the adoption of Resolution n.1593 (2005) is it possible to reconstruct a will in this sense of SC. The teleological interpretation of Resolution on which some have relied on to support the immateriality of Al Bashir's immunity for the cooperation of States with the ICC appears to force too much the scope of SC decision. The latter seems to affect only the relationship between ICC and Sudan. Relations between States Parties to the Statute and Sudan remain regulated by art. 98 StICC. Such a situation could only be changed through a SC Resolution aimed at clearly placing an obligation to cooperate with ICC which implies for the States a lack of recognition of the immunity of the Sudanese President. In this case due to the effect of art. 103 of the UN Charter, the States Parties could not invoke art. 98 of the Statute to escape ICC's request.

The question of the effects of Resolution n.1593 (2005) on States' cooperation obligations remains highly controversial, however. Over the past few years, indeed, following the ICC's pronouncements and its insistence in trying to obtain the cooperation of States Parties and SC for the arrest and surrender of Al Bashir, several States have had the opportunity to take position on the extent of the obligations imposed on Sudan through Resolution n.1593 (2005) and the effects of these on the immunities of the Sudanese organs.

Some SC Member States have made a clear opposition to the hypothesis of a lapse of immunity rules as a consequence of Resolution n.1593 (2005). In several sessions of SC concerning the situation in Sudan, the Sudan federation stressed for example that the obligations of cooperation with ICC, deriving from SC resolutions must be respected "while complying with norms of international law in the matter of immunity of senior state officials"[425]. More recently and in a manner within SC, "the obligation to cooperate, as set forth in Resolution n.1593 (2005), does not mean that the norms of international law governing the immunity

[425]UN Doc. S/PV.6887, 13 December 2012, p. 16.

of government officials of those States not party of the Rome Statute can be repealed and presuming the contrary is unacceptable"[426]. Even among African SC Member States there are those who have expressed similar positions. For example, Egypt strongly argued that ICC "must respect the provisions of international law relating to the immunity accorded to Heads of State and other senior officials during their tenure"[427].

Other States on the contrary have hinted that the cooperation obligations of States Parties to the Statute are not hindered by the immunity of the Sudanese president. France, Sweden and United Kingdom, for example, said in similar terms concerned that President Al Bashir and others indicted by the Court are able to continue to travel internationally, including States Parties to the Rome Statute"[428].

The United States also believe that is "unaccceptable that president Al-Bashir still travels and receives a warm welcome from certain authors of the world"[429] and Ukraine invites all States involved "to fully comply with all their commitments and obligations without exception and ensure full cooperation with ICC"[430].

In light of this brief analysis of states positions, it is not surprising how regrettable the inertia of SC in the face of the multiple and pressing requests for intervention from ICC organs and in particular from ICC Prosecutor[431]. The clear contrast that emerges within SC also particularly highlights how controversial the matter is and how much this derives from the peculiarity of art. 98. Indeed, this provision seems to represent an extremely complex attempt at integration between two different models which inspired the statutory regulatory framework for cooperation[432]. Art. 98 protects against interstate relations by giving expression to

---

[426]UN Doc. S/PV.7963, 8 June 2017, p. 12.

[427]Also the delegate of Egypt sustains that "we reject any action taken against any African country under the pretext that it has not complied with its obligations under the Rome Statute or on the basis of its non-cooperation pursuant to SC Resolution n.1593 (2005)". See, UN Doc. S/PV.7963, 8 June 2017, p. 8. Alternatively and as already partially seen, some States have invoked the suspension of the proceedings against Al Bashir through an exercise by SC of the deferral power.

[428]These are the words of the Swedish representative but in similar terms see France (p. 139 and United Kingdom (p. 5).

[429]UN Doc. S/PV.7963, 8 June 2017, p. 9.

[430]UN Doc. S/PV.7963, 8 June 2017, p. 10.

[431]In addition to the numerous and already mentioned reports SC on the situation in Sudan, the statements made within SC itself in occasion of the meetings just mentioned. See: UN Doc. S/PV.6887, 13 December 2012, pp. 1-3 and UN Doc. S/PV.7963, 8 June 2017, pp. 1ss.

[432]Many have pointed out that in StICC two different models of cooperation coexist: The horizontal or interstate and the vertical or supranational. In principle, in the first there is no general and absolute obligation of cooperation, the latter is rather the result of possible agreements between States. According to which the functioning of the ad hoc tribunals is inspired, States have an unconditional obligation to assist the Court and execute the requests addressed to them. See for further analysis in argument: B. SWART, G. SLUITER,

a so-called model horizontal. More precisely, the provision is aimed at preserving the relations between the States Parties of the Statute, to which ICC may request the delivery of individuals suspected of the Commission of international crimes and States not part of the Statute whose organs enjoy a series of immunity that art. 98 takes care to safeguard. On the other hand, the rule is part of a system of rules relating to cooperation between States and ICC which appears instead inspired by the opposite model, the vertical one which ends up centralizing in ICC the power to decide what cooperation obligations it can impose on States. In light of art. 98 the decision about the compatibility between the requests of ICC and the rules on immunity in relations between States Parties and third States rests in ICC[433].

Ultimately, the Statute through art. 98 has already protected States from the risk of incurring liability for violations of a series of particularly important rules, such as those relating to immunity. The importance of these norms derives from their politically sensitive nature: They are placed to protect state sovereignty. In fact, immunity rules represent a fundamental prerequisite for keeping diplomatic channels open between States and, more generally, for guaranteeing the stability of international relations and therefore peace and international security. Just think of the impact that the arrest of an incumbent head of State could have. The power vacuum caused by the removal of the highest representatives of the State or the isolation caused by the inability to maintain diplomatic ties with other States can cause greater instability than that already produced by past or ongoing violence. The importance of maintaining peace and political sensitivity, and therefore of the decision to impose on States the arrest of a head of State or government in office, seems all the more reason to require action (and consequent assumption of responsibility) of SC[434]. The latter should provide

---

The international criminal court and international criminal co-operation, in H.A.M. VON HEBEL, J.G. LAMMERS, J. SCHUKKING, Reflections on the international criminal court: Essays in honor of Adriaan Bos, T.M.C. Asser Press, The Hague, 1999, pp. 92ss.

[433]There are those who have stressed the problems that this can pose in terms of the international responsibility of States Parties. See in argument: M. BENZIG, Bilateral non-surrender agreements and article 98 of the statute of the international criminal court: An exercise in the law of treaties, in Max Planck Yearbook of United Nations Law, 8, 2004, pp. 200. G. SLUITER, International adjudication and the collection of evidence: Obligations of states, Antwerp, Oxford, New York, 2002, pp. 172ss. H.A.M. VON HEBEL, J.G. LAMMERS, J. SCHUKKING, Reflections on the international criminal court: Essays in honor of Adriaan Bos, T.M.C. Asser Press, The Hague, 1999, pp. 432ss.

[434]It is clear that the current situation is significantly frustrating the repressive action of ICC for the crimes committed in Darfur. However, it should also be noted that the protection granted to heads of State and government and foreign ministers lapses when the body in question has ceased to perform its function and therefore that the personal immunity enjoyed by these bodies does not precludes the possibility of proceeding to arrest and surrender these individuals to ICC. It is true that these would still be protected by the rules on functional immunity but the evolution of customary international law in this area seems to be able to more easily lead to affirming the formation of an exception in the case of Commission of international crimes. The subject is extremely complex and it is impossible here to trace the relevant practice and the variety of positions taken by the

clear indications of the States of behavior to be followed with respect to organ immunities. In view of a correct division of functions and in consideration of the uncertainty that characterizes the issue examined here in the light of the Rome Statute, ICC should instead appear particularly cautious in order to avoid excessive politicization of its jurisdictional activity and to create tensions difficult to heal in their relations with States in the field of cooperation and mutual legal assistance.

Courts and in doctrine. To shed light, however, on the different approach to the two forms of immunity, a Resolution of the Institut de Droit International on the subject can be recalled where it is stated that: "Non immunity from jurisdiction other than personal immunity in accordance with international law applies with regard to international crimes". See: Institut de Droit International, Resolution on the immunity from jurisdiction of the state and of persons who act on behalf of the State in case of international crimes, Rapporteur: Lady Fox, Naples session, 2009, art. III, par. 1 moreover, the latest work on the special rapporteur of the ILC comes to similar conclusions Escobar Hernàndez, Fifth report on immunity of state officials from foreign criminal jurisdiction, 14 June 2016, A/CN.4/701, pp. 15ss: "(..) e) with one exception, States have supported full or absolute immunity ratione personae for the Head of State, the Head of government and the Minister for Foreign Affairs, with no exception even for international crimes, during their term of office and f) however, a large number of States have supported the existence of various exceptions to immunity ratione materiae, the main one being the Commission of the most serious crimes of concern to the international community as a whole (...)".

Chapter 4
Security Council powers in relation to the crime of aggression

1. The crime of aggression in StICC. Reference to UN Charter

Another regulatory element contained in StICC that expresses the needs to link SC activity and that of ICC, concerns the crime of aggression. It is not possible to retrace here the long and complex path that led to the definition of this crime. However, it can be remembered in general that one of the reasons behind the difficulty of including such criminal conduct among those subject to ICC jurisdiction was precisely the lack of a shared and sufficiently precise definition of the criminally relevant behaviors and of the state acts underlying the individual crime[435].

A further element of complexity, also at the origin of the obstacles to the inclusion of the crime of aggression in the ICC ratione materiae competence, concerns the relationships between individual and state responsibility. The crime of aggression, by definition, the expression of a decision taken by the leaders of the political or military apparatus of a State also presupposes a responsibility for the latter. To tell the truth, other international crimes also tend to be committed by an individual-body therefore attributable to the State of belonging of the author of the illegal conduct and in any case present a collective and, so to speak, political dimension: The systematic attack on crimes against the humanity, the planning of war crimes, the intent to target a group as such in the case of genocide. No other international crime has, however, as it will now be better said, a presupposition and condition of the same evidence of individual criminal conduct, a state offense.

The origins of a particularly close relationship between individual and state responsibility for aggression are already clearly visible in art. 16 of the project of crimes against peace and humanity drawn up by ILC in 1996. In light of that provision, in fact, an individual would have been held responsible for the crime of aggression if "as a leader or organizer, participates in or orders the planning, preparation, initiation or waging of aggression committed by a State"[436].

---

[435]B. BONAFÉ, The relationship between state and individual responsibility for international crimes, Martinus Nijhoff Publishers, Leiden, Boston, 2009.

[436]Draft Code of crimes against the peace and security of mankind, in Yearbook of the International Law Commission, 1996, vol. II (part two).

In this perspective, in short, a necessary condition for the existence of individual crime was the commission of an act of aggression by a State. Moreover, also in light of the aforementioned art. 23 of the draft Statute, drawn up by ILC in 1994, the individual crime of aggression presupposes that a State had been held to have committed aggression[437].

Given these assumptions it was difficult to imagine that the Rome Statute did not provide for this particular crime a connection with the UN Charter and that the relationship between the two forms of responsibility was not made explicit in any way. It is almost superfluous to remember that art. 39 of the UN Charter grants SC the power to investigate interstate attacks. For this reason, in addition to the need for a general connection with the provisions of UN Charter, the most specific emerged and here it is of extreme interest and importance to connect the jurisdictional activity of ICC inherent in SC.

Since no shared solution was found at the Rome Conference on the modalities of such coordination between ICC and SC, art. 5 (2) StICC[438], after having precisely ordered that the exercise of jurisdiction over the crime of aggression be postponed to the future adoption of a definition of the crime by the determination of the conditions of activation of ICC, limited itself to recommending in completely generic terms, that this provision however, it must be "consistent with the relevant provisions of the UN Charter"[439]. Now, however incidentally it may appear "redundant but not superfluous"[440], it testifies and anticipates the main question still to be resolved, namely, the need to coordinate the ICC's judicial activity in repressing the individual crime of aggression with the competence of SC to ascertain the commission of a state act of aggression.

Even more than the difficulties related to the definition of the crime of aggression were precisely the conditions of prosecution of the crime, also referred to in art. 5 (2), which led to the decision to postpone the exercise of ICC's jurisdiction over the crime of aggression to a future revision of the Statute[441]. In

---

[437]Draft Statute of the international criminal court with commentaries, in Yearbook of the International Law Commission, 1994, vol. II, part two, 1994, pp. 44ss.

[438]O. BEKOU, The International Criminal Court, op. cit.,

[439]O. BEKOU, The International Criminal Court, op. cit.,

[440]B. BONAFÉ, The relationship between state and individual responsibility for international crimes, op. cit.,

[441]Report of the Preparatory Committee on the establishment of an international criminal court, vol. I, UN Doc. A/51/22, 1996, p. 19. Many Arab and African States already suggested adopting the definition of aggression contained in Resolution n.3314 of 1974 while other States (such as Germany) suggested a definition that best suited the requirements of penal repression, as far as the role of SC is concerned, however the positions seemed even more distinct. See: Report of the ad hoc Committee on the establishment of an international criminal court, A/50/223, 1995, pp. 13-15, it is also evident that some States believed that the crime of aggression was already at least in one of its existing essential nuclei. The fact that the crime of aggression is provided for in the statutes among those subject to ICC jurisdiction ratione materiae but that its actual and concrete persecution was postponed to a future revision intended to define its content and

other words, it was a question of determining to what extent the repression of the crime of aggression by ICC could be conditioned by the powers attributed to SC for the purpose of maintaining peace and in particular of the ascertainment that that body is entitled to in the light of art. 30. All debates relating to the conditions of prosecution of the crime of aggression essentially revolve around the degree of autonomy which with respect to any assessment of SC should have been guaranteed to the Prosecutor for the purpose of opening the investigations and to the other ICC bodies for the purpose of attributing individual criminal liability for this particular criminal conduct.

2. The debates preceding the adoption of the Statute

The debates prior to the adoption of the Rome Statute offer some indications of what were the terms of the issue that we intend to address here. In particular, with regard to the repression of the crime of aggression, it can only start from the repeatedly called art. 23 of the Statute of the ILC Project of 1994. Par. 2 of this provision stipulated that a case relating to the crime of aggression could not be subject to ICC jurisdiction "unless SC has first determined that a State has committed the act of aggression which is the subject of the complaint. The initial orientation of ILC was therefore to attribute to SC a preliminary and unavoidable competence to determine the commission of an act of aggression by a State's party in order to proceed with the repression of individual crime[442]. Within ILC there were opposite or at least skeptical positions with respect to this solution[443]. Several States then opposed an exclusive competence of the political body in determining the existence of a state of aggression. States opposed to such an incisive role of SC rather claimed the need to guarantee the autonomy and independence of ICC and therefore to recognize the latter's power to proceed even in the absence of an assessment by the political body[444]. It can be said in general

---

conditions of admissibility has usually made the report speak. To this period so to speak of transition of dormant jurisdiction over the crime of aggression see the expression of P. KIRSCH, D. ROBINSON, Reaching agreement at the Rome conference, in A. CASSESE, P. GAETA, J.R.W.D. JONES, The Rome statute of the international criminal court. A commentary, Oxford University Press, Oxford, 2002, pp. 68ss.

442See, Report of the international law Commission on the work of its forty-sixth session, UN Doc. A/49/10, 2 May-22 July 1994, pp. 86: "(...) any criminal responsibility of an individual for an act or crime of aggression necessarily presupposes that a state had been held to have committed aggression, and such a finding would be for the Security Council acting in accordance with Chapter VII of the UN Charter to make". For further analysis see: M. SCHUSTER, The Rome statute and the crimes of aggression. A gordian knot in search of a sword, in Criminal Law Forum, 14 (1), 2003, pp. 36ss. T. MERON, Defining aggression for the international criminal court, in Suffolk Transnational Law Review, 25, 2001, pp. 13ss.

443See the positions of Pellet and Bennouna, in ILC Yearbook 1994, vol. I, 2358 meeting, p. 209 and 2361, meeting, p. 227.

444See in particular Bahrein (UN Doc. A/C.6/49/SR17, p. 4) and the Netherlands (UN Doc.

terms that the notion of aggression[445] reflects the inability made by ILC to "divorce form its political nature".

The divergences that emerged during the Commission's work were then repeated in the subsequent Preparatory Commission work, with a clear favor still for a rather marked protection of SC prerogatives with respect to the guarantees of independence and autonomy of ICC (art.10 of the project). A full option included two distinct hypotheses. By virtue of the first, the ICC could not have exercised its jurisdiction only if the SC had expressly denied that the situation brought to the attention of ICC could be classified as aggression. In light of the second hypothesis, however, ICC jurisdiction would always have depended on an explicit assessment made by SC on the basis of Chapter VII of the UN Charter, aimed at determining the commission of an act of aggression by a State[446]. In a second proposal, in more general terms, it provided for the compulsory nature of any finding made by SC on the commission or not of an act of aggression by a State. However, it was not clear in this different scenario what would have happened in the absence of SC determinations.

Then there was a paragraph, aimed at protecting the jurisdictional activity of ICC which sanctioned the principle according to which any decision of SC “shall not be interpreted as in any way affecting the independence of the Court in its determination of the criminal responsibility of the person concerned"[447]. To tell the truth, this statement appears to be aimed at affirming an obvious principle of independence of the judicial function in ascertaining individual responsibilities. However, it does not seem to guarantee an autonomy of the Court with respect to SC in the event of an overlap of the action of the two bodies. It is quite evident in fact that if SC has the power to limit or initiate the exercise of ICC's jurisdiction over the crime of aggression, then preventing its activation through a negative determination about the existence of an act of aggression by part of a State it wants to subordinating the exercise of jurisdiction to a prior positive assessment regarding the commission of a crime, ICC independence to prosecute criminally responsible individuals is subject to the political assessment made by SC, which has in fact the power to preclude the action of the jurisdictional organ.

The divergences that emerged on the definition of the crime of aggression and on the role that SC should have played in the repression of the same ICC

A/C.49/SR/SR.17, p. 18), but also the rather critical attitudes of Greece (UN Doc. A/C.6/49/SR.17, p. 18), France /UN Doc. A/C.6/49/SR.19, p. 9), Israel (UN Doc. A/C.6/49/SR.20, p. 6) and Chile/UNDoc. A/C.6/SR.21, p. 6).

[445]A.C. CARPENTER, The international criminal court and the crime of aggression, in Nordic Journal of International Law, 64, 1995, pp. 234ss.

[446]Preparatory Committee Draft Statute n.110, par. 4 in its first option reads: 4. option 1 (Accompanied of or directly related to (an act) (a crime) of aggression (referred to in art. 5) may (not) be brought (under this Statute) unless the SC has first (determined) (and formally decided) that the act of a State is the subject of the complaint (is) (is not) an act of aggression (Chapter VII of the UN Charter).

[447]A.C. CARPENTER, The international criminal court and the crime of aggression, op. cit.,

reappeared, as a part mentioned also at the Rome Conference. To mark a decisive moment of the debate was an interesting proposal from Cameroon that while admitting the necessary pre-eminence of SC in ascertaining the crime of aggression was aimed at guaranteeing a margin of discretion to ICC action at least in the case of inertia of the political body. With this proposal it was essentially suggested that before ICC exercises its jurisdiction over the crime of aggression, "SC shall determine the existence of aggression in accordance with the pertinent provisions of the UN Charter"[448]. However, and herein lies the most interesting element especially for the influence it will have in subsequent developments in the matter, it was envisaged that SC had delayed to make its own assessment on the commission of a state act of aggression following a request by the Prosecutor to do so. The latter could have initiated "an investigation for the purpose of establishing whether a crime of aggression within the meaning of the present statute exists"[449].

As mentioned at the Rome Conference, it was decided to postpone the matter to a future revision of the Statute and a special Preparatory Commission was established for this purpose[450]. The impression of many was that the ICC's jurisdiction over aggression crime "was still born". And according to some, its birth would never have happened.

3. The work following the entry into force of the Statue and the first review Conference

Starting in 2002, the Assembly of States Parties brought together the work of the Preparatory Commission into a special working group. It was the work of the latter body that laid the foundations for the subsequent debate that took place in the first statute review Conference. It is therefore appropriate to briefly analyze some of the proposals put forward by the States at that time, always naturally with a view to assessing the degree of autonomy that was intended to leave to ICC bodies with respect to SC decisions.

The motions of some States aimed at limiting the role of SC seem to be of particular interest, providing for the possibility of autonomous although limited ICC action or even the involvement of other UN bodies. A first hypothesis put forward by France and Portugal suggested that ICC could exercise its jurisdiction as well as in the event that the SC had already pronounced in this sense pursuant

---

[448]UN diplomatic conference of plenipotentiaries on the establishment of an international criminal court, Rome, 15 June-17 July 1998, official records, vol. I, UN Doc. A/CONF.183/C.1/L.39.

[449]A.C. CARPENTER, The international criminal court and the crime of aggression, op. cit.,

[450]He was assigned to this body to draw up a series of proposals for a provision on aggression, including the definition and elements of crimes of aggression and the conditions under which the ICC shall exercise its jurisdiction with regard to this crime. See, par. 7 of the Resolution adopted by the UN Diplomatic Conference of plenipotentiaries on the establishment of an international criminal court, 17 July 1998.

to art. 39 also following a request for assessment from the same Court and addressed to SC, which was disregarded for a period of 12 months[451]. An idea that suggested by the two States that took up the Cameroonian proposal and destined as already anticipated to a certain success. Unlike another hypothesis perhaps too ambitious submitted to the working group by Bosnia-Herzegovina, New Zealand and Romania which contemplated in an evident attempt to limit the role of SC, the involvement of GA and ICJ[452]. According to this proposal, always SC had not pronounced on the possible aggression within 12 months from the request of ICC or had not decided to endorse the turnaround of ICC using the power provided by art. 15 StICC[453], the ICJ could have notified the GA of the situation before the Court and invite it to request to it in accordance with article 96 of the existence or otherwise of an act of aggression by the State concerned[454]. Only in the event that the opinion of the ICJ recommended an action by ICC, could the latter have proceeded in ascertaining individual liability.

The results of the numerous discussions that took place within the working group[455] then merged into three distinct documents, commonly called chairman's papers. These works highlight a certain convergence of states in relation to the definition of crimes while they still present different options regarding the UN organ to which the competence should have been attributed to carry out this assessment. In other words, discussions continued on whether to allow the Prosecutor to act even in the absence of an assessment, carried out by a body external to the statute system relating to the commission of an act of aggression by a State. In the event that it was wished to preclude this possibility, it remained to be decided which body between SC, GA and ICJ should be invested with this competence[456].

---

[451]Working group on the crime of aggression, proposal submitted by Greece and Portugal, PCNICC/2000/WGCA/DP.5, 28 November 2000.

[452]D. LIAKOPOULOS, La tutela cautelare nella Corte internazionale di giustizia. Aspetti processuali e comparati, ed. Amon, Firenze, 2012.

[453]W.A. SCHABAS, The international criminal court. A commentary to the Rome statute, op. cit.,

[454]Working group on the crime of aggression, proposal submitted by Bosnia and Herzegovina, New Zealand and Romania, PCNICC/2001/WGCA/DP.1, 23 February 2001.

[455]Assembly of States Parties, special working group on the crime of aggression, 30 November-14 December 2007, New York, informal inter-sessional meeting of the special working group on the crime of aggression, ICC-ASP/6/SWGCA/INF.1, 25 July 2007.

[456]See the diverse options contained in the discussion paper on the crime of aggression proposed by the Chairman, ICC-ASP/5/SWGCA/2, 1st February 2007; Discussion paper on the crime of aggression proposed by the Chairman, ICC-ASP/6/SWGCA/2, 14 May 2008 and discussion paper on the crime of aggression proposed by the Chairman, ICC-ASP/SWGCA/INF.1, Annex, 19 February 2009. For further analysis see: O. SOLERA, The definition of the crime of aggression: Lessons not learned, in Case Western Reserve Journal of International Law, 42, 2010, pp. 808ss. T. LAVERS, Aggression, intervention and powerful feminist methodologies on peace and security issues, in Amsterdam Law Forum, 5 (2), 2013, pp. 127ss.

The whole debate sheds more light on the real issue being disputed, namely whether the SC should be given a monopoly, so to speak, in assessing the commission of aggression between States or, instead, we can imagine that this task is shared with other UN bodies or even at least for the purposes of the criminal repression left to the decision-making autonomy of an international tribunal established through a treaty. Despite the widespread skepticism about the concrete possibility of reaching a shared solution regarding the conditions for exercising ICC jurisdiction, the first statute review Conference held in Kampala (Uganda) in 2010 marks the historic compromise[457], which opens the way for the permanent exercise of jurisdiction over this international crime by the permanent criminal court. The same Resolution adopted at the review Conference in 2010 stipulated that jurisdiction over the crime of aggression could only be activated if after the 1st January 2018, a decision had been taken to that effect in the Assembly of States, part of the majority required to amend the Statute (two thirds). In addition, ICC could have prosecuted the crime only one year after thirty States Parties to the Rome Treaty ratified or accepted the amendment. Thirty ratifications have been reached and in December of the last year, the Assembly of States Parties decided to activate ICC's jurisdiction over this particular crime as of 17 July 2018[458]. It is necessary to examine what changes were introduced following the review Conference.

The document presented in Kampala, the so-called Conference Room Paper[459], proposed the elimination of art. 5 (2) and the inclusion of three different provisions. Art. 8 bis, concerning the definition of the crime of aggression, art. 15 bis relating to the conditions of prosecution against this crime in the event of a referral of a State Party or of an action proper to the Prosecutor and concerning the possibility of the referral being exercised by SC.

It is worth mentioning that art. 8 bis (1) defines the crime of aggression as "the planning, preparation initiation or execution by a person effectively in a position to exercise control over or to direct the political or military action of a State, of an act of aggression which by its character, gravity and scale constitutes a manifest violation of the UN Charter"[460]. The conduct that can generate individual responsibility for the crime of aggression therefore presupposes, as had

---

[457]N. BLOKKER, C. KRESS, A consensus agreement on the crime of aggression: Impressions from Kampala, in Leiden Journal of International Law, 20, 2010, pp. 890ss. The revision Conference was convened on par. 1 of art. 121 which provides for the possibility of proposing amendments to the statutes at the end of the seven years from its entry into force.

[458]Assembly of States Parties, Draft Resolution proposed by the Vice-Presidents of the Assembly activation of the jurisdiction of the Court over the crimes of aggression, ICC-ASP/16/l.10, 14 December 2017.

[459]Conference Room Paper on the crime of aggression, Doc. RC/WGCA/1, 25 May 2010. P. WEBB, International judicial integration and fragmentation, Oxford University Press, Oxford, 2013. H.H. KOH, T.F. BUCHWALD, The crime of aggression: The United States perspective, in American Journal of International Law, 109 (2), 2015, pp. 260ss.

[460]P. WEBB, International judicial integration and fragmentation, op. cit.,

already emerged in previous attempts to define this criminal case, an act of aggression by the State for which the individual acts[461]. Art. 8 bis (2) provides for a list of which state conduct may constitute a prerequisite for the suppression of the crime.

With regard to the conditions of prosecution, the proposals contained in the document have shown all the complexity and the composite nature of the debate and the positions taken by the States. The final document distinguishes two different situations as just highlighted: The activation of the jurisdiction upon notification of a State Party or on the initiative of the Prosecutor on one side and the referral of SC on the other. It is obvious that the latter case does not pose particular problems in principle. If the SC reports a situation to ICC, the assessment of individual responsibilities is functional and complementary to the action of the political body itself. As for the first two hypotheses, however, the reporting of a State Party or the action proper motu of the Prosecutor element of extreme importance of the historical Resolution adopted on the evening of 11 June 2010 in Kampala is the fact that the assessment of SC is not indispensable condition for ICC to exercise its jurisdiction over the crime of aggression. Such a solution undoubtedly represents a success of the majority of the States towards the permanent members of SC and appeared to the majority to guarantee a greater probability that the crime of aggression will actually be pursued in the future. Even more if we take into account the known reticence of SC to pronounce on the existence of a situation of aggression. Such a solution undoubtedly represents a success of the majority of the States towards the permanent members of SC and appeared to the majority to guarantee a greater probability that the crime of aggression will actually be pursued in the future. Even more if we take into account the known reticence of SC to pronounce on the existence of a situation of aggression. However, we cannot ignore the rather evident fact that this solution presents greater possibilities of generating opportunities for conflict between the judicial and political body.

Specifically, in light of paragraphs 6, 7 and 8 of the new art. 15 bis of the Rome Statute, the Prosecutor before starting an investigation for a crime of genocide proper motu or on the basis of a report by a State must verify that SC has carried out an investigation according to Chapter VIII of the UN Charter, of the Commission of a state act of aggression. If SC does not make this determination during the six months following the notification (and the transmission of all the relevant documents) to the UN General-Secretary on behalf of ICC regarding the situation on which the opening of the procedure is expected, the Prosecutor can independently carry out the investigation, subject to an authorization from the pre-trial division and unless SC decides to use its referral power.

Despite the compromise reached, it is appropriate to recall here some important limits on the exercise of jurisdiction over the crime of aggression by

---

[461]The amendment to the Statute also provides for a fairly high threshold of severity for the inter-state infringement, as this should represent a manifest violation of the UN Charter.

ICC. In fact, when the ICC action is activated, through the exercise of the referral power of SC there are no distinctions between States that are part or not of the Statute, if instead the investigations are undertaken precisely by the Prosecutor or on the impulse of a State Party, ICC cannot exercise its jurisdiction over a crime committed by a citizen or on the territory of a State not part of the Statute[462]. Finally, as regards the States Parties, they can decide through a specific declaration filed by the Registrar not to accept ICC competence for the sole crime of aggression[463].

In conclusion to the most important question of the entire debate on the role of SC with respect to the repression of the crime of aggression, that is whether or not an organ should be recognized as an organ in the assessment of the existence of an aggression must be given a negative answer. From the point of view of ICC this is reflected in a considerable degree of autonomy of the Prosecutor in proceeding even in the absence of an assessment by the political body. On the other hand, it had already been recognized on several occasions that the primary responsibility attributed to SC of art. 24 of the UN Charter for the maintenance of peace and security must not be considered exclusive and that some functions in this area can also be exercised by other political or judicial bodies. A reading in this sense had already emerged in the General Assembly during the adoption of the Resolution uniting for peace. In that particular context, it was found that art. 10 of the UN Charter gives the General Assembly the power to discuss any questions or any matters within the scope of the present Charter in particular if SC does not exercise the powers attributed to it[464].

Furthermore, in light of articles 12 and 14 of the UN Charter[465], GA can make recommendations regarding the measures to be adopted for a peaceful settlement of any controversy that could prejudice the peaceful relations between the States except in the case in which SC itself is dealing with the question. In short, a residual and secondary responsibility of the general assembly in matters of maintaining peace and security is now considered well established.

Similar reasoning can be made towards the Courts. The same ICJ as it is

---

[462]See par. 5 of art. 15 bis.

[463]See par. 4 of art. 5 bis.

[464]Resolution n.377 (V) (1950), Uniting for peace (3 November 1950) this is the most well-known and relevant step: "if SC because of lack of unanimity of the permanent members, fails to exercise its primary responsibility for the maintenance of international peace and security in any case where appears to be a threat to the peace, breach of the peace, or act of aggression, the GA shall consider the matter immediately with a view to making appropriate recommendations to members for collective measures, including in the case of a breach of the peace or act of aggression the use of armed force when necessary to maintain or restore international peace and security. If not in session at the time the GA shall therefore meet in emergency special session within twenty-four hours of the request. Such emergency special session may be called if requested by SC on the vote of any members (nine since 1965) or by a majority of the UN members (...)".

[465]W.A. SCHABAS, The international criminal court. A commentary to the Rome statute, op. cit.,

known has expressly ruled that the liability provided for by art. 24 "is primary, not exclusive"[466] and on more than one occasion recalled the different roles that a Court and a political body play and affirmed the idea and the principle of the possible parallel exercise of their respective functions[467]. The recognition of an autonomous prerogative of assessment in relation to the Commission of state acts of aggression also seems in line with these reconstructions. On the other hand, while inevitably overlapping the action of SC in the context of the maintenance of international peace and security, the function assigned to ICC maintains its own distinct and precise specificity: The repression of an individual crime.

4. Possible coordination problems between ICC and SC in the repression of the crime of aggression

4.1. Procedural issues: Articles 15a and 15b

The fact that an investigation by SC regarding the Commission of a state act of aggression is not an essential precondition for prosecution undoubtedly represents an important guarantee of autonomy for ICC in the repression of the

---

[466]International Court of Justice, Certain United Nations expenses (article 117, par. 2 of the charter), opinion of 20 July 1962, in ICJ Reports 1962, pp. 163ss. For further analysis see: M. RUDA, Nulidad de los tratados, in Y. DINSTEIN, M. TABORY, international law at a time of perplexity. Essays in Honour of Shabtai Rosenne, ed. Springer, Dordrecht, Boston, London, 1989, pp. 150ss.

[467]International Court of Justice, Military and paramilitary activities in Nicaragua and against Nicaragua (Nicaragua v. United States), par. 95, "the Council has functions of a political nature assigned to it, whereas the Court exercise purely judicial functions. Both organs can therefore perform their separate but complementary functions with respect to the same events"; case concerning the application of the convention on the prevention and repression of the crime of genocide (Bosnia-Herzegovina v. Yugoslavia (Serbia and Montenegro), order of 13 September 1993, in ICJ Reports, par. 33. Armed activities in the territory of Congo (Republic Democratic of Congo v. Uganda), order of 1st July 2000, in ICJ Reports 2000, par. 36. The idea that the ICC could legitimately contribute to determining the situations of aggression, independently of an assessment made by SC, was widely affirmed even before the Rome Conference. See in argument: P. ESCARAMEIA, The ICC and the Security Council on aggression: Overlapping competencies, in M. POLITI, G. NESI, The International Criminal Court: A challenge to impunity, Ashgate Publishing, Aldershot, 2001, pp. 134ss. M.S. STEIN, The Security Council, the international criminal court and the crime of aggression: How exclusive is the Security Council's power to determine aggression?, in Indiana International and Comparative Law Review, 16 (1), 2005, pp. 4ss. N. BLOKKER, A consensus agreement on the crime of aggression: Impressions from Kampala, op. cit., pp. 892ss. S. BARRIGA, C. KRESS, The travaus preparatoires of the crime of aggression, Cambridge University Press, Cambridge, 2012. J. D VAN DER VYVER, Prosecuting the crime of aggression in the ICC, in University of Miami National Security & Armed Conflict Law Review, 2010-2011, 1, pp. 17ss. M. MCCABE, Balancing aggression and compassion in international law: The crime of aggression and humanitarian intervention, in Fordham Law Review, 83 (2), 2014, pp. 999ss. C. MCDOUGALL, The crime of aggression under the Rome statute of the International Criminal Court, Cambridge University Press, Cambridge, 2013, pp. 215ss.

crime of aggression. Compared to other ICC related crimes, however, more and more stringent conditions for exercising jurisdiction are provided for this particular crime[468].

Although not all closely related to the interactions between ICC and SC, these limits to ICC jurisdiction are a clear consequence of the autonomy recognized by the Prosecutor in pursuing the crime of aggression. It is therefore worth mentioning it briefly.

Indeed, as regards the possibility of a report by SC, the changes do not present particular elements of novelty with respect to what is foreseen in relation to the other crimes covered by the ICC's jurisdiction. By virtue of art. 15 ter StICC, SC can exercise its referral power as provided for in art. 13 b) also in relation to the crime of aggression. As emerged during the first chapter, the possibility that SC indicates which crimes it believes have been committed in a given situation does not prevent the ICC bodies from qualifying a certain conduct differently. Similar reasoning can be performed in the event that a SC decision, through which it exercises its power of referral, expressly ascertains the Commission of a state act of aggression. This latter aspect is further highlighted from par. 14 of art 15 ter, which states that the assessment of an act of aggression "by an organ outside the Court shall be without prejudice to its own findings under this Statute"[469]. In particular ICC could decide not to precede in the repression of the crime, believing differently from what hypothetically stated by SC in its report that there has been no state act of aggression or that despite this act has occurred it is not possible to ascertain a corresponding individual liability[470].

As in part anticipated, the differences compared to the conditions of prosecution against the other crimes under ICC jurisdiction emerge instead in the hypotheses of referral of a State Party or of the Prosecutor's action. The amendments made to the Statute provide that ICC cannot exercise its jurisdiction over citizens or crimes committed on the territory of the aggressor State that has previously declare that it does not accept such jurisdictions by lodging a declaration with the register (art. 15 bis (4))[471]. The ICC cannot exercise its jurisdiction over the crime of aggression perpetrated by an upright citizen against the territory of a State Party to the Statute. Similarly, the exercise of ICC jurisdiction over the aggression committed on the territory of a State not part of the Stature by a citizen of a State Party is excluded. These particular limitations which distinguish the extent of ICC jurisdiction over the crime of aggression in relation to the other three categories of crimes in a rather incisive way, do not

[468]It highlights the costs of the choice made in Kampala. C. STAHN, The "end", the "beginning of the end" or the "end of the beginning"? Introducing debates and voices on the definition of aggression, in Leiden Journal of International Law, 23, 2010, pp. 880ss.

[469]P. WEBB, International judicial integration and fragmentation, op. cit.,

[470]In this sense the first comments related to ILC Project of 1994 of the Statute already went. For further details see: A.C. CARPENTER, The international criminal court and the crime of aggression, op. cit., pp. 236ss.

[471]O. BEKOU, The International Criminal Court, op. cit.,

apply in the case of a referral from SC. In practice, if the latter hypothesis is excluded, the ICC can exercise its jurisdiction only when a State Party to the Statute attacks another one.

In general terms, it is evident that with respect to the referral of a State Party or to the own action of the Prosecutor, the activation of ICC by SC envisaged by art. 15b, prefigures exactly as for the other cases of exercise of the power of referral a hypothesis of convergence between the action of the political body and that of the permanent tribunal. It is important to underline, however, that in this case the SC is not required to carry out an assessment of any state aggression that is the basis of its referral. As expected from art. 13 b) in fact, SC can limit itself to reporting a situation in which one of the crimes under ICC jurisdiction has been committed. In short, the time when SC decides to start the Prosecutor's investigations into a specific context of violence, ICC bodies will then ascertain whether the aggression is among the crimes committed.

The main problems of coordination between the SC action and ICC jurisdictional activity evidently arise in the hypotheses provided for by art. 15 bis relating to the referral of a State Party and to the proprio motu of the Prosecutor. As already anticipated, it is clear that having guaranteed an autonomy to ICC in ascertaining the Commission of a state act of aggression as a prerequisite for the corresponding individual crime, is at the origin of possible conflicts between the two organizations in these hypotheses.

In principle, a convergence in the action of the two organs is also possible in the case of referral of a State Part or an action proper to the Prosecutor. The SC could, without exercising its power of referral, explicitly ascertain the Commission of a state act of aggression thus allowing the Prosecutor to proceed with the investigation (art.15 bis (7))[472]. Even in this hypothesis it is possible ICC and SC reach different conclusions. The changes made to the Statute confirm with the same language of art. 15 ter, that ICC is not binding on the assessments made by bodies external to its system (art. 15 bis (9))[473]. It can therefore be imagined that despite the assessment made by SC, the Prosecutor decides not to request the opening of the investigations or this is denied by the pre-trial division. In order to avoid such a scenario of open contrast between ICC and the political body, SC could then choose to exercise its referral power provided by art. 15 ter[474]. As just noted in the exercise of this power, the SC is not required to make any express assessment of the specific state acts of aggression underlying its reporting. He may prefer to initiate investigations on a particular criminal context without exposing himself to a conflict with the ICC as to whether or not an attack by one State is damaging to another.

---

[472]O. BEKOU, The International Criminal Court, op. cit.,

[473]W.A. SCHABAS, The international criminal court. A commentary to the Rome statute, op. cit.,

[474]S. BARRIGA, N. BLOKKER, Conditions for the exercise of jurisdiction based on state referrals and propio motu investigations, in C. KRESS, S. BARRIGA, The crime of aggression: A commentary, Cambridge University Press, Cambridge, 2017, pp. 662ss.

Although the hypothesis is unlikely, one can also ask what happens in the event that SC expressly establishes that in a given context no state act of aggression has been committed. Art. 15 bis does not contemplate this hypothesis since the verification that the Prosecutor is called to perform in relation to SC action concerns the possibility that the latter has made a positive assessment about the Commission of an act of aggression by a State. The provision does not seem to preclude the possibility of ICC proceeding against a crime of aggression even in the face of a clear position taken by SC aimed at denying the assumption of the state act of aggression. In other words, the hypothesis of a negative assessment of SC about the conduct of aggression if they believe, unlike the SC, that a state act of aggression was instead committed.

It is worth pointing out that within art. 15 bis[475], at least two elements seem to balance to a certain extent the absence of any form of control of SC over the ICC's judicial action on aggression. In the first place even if the wording appears superfluous art. 15 bis (8) reminds that the SC can always request the suspension of the investigation or of a proceeding pursuant to art. 16 StICC[476]. Secondly, always with a view to balancing the absence of a filter by SC with respect to ICC action, then the same art. 15 bis (8) entrusts the task of authorizing the opening of investigations with respect to the crime of aggression to the pre-trial division, rather than as foreseen for the other crimes to one of the preliminary chambers.

4.2. Substantial issues: Art. 8 bis

The definition of crime of aggression contained in art. 8 bis largely follows the Resolution n.3314 of 1974, adopted by the UN General Assembly. However, the basic approach of the changes prepared through the review conference and some specific editorial choices mark important differences compared to the definition drawn up at the general meeting.

Art. 8 bis (2) StICC reports with identical letter only art. 3 of the definition contained in Resolution n.3314 of 1974. However, while in the Resolution of GA, state behavior was considered as presumptively constituting aggression in art. 8 bis every single conduct constitutes an act of aggression. In fact, an attempt was made at GA to protect as much as possible the role of SC that could have considered those same conduct not sufficiently serious to configure a hypothesis of state aggression[477]. In the Rome Statute, on the other hand, the

[475]O. BEKOU, The International Criminal Court, op. cit.,

[476]See in argument: C. WENAWESER, Reaching the Kampala compromise: The chair's perspective, in Leiden Journal of International Law, 23 (4), 2010, pp. 888ss.

[477]S.D. MURPHY, The crime of aggression at the international criminal court, in M. WELLER, The oxford handbook of the use of force in international law, Oxford University Press, Oxford, 2015, pp. 542ss. E.P. REALE, Chronicles from Kampala amending the Rome statute, in Revue Internationale de Droit Pénal, 82, 2011, pp. 258ss. P. GRZEBYK, Criminal responsibility for the crime of aggression, op. cit., C. MCDOUGALL, The crime of aggression under the Rome Statute of the International Criminal Court, op. citpp. 258ss.

assessment of the seriousness of the violation of the rules on the use of force as a constituent element of the definition of aggression contained in art. 8 bis (1) is remitted to ICC bodies.

Art. 8 bis also does not contain a provision similar to art. 4 of Resolution n.3314 which recognizes SC power to ascertain that other acts constitute aggression beyond the terms expressly contained in the definition. The inclusion of this part of Resolution n.3314 of 1974 in the Rome Statute would have posed many compatibility problems with the principle of legality. It would have opened the way to the possibility of punishing an individual on the assumption of state conduct qualified by SC as an act of aggression only at a time after the entry into force of the rule[478]. In art. 8 bis, there are also no references to the irrelevance of political, economic, military or other reasons that can be justified by the act of aggression (art. 5 of Resolution n.3314 of 1974) nor is the need to preserve the principle of self-determination of peoples. All these choices mark the attempt to adapt the definition elaborated by the general assembly to the jurisdictional function of ICC. No longer essentially the typical language of the policy-contextual mode of decision making of SC but rather the textual rule based on ICC decision[479]. In other words, the editorial choices made at the review Conference reflect the need for legal certainty and to reduce, as far as possible, the space for political evaluations by the ICC bodies.

Precisely because of the different nature of the functions that perform the assessment that ICC and SC are called to perform in the matter of aggression, it is based on partially distinct legal bases. The DSC, as the Resolution n.3314 of 1974 well points out, enjoys an extremely wide discretion in establishing state acts that may fall into the category of aggression. ICC is required to verify the implementation of one of the specific conduct envisaged by its statutes. This does not detract from the fact that art. 8a StICC is couched in open-ended, valutative language[480]. In this regard, it may be sufficient to remember that the act of aggression underlying the individual crime must by its character, gravity and scale constitute a manifest violation of the UN Charter. These are rather flexible regulatory parameters that are not easy to define and that ultimately imply a judicial choice that can have very significant political repercussions. The point is essentially that as far as art. 8 bis attempting to frame the crime of aggression in a list of determinable conduct the prerequisite for repression in a list of determinable conduct the prerequisite for the criminal repression of that individual behavior remains a state conduct likely to be implemented in the

---

[478]F.P. KING, The crime of aggression: Is it amenable to judicial determination?, in B.S. BROWN, Research handbook on international criminal court, Edward Elgar Publishers, Cheltenham, 2011, pp. 128ss.

[479]W.M. REISMAN, Reflections on the judicialization of the crime of aggression, in The Yale Journal of International Law, 39, 2014, pp. 72ss.

[480]D. SCHEFFER, Amending the crime of aggression under the Rome Statute, in C. KRESS, S. BARRIGA, The crime of aggression: A commentary, Cambridge University Press, Cambridge, 2012, pp. 1480ss.

context of hugely important political-military events.

Beyond these general considerations on the particularly complex role that the ICC will be called upon to play in the suppression of the crime of aggression, a series of coordination problems between the exercise of jurisdiction and SC action can more concretely emerge in the light of the specific content of the assessment and possibly made by SC and the meaning that ICC bodies intend to attribute to that determination.

Some problematic aspects may concern the subjects involved in the act of aggression. It can be imagined that SC, as already happened, condemns an act of armed aggression towards a State without identifying the aggressor State or the relationship existing between the mercenary groups responsible for those conducted with a specific state entity[481]. Art. 8 bis (2) (g) StICC states that in relation to the sending of irregular groups to the territory of a State there must be at least a substantial involvement of the aggressor State. In the absence of a clear assessment of SC relating to the attribution to a State of the illegal conduct configuring the act of aggression it could then be the ICC in full autonomy recognized by the Statute to proceed in this delicate work of identification of the aggressor State and the individuals responsible for the illegal act[482]. Similar difficulties may also arise in relation to the victim of the attack. Art. 8 bis establishes that aggression must be directed against a State. Even in this case, it may happen that SC does not identify the State of these attacks in its assessment of the Commission of a series of acts of aggression. Once again, ICC having satisfied the assumption relating to the determination of SC regarding the Commission of a state act of aggression, could find itself having to identify the victim of aggression in order to be able to determine its jurisdiction over illegal conduct.

Another series of problems can arise in relation to the content of the specific illegal state conduct subject to the assessment made by the political body. No question if SC uses the terms contained in art. 8 bis (2) by explicitly qualifying a state conduct such as invasion, military occupation, bombardment or any of the illegal conduct listed in the provision. This, moreover, has already occurred in the past. In resolution n.424 of 1978 SC condemned for example the invasive armed of Zambia by Rodesia of Sud as a consequence of the continuance of its acts of aggression. On another occasion through Resolution n.546 of 1984 SC condemned South Africa "for its renewed, intensified, premeditated and unprovoked bombing, as well as the continuing occupation of parts of the territory of Angola"[483]. The following year, for example, SC again stigmatized "South

---

[481]See in particular the resolutions relating to the situations in Benin and the Seychelles: Resolutions 405 of 14 April 1977 and 496 of 15 December 1981.

[482]N. STRAPATSAS, The practice of the Security Council regarding the concept of aggression, in C. KRESS, S. BARRIGA, The crime of aggression: A commentary, Cambridge University Press, Cambridge, 2012, pp. 184ss.

[483]N. STRAPATSAS, The practice of the Security Council regarding the concept of aggression, in C. KRESS, S. BARRIGA, The crime of aggression: A commentary, op. cit.,

Africa's (...) unprovoked and unwarranted military attack on the capital of Botswana as an act of aggression"[484]. Israel's air raid on Tunisian territory of 1st October 1985 was also classified by SC as an act of armed aggression[485] and could fall under the letter of art. 8 bis (2) (g), as an attack by "(...) the armed forces of a State on the land (...) or of another State"[486]. As expressly clarified in the amendments made to the elements of the crimes, in fact each of the conduct listed from art. 8 bis (2) represents an act of aggression. In these cases, the prosecutor should not have particular problems in considering the SC's assessment in relation to the Commission of a state act of aggression satisfied. More problematic is the hypothesis in which SC does not use a terminology corresponding to the statutory data. In the past, for example, SC condemned the economic blockade or military threats from Rhodesia of South to Zambia as provocative and aggressive acts[487]. State deeds that are not contained in art. 8 bis (2) of the articles of association and against which the ICC may therefore decide not to exercise its jurisdiction as state conduct irrelevant to the detection of the crime of aggression[488].

Furthermore, SC could limit itself to ascertaining in general terms the Commission of an act of aggression without however specifying the state conduct attributable to that particular violation of the use of force. For example in Resolution n.386 of 31 March 1976 the SC condemned in general "the acts of aggression committed by South Africa against Angola in violation of its sovereignty and territorial integrity"[489]. In these hypotheses, the Prosecutor would certainly be entitled to start its investigation activities without waiting for the six-month period foreseen in the event of failure to ascertain by SC and the subsequent authorization of the pre-trial division. The ICC bodies will then have to identify the specific conduct, among those provided by art. 8 bis (2) which is attributable to that specific aggression. Vice versa, SC could establish that one of the specific conduct contained in art. 8 bis (2) without expressly qualifying those behaviors as acts of aggression. The most obvious case concerns the invasion of Kuwait by Iraq. In that context, in fact, while condemning the invasion, the armed attack and the illegal occupation of the territory of Kuwait, SC has never used the term aggression or acts of aggression with respect to those conducted and considering

---

[484]Resolution of Security Council 568 of 21 June 1985. For further analysis see: T. RUYS, O. CORTEN, A. HOFER, The use of force in international law: A case-based approach, Oxford University Press, Oxford, 2018, pp. 397ss.

[485]Resolution of Security Council 573 of 4 October 1985. T. RUYS, O. CORTEN, A. HOFER, The use of force in international law: A case-based approach, op. cit.,

[486]N. STRAPATSAS, The practice of the Security Council regarding the concept of aggression, in C. KRESS, S. BARRIGA, The crime of aggression: A commentary, op. cit.,

[487]Resolution of Security Council 326 of 26 February 1976. T. RUYS, O. CORTEN, A. HOFER, The use of force in international law: A case-based approach, op. cit.,

[488]N. STRAPATSAS, The practice of the Security Council regarding the concept of aggression, in C. KRESS, S. BARRIGA, The crime of aggression: A commentary, op. cit., pp. 184ss.

[489]N. STRAPATSAS, The practice of the Security Council regarding the concept of aggression, in C. KRESS, S. BARRIGA, The crime of aggression: A commentary, op. cit.,

them rather as violations of use of force[490]. The situation is in this more complex hypothesis. It could be considered that the condition relating to the determination of SC is not satisfied. In this case, the Prosecutor may wait for the six-month period required to obtain an explicit assessment of SC and failing that, ask the pre-trial division to be able to proceed with the investigation activities. ICC could therefore qualify the behaviors identified by SC as true state acts of aggression in light of art. 8 a (2).

5. The proposals put forward regarding the involvement of UN bodies regarding the definition of the conditions of prosecution towards aggression

The problem of SC role for the purpose of exercising ICC jurisdiction in the matter of aggression concerns only the hypotheses of activation of the criminal proceeding on the initiative of a State Party of StICC or of the Prosecutor proprio motu, given that SC action based on Chapter VII of the UN Charter, it is generally competent to submit to the ICC any situation in which it believes that crimes within the scope ratione materiae of the same have been committed[491]. In both situations indicated above on the basis of the proposals that emerged in the context of the working group on the crime of aggression set up by the Preparatory Commission, when an accusation of aggression comes to the fore, ICC would be required and recognize a right of precedence to SC evaluations in relation to the existence of a state act of aggression. Starting from this common premise, the advanced solutions suggest, alternatively, several options regarding the hypothesis in which SC, after a certain period of time, does not take a position[492]. In this context, the crucial point is therefore given by the determination of the value to be attributed to SC silence[493].

---

[490]See the resolutions of SC n. 660 of 2 August 1990, 661 of 6 August 1991, 662 of 8 August 1990, 665 of 25 September 1990, 674 of 29 October 1990. For further analysis see: T. RUYS, O. CORTEN, A. HOFER, The use of force in international law: A case-based approach, op. cit.,

[491]Art. 13, lett. b) StICC.

[492]In the sense in which SC does not rule in relation to ICC's request to ascertain the existence of an act of aggression pursuant to art. 39 of the Charter. The options suggested in par. 5 of the consolidated proposal can thus be established: "1.The ICC could in any case exercise its jurisdiction; 2.The ICC would find itself in the impossibility of exercising its jurisdiction; 3.The ICC could ask the General Assembly to rule in the institution of the Security Council being able to exercise its jurisdiction only in case of ascertaining the existence of an act of aggression by this last one; 4.The ICJ could be called in a consultive manner to rule in the substitution of the Security Council enabling in the event of a positive reply, the ICC at the jurisdiction of the jurisdiction; 5.The ICJ could exercise its jurisdiction after verifying that the ICJ has previously ascertained, in the context of its concurrent competition, the existence of an act of aggression".

[493]R. KHERAD, La question de la dèfinition du crime d'aggression dans le statute de Rome. Entre pouvoir politique du Conseil de sècuritè et compètence judiciaire de la cour pènale internationale, in Revue Gènèrale de Droit International, 109 (2), 2005, pp. 355ss.

The solution that this silence should in any case be interpreted as an obstacle for ICC jurisdiction does not seem to be acceptable[494]. The practice demonstrates how the inertia of SC, precisely in light of the predominantly political criteria, which oversee the functioning of the body, can be explained in widely different terms depending on the situations that arise with the consequence that it would be unreasonable and arbitrary to attribute to it, in the context currently under examination a univocal meaning, even more so when the chosen meaning leads to such drastic consequences as the paralysis of criminal proceedings against crimes of exceptional gravity[495].

As far as the subject of this work is concerned, it is interesting to note that as part of the attempts to identify a more suitable balance in the relations between SC and ICC in order to ensure a balanced division of labor in terms of assessing the aggression in its dual configuration respectively of state and individual crime, some States have penalized the usefulness of attributing precisely to ICJ a role of intermediation between the two instances, given that the latter would be called to intervene in order to verification of the existence of acts of aggression, not to correct the assessment of SC but to replace the latter to remedy its possible inaction, when it does not pronounce, within the terms established upon ICC solicitation.

We refer in this case to a proposal submitted to the attention of the Preparatory Commission from Bosnia and Herzegovina, New Zealand and Romania[496] (tripartite proposal). The proposal is structured as a cascade system of competences if a case of aggression is brought to the attention of ICC (ex artt. 14 an 15 of the Statute)[497], the latter must notify SC, which in turn has six months to take a position on the matter[498]. In the event of inertia, after the indicated deadline has elapsed, CC may invite GA to refer the question of the existence of

---

[494]G. GAJA, The respective roles of the ICC and the Security Council in determining the existence of aggression, in M. POLITI, G. NESI, The International Criminal Court: A challenge to impunity, Ashgate Publishing, Aldershot, 2001, pp. 124ss.

[495]This solution is supported by the statement contained in the opinion on Namibia for which: "le fait que telle ou telle proposition n'ait ètè adoptèe par un organe international n'implique pas nècessarirement quìune dècision colelctive inverse ait ètè prise. Le rejet ou la non-approbation d'une proposition peut tenir à de nombreux motifs (...)" (par. 69)

[496]UN Doc. PCNICC/2001/WGCA/DP.2/Add. 1, 27 August 2001. This is the reworking of a proposal already advanced by these States in February 2001 (UN Doc. PCNICC/2001/WGCA/DP.1, 23 February 2001) and which in its substance maintains its original layout, with the exception of a few exceptions. R. KHERAD, La question de la dèfinition du crime d'aggression dans le statute de Rome. Entre pouvoir politique du Conseil de sècuritè et compètence judiciaire de la cour pènale internationale, op. cit., pp. 358ss. T. DANNENBAUMN, The crime of aggression, humanity and the soldier, Cambridge University Press, Cambridge, 2018.

[497]O. BEKOU, The International Criminal Court, op. cit.,

[498]Note that the six-month limit set in the proposal in question (UN Doc. PCNICC/2001/WGCA/DP.2/Add.1, par. 5) raised in the first version to twelve months (UN Doc. PCNICC/2001/WGCA/DP.1, par. 4)

an act of aggression in the present case to ICJ[499]. If ICJ responds positively to the question, then the ICC can proceed against the alleged perpetrator of the crime[500].

In its version, the proposal from Bosnia Herzegovina, New Zealand and Romania in par. 6, lett. b) also allows ICC to exercise its jurisdiction over a case of assault even in the event that the attempt to obtain the assessment required by art. 39 of the Charter, this assessment is made by ICJ during a litigation procedure. The project in question was also accepted in the latest version of the coordinator's discussion paper[501], not the further variant that the intervention of ICJ in the consultative session could be solicited as well as by GA, on the basis of a Resolution with a majority of nine votes, excluding the application of the veto right of permanent members[502].

---

[499] O. DELEAU, L'examen du rôle de la CIJ par l'Assemblèe gènèrale des Nations Unies, in Annuaire Français de Droit International, 16, 1970, pp. 4ss.

[500] In the original formulation the proposal provided that once the ICJ activated the procedure before ICC (UN Doc. PCNICC/2001/WGCA/DP.1, par. 5). In the second elaboration this intermediate phase is instead eliminated foreseeing directly to the competence of ICC once the investigation of the aggression by ICJ has taken place (UN Doc. PCNICC/2001/WGCA/DP.2/Add.1, par. 6, letter a)). In the comment to the indicated provision the proposing states raised the question of the attribution to ICC of a permanent authorization by GA regarding advisory questions to ICJ, a solution that would allow to simplify and depoliticize the whole procedure but the whose possibilities of realization are in the State canceled by the circumstance that art. 96, par 2 of the UN Charter expressly restricts the circle of potential beneficiaries of this authorization to the organs and organizations of the UN system. The attribution to ICC of a direct competence with regard to the request for advisory opinions to CJ is also the subject of some proposals put forward as part of the work on the draft agreement on relations between ICC and UN organization. For further analysis see: T. DANNENBAUMN, The crime of aggression, humanity and the soldier, op. cit.

[501] As you can see, the tripartite proposal is based on two main assumptions: 1. The primary, but not exclusive, nature of the role of SC in terms of ascertaining aggression; 2. The incompetence of ICC to express assessments pertaining to the responsibility of the States. D.N. NSEREKO, Aggression under the Rome statute of the international criminal court, in C. MCDOUGALL, The crime of aggression under the Rome Statute of the International Criminal Court, Cambridge University Press, Cambridge, 2013, pp. 517ss.

[502] The solution to request for the approval of the opinion by SC a majority of nine votes originates from a proposal formulated by the Netherlands (UN Doc. PCNICC/2002/WGCA/DP.1 of 17 April 2002). The opportunity of introducing the described modification has raised some doubts: It has been argued in this regard that it would include an element of doubtful legitimacy in the tripartite proposal, but above all it would regret meeting the strong, if not insurmountable, opposition of the permanent members. C.E. ESCOBAR HERNÁNDEZ, Corte penal internacional, consejo de seguridad y crimen de agresiòn un equilibrio dificil e inestable, in F.M. MARIŇO MÉNENDEZ, El derecho internacional en los albores del siglo XXI. Homenaje al profesor Juan Manuel Castro-Rial Canosa, ed. Trotta. Fundaciòn Juan March, 2002, Madrid, pp. 262ss. C. MCDOUGALL, The crime of aggression under the Rome statute of the International Criminal Court, op. cit., In reality the perplexity highlighted does not appear completely justified. With this precisation, the proposing delegation intended to resolve the

The solution briefly described presents unquestionable with respect to the other proposals put forward regarding the definition of the trigger mechanism to be applied in the matter of aggression. In particular, the options that tend to attribute to political bodies, especially to SC and GA an exclusive role in the activation of ICC jurisdiction over the crime of aggression, despite the formal assurances that the decisions of these bodies: "Shall not be interpreted as in any way affecting the independence of the Court"[503], are in no way suitable for safeguarding the autonomy and independence of the criminal jurisdiction[504]. ICJ intervention would allow to define the conditions of prosecution in the matter of aggression on the basis of legal parameters, evidently more suited to the type of issue dealt with. Furthermore, taking into account the fact that the individual crime of aggression necessarily implies the existence of a state crime, the referral in case of inertia of SC to ICJ would have the merit of avoiding the direct involvement of ICC in an interstate dispute and at the same time would make it possible to better guarantee the uniqueness and coherence of the international legal system, attributing to a single judicial body the task of ruling on matters relating to the responsibility of states for serious injuries to the essential values of international society[505].

On the contrary, the objection raised against the described proposal does not convince, which essentially hinges on the risk of politicization of the ICJ's activity which could result from its participation in the definition of the conditions of prosecution towards the crime of aggression. In this regard, apart from the completely inconsistent thesis in our opinion that the determination of an act of aggression far from configuring a legal question would be solely "a question of fact"[506], it was highlighted how ICJ would be in substance called to pronounce in

---

controversial issue a priori to be applied to the adoption of requests for opinions. Since the setting therein coincides in fact with the general solution, not only do the doubts of the above mentioned doubts lose consistency from our point of view, but rather it is clear in the greater clarity that results from the modification indicated (in order to determine the activation modalities) of the advisory procedure) an element to be evaluated in positive terms.

503The solution is taken from the text of art. 10 of StICC project presented by the Preparatory Commission to the Rome Conference.

504J. TRAHAN, Defining "aggression": Why the Preparatory Commission for the International Criminal Court has faced such a conundrum, in Loyola of Los Angeles International and Comparative Law Review, 24, 2002, pp. 462ss, which is affirmed that "the credibility of ICC regarding prosecutions for aggression would very much depend on the way the SC and/or GA make determinations as to state responsibility".

505D.N. NSEREKO, Aggression under the Rome statute of the international criminal court, op. cit., pp. 518ss.

506J.N. BOEVING, Aggression, international law and the ICC: An argument for the withdrawal of aggression from the Rome Statute, in Columbia Journal of Transnational Law, 43 (2), 2005, pp. 538ss. The author argues that the involvement of ICJ in the issues currently under examination would be excluded from the Rome Statute itself, which would provide for the latter only to resolve, to the sens of art. 119, the disputes between States Parties relative to the interpretation of the same Statute. Indeed, this argument seems even

a consultative session on a bilateral dispute (between the attacked and the aggressor State) and that it would be unlikely that the States involved (especially the accused State) would accept that ICJ itself will deal with it[507]. The objection indicated actually confuses advisory and contentious jurisdiction and can be easily dismissed in light of the constant ICJ jurisprudence which clearly shows that ICJ has never attributed decisive importance, for the admissibility of a request for an opinion, to the the politicity of the question, let alone the fact that this concerned an interstate dispute with respect to which the parties had not both consented to its jurisdiction. On the other hand, the same configuration of the issues related to the Commission of acts of aggression in terms of purely bilateral disputes (which is at least implicitly apparent from this objection) lends itself, in the light of the considerations developed previously regarding the obligations of erga omnes and international crimes he has been to considerable criticism.

Nor could an obstacle to the involvement of ICJ at the request of GA be identified in hypotheses of this kind in art. 12 of the Charter. The problem of the value to be attributed to the rule indicated for the purpose of determining GA's competence to activate the consultative procedure has already been addressed and resolved (also in the light of the clear stance taken on this point by ICJ in the opinion on the legal consequences of the construction of a wall in the occupied Palestinian territories) in negative terms so there is no need to go back to the issue here again[508]. It is sufficient to note here that the objections that the participation of GA in the indicated proceeding could constitute a violation of the division of responsibilities for the maintenance of international peace and security outlined by the Charter are not in our opinion absolutely relevant[509].

Also the argument, undoubtedly of greater interest, according to which GA's intervention (but these observations are valid mutatis mutandis also with regard to SC role in the version presented in the consolidated proposal of the coordinator of the crime working group of aggression of the Preparatory Commission), resolving itself in the discretionary decision of the latter to activate

---

weaker than the one we criticized in the text, as well as being absolutely unfounded from a logical point of view, given that the attribution of a specific competence in a given field is not at all apt to exclude further exceptions attributions in different sectors. Nor does it make any sense to censor the proposal in question on the absence of the relief that the defendant would have no way of defending his position before ICJ. This objection, in addition to lending itself to a similar use also with regard to the eventual assessment opted from SC, has no real value, however it concerns an assessment that in the context currently under examination has only a procedural and not substantial scope.

[507]T. MERON, Defining aggression for the International Criminal Court, op. cit., pp. 14ss. D.N. NSEREKO, Aggression under the Rome statute of the international criminal court, op. cit., pp. 520ss. D.S. MATHIAS, Remarks on the definition of aggression and the ICC, in ASIL Proceedings, 96, 2002, pp. 182ss.

[508]M. SCHUSTER, The Rome statute and the crime of aggression. A gordian knot in a search of sword, op. cit., pp. 45ss.

[509]M. SCHUSTER, The Rome statute and the crime of aggression. A gordian knot in a search of sword, op. cit., pp. 46ss.

or not the consultative procedure before ICJ would not however be suitable to neutralize the risks of politicization of the procedure and to adequately safeguard the independence of ICC[510], in our opinion not it must be dramatized, given that the influence on the criminal proceeding with regard to the crime of aggression of political elements probably constitutes an absolute factor that cannot be eliminated, but whose scope can only be mitigated, what the proposal currently under consideration seems to us to actually achieve[511].

On the other hand, the question of the relationship between ICC and SC in this area has been framed by us from the outset in terms of harmonization and balancing of potentially conflicting needs, i.e. peacekeeping (in a perspective mainly inspired by considerations of a political nature) and repression of international crimes (in a perspective on the contrary of strict respect for legality and law enforcement).

The compatibility of the six-month limit within which SC should respond to the request of ICC with respect to the charter rules pertaining to its functioning and competences, that are based on the widest discretion in favor of the latter. The rule could be partially correct by providing for an extension in favor of SC in the event that the latter or the Secretary General decides to start an investigation to shed light on the facts in question. On the contrary, no delay in the expected times would seem to be justified in the case of simple negotiations or other diplomatic dispute resolution procedures, and this in consideration of the seriousness of the crime and its consequences. In any case, SC would always have the power attributed to it, pursuant to art. 16 StICC to block the exercise of jurisdiction of the latter[512].

As for the effects to be linked to the involvement of UN bodies in the determination of the conditions of prosecution in the matter of aggression, is discussed whether these should be merely procedural or even substantial. If this second perspective prevails, the determination made in the first instance by the indicated bodies would also condition the conduct of the criminal trial on the

---

[510]J. TRAHAN, Defining "aggression": Why the Preparatory Commission for the International Criminal Court has faced such a conundrum, op. cit., pp. 462ss, the risk of politicization of the issue would be linked in practice to the fact that GA "apparently would retain the option of referring the issue (...)".

[511]With a view to resizing the possibilities of politically motivated determinations, the modification of the present proposal is to be placed, which in its second formulation neutralizes the risk inherent in the first version that following the pronouncement of the ICJ attesting to the existence of acts of aggression, the General Assembly arbitrarily decides not to refer the matter to the ICC. The original formulation actually attributed to the appeal to the ICJ a purely instrumental character with respect to the competences of the General Assembly. In the version currently under examination, instead, once the ICJ has taken up the question, it has ruled on the existence of an act of aggression, the ICC can proceed immediately with the case. In this way, the role of filter of the General Assembly (and mutatis mutandis of the Security Council) is limited only to the activation phase of the ICJ advisory procedure.

[512]O. BEKOU, The International Criminal Court, op. cit.,

merits, as ICC cannot deviate from the assessment expressed in terms of state liability. In this way, the indicated assessment would constrain the decision regarding the existence of the individual crime by ICC itself, limiting the latter's margin of judgment to the assessment and determination of the degree of involvement of the accused in the participation, planning and organization of the aggression[513].

Although it is undeniable that a prior determination of the existence of a state act of aggression is likely to produce a tremendous impact on the criminal trial[514], the first solution is certainly favored in our opinion[515]. It allows to guarantee the application of some fundamental principles that must inspire the criminal trial before ICC. We refer above all to the presumption of innocence, expressly provided for by art. 66 StICC, which would be disregarded in the event that the determination made by UN bodies also constrained the merits of ICC assessments[516]. By adopting the solution of the merely procedural nature of the intervention of UN organs instead, the procedural guarantees in favor of the accused would be reserved and ICC would be recognized the possibility of pronouncing in total independence regarding the existence of the crime and the degree of the accused's responsibility[517]. The consideration that the standard of proof in the criminal trial is notoriously higher than that required for state liability[518] also supports the thesis accepted here. Nor is the objection that, in the event that SC has previously ascertained the existence of an act of aggression, the determination made on the basis of art. 39 would be binding on Member States under the terms of art. 25 of the Charter, for which the latter would be required to accord the evaluation of SC prevalent character with respect to ICC judgment and this by virtue of the provisions of art. 103 of the Charter[519]. In our opinion, it does

---

[513]I.K. MÜLLER-SCHIEKE, Defining the crime of aggression under the statute of the international criminal court, in Leiden Journal of International Law, 14 (2), 2001, pp. 428ss.

[514]S.A. FERNÁNDEZ DE GOURMENDI, The working group on aggression at the preparatory commission for the international criminal court, in Fordham International Law Journal, 25, 2001-2002, pp. 606ss.

[515]D. SAROOSHI, Aspects of the relationship between the international criminal court and the United Nations, in Netherlands Yearbook of International Law, 32, 2001, pp. 28ss.

[516]In this orientation see: W.A. SCHABAS, Follow up to Rome: preparing for entry into force of the international criminal court Statute, in Human Rights Law Journal, 20, 1999, pp. 158ss, "(...) an accused could arrive before the court with the central factual issue in the charge already determined and not subject to change (...)".

[517]V. GOWLLAND-DEBBAS, The relationship between political and judicial organs if international organizations: The role of the Security Council in the new international criminal court, in L. BOISSON DE CHAZOURNES, C.P.R. ROMANO, R. MACKENZIE, International organizations and international dispute settlement. Trends and prospects, Martinus Nijhoff Publishers, 2002, pp. 108ss.

[518]A. NOLLKAEMPER, Concurrence between individual responsibility and state responsibility in international law, in International and Comprative Law Quarterly, 52 (3), 2003, pp. 616ss.

[519]M. SCHUSTER, The Rome statute and the crime of aggression. A gordian knot in a search of sword, op. cit., pp. 40ss.

not make sense to extend the scope of application of art. 103 also to the activity of mere verification carried out by SC pursuant to art. 39[520]. This activity is essentially procedural in Chapter VII of the Charter, constituting a necessary precondition for the adoption of coercive measures aimed at peacekeeping[521], therefore it does not impose any legal obligation in the proper sense on Member States, likely to enjoy the prevalence granted by the aforementioned provision[522].

For the sake of completeness, it should be noted that the indicated solution, favorable to the independence of the ICC's assessments with respect to those made in terms of state liability, lends itself to raising very difficult consequences to be regulated in the event that these are made by ICJ, according to the model proposed by the tripartite proposal. If accepted as a solution of general application, the idea of the merely procedural nature of the prior determination of an act of state aggression is clear that the risk of conflicts between the assessments of ICJ and those of ICC presents extremely serious profiles[523]. In this regard, a situation of connection would appear to arise between proceedings in progress before international courts, with respect to which international practice is not currently able to provide adequate answers, given the absolute novelty of a situation of this kind. In this regard, the above question is immediately closely linked to the highly discussed issue, at a purely theoretical level, in the configurability of a hierarchy of dispute resolution procedures at international level. It must be said that in a more general perspective, the risk of contradictory solutions regardless of the choices made regarding the involvement of other bodies in defining the conditions of prosecution towards the crime of aggression, already exists at present due to the existence to which we have previously referred a plurality of international bodies authorized, albeit with regard to different purposes and in specific institutional contexts, to ascertain the existence of acts of aggression.

6. Concluding remarks

Several proposals have been made with a view to involving the UN bodies in SC first in determining the existence of the crime of aggression, in order to avoid a dangerous overlap in such a sensitive and politically sensitive matter of UN activity to protect peace and that of ICC in the field of repression of the most serious crimes under international law[524].

---

[520]O. BEKOU, The International Criminal Court, op. cit.,

[521]S. YEE, A proposal to reformulate article 23 of the ILC draft statute for an international criminal court, in Hastings International and Comparative Law Review, 19, 1995-1996, pp. 534ss.

[522]D.N. NSEREKO, Aggression under the Rome statute of the international criminal court, op. cit., pp. 508ss.

[523]C.E. ESCOBAR HERNÁNDEZ, Corte penal internacional, consejo de seguridad y crinen de agresiòn un equilibrio dificil e inestable, in F.M. MARIŇO MÉNENDEZ, El derecho internacional en los alores del siglo XXI. Homenaje al profesor Juan Manuel Castro-Rial Canosa, op. cit. pp. 262ss.

[524]It is clear that the question of the relationship between ICC and SC in this area is

The initial idea is that since the crime of aggression necessarily presupposes the existence of an act of aggression, that is to say a particularly serious offense attributable to a State[525], a SC definition regarding the ascertainment of the existence of such this case would in principle always be desirable for ICC to exercise its jurisdiction over the alleged offender.

Pursuant to art. 5, par. 2 StICC the definition of the conditions under which ICC can exercise its jurisdiction over the crime in question must be in

---

intimately linked to the problem related to the definition of the crime of aggression itself. Suffice it to note the aspects that are likely to strongly encapsulate the solution to be attributed to the question of the involvement of UN organs in determining the conditions of transferability in relation to the crime under consideration. On the one hand the idea that the rape of aggression necessarily concerns individuals that are at the political and military levels of a state (M. POLITI, G. NESI, The international court and the crime of aggression, ed. Routledge, Burlington, 2004) and, on the other, that for which aggression could only be prosecuted if actually carried out thereby excluding the criminalization of mere preparatory acts. With regard to the definition of the case to be included in this notion, various principal orientations have emerged up to now, depending on whether a formulation is privileged in general and abstract terms of the case, centered on the prohibition of the armed force supported by art. 2, par. 4 of the UN Charter; or an example of cases similar to the same model based on Resolution n. 3314 (XXIX) of 1973 of GA; or finally a narrow definition of crime, limited only to the war of aggression. For further details see: J. TRAHAN, Defining aggression. Why the preparatory commission of the international criminal court has faced such a conundrum, op. cit., pp. 440ss. R.S. CLARK, Rethinking aggression as a crime and formulating its elements. The final work-product of the preparatory commission for the international criminal court, in Leiden Journal of International Law, 15 (4), 2002, pp. 860ss.

[525]I.K. MÜLLER-SCHIEKE, Defining the crime of aggression under the statute of the international criminal court, op. cit., pp. 410ss, "(...) the crime of aggression is inherently a state crime. Although the idea of initiating an armed conflict originates and develops in the minds of individuals the aggressive act emanates as an act of the State, not of its intellectual initiators (...)". See also in argument: C.E. ESCOBAR HERNÁNDEZ, Corte penal internacional, consejo de seguridad y crinen de agresiòn un equilibrio dificil e inestable, in F.M. MARIŇO MÉNENDEZ, El derecho internacional en los alores del siglo XXI. Homenaje al profesor Juan Manuel Castro-Rial Canosa, op. cit., pp. 244ss, which correctly highlights how the determination of the existence of a state act of aggression would necessarily be configured as "condiciln de procedibilidad bàsica de toda actuaciòn de la CPI (...)". This consequence would be derived neither from the UN Charter nor from StICC, but from the "proper conception and internal development" of the crime. The same jurisprudence of individuals for acts of aggression always presupposes a state responsibility state to which the acts in question should be imputed. In this direction see art. 2, par. 2 of the project of the code of crimes against peace and security of humanity, in the Annuarie de la Commission de Droit Internationale, 1996, II, 2, p.15ss and par. 4 of the comment of art. 16 of the same project. The described approach that is established in the works on the definition of ICC jurisdiction in relation to the crime of aggression excludes the possibility of criminalizing in these same terms certain devastating forms of terrorism, planned and implemented by non-state entities and not connected to a State on the basis of the traditional criteria of imputation due to international law (but which in terms of size and effects, can be equated with real aggressions).

harmony with the relevant provisions of the UN Charter. The dominant opinion is that this clarification was intended precisely to safeguard the prerogatives of SC of ex chapter VII of UN Charter and highlight the absolutely pre-eminent role[526]. On the other hand, this statement constitutes an essential starting point if it wants to develop a proposal that is politically acceptable and in consideration of the very stringent conditions required for its adoption, it can count on a substantial support from the States.

Given that therefore a certain role to SC in this matter must be ensured and guaranteed, given the logical link in terms of aggression between state responsibility and criminal liability of the individual, the next step is to determine specifically what this role consists of and what consequences it leads to ICC operation. It is clear that the involvement of SC in the functioning of the court mechanism poses a serious threat to the independence and autonomy of the Court. Essential requirements for the correct and effective performance of judicial functions. The same principle of equality of individuals before the law would risk undergoing unacceptable compressions, given that SC members of exercising their right of veto could remove from ICC jurisdiction cases involving their own citizens or in which their interests result in various title involved[527].

The definition of the conditions of prosecution towards the crime of aggression requires a delicate work of harmonization between the competences and the operating methods of ICC and SC[528]. In other words, a difficult balance must be found between the objectives of promoting international criminal justice and protecting the peace. While in a first phase (which we can temporarily place in the context of the negotiation that preceded the Rome Conference), the need

---

[526]M.H. ARSANJANI, The Rome statute of the International Criminal Court, op. cit.,, pp. 22ss. H.A.M. VON HEBEL, D. ROBINSON, Crimes within the jurisdiction of the court, in S.K. LEE, The International Criminal Court. The making of the Rome statute. Issues, negotiations, results, Martinus Nijhoff Publishers, The Hague, Boston, London, 1999, pp. 80ss. T. MERON, Defining aggression for the International Criminal Court, op. cit., pp. 2ss. M. SCHUSTER, The Rome statute and the crime of aggression. A gordian knot in a search of sword, op. cit., pp. 4ss. L. YEE, Not just a war crimes court: the penal regime established by the Rome statute of the International Criminal Court, in Singapore Academy of Law Journal, 10, 1998, pp. 322ss., the engraving contained in art. 5, par. 2 of StICC intends to guarantee against any pronouncements of ICC in contrast with previous assessments of SC pursuant to art. 39 of the UN Charter.

[527]C. CARPENTER, The international criminal court and the crime of aggression, op. cit., pp. 224ss. I.K. MÜLLER-SCHIEKE, Defining the crime of aggression under the statute of the international criminal court, op. cit., pp. 426ss. R. PIERCE, Which of the preparatory commission's latest proposals for the definition of the crime of aggression and the exercise of jurisdiction should be adopted into the Rome Statute of the International Criminal Court?, in Brigham Young University Journal of Public Law, 15, 2000-2001, pp. 282ss. G. GAJA, The long journey towards repressing aggression, in A. CASSESE, P. GAETA, J.R.W.D. JONES, The Rome statute of the international criminal court. A commentary, Oxford University Press, Oxford, 2002, pp. 434ss.

[528]I.K. MÜLLER-SCHIEKE, Defining the crime of aggression under the statute of the international criminal court, op. cit., pp. 424ss.

for involvement in this area of SC was mostly motivated on the basis of the assertion of the absolute exclusivity of competences of this body regarding the assessment of the case in question (for which a prior assessment pursuant to art. 39 of the Charter was indicated as an indispensable condition for the exercise of ICC jurisdiction)[529], from the proposals subsequently discussed in the context of

[529]The draft of the Statute of 1994 (in Rapport de la Commission du droit international, quarante-sixième section (2 mai-22 juillet 1994), in Annuaire de la Commission de Droit Internationale proposing a sheme followed already by the provisional version of the project of crimes against the peace and security of humanity adopted in 1991 guaranteed the SC exclusive competence by establishing in article 23, paragraph 2 that "une plainte ne peut être dèposèe en vertu du prèsent statut pour un acte d'agression ou en liaison directe avec un tel acte que si le conseil de sècuritè a constatè au prèable qu'un État a commis l'acte d'agression faisant l'objet de la plainte". Paragraph 3 of the same provision further strengthens the board's position with respect to ICC by providing that: "aucune poursuite ne peut être engagèe en vertu du prèsent statut à raison d'une situation dont le Conseil de sècuritè taite en tant que menace contre la paix ou rupure de la paix ou acte d'agression aux termes du chapitre VII de la Charte des Nations Unies, à moins que le Conseil de sècuritè n'en dècide autrement". In line with this first formulation strongly defended above all by the SC permanent members the project of the Statute elaborated in the Preparatory Commission of 1998 confirmed in principle slightly attenuating the scope, this same approach. Article 10 provided that no provision could be initiated in the event that SC was exercising its functions under the terms of Chapter VII of the UN Charter unless expressly authorized by it, with the consequence that the exercise of ICC jurisdiction to the crime of aggression was allowed only in the hypothesis in which it had determined that the relative state action integrated the extremes of an act of aggression (Report of the Preparatory Committee on the establishment of an international criminal court, UN Doc. A/CONF.183/2/Add. 1, 14 April 1998). Already in the phase preceding the Rome Conference the question began to be more controversial. The related debate soon resulted in an open and clear opposition between SC permanent members and other States. Also in the light of these contrasts, the proposals relating to the aspects indicated began to present far more articulated schemes while continuing to essentially preserve a leading role for SC. In this sense, see also the proposal of Cameroon during the Rome Conference in which, although recognizing the priority of SC role in assessing the crime of aggression, the possibility for ICC to initiate an investigation was admitted on a subsidiary basis. If SC within a reasonable period of time had not responded to the request, addressed by the Court to express its opinion regarding the existence of the case in question (UN Doc. A/CONF/.183/C.1/L.39, 2 July 1998, Option B, par. 4) and similarly that presented by Algeria, Saudi Arabia, Arab Emirates, Iraq, Kuwait, Lebanon, Libya, Oman, Syria, Sudan, Tunisia and Yemen (A Doc. A/CONF.183/C.1/L.56, 8 July 1998). The prospect favorable to the importance of SC political role continued to find expressions of support even after the approval of the Statute of Rome emblematic results were put forward in the Preparatory Commission by the Russian Federation (UN Doc. PCNICC/1999/DP.12, 29 July 1999) and of Germany (UN Doc. PCNICC/1999/DP.13, 30 July 1999). For further details see also: R. WEDGWOOD, The international criminal court: An American view, in European Journal of International Law, 10, 1999, pp. 94ss. D.S. MATHIAS, J.N. BOEVING, Aggression, international law and the ICC: An argument for the withdrawal of aggression form the Rome Statute, in Columbia Journal of Transnational Law, 43, 2005, pp. 576ss. N. KOURSAMI, The contextual elements of the crime of genocide, ed. Springer, Berlin, 2018,

the tendency to reduce the centrality of the SC role emerged from the Preparatory Commission and the working group on the crime of aggression, thus favoring the independence of the functions assigned to ICC itself in this matter[530].

This approach appears undoubtedly preferable. It is based on the widely acceptable assumption of the denial of the exclusivity of SC assessment powers in the matter of aggression[531]. The validity of this solution, on the other hand, is largely supported, in relation to the division of competences within the UN system from the examination carried out so far, especially in light of the role that in this regard is attributed to ICJ itself and to the autonomy of the functions of the latter compared to those of the other bodies of the Organization. In fact, the main judicial UN body can without a doubt also have a say in the matter of aggression, both in the context of the consultative function (being able to pronounce on any legal issue) and in the context of the contentious function (by virtue of the broad definition of the notion of legal disputes resulting from art.36 of the Statute). Far from remaining purely theoretical, this competence has actually been recognized and exercised by ICJ in practice: The Nicaragua case[532], the appeals of Yugoslavia

---

pp. 126ss.

[530]In this direction the text proposed by Greece and Portugal according to which ICC jurisdiction in matters of aggression should be subordinated to a prior determination made by SC pursuant to art. 39 of the Charter but this determination could be solicited directly by ICC itself with the result that, if SC does not pronounce itself within 12 months from the request (in favor or against as to the existence of an aggression or by issuing a Resolution, ex art.16 of the ICC Statute), ICC could proceed with the examination of the case (UN Doc. PCNICC/1999/2000WGGA/DP.2, 7 December 1999). For similar solutions see the proposal of Colombia (UN Doc. PCNICC/2000/WGCA / DP.1) and (UN Doc. PCNICC/2000/WGGA/DP.2, 17 March 2000 and the one developed by Bosnia and Herzegovina, New Zealand and Romania (UN Doc. PCNICC/2001/WGCA/DP.2/Add. 1, 27 August 2001). This is the reworking of a proposal already put forward by these same States in February of 2001 (UN Doc. PCNICC/2001/WGCA/DP.1, 23 February 2001) and that in substance it maintains the original plant except for a few exceptions. For a comment see: R. KHERAD, La question de la dèfinition du crime d'agression dans le statue de Rome. Entre pouvoir politique du Conseil de sècuritè et compètence judiciare de la cour pènale internationale, op. cit., pp. 358ss. The trend highlighted in the text is also confirmed also in the work of the special working group on the crime of aggression established by the Assembly of States Parties. The proposal made by Cuba foresees in par. 2 that: "The lack of a determination shall not impede the exercise of the court's jurisdiction with respect to a case referred to it", ICC.ASP/2/SWGCA/DP.1, 4 September 2003.

[531]In the sense that SC is not accorded pursuant to the same UN Charter, the monopoly of ascertaining acts of aggression. S.M. YENGEJEH, Reflection on the role of the Security Council in determining an act of aggression, in M. POLITI, G. NESI, The international criminal court and the crime of aggression, op. cit., pp. 128ss.

[532]M. SCHUSTER, The Rome statute and the crime of aggression. A gordian knot in a search of sword, op. cit., pp. 48ss, who draws from it the incompetence of ICJ to decide issues that fall within the discretionary competences of SC, ex Chapter VII. On the other hand, the competences of SC regarding the verification of acts of aggression pursuant to art. 39 of the UN Charter is justified exclusively in view of the potential assumption of concrete measures aimed at restoring peace and internal security. On the contrary, SC does

against some NATO countries regarding the lawfulness of the use of force or even the cases brought by the Democratic Republic of Congo against neighboring states accused of committing acts of armed aggression on the applicant's territory.

If ICJ is a UN organ, it retains its own autonomous competence in the matter, but is not clear how the powers attributed by SC of Chapter VII of the UN Charter can determine an overall barrier for the jurisdiction of an organ competence on the repression of individual crimes[533], and established on the basis of a treaty formally completely independent from the UN Charter[534]. On the other hand, the same relations between SC and ad hoc tribunals set up by it are not expressive of an absolute primautè of the former with respect to the latter, as in the jurisprudence relating to the Tadić and Kanyabashi cases amply testifies.

The non-exclusive nature of SC competences in the matter of ascertaining the case in question is further confirmed by the powers exercised in this area by GA. Finally, it was found that pursuant to art. 51 of the Charter any State (not only the one that suffers the aggression, but also all the other States, acting in collective legitimate defense) would in fact be empowered to operate this qualification[535].

---

not at all have the power to decide on the basis of the aforementioned assessment, the conditions for the exercise of criminal jurisdiction against individuals. Emblematic in the perspective described are the observations of dissident judge Scwebel on the sidelines of the sentence of 1986 on military and paramilitary activities in Nicaragua, ICJ Reports, 1986, p. 290, par. 60, "(...) while SC is invested by the Charter with the authority to determine the existence of an act of aggression, it does not act as a Court in making such a determination. It may arrive at a determination of aggression-or, as more often is the case, fail to arrive at a determination of aggression (...) for political rather than legal reasons (...)".

[533]G. GAJA, The long journey towards repressing aggression, in A. CASSESE, P. GAETA, J.R.W.D. JONES, The Rome statute of the international criminal court. A commentary, op. cit., pp. 434ss. G. GAJA, The respective roles of the ICC and the Security Council in determining the existence of aggression, in M. POLITI, F. NESI, The international criminal court and the crime of aggression, op. cit., pp. 124ss. L.J. SPRINGROSE, Aggression as a core crime in the Rome statute establishing an international criminal court, in Saint Louis-Warsaw Transnational Law Journal, 99, 1999, pp. 152ss. I.K. MÜLLER-SCHIEKE, Defining the crime of aggression under the statute of the international criminal court, op. cit., pp. 426ss.

[534]The considerations developed in the text confirm the possibility at least in principle of involving ICJ in the process of defining the conditions of admissibility with regard to the crime of aggression on a concurrent basis, at the most subsidiary to the role attributed to SC in this scope. At the same time they highlight the risk of inconsistencies and contrasts between ICJ's jurisprudence on the subject and the future ICC positions. C.E. ESCOBAR HERNÁNDEZ, Corte penal internacional, consejo de seguridad y crinen de agresiòn un equilibrio dificil e inestable, in F.M. MARIŇO MÉNENDEZ, El derecho internacional en los alores del siglo XXI. Homenaje al profesor Juan Manuel Castro-Rial Canosa, op. cit., pp. 250ss.

[535]For these conclusions see also the document on the historical analysis of the facts concerning the aggression, drawn up from the UN General Secretary (PCNICC/2002/

A further consideration is necessary: The SC has traditionally shown that it is not very inclined to express itself in favor of the existence of an act of aggression, preferring to refer rather to the politically more neutral notion of threat to peace[536]. This choice must be ascribed to the type of variables that SC takes into consideration when carrying out this type of evaluation and to the crucial role that realpolitik factors play between them. Qualifying the conduct of a State in terms of aggression is the most serious condemnation that a State can be imposed. It follows that a determination of this content may in many cases even be incompatible with the pacification effort carried out by SC through the conduct of negotiations and good offices, as well as further stiffen the position of the aggressor State[537].

The absolutely central (if not preponderant) relevance of the methods of political management of the aggression would find its rationale in the reversibility of the crime in question, reversibility which constitutes a completely peculiar and specific characteristic of the case in question compared to the other crimes falling within the ICC competence[538]. Add to this the SC Member States themselves may have an interest in not compromising their relations with the responsible state for which they could prevent avoiding the reference to the notion of aggression.

It is therefore evident that subordinating the exercise of ICC jurisdiction in the matter of aggression to a prior assessment by SC would generally end up making the application of the provisions of the Statute relating to this crime completely uncertain[539], making it ultimately dependent analysis from purely

---

WGCA/L.1, 24 January 2001).

[536]G. GAJA, The long journey towards repressing aggression, in A. CASSESE, P. GAETA, J.R.W.D. JONES, The Rome statute of the international criminal court. A commentary, op. cit., pp. 124ss. P. ESCARAMEIA, The ICC and the Security Council on aggression: Overlapping competences?, in M. POLITI, F. NESI, The international criminal court and the crime of aggression, op. cit., pp. 133, 140ss.

[537]C. ANTONOPOULOS, Whatever happened to crimes against peace?, in Journal of Conflict and Security Law, 6 (1), 2001, pp. 33ss.

[538]C. ANTONOPOULOS, Whatever happened to crimes against peace?, op. cit., pp. 49, 61.

[539]C. ANTONOPOULOS, Whatever happened to crimes against peace?, op. c it., pp. 48ss. G. GAJA, The respective roles of the ICC and the Security Council in determining the existence o aggression, in M. POLITI, F. NESI, The international criminal court and the crime of aggression, op. cit., pp. 124ss. D.N. NSEREKO, Aggression under the Rome statute of the international criminal court, op. cit., pp. 515ss. On the contrary, it seems rather naive to expect that the attribution of the power to activate ICC jurisdiction against the material perpetrators of aggression can determine in itself a greater propensity of SC to refer to the notion indicated in the context of the assessment, ex art. 39 of the Charter. I.K. MÜLLER-SCHIEKE, Defining the crime of aggression under the statute of the international criminal court, op. cit., pp. 424, which is affirmed that "(...) it would be illusory to believe that the court might serve as a catalyst for a clear pronunciation by the Council on the concept of aggression". M. SCHUSTER, The Rome statute and the crime of aggression. A gordian knot in a search of sword, op. cit., pp. 42ss.

political considerations[540].

The idea of involvement of the main UN judicial bodies in this field appears in principle to be assessed in positive terms, and meets with some favor in doctrine[541]. Its main limitation is linked to the duration of the consultative procedure before ICJ, whose participation in the determination of the conditions of prosecution towards the crime of aggression could effectively lead to an excessive dilation of the criminal trial[542]. On the other hand, we do not want to deny that the proposal indicated also has further weaknesses and therefore needs to be properly corrected and enhanced.

An overall judgment cannot be separated from some more general reflections: The question of the definition of aggression has always been one of the thorniest and most controversial issues of international law[543].

The problems raised by this situation have therefore led some to believe that it was even preferable to eliminate any reference to the crime of aggression from StICC[544]. In support of this perspective, it was stressed that ICC is already competent under the Statute to prosecute other crimes that are committed in the course of armed conflicts due to their characteristics, so even if the jurisdiction of the same towards aggression is not foreseen directly those responsible for this

---

[540]C. ANTONOPOULOS, Whatever happened to crimes against peace?, op. cit., pp. 49ss. I.K. MÜLLER-SCHIEKE, Defining the crime of aggression under the statute of the international criminal court, op. cit., pp. 426ss. D.N. NSEREKO, Aggression under the Rome statute of the international criminal court, op. cit., pp. 514ss.

[541]S.M. YENGEJEH, Reflection on the role of the Security Council in determining an act of aggression, in M. POLITI, G. NESI, The international criminal court and the crime of aggression, op. cit. pp. 130ss, which believes that the option described has at least two advantages: "(...) First it is based on the Charter provisions. Second, ICJ is the judicial organ of the organization and has the competence to provide an impartial and independent advisor opinion (...) seems to be the best equipped for that, as the principal judicial organ of UN" and more laconically J.F.E. ESCUDERO ESPINOSA, Los poderes del Consejo de Seguridad y la corte penal internacional en el estatuto de Roma, in Annuario de Derecho Internacional, 19, 2003, pp. 257ss, it should be noted that a part of the doctrine can deny the opportunity of introducing the system described with regard to ICC jurisdiction in terms of aggression, it also believes that the tripartite proposal contains interesting ideas that should be valued rather in the management of the possible issues of legitimacy of SC action pursuant to articles 13, lett. b) and 16 StICC, which could be highlighted in the course of a criminal investigation. I. PETCULESCU, The review of the United Nation Security Council decisions by the International Court of Justice, in Netherlands International Law Review, 52 (2), pp. 194ss.

[542]M. SCHUSTER, The Rome statute and the crime of aggression. A gordian knot in a search of sword, op. cit., pp. 50ss.

[543]W.A. SCHABAS, The unfinished work of defining aggression: How many times must the cannonballs fly, before they are forever banned?, in D. MCGOLDRICK, P. ROWE, E. DONNELLY (ed. by), The Permanent International Criminal Court. Legal and policy issues, Hart Publishing, Oxford & Portland, Oregon, 2004.

[544]J.N. BOEVING, Aggression, international law and the ICC: An argument for the withdrawal of aggression from the Rome statute, op. cit., pp. 560ss.

crime could always be prosecuted on the basis of other charges.

This is actually a very dangerous idea in itself: As it has been pointed out, giving up the ICC's jurisdiction over aggression would create the very serious feeling that "individual perpetrators of aggression may act with impunity"[545] and would mean repudiating the inheritance of Nuremberg with serious damage to the credibility and prestige of ICC itself. On the other hand, the inclusion of aggression in ICC ratione materiae powers retains a fundamental and not negligible symbolic value and in reflecting the will of the majority of States to pursue this crime, produces a deterrent effect that should not be underestimated[546]. Furthermore, the fact that the most serious abuses are committed in the course of arm conflicts does not justify but rather sets against any attempt to remove the aggression from the criminal cases to which the ICC's jurisdiction extends. This elimination "should be tantamount in many cases to treating mere symptoms while ignoring the pathogenic cause"[547].

As far as this investigation is concerned more directly, the perspectives examined in the previous paragraphs regarding a more articulated division and work between the organs of UN and ICC in the persecution of the crime of aggression are once again expressive of an attempt aimed at identifying a as balanced as possible solution to the eternal conflict between the reasons of legality and justice on the one hand and the logic of politics and power on the other and it is above all with a view to the aim assumed that this effort must be evaluated and in our opinion encouraged.

---

[545] J. TRAHAN, Defining aggression. Why the preparatory commission of the international criminal court has faced such a conundrum, op. cit., pp. 466ss.

[546] F. BERMAN, The international criminal court and the use of force by states, in Singapore Journal of International and Comparative Law, 3, 2000, pp. 480ss.

[547] L.S. SUNGA, The crimes within the jurisdiction of the international criminal court (Part II, Articles 5-10), in European Journal of Crime, Criminal Law and Criminal Justice, 6, 1998, pp. 64ss.

Chapter 5
Forms and coordination tools in the interaction between ICC and Security Council

1. Introduction

With this last chapter we aim to explore the interactions between ICC and SC in a broader perspective. The attempt is to transpose the specific problems that emerged during the investigation, related to the different areas of interaction between ICC and SC in the more general framework of tools that can favor an adequate coordination of the action of the two bodies. The analysis is therefore aimed at examining on the one hand the various possibilities and methods of intervention of SC on the activity of ICC and on the other the extent and nature of the judicial control that ICC can oppose to the action of the body politic.

This part of the investigation will focus mainly on hermeneutic techniques and the other tools that the two bodies have at their disposal to resolve any conflicts and to guarantee the performance of the other's prerogatives in the exercise of their functions. The discussion will be developed through two distinct sections, in order to separately examine the perspective of SC and ICC (section 2).

in the first part, we will try to investigate the possible impact of SC action on the jurisdictional activity of ICC. In order to proceed with this analysis, the legal basis of the powers recognized by the Rome Statute must be examined. In light of the particular nature of the powers attributed to SC, an attempt will then be made to verify the existence of any limits to the possibility of influencing ICC jurisdictional activity imposed on the action of the political body. In this perspective linked to the potential effects produced by SC Resolutions on the jurisdictional activity of ICC it will be necessary to analyze the relevance of art. 103 of the UN Charter. Finally, it will be seen that through the exercise of the prerogatives attributed to it by the Rome Treaty, SC inevitably exercises a power to interpret the relevant statutory rules. It will be a matter of understanding whether and in what way, the interpretative and applicative practice of SC can affect the interpretation that ICC bodies must give to the provisions of the Rome Treaty.

The second section will focus on the eventuality that ICC has to operate some form of control over SC decisions. In the first place it will therefore be necessary to draw a picture of the interpretative rules that can guide ICC bodies in determining the content of SC Resolutions. It will be seen how the traditional rules on interpretation must be adapted here to the particular nature and procedure of adoption of SC decisions. Of some importance even if the operation may not be easy, it is also to determine the purpose and object of the relevant Resolutions, through an analysis of the preambles and more generally of the political context in which the art was adopted.

Once a framework of the elements that can guide the interpretative activity of the ICC bodies with respect to SC decisions has been outlined, some attention will be paid to a particular hermeneutic principle, whose function of composition of possible regulatory conflicts can be extremely relevant in this context. This is the principle of systematic interpretation, contained in art. 31 (39 c) VCLT[548], from which it seems to deduce a presumption of conformity with the Rome Treaty of SC decisions aimed at affecting ICC action. The principle of conforming interpretation and the presumption of conformity can be particularly useful for circumventing interpretations of SC decisions incompatible with the provisions of the Statute.

It is clear that it is not always possible, through the principle of conforming interpretation, to avoid possible conflicts between SC Resolutions and regulatory parameters of the Statute. It is a question of understanding whether ICC bodies can make some form of validity union on SC Resolutions and somehow limit their effects. If the admissibility of this control is demonstrated, it will then be necessary to determine in the light of which regulatory parameters the union of validity can be experienced and to what extent the verification of the legitimacy of the decisions made by SC can go.

After having clarified what is meant in this particular context by union of validity, we will then propose an analysis of the jurisprudence of the international criminal courts that have found themselves examining the legitimacy of some decisions taken by SC. Although the issue is not peaceful, some propensity can be signaled at least by some international criminal jurisdictions to operate some form of control of the validity of SC decisions. A crucial role in this jurisprudence is played by the Kompetez-Kompetenz principle which is the foundation and guarantee of the independence of the judicial function. It can be anticipated here that precisely by virtue of the Kompetenz Kompetenz principle, a validity check by ICC on SC Resolutions appears possible in light of the rules of the Rome Treaty that delimit the jurisdiction of validity to include a judgment on compliance with Chapter VII of the UN Charter[549], legal basis for requests to activate and suspend the ICC action. The principle in question will be better

[548]I. BUGA, Modification of treaties by subsequent practice, op. cit., D. PEAT, Comparative reasoning in international courts and tribunals, op. cit., M. FITZMAURICE, O. ELIAS, P. MERKOURIS (eds), Treaty interpretation and the Vienna Convention on the Law of Treaties, 30 years on, op. cit., pp. 9ss. G. NOUTE, Treaties and subsequent practice, op. cit., pp. 224ss. E. BJORGE, The evolutionary interpretation of treaties, op. cit.,

[549]D. WHITTLE, The limits of legality and the United Nations Security Council: Applying the extralegal measures model to chapter VII action, op. cit.

explored in the following pages. Reference to that regulatory parameter, made by articles 13 (b) and 16 of the Rome Treaty, seems to imply that SC adoption of Resolutions is incompatible with the assumptions and limits the exercise of powers assigned to it by the UN Charter. This does not only and obviously contradict the Charter itself but also and at the same time entails a violation of the Rome Statute.

A possible union of the validity of SC decisions in the light of Chapter VII of the Charter could then concern on the one hand the respect of the procedural conditions for the adoption of Resolutions and on the other the prerequisites for the action of SC foreseen by art. 39 of the UN Charter[550]. While the verification of compliance with the decision-making procedures of SC does not seem to pose particular problems, the possibility of a judicial verification of the existence of a threat and/or violation of peace or an act of aggression raises necessarily more critical issues as it is potentially aimed at damaging the prerogatives attributed by the UN Charter to SC.

SECTION 1

The impact of SC action on ICC activity

1. The nature and basis of powers recognized to SC by the Rome Statute

ICC autonomy with respect to the UN system has already been highlighted in the introductory part. However, the need always felt to coordinate the judicial action of ICC in the repression of international crimes with that of SC in the context of the maintenance of international peace and security was also underlined. As seen from a legal point of view, this need for connection has materialized in two ways. On the one hand, the Rome Statute recognizes the SC's power to influence the ICC activity in various ways. On the other, as already foreseen by art. 2 of the Statute, ICC and UN have concluded a relationship agreement aimed at formalizing the interactions between the two organizations and in particular between ICC and SC. It is now a matter of understanding in the light of the statutory provisions and of the agreement just mentioned what is the nature and basis of the powers recognized to SC by the Rome Statute.

In the course of the work that led to the conclusion of the ICC founding treaty, one of the biggest concerns was precisely the legitimacy of any extensions or restrictions. Potentially resulting from the rules of the Rome Treaty of the powers attributed to SC of the UN Charter. Already within the ILC, the main concern about the prerogatives that the ICC Statute would have recognized to SC, in fact "was that the Council would be vested with powers additional to those granted to it under the UN Charter"[551]. On several occasions, several members of

[550]O. BEKOU, The International Criminal Court, op. cit.,

[551]ILC., Summary records of the meetings of the forty-sixth session., 2 May-22 July 1994, in Yearbook of the International Law Commission, A/CN.4/SER.A/19994, vol. I, 1994, pp.

ILC have questioned the legitimacy and viability of such a solution. For example, some have pointed out that a treaty concluded between a few states could not modify the SC powers under the UN Charter[552]. Algeria for example observed on one occasion that the powers of activation and suspension of the ICC jurisdictional activity "would substantially increase the power of the Council" and their prediction of fate amount to a re-writing of the Charter[553]. Also in doctrine it has been highlighted that through the Rome Statute, SC powers cannot be expanded or compressed which remain only those attributed to it and governed by the UN Charter.

Perhaps precisely to avoid affecting the prerogatives and functions of SC, the relevant provisions of the Rome Statute seem in fact formulated in a way not to alter the content of SC powers that can exercise on the basis of the UN Charter. In order to understand how the State has tried to reconcile the role recognized by SC in its relations with ICC the powers attributed to it by the UN Charter it appears necessary to make some distinctions according to the different area in which the SC action is bound to affect.

The nature of the references made by the statutory rules to a possible impact of SC on ICC work, in fact, changes according to the scope of intervention and the different importance that the Statute recognizes to the action of the political body towards the judicial activity.

As regards cooperation and judicial assistance, for example, the Statute limits itself to providing for the possibility that ICC notifies SC of a violation of the obligations of the States in this particular area. Following this assessment by ICC, SC does not seem to confer any particular prerogative if not to recognize the possibility of exercising its coercive opinion to States. A similar, albeit more articulated, provision with respect to that established in the framework of judicial cooperation by the Rome Statute is contained in the convention for the prevention and repression of the genocide of 1948. Art. VII of that treaty provides that the contracting parties "may call upon the UN competent organs to take such an action for the prevention and suppression of acts of genocide or any of the other acts enumerated in article III"[554]. As already illustrated in the doctrine, and by ICJ, the circumstance according to which "the action is to be taken by UN organs under the Charter confirms that no addition is intended to the existing powers of those organs". In other words, the provision would have merely "an expository

15, par. 54.

[552]According to the opinion of Christian Tomuschat see the positions taken by some States at the Rome Conference, in particular of Russia and Bangladesh. See also in argument: M. CHERIF BASSIOUNI, The legislative history of the international criminal court: Summary records of the 1998 diplomatic conference, op. cit., pp. 142, 186ss.

[553]Press Release, Debate on proposed international criminal court continues in sixth committee, GA/L/2880, 2 November 1995.

[554] M. CHERIF BASSIOUNI, The legislative history of the international criminal court: Summary records of the 1998 diplomatic conference, op. cit.

character"[555]. Although not explicitly clarified by the relevant statutory provisions, it is clear that SC powers can exercise following the notification of non-compliance coming from ICC are none other than those recognized to it by the UN Charter and in particular the ability to take coercive measures towards States of non-fulfillment with respect to obligations of cooperation with the ICC bodies, if this is justified on the basis of the conditions laid down in art. 39 of the Charter.

Although in different ways, the exercise of referral or deferral powers and the possibility that the SC ascertains the existence of a state act of aggression are instead intended to produce effects not on the Member States but directly on the action of ICC organs. Once again, however, a distinction should be made between two different hypotheses.

The first hypothesis concerns the crime of aggression. The assessment of the commission of an act of aggression by one State against another is expressly part of the prerogatives recognized by the UN Charter to SC. Within the Rome Treaty there is the task of verifying that SC has made this assessment in order to proceed with investigations relating to the commission of a crime of aggression. It was dealing with an algebraic condition which is not essential for the prosecution of the crime of aggression. The Statute links here some possible consequences on the Prosecutor's activity to an assessment that SC is already entitled to perform and may or not carry out in light of a specific provision of the UN Charter, art. 39. Here, in short, SC is not required to address any particular request to ICC bodies but it is the latter and in particular the Prosecutor that can bring down some consequences on their action from the ascertainment of any aggression that may be carried out by SC.

On the other hand, the prerogatives recognized to SC to formulate their own requests to activate the investigations or to suspend the judicial activity pursuant to articles 13 b) and 16 ICC seem to have a different nature. In these latter hypotheses, in fact, the relationship dynamics established between ICC and SC appear more complex. The Statute, expressly recalling the need for the SC action to be based on the relevent Chapter of the UN Charter seems once again to limit itself to attributing to the exercise of those powers some consequences on

---

[555] G. GAJA, The role of the United Nations in preventing and suppressing genocide, in P. GAETA, The UN Genocide convention, Oxford University Press, Oxford, 2009, pp. 400ss. See also: ICJ, Application of the convention for the prevention and repression of genocide (Bosnia Herzegovina v. Serbia Montenegro), order of 8 April 1993, in ICJ Reports, 1993, p. 23, par. 47. C. GRAY, Application of the convention on the prevention and punishment of the crime of genocide (Bosnia and Herzegovina v. Yugoslavia (Serbia and Montenegro)) orders of provisional measures of 8 April 1993 and 13 September 1993, in International and Comparative Law Quarterly, 43, 1994, pp. 705ss. M. STEINFELD, When ethnic cleansing is not genocide: A critical appraisal of the ICJ's ruling in Croatia v. Serbia in relation to deportation and population transfer, in Leiden Journal of International Law, 28, 2015, pp. 938ss, (observing that the Court made ethnic cleansing become "a rather cruel 'trump card' that could be used as a comprehensive defence against any allegation (...) of genocide (...)").

ICC activity. There are those who, however, noted a certain "outer-guidance" on the part of the statutes' editors in recognizing these prerogatives. This arrogance of the editors would be due to the fact that precisely by virtue of the reference made to the powers provided for by the UN Charter, the Statute seems to take for granted that the activation and suspension functions are already among the prerogatives of SC and that these are attributable to Chapter VII of the Charter. The latter, however, does not explicitly provide for powers to activate and suspend the judicial action of ICC or in any case powers to intervene on the activity of a Court. An assessment of the legitimacy of the exercise of these prerogatives in the light of the UN Charter can only be made by the UN itself and in particular by SC itself[556].

At least as regards the activation and suspension of ICC judicial action, the powers granted to SC of the Rome Statute seem to be framed in terms of a conferral through an international treaty of a right or better of a power to a subject not party to the treaty. To be able to materialize, this contribution requires the organization's consent. This complex relationship can be essentially understood and analyzed in the light of the principles of law underlying art. 36 VCLT concluded between States and international organizations[557]. The provision largely reflects the corresponding article of the 1969 Convention concerning the attribution of a right to a third State. However, contrary to the provisions of the first paragraph of the corresponding article contained in 1969 Convention, art. 36 (2) of 1986 Convention excludes the possibility that the organization's consent may be presumed. The reason for this difference would lie in general in the more limited capacity of organizations to act internationally than in States and in particular in the fact that organizations more than real rights exercise functions assigned to them by Member States. Since the organization has thus argued that ILC has committed itself to Member States to achieve the purposes for which those functions have been recognized, it would not be at liberty to modify, through

---

[556]An example that presents some analogy with the hypotheses under examination here concerns the Treaty of Paris of 1947 concluded by Italy with the allied powers. This treaty assigned SC the task of guaranteeing the independence and integrity of the free territory of Trieste, a contrast between Italy and Yugoslavia. To this end SC should have appointed a governor as its representative and responsible for public order in the territory. See articles 2 and 11 of the peace accords of 10 February 1947, Treaties Series, vol. 49, 1950. In this case it is possible to observe how the Treaty does not limit itself to referring to the powers that SC already possesses in the light of UN Charter and whose discipline in a Treaty is almost superfluous or in any case merely declarative. Here we are dealing with a series of more extensive and articulated powers with respect to the generic possibility that the UN organs act in virtue of the powers attributed to them by the UN Charter, provided for by art. VIII of the Genocide Convention or the rules on the cooperation of the Rome Statute.

[557] I. BUGA, Modification of treaties by subsequent practice, op. cit., D. PEAT, Comparative reasoning in international courts and tribunals, op. cit., M. FITZMAURICE, O. ELIAS, P. MERKOURIS (eds), Treaty interpretation and the Vienna Convention on the Law of Treaties, 30 years on, op. cit., pp. 9ss. G. NOUTE, Treaties and subsequent practice, op. cit., pp. 224ss. E. BJORGE, The evolutionary interpretation of treaties, op. cit.,

a purely presumed consent, the rights and powers that the same States have attributed to them, for those specific purposes[558].

As highlighted by the ILC itself, however art. 36 (2) "lays down no special conditions as to the means whereby such consent is to be expressed"[559]. A certain "variety of forms depending on the type of organ of the Organization which accepts the conferral" is emphasized on the ways in which consent can also be expressed by it[560]. What appears decisive in substance is the evidence of the intention rather than the form of the same. This intention seems to be manifested both implicitly, through the concrete exercise of the powers attributed and through a formal agreement between the parties.

In the present case there is obviously no problem in relation to UN consent. First of all, it can be noted in this regard that SC immediately employed the power recognized by art. 16 StICC through Resolutions n.1422 (2002) and 1487 (2003). At that time it could already be argued that SC practice, at least as regards the arrest of ICC's jurisdiction represented a manifestation of the assent given by this body and the UN organization to exercise that particular power recognized by the Statute[561].

A decisive moment to determine the acceptance by UN of the powers recognized to SC, then appears to be the conclusion of the Resolution of 2004 agreement. It can be said that on that occasion the UN expressed their consent to exercise SC the powers conferred by StICC[562]. On the other hand, ILC had already

---

[558]ILC, Draft articles on the law of treaties between States and international organizations or between international organizations, in Yearbook of the International Law Commission, 1982, vol. II, Part Two, op. 43, note 101, which is affirmed that "the exercise by an organization of certain rights is generally also a matter of performing an obligation at least in regard to its members, and for that reason the situation of an organization cannot be fully equated with that of a State (…)".

[559]M. STEINFELD, When ethnic cleansing is not genocide: A critical appraisal of the ICJ's ruling in Croatia v. Serbia in relation to deportation and population transfer, op. cit.,

[560]D. SAROOSHI, Some preliminary remarks on the conferral by states of powers on international organizations, in New York University Jean Monnet working paper, 11, 2004, pp. 11ss.

[561]The consent of SC to exercise those powers, however, could not be considered sufficient. The powers conferred on SC have repercussions for all the UN Member States. If for the States Parties of the Rome Statute and for the SC members (even if not part of the Statute) the consent to the exercise of those powers can be considered manifested through the concrete exercise of the prerogatives of SC; the acceptance of the new prerogatives granted to SC by all the other UN Member States should instead have been ascertained (some reflections of: G. GAJA, The protection of general interest in the international community, in Recueil des cours, ed Brill, Bruxelles, vol. 364, 2011, pp. 84ss). It should be emphasized that in the course of work that led to the conclusion of the ICC founding Treaty, almost all the States (including those that did not ratify the Statute) expressed the conviction that the close connection between the Commission of international crimes and the maintenance of peace and security imposed an active role of SC towards ICC while not sharing the forms that this relationship should have taken.

[562]UN doc. A/RES/58/318, 13 September 2004. The agreement was signed by the first

noted that the agreement that the two institutions would conclude pursuant to art. 2 of the Rome Treaty "would provide, inter alia, for the exercise by the UN of the powers and functions referred to in the Statute"[563].

In the agreement, however, the two organizations recognize the mutual and generic obligations of cooperation (articles 3 and 17) and consecrate as said the principle according to which UN and ICC "respect each other's statutes and mandate" (art. 2 (3)). The agreement therefore seems to sanction the UN's commitment to exercise the powers conferred on its bodies in compliance with the Rome Statute and ICC prerogatives.

The principles set out in the agreement also relate to another plan which concerns the possible limits of SC action when acting on the basis of the powers attributed to it by the Statute. As established by art. 36 (3) VCLT in order to produce the effects attributable to the right attributed through the trait, the organization "shall comply with the conditions for its exercise provided for in the Treaty or established in conformity with it"[564]. This provision is identical to the respective art. 36 (2) VCLT on the conferral of a right to a third State. In relation to this particular hypothesis, the ILC noted that in the event that the third party intends to exercise a right or an option attributed to it by a treaty, it will also be required to suffer "the corresponding disadvantages or disabilities"[565]. In particular, if the exercise of that right is subject to certain conditions, the fulfillment of the same "may give rise to a claim to exercise rights or enjoy benefits"[566].

In light of the principles set out in the work of ILC, it can therefore be stated that when SC intends to exercise the powers attributed by the Rome Statute, it is also required to comply with the operating conditions provided therein, in the same way if it exercises those powers in compliance with these limits and

---

president of ICC, Philippe Kirsch and by the then UN Secretary General, Kofi Annan. The Assembly of States Parties to the Statutes also expressed its willingness to conclude the treaty through a Resolution of 7 September 2004, ICC-ASP/3/Res. 1. For further details see: M. RAMSDEN, Uniting against impunity: The United Nations General Assembly as a catalyst for action at the International Criminal Court, in The International & Comparative Law Quarterly, 66 (4), 2017, pp. 98ss. J.M. ISANGA, The International Criminal Court ten years later: Appraisal and prospects, in Cardozo Journal of International & Comparative Law, 21, 2013, pp. 238ss.

[563]Draft Statute for an international criminal court with commentaries, in Yearbook of the International Law Commission, 1994, vol. II, part two, p. 28.

[564]M. RAMSDEN, Uniting against impunity: The United Nations General Assembly as a catalyst for action at the International Criminal Court, op. cit.,

[565] I. BUGA, Modification of treaties by subsequent practice, op. cit., D. PEAT, Comparative reasoning in international courts and tribunals, op. cit., M. FITZMAURICE, O. ELIAS, P. MERKOURIS (eds), Treaty interpretation and the Vienna Convention on the Law of Treaties, 30 years on, op. cit., pp. 9ss. G. NOUTE, Treaties and subsequent practice, op. cit., pp. 224ss. E. BJORGE, The evolutionary interpretation of treaties, op. cit.,

[566]Sir Gerald Fitzmaurice, Fifth Report on the law of treaties (treaties and third States), in Yearbook of the International Law Commission, 1980, vol. II, A/CN.4/130, p. 77.

conditions, SC will be able to claim against ICC the consequences connected by the Rome Statute to its action. In other words, if SC exercises the powers that the Rome Treaty recognizes in compliance with the Statute, ICC has the corresponding obligation to give effect to decisions aimed at affecting its action[567]. It should be specified in this regard that while in the case of the exercise of the power of deferral the obligation consequences is to suspend the investigation activities and the courses, i.e. the referral of SC does not require ICC to open the investigations. However, the Prosecutor may be deemed to have an obligation to evaluate in good faith the consistency and substantiation of the notitia criminis acquired upon notification by SC.

2. The limited relevance of art. 103 of the UN Charter in the relationship between Security Council and ICC

The analysis carried out in the previous paragraph therefore leads to believe that the powers attributed to SC to activate or suspend the ICC judicial activity must respect in order to produce the effects envisaged by art. 13 (b) and 16 StICC, the conditions and operating limits set by the Rome Treaty.

In the introduction to this work, mention was made of the possibility sometimes even banned in doctrine[568], of reconstructing the interactions between ICC and SC with a view to guaranteeing a prevalence of the action of the political body over the ICC jurisdictional activity, independently by the limits set by the Rome Statute. This possible reconstruction of the relationship between SC and ICC usually relies on the role that could be played in this area of art. 103 of the UN Charter.

The hypothesis of a relevance of art. 103 of the UN Charter to legitimize a possible jurisdiction or an extension by the SC beyond what is foreseen by the Statute, infact have already been envisaged in at least two distinct circumstances. During the adoption of Resolution n.1423 of 2002 relating to the renewal of the UN mission in Bosnia Herzegovina, some States affirmed that the possibility of permanently and automatically renewing the effects produced by the exercise of the power of deferral envisaged by art. 16 of the Statute would be "within SC's authority"[569]. According to these positions, this SC power to extend the suspension of the ICC's judicial activity beyond the 12 months established by the

---

[567]M. FITZMAURICE, E. ELIAS, Contemporary issues in the law of treaties, Eleven Publishing International, The Hague, 2005, pp. 284ss.

[568]In addition to the authors already mentioned in the introduction, here we can further report some theses aimed at recognizing art. 103 the effect of attributing for the purposes of the UN Charter and in particular to the maintenance of international peace and security the nature of "international public order to which other treaty regimes and the international organizations giving effect to them must conform". See: D. SHELTON, International law an "relative normativity", in M. EVANS, International law, Oxford University Press, Oxford, 2006, pp. 178ss.

[569]UN Doc. S/PV.4568, p. 23.

Statute, would derive directly from the effects of art. 103 of the UN Charter for the mere fact that this provision "provided for charter obligations to prevail in the event of a conflict between them and other international obligations"[570]. Even in doctrine it is possible to find some critical positions regarding the scope of art. 16 and the time limit provided therein. The impossibility of suspending ICC jurisdiction for a period longer than 12 months set by that provision raises, according to some, a series of perplexities in particular on the fact that "the Rome Statute can constitutionally limit the Council's powers"[571]. These criticisms are still based on a generic reference to art. 103 and the prevalence that this rule attributes to the obligations deriving from the UN Charter. More general according to these reconstructions this provision should allow SC to exercise "its plenary powers (...) to act decisively in many matters affecting international peace and security"[572].

Also in the report to the UN Secretary-General of 2005 sent by the Commission of experts for the repression of crimes committed in East Timor, the hypothesis was put forward that SC adapts the Rome Stature to the contingent repressive needs that emerged in that particular contest. The possibility of extending ICC's jurisdiction ratione temporis to include crimes committed in East Timor at the end of the 1990s was discussed in a period preceding the entry into force of the Statute. According to the Commission of experts, in fact Chapter VII and art. 103 of the UN Charter would represent "a legal basis upon which SC could legitimately extend the scope of the temporal jurisdiction of ICC"[573].

In support of solutions similar to those just mentioned, some authors believe that the measures adopted by the SC "are binding also for ICC and art. 103"[574]. In other words, if the measures adopted by SC respect the limits of the exercise of powers recognized by the UN Charter of the UN, their possible incompatibility with the Rome Statute "is irrelevant" and SC decisions would in practice enjoy a true and its priority over conflicting Rome Statute obligations of ICC and its Member States[575]. The prevalence of obligations deriving from the

---

[570]M. RAMSDEN, Uniting against impunity: The United Nations General Assembly as a catalyst for action at the International Criminal Court, op. cit.,

[571]R. WEDGWOOD, The international criminal court: An American view, op. cit., pp. 98ss.

[572]R. WEDGWOOD, The international criminal court: An American view, op. cit., pp. 98ss. M. RAMSDEN, Uniting against impunity: The United Nations General Assembly as a catalyst for action at the International Criminal Court, op. cit.,

[573]Report to the Secretary-General of the Commission of experts to review the prosecution of serious violations of human rights in Timor-Leste (Then East Timor) in 1999, S/2005/458, 26 May 2005, par. 455.

[574]J. PICHON, Internationaler Strafgerichtshof und Sicherheitsrat der Vereinten Nationen, ed. Springer, Heidelberg, 2011, pp. 352ss.

[575]Some reconstructions tend to attribute a role to the relationship agreement and to the recognition of UN responsibilities in order to confirm the prevalence of SC action on that of ICC. In particular, according to these arguments, the 2004 Agreement Report "does not validate any aspect of ICC work that would purport to override the established mechanisms

UN Charter would therefore not be granted only with respect to the obligations deriving from the Rome Treaty for the States Parties but also to the obligations that derive from the Statute for the ICC organs.

If, also in light of the provisions of the 2004 agreement, there is no doubt that ICC, like any other legal entity, is required to comply with the principles and rules of a customary nature contained in the UN Charter, however, it is more complicated to make descend by art. 103 an automatic supremacy of the SC's action over the ICC jurisdictional activity. These references to art. 103 of the UN Charter do not seem to adequately take into consideration the letter of the provision and what has so far been its concrete application. In other words, art. 103 would not be aimed at sanctioning the prevalence of the UN Charter over any other international treaty but would simply be a rule for the solution of possible conflicts between obligations of States. Unlike what the above mentioned reconstructions suggest, in fact, art. 103 seems clearly aimed at determining the prevalence for the States and not for all the subjects of the international legal system of the obligations deriving from the UN Charter. Despite the universal nature of some principles expressed in the UN Charter and the commitment made by ICC itself to respect its content and purposes, the ICC is not subject to a rule aimed at regulating hypotheses of conflicts between obligations that could potentially arise for UN Member States.

It cannot be ignored and this aspect has already emerged during the discussion of the possible effects of art. 103 on the effectiveness of the ICC's action, in particular in the field of cooperation and judicial assistance. Indeed, the fallout of possible SC Resolutions aimed at limiting or preventing the cooperation of States with the international tribunal, can evidently whip its repressive action. Art. 103 of the UN Charter in other words guaranteeing a prevalence of the obligations deriving from the decisions of SC over the contractual obligations assumed by the States towards ICC, could prevent or in any case hinder the execution of ICC decisions. This provision may ultimately allow SC to hinder the collaboration of states with the ICC and actually compromise the effectiveness of the action of the Court.

3. Security Council power to interpret the Rome Statute

In the exercise of the functions assigned to it, the SC regularly interpreted the meaning and scope of the provisions of the UN Charter to which its powers are attributable[576]. As the same ICJ pointed out in the opinion on certain expenses

---

of maintenance of international peace and security centered on the leading role of the UN Security Council in situations endangering peace and security". See in argument: J. DORIA, Conflicting interpretation of the ICC statute. Are the rules of interpretation of the Vienna Convention still relevant?, in M. FITZMAURICE, O. ELIAS, P. MERKOURIS, Treaty interpretation and the Vienna Convention on the law of treaties: 30 years on, ed. Brill, Leiden, Boston, 2010, pp. 312ss.

576M.C. SOHN, The UN system as authoritative interpreter of its law, in O. SCHACHTER,

of UN, in fact, any body not only the courts "must in the first place at least, determine its own jurisdiction"[577]. The bodies operating within the international organizations are constantly called upon to interpret their founding Treaty. In many cases, however, through the application practice these bodies end up affecting the interpretation itself of the rules that regulate the functioning and the scope of the powers[578]. In addition to the rules of its founding Treaty, the bodies of international organizations may sometimes be called upon to apply (and therefore interpret) treaties concluded between States. In fact, the same SC has over time interpreted the content of international agreements other than the UN Charter. The Resolution n.541 of 1983, through which the SC sanctioned the incompatibility of the declaration of independence of the Turkish authorities of Cyprus with the Alliance and guarantee treaties concluded in 1960, can only be referred to as an example.

When it uses the powers of intervention on ICC jurisdictional activity recognized to it by the Rome Statute, it is therefore inevitable that the SC also exercises an interpretative power about the content of the statutory rules relevant for the purpose of its action by determining the limits and extension of what it believes to be its prerogatives.

Moreover, it has already been noted that the SC has more or less expressly referred to the provisions of the Rome Statute which is considered relevant for the exercise of the powers attributed to it. On the occasion of the Resolutions n.1422 (2002) and 1487 (2003) for example SC has considered its action consistent with article 16 of the ICC Statute. While not expressly referring to the Rome Statute with the Resolution n.1593 (2005), SC has then manifested, using the language of art.13 b), its intention to refer the situation in Darfur to ICC. In an even more explicit way in that part of Resolution n.1970 (2011) entitled "ICC referral", the SC then reported to ICC Prosecutor the crimes against

---

C. JOYNER, United Nations legal order, Cambridge University Press, Cambridge, 1995, pp. 204ss. R. HIGGINS, P. WEBB, D. AKANDE, Oppenheim's international law: United Nations, Oxford University Press, Oxford, 2018. D.M. MALONE, The Security Council in the post-cold war era: A study in the creative interpretation of the UN charter, in Security Dialogue, 28 (4), 1997, pp. 489ss. Even if the debate is wide and the risk of obvious abuse can be noted that some authors tend to emphasize the inherent advantages of the SC's ability to adapt, through its own interpretative activity, the provisions of the Charter to the changing dynamics of international security. “There has been an evolution in SC's interpretation of the rules that shows the ability of the system to adapt (...)”. J.E. STROMSETH, Law and force after Iraq: A transnational movement, in American Journal of International Law, 97, 2003, pp. 634ss. C. GRAY, International law and the use of force, Oxford University Press, Oxford, 2018.

[577]International Court of Justice, certain United Nations expenses, opinion of 20 July 1962, in ICJ Reports 1962, pp. 176ss.

[578]It is possible to report what was noted in the doctrine concerning the acts of the general secretary of the UN: “chacune des dècisions qu'il est amenè à prendre constitue concrètement une interpètation de son mandat”, in M. VIRALLY, Les Nations Unies et l'affaire du Congo en 1960, in Annuaire Français de Droit International, 6, 1960, pp. 572ss.

humanity committed in Libya since 16 February 2011[579]. In these circumstances, the political body has not only exercised the powers attributed to it by the Statute but has also proposed in fact its own interpretation of the relevant provisions and more generally of the extent and limits of its prerogatives to intervene on ICC action.

In the light of the rules regarding the interpretation of the treaties, SC is the principle called to determine the scope of its powers based on the Rome Statute through a good faith interpretation of the relevant rules, giving importance to the ordinary meaning to be attributed to the terms employees and taking into account the context, as well as the object and purpose of the Treaty. On the relevance of the literal interpretation criterion in this context, we can limit ourselves to observing to give some examples that the time limit of 12 months expressly provided for by art. 16 does not seem to leave particular room for interpretation regarding the maximum duration of the suspension of the judicial action that can be requested from SC to ICC. The same could be said for the basis of the decisions to activate or stop the activity of ICC which must necessarily be identified in Chapter VII of the UN Charter[580]. Beyond some conditions expressly provided for by the Rome Treaty, the provisions relating to the powers of activation and suspension of the ICC action are however drawn up as widely highlighted in a rather concise manner, sometimes presenting uncertainties and ambiguities. The possibility still to give some examples of delimiting the geographical dimension or the time span (as long as I include a period after the entry into force of the Rome Treaty) of the situations that can be referred to the Prosecutor is not specifically regulated by the Statute. Just as it is not easy to determine how much an attempt has been made to offer some interpretative solution in the light of the ratio of the provision and the preparatory work if and in what way the SC can delimit the ICC competence ratione personae.

It may be asked whether SC through the concrete exercise of the referral and deferral powers could affect the interpretation to be given to the relevant provisions of the Statute. For the purposes of this question, art. 31 (3) b) VCLT[581]. In light of this provision, a role for the interpretation of the treaties can be played by subsequent practice to the extent that it is possible to derive from it the existence of an interpretative agreement between the parties[582]. In the light of this

---

[579]O. BEKOU, The International Criminal Court, op. cit.,

[580]D. WHITTLE, The limits of legality and the United Nations Security Council: Applying the extralegal measures model to chapter VII action, op. cit.

[581]I. BUGA, Modification of treaties by subsequent practice, op. cit., D. PEAT, Comparative reasoning in international courts and tribunals, op. cit., M. FITZMAURICE, O. ELIAS, P. MERKOURIS (eds), Treaty interpretation and the Vienna Convention on the Law of Treaties, 30 years on, op. cit., pp. 9ss. G. NOUTE, Treaties and subsequent practice, op. cit., pp. 224ss. E. BJORGE, The evolutionary interpretation of treaties, op. cit.,

[582]For further details see: A. MARSCHIK, Legislative powers of the Security Council in R.S.J. MACDONALD, D.M. JOHNSTON, Towards world constitutionalism. Issues in the legal ordering of the world community, ed. Brill, Leiden, Boston, 2005, pp. 464ss. K. ZEMANEK, The legal foundations of the international system, in Recueil des cours, ed.

interpretative rule, SC practice insofar as it contributes to the application of certain rules of the Rome Statute, could in principle be used to affirm evolutionary interpretations or even as far as the distinction between the two hypotheses is not always easy amendments to these provisions.

In order to determine the interpretative relevance of SC practice, it is necessary to first take into consideration the particular institutional context in which the interactions between SC and ICC are inserted[583]. It can be considered that the very notion of application practice is in the complex institutional architecture designed by the Rome Statute in some way broader and in more difficult assessment. This is essentially due to the plurality and heterogeneity of the subjects potentially involved in the application and interpretation of the Treaty not only the States Parties to the Statute but precisely SC and of course the ICC bodies themselves.

In this regard, the first element to highlight is that the CS practice does not per se but only insofar as it allows to detect the existence of a consensus between the States Parties to the Treaty. An indication in this sense can be obtained from the opinion of the ICJ in the case of the legal consequences for the States of the continuous presence of Southern Africa in Namibia (African Southwest), despite the Resolution n.276 (1970). According to ICJ, a body's practice can in principle be used to interpret the content of the organization's founding treaty if such practice is generally accepted by the Member States of the organization[584]. The opinion refers to the practice of the bodies created by the treaty establishing the organization within which those bodies operate. Although it is a question here of giving relevance to the behavior of a body external to the treaty establishing the Court, reasoning similar to that made by the ICJ can however be made to establish the impact of SC practice for the purposes of interpretation of the Rome Statute. The containment of the States in relation to a specific interpretation of the Rome Statute put forward by SC can in fact point out as an indicative element of a possible agreement between these regarding the meaning that must be attributed to the rules of the Treaty. In other words, a generalized consent of the States

---

Brill/Martinus Nijhoff Publishers, Bruxelles, vol. 269, 1997, pp. 96ss. G. NOLTE, Subsequent practice and treaties, Oxford University Press, Oxford, 2013. S. BREAU, The responsibility to protect in international law: An emerging paradigm shift, ed. Routledge, London & New York, 2016. I. GOVAERE, S. GARBEN, The interface between European Union and international law: Contemporary reflections, op. cit., pp. 86ss. R. COLLINS, The institutional problem in modern international law, ed. Bloomsbury, New York, 2016.

[583]C.M. BRÖLMANN, Specialized rules of treaty interpretation: International organizations, in D.B. HOLLIS, Oxford guide to treaties, Oxford University Press, Oxford, 2012, pp. 508ss. R.K. GARDINER, Treaty interpretation, Oxford University Press, Oxford, 2015, pp. 127ss.

[584]International Court of Justice, Legal consequences for the States of the continued presence of Southern Africa in Namibia (South-West Africa) despite the Resolution n.276 (1970), opinion of 21 June 1971, in ICJ Report, 1971, pp. 22. J.A. FROWEIN, The international and external effects of resolutions by international organizations, in Zeitschrift für ausländisches öffentliches Recht und Völkerrecht, 49, 1989, pp. 790ss.

Parties to the Rome Treaty with respect to a specific CS practice could be indicative of a new understanding regarding the interpretation to be given to a certain statutory provision.

The point just outlined already offers a first interesting element of evaluation of the practice developed to date by SC in relation to the exercise of the powers assigned to it by the Rome Statute. In particular, it is interesting to note here that certain positions of SC have raised critical reactions from a substantial number of States, including SC Member States. As highlighted in the previous chapters on the practice of sanctions by the ICC jurisdiction for peacekeeping personnel, arranged over the years on several occasions by SC, it has encountered a widespread opposition between the States Parties of the Statute[585]. The state's protest reaction to certain consequences of this practice has gone so far as to prefigure at least for the limitations envisaged with regard to the exercise of the criminal action by the national courts the impossibility of being able to execute the parts of the device of the SC decisions regarding the above exemptions[586]. The particular circumstance that in the Resolution n.1970 (2011) of activating the investigations of the Prosecutor with respect to the crimes committed in Libya, the exclusive jurisdiction of the sending State prepared for personnel of the States not part of the Statute has found at the moment to support an affirmation of this particular practice. The widespread belief among States of the need for military intervention in Libya seems, however, in that particular context to have overshadowed the critical issues relating to the exercise of the criminal action by ICC. In short, it can be argued that the attitudes of States Parties to the Rome Treaty with respect to the exemptions provided by SC considerably limit the relevance that can currently be attributed to this practice for the purpose of interpreting the Statute.

The interpretative relevance of SC practice does not seem to depend only on the attitude taken by the States. In the articulated dynamic of relationship crest from the Rome Treaty, other actors who exercise their own determinant potestas interpretandi are naturally the ICC organs[587]. The fact that the Rome Treaty

---

[585]Here we can resume only to give some examples the positions expressed by the Member States of the Rio Group in debates that preceded the adoption of Resolution n.1422 (2002) which is affirmed that "the entire peace-keeping system might be jeopardized by an erroneous interpretation of the provisions of the Rome Statute" UN Doc. S/PV.4568, p. 15 and from Mexican delegate which affirmed that "the Council would be interpreting the scope of article 16 very broadly, since the article was designed for specific situations". Or you can remember the words of Jordan at the time of the adoption of the Resolution n.1487 (2003) "the Council's interpretation of article 16 does not accord with the drafting history of that article", UN Doc. S/PV.4772, p. 6.

[586]We recall the positions taken by France, Germany and Denmark at the time of the adoption of the Resolution n.1497 (2003).

[587]D. SIMON, L'interpretation judiciaire des traitès d'organisations internationales, ed. Pedone, Paris, 1981. Y.T., CHANG, The interpretation of treaties by judicial tribunals, Columbia University Press, London, 1933. K. BERNER, Authentic interpretation in public international law, in Zeitschrift für ausländisches öffentliches Recht und Völkerrecht, 74,

establishes a particular international organization, an international tribunal implies a centralization in the judicial organs of interpretative activity. In fact, the ICC bodies not only have the power inherent in the function they exercise, to determine the scope of their jurisdiction, but they also tend to focus on themselves the decision-making power regarding any interpretative issue that could potentially emerge in relation to the rules contained in its institutional treaty. This means in practice that the interpretation of the Rome Statute adopted by SC cannot be considered binding for the ICC bodies. Although endowed with its own interpretative power in the exercise of this power, SC will find itself essentially subject to a form of control by ICC. More generally, it is the activity of SC that appears likely to be subject to a control not only of compliance with the Rome Statute but also possibly with high rules and principles of international law.

In conclusion, it can therefore be argued that the legal relevance in the practice of SC that can take for the interpretation of the Rome Statute appears limited. On the other hand, it is necessary that this interpretative practice corresponds to a generalized consensus of the States that demonstrates the need for an agreement between the latter regarding the interpretation of the Statute adopted by SC. On the other hand, ICC bodies will tend to attribute the decisive word for the interpretation of the Statute.

A different discussion regards the relevance that SC Resolutions can take on. The authority and political weight of the decisions taken by SC could in fact induce ICC to avoid such word-of-mouth interpretative solutions in a position of open contrast with the political body. And this not only to avoid generating tensions and insoluble inter-institutional conflicts, once again in fact and more concretely for ICC it could prove to be particularly costly to break up relations with SC and expose themselves to the risk of not being able to rely on the collaboration of this last in the repression of the crimes within its jurisdiction.

SECTION 2

ICC control on Security Council activity

1. The interpretation of Security Council resolutions

In order to determine the effects of SC Resolutions on its action, ICC will first have to interpret its content. However, the interpretation of SC decisions can be particularly complex. These are heart attacks often characterized by a certain ambiguity of language resulting from the political compromises necessary to reach a shared position among the Member States.

A further complicating element is given by the fact that the rules of interpretation relevant for establishing the meaning to be attributed to SC Resolutions have never been the subject of specific regulations or attempts to codify. On the matter, ICJ has provided, through two well-known opinions, some

---

2016, pp. 876ss.

important indications. On the first occasion (the opinion on the legal consequences of the prolonged presence of South Africa in Namibia) the ICJ had limited itself to affirming without referring to the rules on the interpretation of the treaties that to define the binding nature of a SC Resolution, it is necessary to take into account "the terms of the Resolution to be interpreted the discussions leading to it, the charter provisions invoked and in general to the circumstances that might assist in determining the legal consequences of the Resolution of their SC"[588]. In the most recent opinion on the compliance with the international declaration of independence with regard to Kosovo, ICJ expressly recognized that the rules on the interpretation of the treaties contained in articles 31 and 32 of the VCLT may provide guidance[589]. This prudence of ICJ in recalling the rules on interpretation is immediately explained by the subsequent affirmation that the differences between treaties and SC Resolution[590] require that in order to establish the meaning of the latter it is necessary to take into consideration additional elements with respect to to those covered by VCLT[591]. In particular according to ICJ, SC decisions, as an expression of the will of a collective body and result of a peculiar adoption process, may require to analyze statements by representatives of SC members made at the time of their adoption on the same issue as well as the subsequent practice of relevant UN organs and of States affected by those given

---

[588]International Court of Justice, Legal consequences of the continued presence of South Africa in Namibia (South-West Africa despite the Resolution n.276 (1970), opinion of 21 June 1971, in ICJ Reports 1971, par. 114.

[589]International Court of Justice, Compliance with international law of the declaration of independence with regard to Kosovo, opinion of 22 July 2010, in ICJ Reports 2010, par. 94. For further details see: M.C. WOOD, The interpretation of Security Council resolutions, in Max Planck Yearbook of the United Nations, 2, 1998, pp. 73ss, which is affirmed that: "such general principles of interpretation as exist in international law need to be applied to different kinds of instruments having regard to their particular nature" and the same author: M.C. WOOD, The interpretation of Security Council resolutions, revisited, in Max Planck Yearbook of United Nations Law, 20 (1), 2017, pp. 5ss. Here it is worth mentioning also that ICTY also made extensive use of the hermeneutical criteria established by VCLT in order to interpret its own statute which, as is known, is not an international treaty but is attached to a SC Resolution. See in particular the note: Decision on the defence motion for interlocutory appeal on jurisdiction, Appeals Chamber, IT-94-1-AR72, Appeals Chamber, 2 October 1995. In argument see also: J.M. SOREL, V. BORÉ EVENO, Article 31, O. CORTEN, P. KLEIN, The Vienna conventions on the law of treaties, Oxford University Press, Oxford, 2011, pp. 822ss.

[590]H. THIRLWAY, The law and procedure of the international court of justice 1960-1989, in British Yearbook of International Law, 72 (1), 1996, pp. 29ss. One of the differences obviously lies in the very nature of the Resolutions "more akin to a unilateral act than a Treaty". See in argument: R.K. GARDINER, Treaty interpretation, op. cit., pp. 129ss.

[591] I. BUGA, Modification of treaties by subsequent practice, op. cit., D. PEAT, Comparative reasoning in international courts and tribunals, op. cit., M. FITZMAURICE, O. ELIAS, P. MERKOURIS (eds), Treaty interpretation and the Vienna Convention on the Law of Treaties, 30 years on, op. cit., pp. 9ss. G. NOUTE, Treaties and subsequent practice, op. cit., pp. 224ss. E. BJORGE, The evolutionary interpretation of treaties, op. cit.,

Resolutions"[592].

Beyond the relevance in this context of the typical methods of interpretation of the treaties and of the pre-eminence generally accorded to the literal criterion, it appears however inherent to the legal reasoning itself "to start first with the document under construction and only to look beyond it in hard cases"[593]. Thus, to recall a particularly stringent example of the regulatory context in question, if SC makes a request for suspension to ICC for a clearly determined period of time, it is not clear how other parameters can be detected to establish the content of that particular element of the decision.

The so-called contextual elements identified by the international court of justice are evident especially when the meaning of a Resolution or some of the terms used is ambiguous.

Among the elements referred to by ICJ, some attention must be paid as seen to the positions expressed by the representatives of the States within the SC regarding the interpretation that must be given to the content of SC decisions. The relevant practice for the purpose of this investigation provides numerous examples of potentially useful interventions in order to reconstruct the meaning to be given to a SC Resolution. The position expressed by the EU regarding the intention formulated by the SC through the Resolution n.1422 (2002) and 1487 (2003) to annually renew the suspension of jurisdiction of ICJ is emblematic in this regard. The EU representative noted on this specific aspect that this part of the device "cannot be interpreted as permitting the automatic renewal of that Resolution without taking into account the specific conditions under which such a request is being made"[594]. The same point of view expressed in the same meeting by the Dutch delegate according to which precisely the Resolution "should not in any way be interpreted as moving in the direction of automatic yearly renewal"[595]. These positions are aimed at excluding interpretations of the Resolutions in question which favor the idea of an automatic renewal of the suspension of the court jurisdiction. Any extension of this measure must instead be reconsidered in the light of the circumstances existing at the time when SC request was addressed to the Court.

Also with regard to the issue of the exclusive jurisdiction of the status of dispatch on their citizens engaged abroad in missions established or authorized by UN raised by some SC Resolutions, there are emerging statements of States aimed at potentially affecting the interpretation that the organs of the Court could give to that particular measure. In the debate prior to the adoption of the Resolution n.1593 (2005) for example, Tanzania stated that it could not accept "that the

[592]International court of justice, Compliance with international law of the declaration of independence with regard to Kosovo, opinion of 22 July 2010, in ICJ Reports 2010, par. 94.

[593]C. MCLACHLAN, The principle of systemic integration and article 31 (39 (c) of the Vienna Convention, op. cit., pp. 288ss.

[594]UN Doc. SP/V.4772, p. 9.

[595]UN Doc. SP/V.4772, p. 20.

Resolution should in any way be interpreted as seeking to circumvent the jurisdiction of the Court"[596]. Unlike the renewal hypothesis however, in the light of the clarity of the text of the decision, it appears difficult to interpret that part of the device of Resolution n.1593 (2005) so as not to affect ICC jurisdiction.

Finally, also as regards the relationship agreements concluded on the basis of art. 98 (2) StICC to which, as seen in SC Resolution n.1593 (2005), reference can be made to useful elements to reconstruct the meaning to be attributed to the content of the decision. Denmark, for example, stressed that the resolution "is merely referring to the existence of such agreements" and that therefore "in no way impinges on the integrity of the Rome Statute"[597]. In other words, the recognition of the existence of these agreements should not, in the opinion of this State, affect the powers of ICC bodies and the obligations assumed by the States Parties to the Rome Treaty.

For the purposes of this investigation, a further element of interest resulting from the indications offered by ICJ in the opinion of 2010 concerns the subsequent practice of the other UN bodies. It will be remembered that the UN Secretary-General expressed himself on the first Resolutions adopted by SC in the name of the powers conferred on it by art. 16 StICC[598] has severely criticized this practice and invited to stop its repetition. The Secretary-General expressed in particular his concern about its conformity with article 16 of the Rome Statute[599] and revealed for what interests him most, his fear that the practice of SC could be interpreted "as meaning that the Council wished to claim absolute and permanent immunity for people serving in the operations it establishes or authorizes"[600]. The annual suspension of ICC's jurisdiction over certain categories of individuals then effectively ceased. These passages of the declarations made by the Secretary-General, however, reinforce the aforementioned position statements of some States and lead us to believe that ICC could have interpreted those Resolutions in the sense of denying the permanent character through an automatic renewal of the suspension ordered by SC.

A final element that can take on some significance for interpretative purposes naturally concerns the purpose of Resolutions. In particular, reconstructing the objective of SC decision, in the case of a peacekeeping action of ex chapter VII, can be useful in identifying the reasons and assumptions underlying the measures adopted.

Particular attention can be paid to the preamble of the act in question to determine the purposes that the decisions of the SC set. As critically noted in the doctrine, however, the preambles of the Resolutions must be interpreted with

---

[596]UN Doc. SP/V.5158, p. 9.

[597]UN Doc. SP/V.5158, p. 6.

[598]O. BEKOU, The International Criminal Court, op. cit.,

[599]UN Secretary-General Kofi Annan, statement to UN Security Council. Open debate on the proposed renewal of the provisions of SC Resolution n.1422, SG/SM/8749, SC/7790, 12 June 2003.

[600] R.K. GARDINER, Treaty interpretation, op. cit.,

caution since often among the representatives of the States there is no conscious effort to ensure that the object and purpose of each operational provision is reflected in the preamble. More generally, it is always good to keep in mind that the SC "is not a judicial body set up to give a purely juridical response to a problem" and that in determining the attitudes of state representatives and the decisions taken by international law does not always have a decisive role[601]. Often, therefore, only an understanding of the broader political context in which SC Resolutions are adopted can help establish its purpose and presuppositions.

The latter considerations are of particular relevance in trying to trace a link between the exemptions set out in Resolutions n.1422 (2002) and 1487 (2003) and the interest set out in the preamble to those decisions to ensure the participation of States in peacekeeping missions and more in general, the maintenance of international peace and security. According to some reconstructions it has already been seen, this preamble, highlighting the true purpose of the Resolution, would also indicate the content of the threat to peace identified by SC as the basis for its suspension request. This threat would essentially be represented by the possibility that ICC exercises its repressive power towards individuals (citizens of States not part of StICC) engaged in missions established or authorized by UN. We have already mentioned in part and we will return in the next pages to the difficulty of framing these Resolutions in Chapter VII precisely because it is impossible to trace what the threat to peace is that is the basis of SC decisions. Here, in order to interpret the basis of SC decisions in light of their purpose, we can limit ourselves to pointing out that this threat is not expressly indicated in the Resolution. The preamble is limited to recalling a general interest of the international community in favoring the participation of UN states in operations. This statement in truth seems to have a purely political value rather than identifying a specific threat to peace which is the basis of the request for suspension of ICC action. The reference to the interest of the international community in the participation of States in peacekeeping operations is essentially nothing other than recognition of the particular political context, more precisely of a condition placed by the United States for its adhesion to UN missions which led to the adoption of those Resolutions.

Finally, it is good to underline that in principle the SC could also offer an authentic interpretation of one's own acts. It is customary to report on the subject the words of the permanent court of the international justice according to which "it is an established principle that the right of giving an authoritative interpretation of and legal rule (le droit d"interprèter authentiquement) belongs solely to the person or body which has the power to modify or suppress it"[602]. To date, it is not

---

[601]A. PRANDLER, The Security Council and international law, in Acta Juridica. Academiae Scientiarum Hungaricae, 15, 1973, pp. 179ss.

[602]Permanent Court of international justice, Delimitation of the Polish-Czechoslovakian frontier (Question of Jaworzina), advisory opinion, 6 December 1923, PCJI, series B, n. 8, p. 37. For further details see also: K. BERNER, Authentic interpretation in public international law, op. cit., pp. 846ss.

possible to find authentic interpretations of SC of the Resolutions intended to affect the interpretative activity of ICJ. It can be noted here that in the abstract this power can be particularly relevant to clarify some controversial elements of the SC's decisions regarding cooperation and mutual legal assistance. As seen, a long and complex interpretative controversy has been going on for some time in relation to the possibility that ICC asks the States Parties to the Statute to hand over a head of government of a third State against a SC decision that in addition to reporting the Commission of crimes on the territory of the third country concerned also requires the latter to cooperate fully with ICC. Beyond the difficulty of interpreting the relevant statutory provisions, it is not clear whether through its request for full cooperation addressed to Sudan by SC the latter also intended to force that State to renounce the protection offered to its organs by the rules on immunity. An authentic interpretation of the particular purchase aspect of the decisions in question could resolve the interpretative question and possibly constitute a more solid legal basis for the requests for delivery addressed to States Parties and which have remained unfulfilled to date.

2. The presumption of conformity of Security Council Resolutions to the Rome Statute

Among the rules regarding the interpretation of the treaties, particular importance is attached in this context to art. 31 (3) c) VCLT[603]. As known, this provision attributes a role for the purpose of interpretation to any relevant rules of international law applicable in the relations between the parties. Art. 31 (3) c) in fact envisages treaty interpretation against the whole background of international law[604]. As is well known, the standard reflects the customary principle of systemic interpretation which, although neglected for a long time in recent years, seems to have become fundamental for connecting the various legal systems that make up the international system to each other and more generally guarantee greater unity and coherence of the ordering itself[605]. The principle more generally underlies the idea of an international law understood as a system[606].

By virtue of this fundamental function recognized in the principle under consideration, art. 31 (3) c) would in fact have the ability to become applicable in

---

[603] I. BUGA, Modification of treaties by subsequent practice, op. cit., D. PEAT, Comparative reasoning in international courts and tribunals, op. cit., M. FITZMAURICE, O. ELIAS, P. MERKOURIS (eds), Treaty interpretation and the Vienna Convention on the Law of Treaties, 30 years on, op. cit., pp. 9ss. G. NOUTE, Treaties and subsequent practice, op. cit., pp. 224ss. E. BJORGE, The evolutionary interpretation of treaties, op. cit.,

[604] M.E. VILLIGER, The Vienna convention on the law of treaties-40 years after, ed. Martinus Nijhoff Publishers, The Hague, 2009, pp. 124ss.

[605] C. MCLACHLAN, The principle of systemic integration and article 31 (39 (c) of the Vienna Convention, op. cit., pp. 280ss.

[606] ILC, Report of the international law Commission fifty-seventh session, A/60/10, 29 July 2005, p. 214, par. 467.

a greater variety of circumstances than its origins would suggest[607]. For example, it can be considered a real corollary of the principle of systemic integration, the principle of conforming interpretation or the hermeneutic technique that tries to attribute to an act or a norm the meaning that best accords with the other rules relevant for the solution of the specific case. Indeed, conforming interpretation is often considered a subspecies of the traditional canon of systematic interpretation as an interpretative tool aimed at making all the rules of an order coexist in the best possible way.

In other words, the principle of conforming interpretation is a useful tool for the purpose of settling possible regulatory conflicts and its use should guarantee a harmonious integration between different legal systems as required precisely by the principle enucleated in art. 31 (3) c) VCLT[608]. What in this particular regulatory context is obviously to reconcile is the content of SC decisions with the norms of the Statute and more generally with the rules and principles relevant for the correct administration of criminal justice at international level. Here emerges in practice the need to harmonize different spheres of legality: the UN one at the basis of SC Resolutions and that of the Rome Statute which guides ICC action. On the other hand, the same relationship agreement concluded in 2004 between UN and ICC explicitly states that the two institutions shall cooperate closely (...) in conformity with the respective provisions of Charter and Statute (...)" (art. 3)[609].

An important declination, or rather from a logical point of view, a precondition for the application of the principle of conforming interpretation itself is the presumption of conformity. In essence, the interpreter is not only called to interpret the relevant external standard in a manner consistent with the treaty being interpreted but must first assume that that standard has been adopted in accordance with the treaty itself, also has not been expressly provided to the contrary. The relevance of the presumption of conformity in the international legal system clearly emerges from the work of the special rapporteur of ILC (Koskenniemi on the fragmentation of international law) where it is expressed in completely general but extremely clear terms the idea that in international law it operates as a strong presumption against normative conflict[610].

---

[607]R.K. GARDINER, Treaty interpretation, op. cit., pp. 290ss. Others have found that the scope of art. 31 (3) c) is usually considered: "Not confined exclusively". See in argument: D. ROSENTRETER, Article 31 (3) c) of the Vienna convention on the law of treaties and the principle of systemic integration in international investment law and arbitration, ed. Nomos, Baden-Baden, 2015, pp. 217ss.

[608]I. BUGA, Modification of treaties by subsequent practice, op. cit., D. PEAT, Comparative reasoning in international courts and tribunals, op. cit., M. FITZMAURICE, O. ELIAS, P. MERKOURIS (eds), Treaty interpretation and the Vienna Convention on the Law of Treaties, 30 years on, op. cit., pp. 9ss. G. NOUTE, Treaties and subsequent practice, op. cit., pp. 224ss. E. BJORGE, The evolutionary interpretation of treaties, op. cit.,

[609]O. BEKOU, The International Criminal Court, op. cit.,

[610]Martti Koskennjiemi, fragmentation of international law: Difficulties arising from the diversification and expansion of international law. Report of the study group of the

The work of settling the regulatory conflicts between different legal systems put into play through the hermeneutic mechanism of the presumption of conformity of the deeds of SC with an international treaty has moreover already consolidated other legal experiences. In the AL-Jedda case, for example, the European Court of Human Rights (ECtHR) stated that in interpreting SC Resolutions, "there must be a presumption that SC does not intend to impose any obligation on Member States to breach fundamental principles of human rights"[611]. Not only in the opinion of ECtHR should the interpretation which is most in harmony with the requirements of the Convention be preferred. The SC in fact thus continues the reasoning of Strasbourg judges would have used explicit language if the intention had been to ask the UN Member States not to respect their international human rights obligations[612].

The jurisprudential practice of some national courts also confirms the relevance of this principle in the interpretation of SC decisions. The Swiss Federal Court, for example in relation to the jurisdictional activity of ICC, stated that the fact that the latter was created through a SC Resolution represents a strong presumption that the procedures within the same comply with the guarantees of the just process and in particular those provided by the International Covenant of Civil and Political Rights of the 1966[613].

The presumption of conformity principle can also be applied in SC Resolutions and StICC Report. Indeed, it can be assumed that SC Resolutions aimed at affecting the jurisdictional activity of ICC have also been adopted in

---

International Law Commission, A/CN.4/L.682, 13 April 2006, p. 25, par. 37.

[611]ECtHR, Al-Jedda v. The United Kingdom, of 7 July 2011, par. 102. For further analysis see also: M. MILANOVIC, Al-Skeini and Al-Jedda in Strasbourg, in the European Journal of International Law, 23 (1), 2012, pp. 124ss.

[612]Interesting reflections on the presumption of conformity are also expressed in the separate opinion of Nigel Rodley in the decision of the Human Rights Committee, Sayadi v. Belgium, CCPR/C/94/D/1472/2006, 29 December 2008. For further analysis see: L. BOISSON DE CHAZOURNES, P.J., KUIJPER, Mr Kadi and Mrs Prost: Is the UN Ombudsman going to find herself between a rock and a hard place?, in H. RIETER, E. WAELE, Evolving principles of international law. Studies in honor of Karel C. Wallens, ed. Brill, Leiden, 2011, pp. 78ss. A. TZANAKOPOULOS, Collective security and human rights, in E. DE WET, J. VIDMAR, Hierarchy in international law: The place of human rights, Oxford University Press, Oxford, 2012, pp. 56ss. M. MILANOVIĆ, Norm conflict in international law: Whither human rights?, in Duke Journal of Comparative and International Law, 20, 2009, pp. 70ss. S. SHEERAN, C. BEVILACQUA, The UN Security Council and international human rights obligations. Towards a theory of constraints and derogation, in S. SHEERAN, N. RODLEY, Routledge handbook of international human rights law, Routledge, London & New York, 2013, pp. 390ss. S. DROUBI, Resisting United Nations Security Council resolutions, ed. Routledge, London, New York, 2014, pp. 12ss.

[613]Federal Supreme Court of Switzerland, Rukundo v. Federal office of Justice, Appeals judgment, cases N. 1A.120/2001 and 1.A.132072001, 3 September 2001, par. 3. For further details see also: C. SOLER, The global proscution of core crimes under international law, op. cit.,

accordance with StICC. The presumption is in this case that the SC does not intend in principle to act contrary to the content of an international treaty which has however recognized some particular prerogatives of intervention on the action of another international organization. It can also be assumed more generally that the SC does not intend, through the main decisions, to breach the obligations assumed towards ICC with which the UN entered into a mutual respect agreement.

This presumption also operates even if SC Resolutions do not contain an explicit reference to the relevant statutory provisions. Infarcts if in some cases SC itself has as explicitly stated to act in accordance with the Rome Treaty there are hypotheses in which the intention of SC to exercise the powers recognized by the Statute does not appear to be of so immediate deduction.

For example, excluding ICC jurisdiction against certain categories of individuals in Resolution n.1497 (2003) relating to the situation of Liberia, SC has recalled art. 16 StICC in a very general way and has not made a formal request for suspension towards the ICC such as the provision provides. In the beginning and as already mentioned in the course of the investigation, it must be considered that SC intended to adopt measures compatible with the letter and the spirit of the Rome Statute, regardless of the absence, for example of an explicit reference to the time limit established by art. 15 StICC[614]. Where possible, ICC must assume that the arrest of its jurisdiction has been ordered by SC in accordance with the relevant statutory provision in the present case, therefore within the time limit of the twelve months provided therein.

The role that the presumption of conformity can then play is particularly emblematic in the context of cooperation and mutual legal assistance. As we have seen, SC in imposing a general obligation of assistance to ICC bodies on Sudan has required this State to fully cooperate with ICC, an expression that refers to art. 86 (1) StICC[615]. As noted by the Prosecutor, the SC has thus imposed on Sudan "any cooperation duties required in the discharge of the court's mandate"[616]. This statement that the content of the SC's request for full cooperation addressed to Sudan should be presumed to correspond to the rules governing the ICC's action in this area.

In matters of aggression, the principle could play an important role in tracing an assessment of SC not perfectly compliant with the letter of art. 8 bis (2) to one of the state conduct envisaged by that provision.

It seems useful to highlight some possible limitations of the presumption of conformity mechanism. In fact, there are those who have highlighted how conform interpretation sometimes tends to reverse the logic behind systematic techniques. According to the reading, this hermeneutic tool would select one or more particular rules within the system against which compliance is required. This approach highlights a problem of considerable importance in the use of this

---

[614]O. BEKOU, The International Criminal Court, op. cit.,

[615]O. BEKOU, The International Criminal Court, op. cit.,

[616]ICC, The Prosecutor v. Omar Hassan Ahmad Al Bashir, pre-trial Chamber II, transcript-open session, ICC-02/05-01/09-T-2-ENG, 7 April 2017, pp. 70ss.

hermeneutic practice, i.e. the interpretation compliant could lend itself to being used as a hierarchical technique rather than harmonization. It could in essence hide the attempt to bend the content of the object to the parameter norm. Beyond these risks to avoid which one can only rely on the wisdom of the interpreter, however, there is an obvious structural limit that this technique cannot necessarily circumvent: One cannot harmonize what is inevitably in contrast. The most delicate problems arise when it is impossible to reconcile SC Resolutions with the regulatory parameters against which the presumption of conformity must operate. In practice compatibility problems of SC Resolutions with the Rome Statute or with other rules international events can be manifested in all their evidence when it is impossible to interpret those decisions in a manner consistent with statutory rules or other principles and rules of international law.

3. ICC power to syndicate the validity of Security Council Resolutions in order to limit the effects that may derive from it based on the Statute

As just mentioned, it is not always possible to interpret the regulatory conflicts that can arise in the interactions between SC and ICC through the techniques of interpretation. It is a matter of understanding what happens when a SC decision is in contrast with the Rome Statute or with other regulatory parameters that can guide the ICC action. We must first ask ourselves whether these bodies can perform some form of validity check on SC Resolutions. If such control is possible, it will then be necessary to determine in light of those regulatory parameters the validity union can be experienced and to what extent the verification of the legitimacy of the decisions taken by the SC can go. Before trying to answer these questions it is necessary to clarify what is meant by syndication of validity of SC Resolutions in this context. It is clear that the ICC does not have the power to ascertain with absolute effect erga omnes the invalidity of a SC Resolution. The judgment of validity referred to here would have only a relative scope. Its consequence would be to exclude that SC Resolutions deemed incompatible with certain parameters could be considered productive of effects towards ICC. In practice, the possibility of a judicial review of ICC on SC decisions is substantiated here in the eventuality that the requests for activation or suspension addressed to it are not considered by ICC bodies to produce effects on their judicial action. In other words, the ICC may deem a SC decision to activate or suspend its judicial action invalid or even partially invalid and limit its effects in whole or only in relation to those parts of the device adopted in contrast with the legal framework laid down by the Rome Statute or with the other relevant regulatory parameters. Of course, this union has no effect on any other obligations for the States deriving from SC decisions or more generally on the validity of these acts tout court.

To establish the existence of a power to syndicate SC decisions by ICC it is necessary to define the jurisdiction of the international court and understand through this operation if and to what extent the possible validity check on the political acts of SC falls within this competence. It can be said that the jurisdiction of international criminal courts is in principle limited to matters relating to the assessment of individual responsibility for the Commission of international crimes. It cannot be excluded that these jurisdictions are also called to pronounce on matters that do not directly concern the ascertainment of criminal responsibility. In particular, it is possible that international criminal courts as well as any other judicial body may have to resolve a series of preliminary questions to determine the scope of their jurisdiction. These issues may also include that relating to the validity of SC Resolutions.

3.1. The recognition of a competence to ascertain the validity of Security Council Resolutions in the jurisprudence of the international criminal courts

The issue just mentioned has actually arisen on more than one occasion over the past few decades before several international or mixed criminal courts. The ICC, for example, to determine the legitimacy of its own institution wondered if SC could invoke Chapter VII of the UN Charter to deal with the situation in the former Yugoslavia and if the creation of the Court could be considered a measure in compliance with the UN Charter for the purposes the maintenance of international peace and security. In order to be able to answer these questions of no small moment, the tribunal was forced even before to question its own competence to answer these delicate questions and therefore its power to syndicate the validity of the decisions taken by SC.

The responses provided by the Court reveal the non-peaceful nature of the matter. At first the pre-trial Chamber in the Tadić case had in fact emphasized that it could not be considered a constitutional Court set up to scrutinize the actions of UN organs[617]. More specifically in the opinion of the pre-trial Chamber, the criminal judge has a series of clearly defined powers that concern a quite specific and limited criminal jurisdiction[618]. For this reason, ultimately the ICTY would have no authority "to investigate the legality of its creation by SC".

In the same case, Tadić, the appeals chamber for the former Yugoslavia, however, accepted a somewhat opposite position destined to mark future jurisprudence on the matter. The second instance judges in fact highlighted that the international legal system is not composed of an integrated judicial system and that therefore very judicial or arbitral organ needs a specific constitutive instrument defining its jurisdiction. In ICTY reasoning a central dimension occupies the Kompetenz-Kompetenz principle. By virtue of this principle, it is up to each court as inherent in its function to determine the content of its institutional act and therefore define the perimeter of its jurisdiction. In the opinion of the

[617]ICTY, Prosecutor v. Tadić, Decision on the defence motion on jurisdiction, trial chamber, IT-04-1-T, 10 August 1995, par. 5.

[618]ICTY, Prosecutor v. Tadić, Decision on the defence motion of interlocutory Appeal on jurisdiction, Appeal chambers, IT-91-1-AR72, 2 October 1995, par. 20.

Appeals Chamber in essence "the first obligation of the Court as of any other judicial body is to ascertain its own competence"[619].

The competence to investigate the foundation and legitimacy of one's founding act would therefore be a consequence of the Kompetenz-Kompetenz principle. The ascertainment of the validity of one's own institution would therefore be one of the elements of the power of each Court to determine its jurisdiction. In the words of the judges, in fact, "the plea based on the invalidity of constitution of the international tribunal goes to the very essence of jurisdiction"[620]. For this reason, the Appeals Chamber believes it should examine "the legality of its establishment by SC solely for the purpose of ascertaining its own primary jurisdiction over the case before it"[621]. Compared to what was established at first instance, the appeals chamber has adopted in practice "an expansive view of its power to determine its own jurisdiction even at the expense of the Council"[622]. In other words, the notion of jurisdiction would include a verification of the validity of the legal basis of the jurisdictional power that ICC itself exercises, consequently a control is imposed on the act to which in this jurisdictional power is attributable a SC Resolution.

The Appeals Chamber stated that the power to decide the scope of its jurisdiction does not need to be explicitly recognized in the instrument establishing ICC and precisely because inherent in the same judicial function, its exercise by the judges can be considered "implicit in SC's intention to set up, not any subsidiary organ but a tribunal"[623]. In essence, it would have been the same

---

[619]Although the jurisprudence of the international court of justice relating to the validity review of SC Resolutions is not always easy to interpret and sometimes leads to uncertain results, some words pronounced by the same international court of justice in the advisory opinion of legal consequences for the States of the continued presence of southern Africa in Namibia (South-West Africa) despite Resolution n.276 (1970), opinion of 21 June 1971, in ICJ Reports, 1971, pp. 45, which is affirmed that: "(...) The Court does not possess powers of judicial review or appeal in respect of the decisions taken by the UN organs concerned. The question of the validity or conformity with the Charter of GA Resolution n.2145 (XXI) or of related SC Resolutions does not form the subject of the request for advisory opinion. However in the exercise of its judicial function and since objections have been advanced for the Court, in the course of its reasoning will consider these objections before determining any legal consequences arising from those Resolutions (...)".

[620]ICTY, Prosecutor v. Tadić, Decision on the defence motion of interlocutory Appeal on jurisdiction, op. cit., par. 12.

[621]ICTY, Prosecutor v. Tadić, Decision on the defence motion of interlocutory Appeal on jurisdiction, op. cit.

[622]J. ALVAREZ, Nuremberg revisited: The Tadić case, in European Journal of International Law, 7 (2), 1996, pp. 248ss. J. ALVAREZ, The likely legacies of Tadić, in ILSA Journal of International and Comparative Law, 4, 1997-1998, pp. 614ss.

[623]ICTY, Prosecutor v. Tadić, Decision on the defence motion of interlocutory Appeal on jurisdiction, op. cit.., par. 14. See also in argument: C. WARBRICK, C. ROWE, The international criminal tribunal for Yugoslavia: The decision of the appeals chamber on the interlocutory appeal on jurisdiction in the Tadić case, in International and Comparative Law Quarterly, 45 (3), 1996, pp. 692ss. R.E. VINUESA, La jurisdicciòn del Tribunal penal

SC through the creation of a judicial body to accept the possible exercise by the same ICC of the power to syndicate the legitimacy of the act placed at the foundation of its institution. In more general terms but in this same perspective it can be remembered that the UN Secretary-General had remarked at the time of the birth of ICC that the new body created by ICC "would of course not be subject to the authority or control of SC with regard to the performance of its judicial functions[624]".

The question just traced about the power of the international criminal courts to determine their jurisdiction by checking the validity of their founding act again arose before ICTR. In the Kanyabashi case, indeed, the ICTR limited itself to responding to the remarks raised by the defendant's defense, observing for example that the conflict in Rwanda undoubtedly represented a threat to peace and that the institution of ICTR was part of the measures that the SC can adopt by virtue of art. 41 of the UN Charter. ICTR has asked itself explicitly about the very existence of the power to express itself on these matters in order to determine its jurisdiction. In this regard, it can be considered that precisely in light of the conclusions reached on the compliance of SC Resolutions with the powers provided for by Chapter VII of the UN Charter the ICTR, it intended to abide on the preliminary question relating to the power to syndicate the validity of the founding act to the persuasive authority of the decision of the Appeals Chamber of the ICC for the Former Yugoslavia[625].

Although based on a different legal basis an agreement between the State concerned and the UN, also the Special Court for Sierra Leone (SCSL) has adopted an approach similar to that of ICTY. The Special Court for Sierra Leone has recognized that it is beyond argument its jurisdiction to decide the lawfulness and validity of its creation[626]. Once again the idea re-emerges that they fall within the concept of jurisdiction over which a Court can be called to express itself all questions relating to the validity of the international act through which the same judicial body was established and exercises its power.

---

internacional para la ex Yugoslavia segùn la decisiòn de la Càmara de Apelaciones en el caso Tadić (sobre competencia), in Hèctor Gross Espiell Amicorum Liber, human person and international law, ed. Bruylant, Bruxelles, 1997, pp. 1802ss.

[624]Report of the Secretary-General pursuant to paragraph 2 of the Security Council Resolution n.827 (1993), UN Doc. S/25704, 3 May 1993, par. 28.

[625]ICTR, Prosecutor v. Kanyabashi, Decision on the defence motion on jurisdiction, trial chamber II, ICTR-96-15-T, 18 June 1997, par. 4. V. MORRIS, Prosecutor v. Kanybashi, Decision on jurisdiction, case n. ICTR-96-15-T: International criminal tribunal for Rwanda, June 18 1997, in American Journal of International Law, 92 (1), 1998, pp. 67ss.

[626]The prosecutor v. Morris Kallon, Sam Hinga Norman, Brima Bazzy Kamara, Decision on constitutionality and lack of jurisdiction, Appeals chamber, SLCS-2004-15-AR72 (E), 13 March 2004, par. 34.

3.2. Critical analysis of the arguments put forward by the Special Tribunal for Lebanon to deny such jurisdiction

The legitimacy of the establishment of the Special Tribunal for Lebanon (STL) was also contested. As occurred at least initially within ICTY, the STL also assumed fluctuating positions on the matter under examination, however ultimately contradicting the conclusions just recalled reached by other international criminal jurisdictions. In the beginning the Appeals Chamber of STL in the wake of the previous ICTY jurisprudence reiterated the centrality of the Kompetenz-Kompetenz principle in order to determine any legal issue of which the tribunal is seized by reason of the mater falling under its primary jurisdiction[627].

Despite the relevance attributed to the Kompetenz-Kompetenz principle in these directions in the subsequent Ayyash case628, the STL not only did not consider it pertinent to recall the power of the judicial bodies to determine the scope of its jurisdiction but expressly distanced itself from what had been the approach taken by the ad hoc courts and albeit in a context other than SCSL[629]. In practice, the question of legitimacy of SCSL "attacks its legal basis or foundation" and therefore requires an investigation of jurisdiction, referring more simply to a judicial body's power or to the right to adjudicate a matter before that judicial body.

Beyond the difficult distinction that can perhaps be made between the two concepts, the reasons given by STSL to claim that a judicial body cannot incidentally exercise its jurisdiction over a preliminary question related to the very legitimacy of the function that is not clear is called to carry out and why this operation cannot fall within the concept of jurisdiction. As will be seen, the reasons for the refusal of a union of validity seem more related to the political nature of the deeds of SC than to the absence of certain regulatory parameters to assess their legitimacy rather than on a real lack of jurisdiction. However, although the restrictive conception of the notion of jurisdiction leads the Court of first instance to assert that it cannot exercise any control over SC decisions, the judges seem to de facto syndicate the latter's power to establish international criminal courts for the purposes of peacekeeping by ultimately concluding that the UN may establish a court or tribunal with specified functions.

---

[627]STL, In the matter of El Msayed, decision on appeal of pre-trial judge's order regarding jurisdiction and standing, appeals chamber, STL-CH/AC/2010/02, 10 November 2010, par. 45. The tribunal considered it possible to rule on the request made by El Sayed to obtain useful evidence to act before the domestic courts against those who accused him of being involved in the attack.

[628]STL-11-01 of 14 February 2005.

[629]STL, The Prosecutor v. Samil Jamil Ayyash, Mustafa Amine Badreddine, Hussein Hassan Oneissi, Assad Hassan Sabra, Decision on the defence challenges to the jurisdiction and legality of the tribunal, trial chamber, STL-111-01-PT/TC, 27 July 2012, par. 29.

The following decision of the Appeals Chamber of the same STL further sharpens the distance from the guidelines of the courts for ICTY and ICTR. Censoring the latest assessments expressed by the court of first instance regarding the legitimacy of the powers exercised by SC and reiterating the impossibility of carrying out any control on the resolutions adopted by the political body, the appeals chamber notes how its founding act defines precisely the STL jurisdiction[630]. On the contrary, and on this aspect the Appeals Chamber seems to insist on legitimizing the solution ultimately adopted, ICTY would have been somehow forced to adopt a wider conception of jurisdiction (and the power to determine it) due to the absence in its own Statute a clear delimitation of its area of competence[631]. In support of this thesis, STL found that even the ad hoc courts, following a clearer delimitation of its jurisdiction based on some changes to the procedural regulations operating by the same ICTY, have changed their attitude by limiting the scope in fact of the validity union of SC Resolutions. This argument is not particularly convincing. As pointed out by the defendants' defenses, the changes made to regulations of the ad hoc courts were rather aimed at avoiding the re-proposal of similar appeals to those previously experienced regarding the legitimacy of the establishment of the courts. Furthermore, when the legitimacy of the SC action was again questioned, ICTY judges did not hesitate to refer to the solution adopted in the Tadić case without giving particular relevance to the changes made in the procedural and trial regulations[632].

To further support its approach, the STL also referred to the jurisprudence of the Court of Justice of the European Union (CJEU) and ECtHR regarding targeted sanctions and in particular the Kadi[633] and Nada[634] cases. The reference

---

[630]M. NIKOLOVA, M.J. VENTURA, The Special Tribunal for Lebanon declines to review UN Security Council action. Retreating from Tadić's legacy in the Ayyash jurisdiction and legality decisions, in Journal of International Criminal Justice, 11 (3), 2013, pp. 626ss.

[631]STL, Decision on the defence appeals against the trial chamber's decision on the defence challenges to the jurisdiction and legality of the Tribunal, Appeals Chamber, STL-111-01, 24 October 2012, par. 14.

[632]ICTY, Prosecutor v. Milosević, Decision on preliminary motions, trial chamber, IT-02-54, 9 November 2001 and Prosecutor v. Karadžić, Decision on the accused's motion challenging the legal validity and legitimacy of the Tribunal, trial Chamber, 7 December 2009, IT-95-5/128-T.

[633]CJEU, joined cases: C-415/05 P, Kadi & Al Barakaat Int'l Foundation v. Council of 8 November 2008, op. cit., For further details see, R. UERPMANN-WITTZACK, Rechtsfragen und Rechtsfolgendes Beitritts der Europäischen Union zur EMRK, in Europarecht, 2012, pp. 167ss. C. NOWAK, Europarecht nach Lissabon, ed. Nomos, Baden-Baden, 2011. D. CHALMERS, G. DAVIES, G. MONTI, EU law, Cambridge University Press, Cambridge, 2014. J. TILLOTSON, N. FOSTER, Text, cases and materials on EU law, Gavedish Publishing, New York, 2013. M. HORSPOOL, M. HUMPHREYS, EU law, Oxford University Press, Oxford, 2012, pp. 552ss. H. SATZGER, International and European criminal law, Hart Publishing, Oxford & Oregon, Portland, 2017. T. OPPERMANN, C.D. CLASSEN, M. NETTESHEIM, Europarecht, C.H. Beck, München, 2016.

[634]ECtHR, Nada v. Switzerland of 12 September 2012, par. 212.

to this case law is also of particular interest here. These are cases in which the question has arisen of the jurisdiction of courts outside the UN system to perform some form of control over SC decisions. This type of situation can occur in particular when such judicial bodies find themselves having to recognize the legal effects which are more or less directly produced by SC decisions within their own legal system. Such a situation is not far from what occurs in the interactions between SC and ICC.

According to STL, the jurisprudence of the "European" courts indicates a clear tendency of the judicial bodies to deny the possibility of syndicating the validity of SC decisions[635]. Without here retracing the various passages of the intricate Kadi case, it is true that the CJEU has in fact limited itself to expressing the compatibility with the fundamental rights of the internal EU acts which implemented those decisions. It is difficult to see in this judgment a clear indication in support of the non-unionization of SC Resolutions. It should be noted that the CJEU insisted on the peculiarity of the case submitted to it and in particular on the existence of an internal act of implementation. It is because of the presence of this internal act that the CJEU has limited the scope of its validity check. The CJEU as already noted in the doctrine did not in principle exclude the possibility of a union on the international act, in this case a SC Resolution, in the absence of a corresponding internal act of implementation. The capacity to produce effects directly in the EU legal system is recognized in this act[636]. From a substantial point of view, then, it seems undeniable that when, as in the case of targeted sanctions, the internal act is limited to producing the international one "the frontier between norms disappears and the judicial review of one entails the parallel evaluation of the other"[637]. In short, as also observed by judge Baragwanath, in his separate and partially dissenting opinion on the decision of STL in the Ayash case, the essential element of the Kadi jurisprudence is the statement of EU judges: "That its own" fundamental law did not permit even such

[635]STL, Decision on the defence appeals against the trial Chamber's decision on the defence challenges to the jurisdiction and legality of the tribunal, Appeals chamber, STL-111-01, 24 October 2012, parr. 47ss.

[636]For further analysis see also: E. CANNIZZARO, P. PALCHETTI, A. WESSEL, International law as the law of European Union, ed. Brill, Leiden, Boston, 2012, pp. 386ss.

[637]L. HINOJOSA MARTÍNEZ, Bad law for good reasons: The contradictions of the Kadi judgment, in International Organizations Law Review, 5 (2), 2008, pp. 342ss, which is affirmed that: "An international regional court which is an institution of an international organization bound by the UN Charter may not say that SC sanctions cannot be implemented because they are incompatible with its particular international (regional) law without questioning the hierarchy of norms in the international legal order" (pp. 346ss) it is worth mentioning that in the epoch the tribunal of European Union of first instance, the current general Court had claimed to be able to review compliance with the jus cogens of the SC Resolutions adopted on the basis of Chapter VII of the UN Charter. See in argument: T-315/01, Yassin Abdullah Kadi v. Council of the European Union of 21 September 2005, ECLI: EU:T:2005:332, II-03649, par. 226. For further details see: S. DROUBI, Resisting United Nations Security Council resolutions, op. cit.,

a powerful norm as is the SC Resolution to infringe it"[638].

Even the Nada case does not seem to actually support the thesis of an impossibility of syndicating the validity of SC decisions. It is true that once again, albeit in a different way than in the Kadi case, the problem has been effectively circumvented. The judges of Strasburg attributed a decisive importance to the margin of discretion that SC Resolution would leave to the States in the implementation of the sanctions regime. In particular according to ECtHR, the State concerned "could not validly confine itself to relying on the binding nature of SC Resolutions, but should have persuaded the Court that it had taken, or at least had attempted to take, all possible measures to adapt the sanctions regime to the applicant's individual situation"[639]. Beyond the problem of not a little account of understanding some is the actual margin of maneuver left to the states by SC decisions, it does not seem possible to deduce from the decision that in the absence of such discretion in favor of the state it is impossible to perform a union on the validity of the same SC Resolutions. Moreover, in their own case law on targeted sanctions both CJEU and ECtHR have repeatedly resorted, albeit in sometimes different forms to the so-called equivalent protection test. Through this particular technique, in fact the European judges have subjected the system of sanctions created by SC to a check on the degree of protection which must precisely be at least equivalent to the protection guaranteed within their own systems of fundamental rights[640]. The test is based on the presumption that the international act from which the obligation for the State derives offers equivalent human rights protection on that of the system within which this act must be implemented. As mentioned by ECtHR, the presumption can however be refuted in the event that the protection of fundamental rights is manifestaly deficient. In this case the Strasbourg judges argue that "the interest of international cooperation would be outweigthed by the convention's role as a constitutional instrument of European public order in the field of human rights (case boshorus hava yolari turizm .... insert as notes). The technique of equivalent protection, in addition to not guaranteeing a supremacy to the obligations deriving from SC Resolutions on international human rights obligations, therefore implies a form of union, albeit indirect and limited, on the decisions of the political body intended to affect the

---

[638]STL, Decision on the defence appeals against the trial chamber's Decision on the defence challenges to the jurisdiction and legality of the tribunal, separate and partially dissenting opinion of judge Baragwanath, Appeals chamber, STL-11-01, 24 October 2012, par. 55. See in argument: J. ALVAREZ, Tadić revisited, in Journal of International Criminal Justice, 16 (5), 2013, pp. 298ss. It is worth mentioning that the judgments in this area of the CJEU have originated several attempts to reform the sanctions regime by the UN demonstrating the fact that the real target of the European judge was the particular practice implemented by the SC and the effects of this on some fundamental rights.

[639]S. DROUBI, Resisting United Nations Security Council resolutions, op. cit.,

[640]E. DE WET, From Kadi to Nada: Judicial techniques favoring human rights over United Nations Security Council sanctions, in Chinese Journal of International Law, 12 (4), 2013, pp. 788ss.

protection of fundamental rights[641].

A brief reference to a tendency to syndicate the validity of SC Resolutions can also be made by some national jurisdictions. It can be recalled in this regard that in the Nada case itself, the Swiss federal court had not hesitated to carry out its own examination of the compatibility of the sanction system with international standards for the protection of human rights[642].

3.3. The indications obtained from the Rome Statute regarding the ICC competence to exercise a union on Security Council Resolutions

Ultimately it can be noted that the issue of validity of the union Resolutions does not lend itself to a univocal solution. The attitudes and assessments of individual courts regarding the scope of their jurisdiction are not always uniform. Beyond the peculiar position taken by STL, we can report a now consolidated propensity of various international (and national) jurisdictions to operate some form of control of the validity of SC decisions. As far as it directly concerns the power of an ICC to determine its jurisdiction through a union of the act placed at the basis of its institution the path indicated by ICTY appears to be the convincing way. It seems in particular that when the assessment of the validity of a SC Resolution constitutes a prerequisite for determining the extent of a court jurisdiction, the Kompetenz-Kompetenz post-foundation principle and guarantee that the independence of the judicial function can justify the exercise of a validity check[643]. Moreover, it has already been said that the ICJ itself has long recognized

---

[641]V. BILKOVÁ, The standard of equivalent protection as a standard of review, in L. GRUSZCZYNSKI, W. WERNER, Deference in international courts and tribunals, Oxford University Press, Oxford, 2014, pp. 282ss.

[642]Swiss Federal Court, Nada v. State Secretariat fro economic affairs and federal department for economic affairs, administrative appeals judgment, 1A 4572007, BGE 133 II 450, 14 November 2007, in particular par. 8.3. See also the decision of the Federal Tribunal of Canada in case: Abdelzarik v. Canada (Minister of Foreign Affairs), 4 June 2009. For further details see also: E. DE WET, A. NOLLKAEMPER, Review of the Security Council decisions by national courts, in German Yearbook of International Law, 45, 2002, pp. 168ss. G. VERDIRAME, The UN and human rights. Who guards the guardians?, Cambridge University Press, Cambridge, 2011, pp. 316ss.

[643]S. ZAPPALÁ, Reviewing security council measures in the light of international human rights principles, in B. FASSBENDER, Securing human rights? Achievements and challenges of the UN Security Council, Oxford University Press, Oxford, 2011, pp. 180ss. L. CONDORELLI, La soumission des organisations internationales aux normes internationales aux normes internationales realtives aux droits de l'homme: Journèe d'ètudes de Strasbourg, ed. Pedone, Paris, 2009, pp. 140ss, which is affirmed that "loisible de soutenir que, du moment que le côntrol de la lègalitè des dècisions du Conseil de sècuritè n'est pas un domaine rèservè à la competènce exsclusive d'un organe dèterminè, il fait alors en infèrer que touyt juge appelè à faire application d'une de ces dècisions, y compris le judge national, doit s'assurer que celle-cci a ètè valablement èmise, tant pour ce qui est des conditions de forme que de fond, c'est-à-dire qu'elle ne contredit pas le principes de la

the importance for any body (and even more so it could be said for a Court) to determine autonomously and in the light of its founding act, the scope of the own competence[644].

The position taken by the ad hoc tribunals established by SC constitutes a valid precedent for assessing the possibility for ICC to exercise a validity check on SC decisions aimed at producing effects on its jurisdiction. Indeed, it can be said that the principles enumerated in ICTY jurisprudence find their further more explicit and clear expression within the Rome Statute of Rome[645].

First of all, the Rome Statute expressly establishes the relevance of the Kompetenz-Kompetenz principle. By virtue of art. 19 StICC, the ICC "shall satisfy itself that it has jurisdiction in any case brought before it". In more general terms art. 119 (2) provided that "any dispute concerning the judicial functions of the Court shall be settled by its decision"[646]. This principle protects the independence of ICC bodies in determining the scope of its competence, also possibly through a union of validity of the SC decisions intended to affect its jurisdictional activity.

Secondly, the scope of the Kompetenz-Kompetenz principle, as far as inherent in the judicial function itself, takes on an even more marked significance in the ICC system. In this context, it is not a question of examining the legitimacy of the act which was the basis for the existence of the international court. A type of control which, as claimed by ICTY, can certainly fall within the broad notion of jurisdiction, but which affects the same origin and legitimacy of the exercise of power and judicial function. In ICC system, the link between ascertaining the validity of the decisions of SC and determining the scope of ICC jurisdiction is even closer and more evident as these decisions are aimed precisely at initiating or limiting the judicial activity.

---

charte, dont ceux relatifs aux droit de l'homme doivent être conçus comme faisant partie (...)". In the same orientation see also: I. BROWNLIE, The decision of political organs of the United Nations and the rule of law, in R.S.J. MACDONALD, Essays in honor of Wang Tieya, Martinus Nijhoff Publishers, Leiden, Boston, 1993, pp. 102ss.

[644]International Court of Justice, certain UN expenses, opinion of 20 July 1962, in ICJ Reports 1962, pp. 176.

[645]See in argument the jurisprudence of ICJ and ICTY came to the conclusion that "(...) there would be seem to be no legal barrier to ICC also conducting such a review where it was strictly limited to the question of determining its jurisdiction in a case (...)". For further analysis see: D. SAROOSHI, The peace and justice: paradox. The international criminal court and the UN Security Council, in D. MCGOLDRICK, P. ROWE, E. DONNELLY (ed. by), The Permanent International Criminal Court. Legal and policy issues, op. cit., pp. 114ss.

[646]D. SAROOSHI, The peace and justice: paradox. The international criminal court and the UN Security Council, in D. MCGOLDRICK, P. ROWE, E. DONNELLY (ed. by), The Permanent International Criminal Court. Legal and policy issues, op. cit.,

4. Rome Statute's respect as a parameter for the validity union of Security Council Resolutions

Once established ICC the virtues of the power to ascertain the scope of its competence that can exercise a form of control over the SC Resolutions, it is a question of establishing in the light of those regulatory parameters this control can be experienced. It has already been said that the exercise of the powers attributed to SC, through the Rome Statute, is conditional on compliance with the statutory provisions that delimit ICC jurisdiction. In other words, in order for those powers to produce effects against the ICC bodies, the SC must exercise its prerogatives within the limits set by the Statute. Consequently and as anticipated in conclusion in the previous paragraph, a validity union of the SC Resolution can be carried out by ICC in the light of the rules of the Treaty of Rome which delimit ICC jurisdiction. Several indications in this sense are moreover contained in the same Rome Statute and in this same direction some statements of the ICC organs can already be read.

Art. 13 StICC states, before listing the mechanisms for activating the investigations of the Prosecutor which includes the possible exercise of referral power by SC, that the ICC must exercise its jurisdiction "in accordance with the provisions of this Statute". Already in the first comments relating to the Draft Stature drawn up by ILC in 1994, it had also been highlighted that "although the SC may initiate proceedings the source of law to be applied will be the same as if the complaint were lodged by a State"[647]. In this same sense, to resume the words of ICC judges when they decide to exercise their referral power, the SC accepts the investigations of the Prosecutor and all related activities "will take place in accordance with the statutory framework provided for in the Statute"[648]. In practice, as for other purposes, it has already been noted, when SC decides to activate ICC jurisdiction "must live within the parameters of the Rome Statute with respect to such matters as jurisdiction"[649].

By virtue of the power to determine the scope of its jurisdiction, therefore the ICC bodies could consider a request of SC invalid and not take action in the sense indicated by the Resolution, if they judge the decision aimed at activating the investigations of the Prosecutor incompatible with the regulatory framework outlined by the Rome Statute. Depending on the content of the decision, however, you can also imagine a different solution. In particular, the ICC bodies involved could instead simply limit the effects of the request for activation of SC to make

[647]J. CRAWFORD, The ILC's Draft Statute for an international criminal tribunal, in American Journal of International Law, 88 (1), 1994, pp. 148ss.

[648]ICC, Prosecutor v. Omar Hassan Ahmad Al Bashir, decision on the Prosecution's application for a warrant of arrest against Omar Hassan Aymad Al Bashir, pre-trial Chamber I, ICC-02/05-01/09-3, 4 March 2009, par. 45.

[649]ICC, Prosecutor v. Omar Hassan Ahmad Al Bashir, decision on the Prosecution's application for a warrant of arrest against Omar Hassan Aymad Al Bashir, pre-trial Chamber I, op. cit.,

use of the competence attributed to them through an adjustment of the scope of the referral such as to ensure compliance with the statutory parameters.

For greater clarity we can try to give shape to these hypotheses. We have already said at the end of the situation contained in art. 13 b) a report from SC concerning certain individuals suspected of having committed international crimes under ICC jurisdiction. In the face of a possible request in this sense, it is first of all possible to imagine and it is the most linear solution that the ICC invalidates the request for initiating investigations tout court. Alternatively, the Prosecutor could decide to proceed anyway with its investigative activity on the wider context of violence covered by the SC decision. In other words it can be assumed that the Prosecutor ignores the specific indication of SC about the suspected individuals of the Commission for crimes, in that it is in contrast with the letter and ratio of art. 13 b), but nevertheless deems its activation valid in general with regard to the criminal conduct for the repression of which the SC has decided to apply to ICC. A solution of this type would come close to a form of conformal interpretation of the Resolution, an interpretation that could be justified within the limits which do not end up distorting the will of SC as expressed by the Resolution itself.

A similar speech can be made in relation to art. 16 StICC[650]. The standard does not expressly provide for a possibility for ICC to review the suspension request from SC. Indeed, as the provision is formulated, one could at first sight believe that this request should be followed by an automatic suspension of the investigation activities or of the ongoing proceedings. However, since the request to stop investigations or to proceed with one or more proceedings interferes "with the normal exercise of the Court's primary jurisdiction under the Statute" the question "should be considered as jurisdictional lato sensu"[651] to be therefore subject of control by the ICC bodies. Again, to give an example, in this case we can imagine that SC asks ICC to suspend an investigation or a proceeding for a period longer than the 12 months foreseen by the Statute. Two solutions can then be proposed once again. The ICC bodies may deem the request invalid because in open contrast to the letter of art. 16. Otherwise a solution that seems preferable in view of the greatest possible cooperation between ICC and the political body, ICC could consider SC's request to produce effects only within the time limits expressly provided for by the Statute and therefore reduce the arrest of own legal action. Although the latter solution cannot be qualified as the possible outcome of a compliant interpretation given the clear textual content of Resolution, it nevertheless appears to be inspired by the same basic need to recognize the SC Resolutions compatible with the framework dictated by the Statute.

Also on other issues it may be interesting to see how ICC will orient itself in interpreting its own Statute and possibly in evaluating the validity of SC Resolutions. In this investigation, for example, it was argued that in light of art. 16, SC may request the suspension of even a specific ongoing proceeding against

---

[650]O. BEKOU, The International Criminal Court, op. cit.,

[651]O. BEKOU, The International Criminal Court, op. cit.,

a particular individual. In the event that the ICC bodies should instead come to a different conclusion and believe that the request for suspension can invest only the broadest contrast of violence to which the repressive action is directed, it should be assumed that instances of SC aimed at suspending a specific proceeding against, for example, a Head of State is considered invalid by ICC not producing effects on the judicial action of ICC and therefore does not affect the ongoing proceedings or investigations.

An example can also be given in relation to a practice already implemented by SC. In fact, it has been seen that in the light of the particularly critical attitudes of States, they do not generally seem to comply with art. 16 StICC the requests of SC aimed at suspending ICC activity in a generic and abstract way without any connection with particular criminal conduct or in relation to specific proceedings or concrete investigation activities. Resolutions n.1422 (2002) and 1487 (2003) to which those criticisms were addressed, could have been considered by the ICC bodies incompatible with their founding treaty and therefore could not be considered impediments, even during the 12 months of suspension of the non-Member States personnel engaged in operations established or authorized by the UN.

5. Validity union of Security Council Resolutions in the light of Chapter VII of the UN Charter

The preceding paragraph investigated the possibility that ICC performs a validity check of SC decisions in the light of the regulatory parameters, aimed at delimiting ICC jurisdiction, contained in the Rome Treaty. Articles 13 b) and 16 StICC recall and therefore incorporate in the Treaty a normative parameter foreseen and disciplined by another international treaty. This is of course the necessary foundation in Chapter VII of the UN Charter for the exercise of referral and deferral powers by SC.

Referring to Chapter VIII of the UN Charter the foundation of the powers of activation and suspension of ICC action, the Rome Statute makes Chapter VII itself a regulatory parameter in the light of which it is possible to syndicate the validity of SC Resolutions intended for affect one's judicial action. In other words and more concretely, the reference made by the Rome Treaty implies that the ICC bodies have the competence to verify in light of Chapter VII of the UN Charter of the legitimacy of SC decisions that adopts in order to activate or suspend ICC's judicial activity[652]. By virtue of the letter of articles 13 b) and 16 StICC, in fact, the adoption by SC of Resolutions incompatible with the conditions and limits to the exercise the powers assigned to it by the UN Charter does not only arise and, of course, in contrast with the same Charter but also involves a violation of the Rome Statute.

If the assumption of the referral and deferral powers by SC is found on

[652]D. WHITTLE, The limits of legality and the United Nations Security Council: Applying the extralegal measures model to chapter VII action, op. cit.

Chapter VII of the UN Charter the validity union on the acts of this body that the ICC is called to perform may in practice concern two different aspects. On the one hand it is necessary that SC decisions are adopted in compliance with the procedural conditions provided for by the UN Charter and in particular by art. 27. On the other hand SC decisions aimed at activating or suspending the judicial activity of ICC must necessarily be based on the assumptions of the action of ex Chapter VII provided for by art. 39 of the UN Charter, i.e. the existence therefore of a threat to peace of a violation of peace or an act of aggression.

As regards the first aspect, the judicial verification of compliance with the procedural conditions for the adoption of SC Resolutions finds a significant precedent in ICJ jurisprudence. In the opinion concerning the legal consequences for the States deriving from the continuous presence of South Africa in Namibia, the ICJ after recognizing that it does not generally have "powers of judicial review or appeal in respect of the decisions taken by the UN organs" stated that if objections are raised during a proceeding regarding the validity of those decisions, the ICJ "will consider these objections before determining any legal consequences arising form those Resolutions"[653]. As noted in doctrine, ICJ opinion on Namibia "reflects a common sense view that once the Court is asked about the effect of a UN organ's Resolution it cannot avoid considering whether it is valid in the first place"[654]. Specifically in the face of South Africa's disputes regarding the validity of the adoption of SC Resolution n.276 of 1970 despite the abstention from the vote of two permanent members, ICJ stated that "uniformly interpreted the practice of voluntary abstention by a permanent member as not constituting a bar to the adoption of Resolutions"[655]. What is most important here is that ICJ has pushed itself to verify the legitimacy of a Resolution in light of the practice of States and SC itself. The Resolutions adopted despite the abstention of two permanent members and in apparent contrast therefore with the letter of art. 27 of the UN Charter. In a completely analogous way, it can be considered that ICC, in determining the correct activation or suspension of its judicial activity, is also entitled to verify that the related decision of SC has been adopted in compliance with the voting procedures required by the UN Charter or with what is believed to be the practice generally accepted by States in this particular area.

The possibility of a syndicate validity on the decisions that SC adopts on

---

[653]International Court of Justice, Legal consequences for states deriving from the continued presence of South Africa in Namibia despite Resolution n.276 of 1970 of SC, Opinion of 21 June 1971, in ICJ Reports, 1971, par. 89. Position expressly supported also in the opinions of judges Onyeama which does not consider compatible with the judicial function "that the Court will proceed to state the consequences of acts whose validity is assumed, without itself testing the lawfulness of the origin of those acts" (parr. 133-134) and De Castro, which affirms that "the Court as a legal organ, cannot cooperate with a Resolution which is clearly void, contrary to the rules of the Charter, or to the principles of law" (par. 180). See also the opinions of judges Petren, Dillard and Fitzmaurice in argument.

[654]G.R. WATSON, Constitutionalisms, judicial review and the world court, in Harvard International Law Journal, 34, 1993, pp. 22ss.

[655]G.R. WATSON, Constitutionalisms, judicial review and the world court, op. cit.,

the basis of conditions laid down by art. 39 of the UN Charter opens up a series of major problems. The admissibility of a judicial review of the assessment made by SC about the existence of a threat to peace of a violation of the peace or an act of aggression could in fact at least in some circumstances prefigure for the judge a delicate work of demarcation between the space of political discretion and that of judicial autonomy. The complexity of this operation is amplified by the indeterminacy of the relevant regulatory parameters.

In order to establish the possibility and possible extension of such a validity union, it is necessary to take up once again the jurisprudence on the matter of the other international criminal courts which have been called in some way to express themselves on the matter.

ICTY's attitude towards the possibility of syndicating SC decisions made on the basis of Chapter VII of the UN Charter was once again at least initially challenged. In the first instance of the Tadić case ICTY stated that the decision to establish an international criminal court due to the existence of a threatening to peace situation "is eminently for SC and only for it" and this is because its evaluation "is certainly not a justiciable issue but one involving considerations of high policy nature"[656]. Through this statement, the pre-trial Chamber seems in practice to allude to the idea that the strictly political nature of the assessments that SC is called to carry out in the context of the maintenance of international peace and security would exclude any possibility of syndicating the validity of SC decisions.

However extremely cautious the position ultimately adopted by the Appeals Chamber is fundamentally opposite. The ICTY judges in this circumstance started from the assumption that SC was not conceived by the UN Charter of as a legibus solutus body[657]. While recognizing the existence of some limits to SC action, the Appeals Chamber shows a considerable deference with respect to the particular assessment that that body can make about the existence of a threat to peace, a violation of peace or of an act of aggression. In ICTY's opinion, SC would enjoy a very wide discretion in this context[658]. Again according to the judges of the Appeals Chamber, the one enjoyed by SC "is not a totally unfettered discretion" since the decision "has to remain, at the very least, within the limits of the purposes and principles of the Charter"[659]. SC discretion would be extremely broad in this context, but not absolute. The limitations existing to

---

[656]ICTY, Prosecutor v. Tadić, Decision on the defence motion of interlocutory Appeal on jurisdiction, op. cit., par. 23.

[657]ICTY, Prosecutor v. Tadić, Decision on the defence motion of interlocutory Appeal on jurisdiction, op. cit., par. 28. In this sense there were already some pronouncements of ICJ as we can see: On the conditions of admission of a State as a UN member, Opinion of 28 May 1949, in ICJ Reports 1947/1948, p. 64, which is affirmed that: "The political character of an organ cannot release it form the observance of the treaty provisions established by the charter when they constitute limitations on its powers or criteria for its judgment (...)".

[658]ICTY, Prosecutor v. Tadić, Decision on the defence motion of interlocutory Appeal on jurisdiction, op. cit.., par. 28.

[659]ICTY, Prosecutor v. Kanyabashi, decision on the motion on jurisdiction, op. cit., par. 20.

SC discretion, as will be seen later, have, in the opinion of ICTY, a series of effects also on the scope of the validity union that can be exercised by the latter.

The ICTR, on the other hand, seems to have taken on a more restrictive approach at least in its first orientation regarding the possibility of syndicating the choices that the SC makes when acting on the basis of the powers provided for in Chapter VII of the UN Charter. In the aforementioned Kanyabashi case, while recalling the limits set by the UN Charter, the pre-trial Chamber believes that the widely discretionary assessments that the SC can make in the context of peacekeeping "are not justiciable since they involve the consideration of a number of social, political and circumstancial factors". According to ICTR, the assessment of the existence of a threat to peace" is a matter to be decided exclusively by SC"[660].

It can be considered that a union on the basis of SC action, ex art. 39 of the UN Charter, was made by SCSL. According to the Appeals Chamber of SCSL it is clear that "SC power to enter into an agreement for the establishment of the Court was derived from the UN Charter both in regard to the general purposes of UN as expressed in article 1 of the UN Charter and the specific powers of SC in articles 39 and 41"[661]. The SCSL in practice judges the conclusion of an agreement between SC and Sierra Leone for the purpose of the situation of a special court, one of the prerogatives provided for in Chapter VII of the UN Charter and the assumption of that action would be attributable to the assessment made by SC about the existence of a lack of peace. It can be noted that if SCSL had deemed the SC decision unquestionable, it would not have proceeded to affirm (and therefore somehow evaluate) compliance with the UN Charter and in particular for what matters most here with art. 39[662].

In the Ayyash case, the STSL argued similarly to what ICTY did at first instance in the Tadić case, the impossibility of a judicial union on SC decisions due to the strictly political nature of the findings made by this body when acting on the basis to Chapter VII of the UN Charter. In the words of ICTY: "The SC's determination as to the existence of a threat to international peace and security is not subject to judicial review"[663]. In particular, this peremptory conclusion would be a direct consequence of the difficulty of establishing any meaningful standard

---

[660]G.R. WATSON, Constitutionalisms, judicial review and the world court, op. cit.,

[661]STSL, Prosecutor v. Charles Chankay Taylor, decision on immunity from jurisdiction, appeals chamber, SCSL-2003-01-I, 31 May 2004, par. 37.

[662]O. BEKOU, The International Criminal Court, op. cit.,

[663]STL, Decision on the defence appeals against the trial chambers, Decisions on the defence challenges to the jurisdiction and legality of the tribunal. Appeals Chamber, SYL 1101/PT/AC/AR90.1, 24 October 2012, par. 35. It is interesting to note that even some national lawsuits have in fact operated a union on the compatibility of SC decisions with the provisions of the UN Charter. For example the district Court of Hague which is affirmed "(...) the inauguration and establishment of the tribunal can be considered to fall within the scope of article 41 of the UN Charter (...)". See district Court of Hague, Milošević v. The Netherlands, 29 June 2001. See also the Swiss Federal Tribunal, Emmanuel Rukundo v. L'office fèdèral de la justice, n. 1A.120(2001, 3 September 2001.

of such review.

There is no shortage of similar positions in the doctrine as well[664]. In light of various reconstructions, the purely political nature of the decision and the absence of precise legal parameters would exclude the possibility of forms of judicial union and control should therefore take place only at political level (through the peculiar voting system around SC and any protest reactions from States)[665].

As can be seen from this analysis, at least a part of the jurisprudence referred to here more or less explicitly recalls the doctrine of the political question or the theory of political acts, which constitutional doctrine has focused a great deal on and which has over time taken on a certain importance in the debate between internationalists[666]. As briefly mentioned in the introduction to the present investigation, it is essentially the idea that some aspects of an act or a political decision cannot be subject to a judicial solution. In particular, the purely political nature of one or more elements subject to the judgment would require judicial bodies to leave the field to the discretion of political power and to refrain from any ruling. It has also been pointed out that the political question theory does not always and necessarily imply the total inadmissibility of a judicial union on political decisions. A particularly interesting aspect of this construction is the impact that it can have on the scope of the judicial union rather than to support its absolute negation. In practice, the scope of judicial review would be all the narrower as the political discretion granted for the particular decision is extended. Thus, while admitting in principle that any issue, including a political one, may be subject to a legality check where the discretion granted to the political bodies is extremely wide, the jurisdictional assessment could be limited to the formal aspects of the decision-making process or intervene only in front of posters abuse of power. We have already said about the formal aspects of this control. It can be more complex to determine its substantial limits.

---

[664]There are those who said that the SC: "Is not bound by any definition or formula as to what constitues a threat to or breach of the peace or act of aggression". See in argument: T.D. GILL, Legal and some political limitations on the power of the UN Security Council to exercise its enforcement powers under Chapter VII of the UN Charter, in Netherlands Yearbook of International Law, 26, 1995, pp. 40. Kelsen already argued in more general terms than SC Resolutions adopted on the basis of Chapter VII of the UN Charter which "the purpose of the enforcement action under article 39 is not to maintain or restore the law, but to maintain or restore peace which is not necessarily identical with the law (...)". H. KELSEN, The law of the United Nations: A critical analysis of its fundamental problems, ed. Praeger, London, 1951, pp. 294ss. In this sense see also the observations of R. HIGGINS, The place of international law in the settlement of disputes by the Security Council, in American Journal of International Law, 64 (1), 1970, pp. 16ss.

[665]J. COMBACAU, Le chapitre VII de la charte des Nations Unies: rèsurrection ou mètamorphose?, in R. BEN ACHOUR, S. LAGHMANI, Les nouveaux aspects du droit international, ed. Pedone, Paris, 1994, pp. 148ss.

[666]T.R.S. ALLAN, Constitutional justice: A liberal theory of the rule of law, Oxford University Press, Oxford, 2003, pp. 162ss.

There is no doubt that SC decisions takes by virtue of the powers recognized to it by Chapter VII of the UN Charter have a strongly political value. It is equally difficult to deny that the ICC itself leaves SC with an extremely wide margin of discretion in determining the conditions for its action and the measures to deal with it for peacekeeping purposes. The political dimension of the decisions taken by SC in this area, however, does not seem to absolutely preclude the possibility of forms of judicial control. In particular, the political discretion enjoyed by SC in taking its own decisions is not sufficient to place the acts that it adopts outside any possible control or judicial assessment. In this regard, it seems particularly fitting that judge Jenning observed in her dissenting opinion on the Lockerbie case and that ultimately all discretionary powers of lawful decision-making are necessarily derived from the law and are therefore governed and qualified by the law"[667].

The political and largely discretionary nature of SC assessment on the existence of a threat to peace and the indeterminacy of the regulatory parameters contained in UN Charter seem to have more than anything else the effect of significantly reducing the space of judicial control, as far as the judicial bodies must be recognized the ability to attribute. Also for example in light of the practice of the same SC, a legal meaning to the notions contained in art. 39 of the UN Charter the possibility of a judicial union appears all the more reduced the greater the discretion left to the political body. On this point, it is particularly interesting how the ICTY assertion has been mentioned that according to what in principle "the wider the discretion of SC under the UN Charter the narrower the scope for the international Tribunal to review its actions" this does not mean that the union power of a Court disappears altogether[668]. The clear attribution to SC of a prerogative of a political and highly discretionary nature therefore does not seem to imply as seen neither the absence of any substantial limit to the decisions taken nor the absolute impossibility of any form of judicial control over them. Although the notions used in Chapter VII of the UN Charter are difficult to determine, it is possible to recognize the possibility for a judicial body to delimit its content.

However, a distinction can certainly be made according to the type of assessment that must be made by SC. As just said, the degree of judicial control is inversely proportional to the extent of the discretion of the political decision. In the interactions between ICC and SC, it is particularly important to distinguish

---

[667]International Court of Justice, Issues of interpretation and application of the 1971 Montreal Convention that followed the Lockerbie plane crash (Libya v. United Kingdom and Libya v. United States) sentence of 27 February 1998, in ICJ Reports 1998, pp. 110ss. There are those who believe it is more correct to claim that SC does not enjoy "un pouvoir discètionnaire, mais d' un marge d'apprèciation". The conclusion is similar since "il est implicite dans le concept même de marge d'apprèciation qui'il ne s'agit opas d'un pouvoir illimitè". See in argument: M. BOTHE, Les limites de pouvoirs du Conseil de Sècuritè, in R.J. DUPUY, The development of the role of the Security Council, Martinus Nijhoff Publishers, Dodrecht, 1993, pp. 70ss.

[668]ICTY, Prosecutor v. Tadić, Decision on the defence motion of interlocutory Appeal on jurisdiction, op. cit., parr. 20-21.

between the assessments relating to the existence of a threat or a rupture of peace on the existence of which the requests for activation and suspension of judicial activity can be based and the determination of a state act of aggression which may instead represent a condition of prosecution of the investigative activity against the related crime.

The extent of a possible syndicate of validity of the assessments made by SC with respect to such situations is once again quite significant as highlighted by ICTY itself. The Appeals Chamber also in the Tadić case found that the assessment of the existence of a threat to peace would be more of a political concept while the notion of aggression more amenable to a legal determination[669]. The Rome Statute tangibly confirms this approach. While in fact on the notions of threat to peace and violation of peace in artcile 13 b) and 16 SCtICC refer exclusively to the discretion recognized to the SC for the purpose of their determination by the letter of art. 39 of the UN Charter, the new provisions on aggression attribute to ICTY bodies the possibility of independently ascertaining, therefore, from an assessment in this sense of SC, the existence of a state act of aggression as a prerequisite for proceed against individuals suspected of having engaged in conduct attributable to the crime of aggression. In other words, the existence of certain legal parameters useful to qualify the state acts of aggression has the effect of extending the possibility of a validity union on the decisions taken by SC with respect to this particular situation. As regards situations of threat to peace and violation of peace, the limits to the judiciary to express itself on the correctness of the choices made by SC are a consequence of the more strictly political nature of those notions.

From a somewhat different perspective, the issue can be seen as a particular attribution of competences made by the UN Charter, under which the power of a judge to ascertain the existence of a threat to peace or a violation of peace is limited by the fact that the jurisdiction to make such a decision has already been allotted elsewhere[670]. In the absence of precise regulatory parameters it would be as already argued in the doctrine "quite wrong for any Court to substitute its own political judgment for that by SC"[671]. A similar position was also taken by judge Lauterpacht in his separate opinion annexed to ICJ order in the case relating to the application of the Convention against genocide (Bosnia Herzegovina v. Yugoslavia). While acknowledging the existence of a syndication power of validity of SC decisions by ICJ, Lauterpacht emphasized that "there can be no less doubt that it does not embrace any right of the Court to substitute its

---

[669]ICTY, Prosecutor v. Tadić, Decision on the defence motion of interlocutory Appeal on jurisdiction, op. cit., par. 29.

[670]R. HIGGINS, Policy considerations and the international judicial process, in The International and Comparative Law Quarterly, 17 (1), 1968, pp. 80ss.

[671]D.W. BOWETT, Judicial and political functions of the Security Council and the International Court of Justice, in H. FOX, The changing constitution of the United Nations, British Institute of International Law, 22, 1973, pp. 84ss. G. WILSON, The United Nations and collective security, ed. Routledge, London & New York, 2014, pp. 192ss.

discretion for that by SC"[672].

It is therefore a question of determining in what circumstances a declaration of SC invalidity represents an undue interference, an invasion of powers, of the judicial body in the prerogatives recognized by the UN Charter to the political body. More concretely, the problem remains of understanding to what extent the wide discretion granted to SC in ascertaining the existence of a threat or a violation of peace reduces (or even excludes) a validity union.

In doctrine there are those who observed investigating the relationship between SC and ICJ that although the ascertainment of the existence of a threat to peace is a matter "d'ordre essentiellement politique, que le chapitre VII de la Charte confie au Conseil"[673], the possibility of a syndicate of validity would not be excluded at least when a judge" qualifierait la constatation arbitrate"[674]. In similar terms, more specifically with regard to the assessment that SC can make in the light of art. 39 of the UN Charter some authors have highlighted that it should be possible at least to identify some factual and logical matrix between the events in question and the Council's determination of threat to, or breach of the peace and that therefore the SC "cannot act arbitrarily, such as by determining literally anything to constitute a threat to peace and international security"[675].

In light of these general considerations on the form and extent that judicial control can take on the assessment made by the Council about the existence of a threat to peace, some assessments can also be made on the extent of the validity union that the ICC can exercise in light of Chapter VII of the UN Charter on SC Resolutions intended to affect one's jurisdiction.

Some criticisms related to the SC's practice of exempting non-statute

---

[672]International Court of Justice, separate opinion of judge Lauterpacht, Application of the convention against genocide (Bosnia Herzegovina v. Yugoslavia), order of 13 September 1993, in ICJ Reports 1993, pp. 439, par. 99. J. QUIGLEY, International Court of Justice as a forum for genocide cases, in Case Western Reserve Journal of International Law, 40, 2008-2009, pp. 244ss.

[673]G. GAJA, Rèflexions sur le rôle du Conseil de Sècuritè dans le nouvel ordre mondial, in Revue Gènèrale de Droit International Public, 97, 1993, pp. 316ss. T.M. FRANCK, Fairness in the international legal and institutional system, in Recueil des cours, ed. Brill, Bruxelles, vol. 240, 1993, pp. 192, which is affirmed that "in extreme cases, the Court may have to be the last-resort defender of UN system's legitimacy is to continue to enjoy the adherence of its members (...)".

[674]G. GAJA, Rèflexions sur le rôle du Conseil de Sècuritè dans le nouvel ordre mondial, op. cit.,

[675]S. LAMB, Legal limits to United Nations Security Council powers, in S. GOODWIN-GILL, S. TALMON, The reality of international law, Oxford University Press, Oxford, 1999, pp. 386ss. G. WILSON, The United Nations and collective security, op. cit., pp. 192ss. S. ELGEBEILY, The rule of law in the United Nations Security Council, decision making process: Turning the focus inwards, ed. Routledge, London & New York, 2017. H. NASU, Chapter VII powers and the rule of law. The jurisdictional limits, in Australian Yearbook of International Law, 26, 2007, pp. 109, which is stated that: "manifest error of the Security Council in using its discretionary powers under chapter VII for an improper purpose"

states personnel engaged in peacekeeping missions have already been highlighted as well as the skeptical positions taken by many States regarding the foundation of Chapter VII of some Resolutions. Beyond the difficulty of seeing a threat to international peace and security in the possible repressive action of the international tribunal against peacekeepers, it is not clear why this threat would derive only from a possible repressive action by ICJ against individuals who are citizens of non-Member States. In general, obstacles to participation in peacekeeping missions could also derive from other criteria of competence that can attribute to a national court the exercise of criminal jurisdiction over foreign citizens who commit international crimes on their territory. The possible exercise of criminal jurisdiction by internal courts against these individuals based, for example, on the principle of universal jurisdiction of a territorial jurisdiction or linked to the nationality of the victims, should also be considered to pose a threat to peace. Conclusion hardly sustainable and that does not find any support in state practice.

But beyond these inconsistencies and perplexities, what is most relevant here is the impossibility itself, at least in the first two decisions aimed at affecting the activity of ICC (Resolutions n.1422 (2002) and 1487 (2003)), to identify the assumption of the use by SC of the powers provided for in Chapter VII of the UN Charter[676]. From a formal point of view, the absence of an assessment of the existence of a threat to peace from a violation of peace or an act of aggression may not be particularly relevant. Although preferably in principle, it does not seem that the SC is required to explain the factual situation underlying its action. As noted by ICJ "when the UN takes action which warrants the assertion that it was appropriate for the fulfillment of one of its stated purposes, the presumption is that such action is not ultra vires"[677]. Judge Morelli, in that same contrast, observed further confirmation of what has been shown so far that in some particularly serious cases the act of an organization can be considered invalid especially in the event of a "Resolution the subject of which had nothing to do with the purposes of the Organization"[678]. Even in the relations between ICC and SC, the idea that "the Court should not limit itself to the formal verification that the SC has made such a determination" seems to be acceptable[679].

---

[676]C. CRYER, N.D. WHITE, The Security Council and the international criminal court: Who's feeling threatened?, in Journal of International Peacekeeping, 19, 2004, pp. 156ss.
[677]International Court of Justice, certain UN expenses (art. 17, par. 2 of the Charter), Opinion of 20 July 1962, in ICJ Reports 1962, pp. 168ss.
[678]E. LAUTERPACHT, The legal effect of illegal acts of international organizations, in Mcnair, Essays in honor of lord McNair, ed. Stevens, London, 1965, pp. 89ss. E. CANNIZZARO, P. PALCHETTI, Ultra vires acts of international organizations, in G. KLABBERS, E. WALLENDAHL, Research handbook on the law of international organization, Edward Elgar Publishers, Cheltenham, 2011, pp. 367ss.
[679]L. CONDORELLI, L. VILLALPANDO, Referral and deferral by the Security Council, in A. CASSESE, P. GAETA, J.R.W.D. JONES, The Rome Statute of the international criminal court. A commentary, op. cit., pp. 642ss. According to the cited authors "should also determine that the SC has acted within the limits of the purposes and principles of the

Indeed, in the decisions under examination it is impossible from a substantial point of view to determine what the objective situation of threat to peace is that moves the SC action[680]. Declaring that through these decisions it wants to encourage States to participate in peacekeeping missions may suggest that a State's unwillingness to contribute to these missions constitutes such a threat[681]. Beyond the fact that the threat would then be represented by the behavior of the state and not that of the ICC, the refusal of states to participate in peacekeeping missions may depend on numerous causes of a political or material nature and this possible inertia or unavailability of the States not was never considered by SC a prerequisite for the adoption of the measures provided for in Chapter VII. Rather, they are political choices that States regularly make and which are inherent in the process of establishing those operations. The total absence of the material assumption underlying the SC's suspensive requests in these hypotheses can lead us to believe that we are faced with decisions of an arbitrary nature and that they have nothing to do with the UN purposes. The ICC bodies in the face of the need to open investigations or proceedings against individuals protected by those exemptions could therefore have ignored the SC requests, considering them invalid as they lack the legal basis in Chapter VII of the UN Charter requested by art. 16 StICC[682].

Finally, some more general considerations on the opportunity of judicial control over the SC decisions. It is clear that admitting a union by ICC on the decisions that the SC makes in the light of the UN Charter is equivalent to recognizing the ICC power to contribute not only to the definition of what are the limits to SC action but more specifically general to the determination of the fundamental principles and purposes of the international system. In this regard, it can be considered that the participation of several subjects in the process of formation and evolution of international law appears from a systemic point of view certainly desirable in order to guarantee that system of weights and counterweights typical of democratic systems. This widespread participation is, however, even more important in an order such as the international one whose democracy (and consequent legitimacy of political choices) is often questioned[683].

Charter, the Court for instance should bear out that the determination of SC in that situation is in accordance with its settled practice and the common understanding of the UN membership in general (...)".

[680]A. ZIMMERMANN, "Acting under chapter VII (...)": Resolution n.1422 and possible limits of the powers of the Security Council, op. cit., pp. 262ss.

[681]J.A. FROWEIN, Issues of legitimacy around the United Nations Security Council, in J.A. FROWEIN, K. SCHARIOTH, I. WINKELMANN, R. WOLFRUM, Verbandeln für den Frieden. Liber amicorum Tono Eite, ed. Springer, Berlin, 2003.

[682]O. BEKOU, The International Criminal Court, op. cit.,

[683]A. BIANCHI, Assessing the effectiveness of the UN Security Council's anti-terrorism measures. The quest for legitimacy and cohesion, in European Journal of International Law, 17 (5), 2007, pp. 912ss, which is stated that "if one takes the doctrine of separation of powers and its ancillary concept of checks and balances not as constitutional law doctrines grounded in nay particular domestic system, but rather as concepts related to an area of

However, a certain tendency can be recalled in constitutional doctrine to believe that the participation of several subjects in the formation of the fundamental laws of an order represents an optimal solution to guarantee a fair balance between the powers of the State[684]. From the point of view of judicial control, it is basically a matter of conceiving the order as a system where, within the limits of its competences, each individual international judge is the depositary of the entire judicial function and ultimately admits the possibility and the need for a union to widespread although limited validity of the political choices made by SC.

Concluding remarks

1. The relevance of the prevalence, autonomy and limited control models in defining the relationships between ICC and Security Council

Through the analysis conducted so far, we have tried to highlight the various critical issues that may emerge in the complex attempt to harmoniously link the political action of SC, aimed at maintaining peace with the jurisdictional one of ICC, aimed at ascertaining criminal responsibility for the International Crimes Commission.

In order to provide some interpretations of this complex relationship, some models of interaction between the two organizations were identified during the introduction. This was done through the prisms of possible immunity or as opposed to the possible submission of the SC action to forms of control exercised by the ICC. In other words, and more concretely, an attempt has been made to frame the possible extensions of political discretion and the corresponding jurisdictional syndicate into three theoretical reference models aimed at representing the forms through which the freedom of SC with respect to the ICC action can be expressed or vice versa. judicial control over political action.

In defining these models, there has inevitably been a simplification of the particularly articulate and complex relations that can be established between the two institutions and more generally, between political and judicial bodies. In fact, as has emerged in part during the last chapter, it is difficult to frame the

---

political though with much wider connotations their inspiring motif and underlying policy rationales are fairly simple. Power must not be concentrated in one entity and must be subject to some control (...)"

[684] J.E. ALVAREZ, Judging the security Council, in American Journal of International Law, 90 (1), 1996, pp. 8ss., which is stated that "what each organ does no matter how solicitous it is of each organ's respective tasks, inevitably forms part of the web of emerging law and practice under the charter and of international law. Making law through a dialogue between judicial interpreter and lawmakers is the essence of constitutional adjudication and cutting of that dialogue seems as unlikely as avoiding instances of overlap all together (...) even more activist forms of judicial review than have appeared to date may prove to be neither utopian nor calamitous, especially if the SC permanent members of come to appreciate that they have long-term interests in pursuing peace through law (...)" (pp. 40ss).

relationship object of this investigation in only one of the prototypes outlined. In different ways and with a variable relevance depending on the type of interaction that can be called to define as well as the nature and object of the potential conflict all three models, prevalence of the politician and the judiciary full autonomy of ICC. The SC action and limited forms of judicial control are useful in capturing some aspects of the intricate dynamics of relations between the two organizations.

For greater clarity, the essential characteristics of the three theoretical models to which reference is being made can be briefly summarized here. The first was aimed at effectively establishing a prevalence of the political dimension over the jurisdictional one. In other words, the decisions that the SC takes to guarantee peace and international security should always be ensured also with respect to the action of an international court that deals with the repression of the most serious international crimes. This solution would be a consequence of the crucial role that must be attributed to art. 103 of the UN Charter and more generally to the constitutional value that must be recognized in that particular international treaty. In this perspective, the ICC's control over the SC decisions would be practically excluded. The ICC bodies would de facto be forced to follow up on any request from the political body in the name of the superior demands of international peace and security maintenance of which the SC is an expression.

The second model focuses instead on the idea of full autonomy of the two legal systems in their mutual interaction. In other words, it is a pluralistic conception of the international order in the light of which each body remains fully free to interpret and apply the rules of its founding treaty and more generally the powers linked to the function it is called to perform. And this regardless of the effects that their decisions are destined to produce towards other subjects of the legal system. With this in mind, the ICC could legitimately verify the validity of SC decisions in the light of any relevant regulatory parameter. Not only therefore the statutory rules but also other rules and principles of international law that may be useful in syndicating the discretion of the chapter VII of the UN Charter, expressly referred to by the Statute in the provisions governing the referral and deferral powers, could become the subject of a validity check of SC decisions aimed at affecting the jurisdictional activity of ICC.

Finally, an intermediate theoretical model, so to speak, is that which seeks to integrate the two systems as far as possible and coordinate the action of the two organs, without always and necessarily guaranteeing a political prevalence of SC, nor protecting regardless of the autonomy of power jurisdiction of ICC. In this case there was talk of a form of limited control. Indeed, through a particular reconstruction of the doctrine of the policy in question, it could be argued that the judicial union can be experienced only within certain limits, where in essence the judge's evaluation does not replace the political discretion deliberately remitted by the UN Charter to SC. This possible model expresses the attempt to reconcile the prerogatives and purposes of SC political action with the exercise of the judicial function. However, it is up to the interpreter to find the difficult task of establishing the boundaries between purely political decisions and issues that can be judged. As seen in the relationship between ICC and SC, this discrimination could be identified on the basis of the regulatory parameter in the light of which the political action must be assessed. More precisely, one could distinguish between strictly statutory parameters on which the ICC would have full control power and parameters which, as referred to by the Statute, are in any case external to the pact system through which the ICC was established and therefore preclude the possibility of a validity union. This naturally refers to the foundation in Chapter VII of the UN Charter on which the SC action must be based for the purpose of activating or suspending the judicial activity.

Before examining the relevance that these models can assume in defining the different forms of coordination of the interactions between ICC and SC, a preliminary observation is appropriate. It is clear that the potential relevance of these theoretical models emerges only when a conflict arises between SC and ICC. In fact, the need to establish which organ and purpose (peace and justice) it is necessary to give prevalence is imposed only if it is impossible to reconcile political action with the judicial function, when, in short, the conflict between the two institutions appears inevitable. As emerged in this part of the discussion, if a coordination of the activities of the two organizations can be resolved on an interpretative level, the problem of establishing a prevalence or a subordination of the action of one organ over the other does not obviously arise. It should be noted that an interpretation solution, however desirable, can be particularly complex. On the one hand, the difficulty of reconstructing the meaning of covenant provisions, those of the Rome Treaty which were not particularly elaborate, has repeatedly been highlighted. On the other hand, as far as the ICC is concerned, the last word on the interpretation of its founding treaty is the subject that can affect the application and interpretation of the Statute through its own behaviors and among these a prominent role is obviously played from the same SC. It is also worth mentioning that in this complex hermeneutic recomposition of the claims and needs of the two institutions, a particularly relevant function was assigned at various points of the investigation to the principle of presumption in conformity and more generally to the need to integrate the sphere of political action with that of the criminal repression of harmonizing the UN law with that of the Rome Statute in a systemic perspective aimed at bringing together the plurality of subsystems that make up the international system.

When this work of hermeneutic recomposition of the potential conflict is impractical, it becomes necessary to grant a prevalence to one of the two collective interests at stake and to guarantee a supremacy to the action of the organ that is its priority scope. In this regard, the absolute centrality of peacekeeping in the international order could the principle ensure freedom of SC with respect to the means and methods of directing and possibly limiting the exercise of the judicial function. However, the reconstruction of the relationship between the two organizations has already led to rejecting the idea of an unconditional prevalence of SC action over the jurisdictional power of ICC. As we have tried to highlight, art. 103 is a rule for solving possible conflicts between obligations of States. It establishes the superiority of the obligations deriving from States participated in UN over any other international obligation. Art. 103 does not however concern relations with other international organizations. The ICC, by virtue of the relationship agreement of 2004 and the universal character of the principles expressed in the UN Charter, is required to respect the fundamental rules and encourage the pursuit of the objectives contained in that particular international treaty. However, it does not seem correct to attribute to art. 103 a different and further scope than that which is its most linear and common interpretation and application. The purpose of this operation would only be to guarantee a primacy to SC over the ICC action by leveraging a rule having the different function of regulating the conflict between the international obligations of States.

In a broader perspective of coordination between ICC and SC that transcends the closest dimension of direct relations between the two organizations, the space that remains for art. 103 of the UN Charter however is not marginal and cannot be ignored. As has sometimes been highlighted in this paper if the necessary involvement of the States is taken into consideration for the full and correct functioning of ICC, the possible effects of art. 103 on the effectiveness of ICC action are of evidence and relevance in particular in the field of cooperation and mutual legal assistance. Faced with conflicting requests from the two institutions and addressed to States, art. 103 guarantees a prevalence of the obligations deriving from SC decisions with respect to the covenant commitments assumed by the States towards ICC and can therefore hamper delay or even legally preclude the execution of ICC decisions. An element that cannot be overlooked if we want to fully understand the broader political and diplomatic space in which the ICC operates and moves. This possible impact of SC decisions on the collaboration of States with ICC can in fact condition the will of ICC to oppose the action of the political body and therefore have an impact relevant to the overall action of the international tribunal influencing the judicial policy that it intends to pursue.

The model focused on the concept of autonomy of the two organizations plays a certainly more significant role in the more limited perspective and at the center of the present investigation of the relationships that can be established between ICC and SC. This model in particular helps to understand the nature of any limits to the action of SC against the jurisdictional activity of ICC, as well as to grasp the possible scope of the corresponding power of ICC to syndicate the political decisions intended to affect its jurisdiction. As seen on the basis of the Kompetenz-Kompetenz principle, it can be considered that the ICC always has the power to determine the scope of its jurisdiction even in the event that this leads it to disregard the decisions through which in the exercise of the powers of activation and suspension of the ICC's activity, the SC starts or stops ICC action. However, some critical aspects of this model can emerge when it comes to establishing the extent of the ICC's validity check on SC decisions in light of regulatory parameters which, although expressly referred to by the Rome Statute, are contained in a different international treaty, the UN Charter. In this regard, it can be observed, for example, that claiming full autonomy and ability of ICC to syndicate the validity of Resolutions that the SC adopts in ascertaining the existence of the conditions laid down in art. 39 of the UN Charter can be particularly problematic. The admissibility of this union risks in fact not taking into due consideration the other rate of politicity that that type of decision implies and ultimately corroding or in any case questioning the priority given to SC in the context of peacekeeping and international security.

To try to overcome these limitations that the pluralist model presents the different type of interaction, the idea of limited control inspired by the doctrine of the political question seems to add some interesting and useful elements for reflection. It can be assumed that the relationship between political discretion and judicial review does not take static and immutable forms but rather must necessarily adapt to the type of assessment subject to potential conflict. In this perspective, it has been highlighted, for example, that the determination of a threat to peace deliberately characterized by a strong political discretion indicates that the possibility of judicial control is rather reduced. In the context of aggression, however, the presence of greater elements of certainty that characterize this state conduct could lead to a possible overlap of the assessments that can be simultaneously carried out by the political and judicial bodies on this area with an extension therefore of the possibility of verification jurisdictional political decisions.

However, even this model does not appear fully satisfactory and still has some limitations. In fact, once established the principle according to which a greater extent of political discretion corresponds to a reduction in the margin of judicial autonomy, the problem remains of establishing a certain perimeter of the spaces of the politician and the judiciary. The idea that this line is changeable according to the degree of politicity of the decision to be taken appears persuasive but offers only an indication of principle for the purpose of identifying the boundary between discretion of political action and extent of judicial control. Moreover, the determination of the legal parameters that define the threat to peace, the violation of peace and the act of aggression are constantly evolving and can over time reduce the rate of politicity of those assessments making them gradually liable to a more intense judicial control.

Not even the attempt to determine a limit to SC discretion contributes to eliminating the area just highlighted. So we tried to demonstrate in this last chapter we can in fact support in the light of some important judicial practices of the attitudes of States with respect to SC action and of numerous and important doctrinal reconstructions that a power to sanction the invalidity of political decisions both to be admitted in the event that the latter are characterized by an arbitrariness such as to believe that the prerogatives recognized to the SC result in a real abuse of power. For example, one can imagine the need for judicial intervention against decisions that are difficult to ascribe to the powers attributed to the SC or acts that cannot be considered functional to the objectives of the UN Charter or that in any case manifestly conflict with the principles and the fundamental rules of international law. However, the concepts of arbitrariness and abuse of power also remain concepts with uncertain boundaries, thus making the determination of the moment in which the limit to political discretion is overstepped elusive.

Ultimately, it seems difficult to draw a precise dividing line between action and judicial control and to be able to evade the dichotomy between political discretion and judicial autonomy. The possible solutions in the face of possible conflicts between the two institutions end up constantly oscillating between the need to protect judicial autonomy in criminal repression and the defense of the strictly political prerogatives that characterize the SC decisions for the purpose of maintaining peace. From the point of view of the proposed models, it does not seem easy to find the balance between the full jurisdictional autonomy expressed by the Kompetenz-Kompetenz principle and the affirmation of a limited control model based on the relevance that the political question theory can assume.

After all, both these constructions start from concepts which, as already pointed out, have a reach from the borders in many ways indefinite. Both the Kompetenz-Kompetenz principle and the doctrine of the political question essentially lend themselves to being invoked to protect political prerogatives or those related to the exercise of the judicial function. The concrete application of these constructions can lead to antithetical solutions according to the role that the interpreter intends to assign them. Thus the Kompetenz-Kompetenz principle could be used to extend the concept of jurisdiction to the point of considering any SC decisions aimed at affecting the ICC action subject to a valid union. The doctrine of the political question, on the other hand, could lend itself to being invoked to maintain that any form of judicial control is precluded from any decision of the SC adopted for the purpose of maintaining peace as undeniably characterized by a strong political connotation.

Finally, in this problematic oscillation between two opposites, other components, so to speak diplomatic, and in some measure of strength that can help to fix at a different point each time the delicate balance between protection of political action and guarantee of judicial independence cannot be ignored. On the one hand, in fact, the ICC bodies cannot neglect the more general political consequences of the exercise of a validity union of the SC decisions. On the other hand, the SC cannot underestimate the consequences of its action in terms of the legitimacy and credibility of its own work in the administration of international criminal justice and of the entire system created through the Rome Treaty. These additional contextual elements can play an important role in determining the attitudes of the two organizations even beyond what are the most correct interpretations of the normative data at the center of the conflict and the relevance that can be attributed to the political nature of the case decision or the need to safeguard the autonomy of the judicial function. The changing nature of these elements of a diplomatic sense side is neither impossible nor definitive in a definitive way, the impact that can only depend on the contingencies of the concrete case on the power relations existing between the two organizations on the credibility of which they may or not enjoy in a given historical moment. The attempt of dominance or the deference of one organization towards the other can therefore through claims of judicial autonomy or claims of politicity of the assessments to be made, vary over time depending on what are the contingencies of the wider political dimension in which the action of the two organs is inserted.

2. The impact of interactions between ICC and Security Council on the effectiveness and legitimacy of the judicial function

The considerations just carried out highlight in particular an aspect of different ways that emerged several times in the course of the investigation which cannot be overlooked when evaluating the activity of ICC and the relationships that it maintains with SC, i.e. the conflictual or post-contexts conflicts in which the repressive action of ICC inevitably makes it an important political actor in the process of restoring international peace and security. On the other hand, it is sufficient to think that the numerous functions that are normally attributed to international criminal jurisdictions in addition to the more traditional ones related to the deterrent effect of the repressive action and the remuneration purpose of the penalty tend to add reconciliation between the parties to the conflict and ultimately the restoration and maintenance of peace. It has not been the subject of this investigation to determine whether the international criminal courts and ICC in particular are actually able to contribute and to what extent to the achievement of such an ambitious goal and to which many actors on the international scene contribute[685]. What is most important here is how this peculiar function, which has always been considered inherent to the prosecution at international level, places the ICC in an extremely delicate position in the complex and intricate management of collective security. In fact, in the particular context in which the ICC operates, the assessment of individual responsibility is part of dynamics and power structures that can decisively condition the performance of the judicial activity and on which the SC action necessarily affects.

Rome Statute as widely seen is based on the assumption that there is a form of complementarity in the action of the two bodies. Moreover, the preamble expressly recognizes that the large-scale international crimes Commission threaten the peace, security and well-being of the world. The legal framework of the Statute is more generally inspired by the need that the exercise of jurisdiction, and therefore the assessment of individual responsibilities and the satisfaction of the victims, is in any case functional to the reconciliation between the parties to the conflict and to the maintenance of peace as ultimate goals even if pursued with different means of action by SC and ICC.

The Rome Statute in establishing precise forms of interaction between ICC and SC also ends up fixing within a predefined regulatory framework the possible space for intervention of the political choices made by SC on the jurisdictional action of ICC. The result is the construction of a complex and delicate balance between the necessary protection of the autonomy of the ICC

---

[685]L.E. FLETSCHER, H.M. WEINSTEIN, Violence and social repair: Rethinking the contribution of justice to reconciliation, in Human Rights Quarterly, 24, 2002, pp. 574ss. P. AKHAVAN, Are international criminal tribunals a disincentive to peace? Reconciling judicial romanticism with political realism, in Human Rights Quarterly, 31 (3), 2009, pp. 624ss.

bodies and the political implications of the exercise of the criminal action at an international level on which the SC evidently fits.

The investigation conducted revealed that the inevitable indeterminacy of the relevant statutory provisions in many ways makes it particularly difficult to circumscribe the scope of political intervention on judicial activity. This regulatory uncertainty can therefore lend itself to opposing claims and possibly lead to real conflicts between the two bodies. Although the indeterminacy of the regulatory data is destined to decrease over time thanks to the interpretative activity of the ICC bodies. The flexibility of some provisions of the Statute is inherent in the need that the relationship dynamics between ICC and SC can somehow adapt to particularly complex and constantly evolving political situations and contexts. In other words, this indeterminacy seems to reflect the need to preserve a certain margin of discretion to ICC bodies and SC in evaluating the forms from time to time of the extent and scope of judicial intervention with a view to always promote peacekeeping. In the perspective of ICC, the flexibility of the statutory data can give the ICC a more or less large space for judicial policy assessments aimed, for example, at extending or compressing its repressive action and which, depending on the case, may be inspired by a total adhesion or contrary to attitudes of resistance if not of open opposition to SC requests[686].

The need to link the judicial activity of ICC with the SC prerogatives is not only linked to the possible superposition of the action of the two bodies but is also the consequence of another and different aspect, i.e. the universal vocation of the repressive action of ICC. If there is no doubt that the task assigned to the permanent tribunal by the Rome Statute is an expression of a collective interest of the international community, it is also true that this universal dimension of the jurisdictional function attributed to ICC is not reconciled with the contractual nature of the founding treaty of ICC. With this in mind, the intervention of SC serves to compensate for this structural limit of the system created by the Rome Treaty. This intervention may be necessary precisely to make that universal vocation effective through the imposition also on states that are not part of the system of ICC jurisdiction or a series of assistance obligations towards the ICC organs.

The reconstruction of the interpretative and application practice of the statute provisions highlights the complexity of the framework just outlined and in particular that delicate balance on which the relationships between ICC and SC are built. The elements of practice that have hitherto characterized the relations between the two bodies in fact show in a tangible way a series of harmonious coordination potentials but also the risk of tensions and conflicts that can manifest themselves in the relations between ICC and SC.

The fact that in these final pages we want to highlight is how this dialectic between the two bodies is capable of profoundly affecting two central aspects of ICC activity, i.e. the effectiveness of the repressive action of international crimes

---

[686] Y. SHANY, Questions of jurisdiction and admissibility before international courts, Cambridge University Press, Cambridge, 2016, pp. 12ss.

and the legitimacy of this work in the eyes of the international community. Not only does the problem of the effectiveness and legitimacy of ICC action go through all the forms of interaction that have been examined in the previous chapters. It constitutes an essential profile for understanding the basic question addressed in this study, i.e. the definition of ICC area of jurisdictional autonomy with respect to the political action of SC.

As seen in chapter I in the referral remake, the SC's choices to initiate the ICC's judicial activity in Darfur and Libya represented first important acknowledgments of the role that the ICC can be called to play in order to restore the peace. In both circumstances, however, recognition of the role of ICC has been accompanied by limitations which risk weakening its effectiveness or highlighting the political constraints in the selection of the objectives of its repressive action. We refer in particular to the removal from ICC jurisdiction of the conduct of individuals from States not part of the Statute engaged in peacekeeping operations or in the Libyan case the limitation ratione temporis placed on the activation of the repressive action. For both Libya and Darfur, the SC then arranged in a way that is difficult to comply with that principle of full cooperation that should inspire the interaction between the two organizations that no expense related to ICC activity is supported by the UN. This choice actually ends up affecting the number and scope of investigations and procedures that the ICC bodies are able to conduct, limiting to some extent the repressive potential of ICC.

Even more problematic is the use of SC to suspend ICC activity as widely seen in Chapter II. Precisely in the practice relating to the exercise of this peculiar and particularly incisive prerogative recognized to SC, from the very first years of existence of the ICC, a series of critical issues and potential opportunities for conflict of no small importance have emerged fatally. In particular, the suspension of the repressive action against citizens of states not part of the Statute engaged in authorized or constituted operations of UN is difficult to reconcile with the same assumptions of the action of SC provided for in Chapter VII of the UN Charter and therefore with the aim of maintaining international peace and security. This practice seems to have contributed to the emergence between some states of the belief, then somewhat heightened by the particular limitations affixed to the requests to start the investigation activity, that the SC through the decisive influence that can be asserted internally by the permanent members intends to model the jurisdictional activity of ICC on the basis of the interests and claims of the great powers.

Also in the context of the cooperation of states with the ICC, the importance that a convergence between the action of the two bodies can have to ensure a full and effective exercise of the repressive action of ICC clearly emerges. However, as seen in Chapter III, numerous and in some ways still insurmountable tensions emerged between the claims of the ICC organs to be handed over by States some of the individuals suspected of the crimes of their competence and the reluctance of SC to take concrete action to impose the necessary cooperation obligations on those States.

More specifically, in the particular context of cooperation and execution of ICC decisions, the deepest conflict between some States that are part of the ICC Statute is taking place. The issue of the immunity of Heads of State from ICC jurisdiction, and in particular the request made by the ICC to States Parties to the Statute to arrest and hand over Sudanese President Al Bashir has indeed provoked a series of rather harsh reactions by ICC[687]. The countries of the African continent essentially perceive the judicial activity of ICC more and more as a threat to the political stability of governments legitimately in power and an instrument in the hands of SC to exercise a real selection of the ruling classes[688].

The Sudanese case shows the costs that the SC's inertia can have on the jurisdictional activity of ICC. The ICC organs are powerless in the face of the refusal of states to cooperate and the current manifestation of this impotence certainly does not attribute to strengthening the centrality of ICC in the repression of international crimes and more generally its role in the international order. Although activated by SC, the ICC was substantially left alone in the subsequent management of this crisis without the SC providing forms of collaboration aimed at ensuring the effectiveness of the repressive action.

Regarding aggression, it is not yet possible to make assessments on the impact of the interactions between ICC and SC on the effectiveness and legitimacy of the exercise of the judicial function. However, as emerged in Chapter IV, several occasions of conflict can be envisaged at least in relation to the assessment of the relevant state conduct. These possible differences may

---

[687]Precisely following the numerous disputes related to the Sudanese case in October of 2018, Burundi was the first state to withdraw its ratification of the Rome Statute. It can also be pointed out that only after a change in the government of the country, Gambia decided to return to being part of the treaty establishing the tribunal which it had previously also denounced; while the continuing participation of South Africa in the Rome Statute still remains uncertain. The High Court had invalidated the withdrawal from the Statute as it was not authorized by Parliament, see High Court of South Africa Democratic Alliance v. Minister of international relations and cooperation and others (Council for the advancement of the South African Constitution intervening), 83145/2016 of 22 February 2017. The African Union in the meantime is also studying a procedure for a collective exit of the states that are part of the organization from the ICC system.

[688]O.A. MAUNGANIDZE, A. DU PLESSIS, The ICC and the AU, in C. STAHN, The law and practice of the international criminal court, Oxford University Press, Oxford, 2015, pp. 67ss. B. SWART, In the eye of the storm: The Keynatta case and the dispute between the African union and the international criminal court, in African Yearbook of International Humanitarian Law, 20, 2015, pp. 134ss. K. AMBOS, Expanding the focus of the African criminal court, in W.A. SCHABAS, MCDERMOTT, HAYES, The Ashgate research companion of international criminal law, Ashgate Publishing, The Hague, 2013, pp. 500ss. F. OKOWA, The Security Council, the African Union and the international criminal court. Anatomy of a problematic relationship, in J. EBBESSON, M. JACOBSSON, M.A. LAMBERG, D. LANGLET, P. WRANGE, International law and changing perceptions of security. Liber amicorum Said Mahmoudi, Hotei Publishing, The Hague, 2014, pp. 226ss. P.S. WEGNER, The International Criminal Court in ongoing intra-state conflicts, op. cit., C. CHINKIN, M. KALDOR, International law and new wars, Cambridge University Press, Cambridge, 2017, pp. 437ss.

evidently end up undermining the relationship between the political body and the judiciary. On the other hand, even a convergence between ICC and SC could generate suspicion at least in some states of a politicization of the repressive action of the Permanent Court.

In essence, beyond the purely political assessments that can be made on the choices of SC, it is clear that the requests that this body addresses to ICC can put it in front of particularly difficult decisions with important repercussions on the effectiveness and legitimacy of the judicial action.

In the hypothesis of SC requests that may appear scarcely compatible with the statutory data and expression of attempts at political exploitation of the action of ICC, it is in fact faced with two alternatives that present potential advantages but also significant costs.

On the one hand, the ICC can decide to comply with the requests of SC, ensuring the support of the only actor who can guarantee its repressive action to overcome the consensualistic principle and the inability of ICC to coercively impose respect for its decisions on States. The risk for the ICC to bow to the will of SC, however, is to be perceived as an ICC enslaved to the political body. The ultimate effect could be a loss of consensus among States and a delegitimization of their role. On the other hand, the ICC may decide instead to oppose some requests of SC by claiming its autonomy and presumably gaining a certain consensus among the States but at the same time risking losing a fundamental political support for the realization of its universal aspirations and of the full and effective performance of the judicial function.

In practice, no real conflicts have yet emerged between ICC action and SC. ICC has in fact not taken any decision to date that has openly questioned the effects of the SC decisions relating to its jurisdiction. This study sought to highlight in a strictly juridical key the possible areas of conflict between the two bodies attempting to offer solutions on how the statutory provisions and indications on the extension that the judicial union of the political choices of the SC can take. Precisely the flexibility of the normative data and the changeability and indeterminacy of the boundaries between the politician and the judiciary allow the ICC bodies a certain amount of movement on the intensity of the control they intend to exercise on SC decisions. In this area of uncertainty and discretion, assessments are inserted which cannot be statically predetermined but which depend on the particular contexts in which the ICC is involved in the authoritativeness and legitimacy rate it enjoys in a given historical moment and ultimately analysis of the power relationships that over time will be established with the SC.

Chapter 6
Thoughts and perspectives of universalism and particularism in international criminal justice

1. Introduction.

When we speak of international criminal law and/or international criminal justice between universalism and particularism it would seem to put more emphasis on a diachronic consideration in which universalism and particularism are two possible tendential ways of manifesting the law that mark its historical evolution and the different systems.

Universalism and particularism as two poles of one of the many internal contradictions that run through juridical experience creating a vital tension and a complex dynamism for which the possibility that a manifestation of universalism mutates in its opposite and *vice versa* is by no means excluded.

Looking at the legal phenomenon or a part of it like that of international criminal law through the lens of opposition between universalism and particularism certainly means placing analysis in a philosophical dimension. This, however, does not imply dispelling the analysis into a conceptual illusionism alien to the reality of the interests and values with which it actually has to do with law. On the contrary, proposing an analysis through the opposition universalism/particularism testifies rather the awareness that international criminal law is more than the verbal expression of a will that has found the way to impose itself. Something that, like every product of the historically manifesting human spirit, lives in the dialectic between universalism and particularism. Two connotations that the law assumes not because it has been decided by the *voluntas legislatoris,* but because in one sense and the other they push the most complex vital forces both internal and external to juridical experience[689].

2. Universalism versus/or particularism?

It is not a peaceful coexistence between universalism and particularism. There is, in both cases, a kind of pretended overpactation/overcodification that creates reasons for tension and disorder, all the more serious the more coercive

---

[689]M. DELMAS-MARTY, Le pluralisme ordonnè, Seuil, Paris, 2006. M. DELMAS-MARTY, Libertès et sûretè dans un monde dangereux, Seuil, Paris, 2010, pp. 196ss.

they are at their disposal. This overburdening tendency can count on the obligatory force of the legal instrument. But in the world of penalties, these dangers are further accentuated by the violence that makes criminal punishment international criminal responsibility available to them. Universalism contrasts the particularism almost imperialistically disavowing its reality, often cloying itself of the disguised form of an irenicism of which it prides itself on crediting. The particularism is even more warlike because not only is opposed to universalism exalting the existential concreteness of its vitality but it triggers a perennial conflict with all the other particularities that it meets on its way. Latent or manifest that the fact remains of an exaggerated conflict that when it can count on the subsidy of the penalty puts at risk the freedom and dignity of the individual.

Hence the imposition of an ethical imperative for a balance of that pluralism ordered as a great challenge of our millennium. An order which, without disregarding the pluralistic diversity of men and peoples, is able to find what joining them allows a peaceful coexistence fertilized by mutual enrichment.

International criminal law also knows this conflictual coexistence of universalism and particularism but it is certainly true that the world of international penalties strongly inclines to particularism. If particularism also means closure towards the other and others, there is no doubt that international criminal law, both consubstantially and historically, implies closure towards man and towards States. Consubstantially what better than the prison walls expresses the particularistic logic of the isolation of expulsion, of the refusal of the individual? Prison embodies the particularistic logic of the conflict opened up by international crime and that of being held in the detention, segregation that certainly does not unite but rather separates the offender materially and ideally from society. There is in international criminal law that we know an innate component of enmity which can be mitigated by re-educational ideologies inspired by social solidarity but it can also degenerate into the grim "international law of the enemy" (which can be the ideologized terrorist but also the common delinquent author of heinous crimes entering into crimes against humanity.

Historically, a persistent manifestation of particularism towards States, in our case of Member States of the Statute of Rome, is the very idea of code so dear to modern international criminal law and to the same penalistic reflection in the national, internal sense. Accredited almost as the very form of modern international criminal law in the historical concreteness the statutes of the international criminal courts is like a code of particularistic affirmation that tends to the (at least theoretically) disregard of all that remains away in the codicistic fence in the sense of domestic law. It is an instrument in which an order of values is closed in order to differentiate it and also impose it on other evaluative systems: whether it originates in the pronouncement of the will of a political subject that imposes itself thus realizing itself, or that it constitutes the nationalistic goal of a demos that has rediscovered itself and its identity by manifesting its deepest essence in the criminal commandments in the national sense as the Spanish code of 1995 that consecrated the rediscovered democratic identity after the Franco dictatorship. But our discourse can not stop here at the observation of this sort of inclination of international criminal law towards particularism. It would be partial and even misleading because even in the field of international criminal law the universalistic vocation is present, if not a cardinal principle in its dynamic balance with the particularistic inclination and with the tendency of one to convert into the other and *vice versa.*

But before entering into the discourse, some clarifying premises are opportune at least to make manifest the path chosen here among the many passable in the intricate forest in which universalism and particularism intertwine their branches, thus enveloping international criminal law.

The meaning of copy universalism/particularism can be understood in a twofold fundamental meaning. In a logical-cognitive sense, of Aristotelian derivation. On the other hand, in an ethical-axiological sense of Kantian derivation. In the first sense, the universal arises as the essence of particular things that allows the latter to be traced back to the same genus (leaving necessarily the unresolved dispute of what genus is in reality and of how the essence can be identified). In the second sense, the universal indicates evaluative assertions that claim to be or that are actually shared in a reference human-social order, which can be spatially and culturally identified and delimited or even coincide with the order of the whole immunity in that such.

In the international criminal law the first gnoseological exception of the contrast between universalism and particularism is especially at stake as a theme of words, almost methodological, of systems and techniques of normative representation of the criminal relevant reality. In the second sense-axiological-evaluative-the contrast refers to a theme and problem of affirmation always historically conditioned by values that manifesting what a will of power are able to impose themselves as deserving of the maximum protection of the law that penalty. Undoubtedly the greatest attention will have to be devoted to the second perspective here, but it may also be appropriate to mention the first concerning penalization techniques. Comparing the atypicalness of the civilian illicit with the typicality and fragmentation characterizing instead of the criminal offense one would be tempted to conclude that only the former is able to grasp the essence of things while the latter is destined to remain trapped in the particular of the fact that cuts and closes that and not another portion of reality. The image of starting and not distensive ideas well expresses the descriptive particularism proper to criminal cases. This idea must however be resized. The modern technique of typing the criminal offense has long since abandoned the exasperated casuistry and the particularistic chaos characteristic of the indictments of medieval statutes and the sources of the *ancien règime*. The happy idea of criminal type represented by the statues of the international criminal courts allows a fruitful balance between a unitary evaluative essence, embodied and expressed in this case and the differentiated particularist multiplicity of concrete manifestations of reality[690]. Exceeded an exclusively subjunctive conception of the norm/fact relationship. On

[690]See in argument: W. HASSEMER, Tabestand und Typus. Untersuchungen zur Strafrechtlichen Hermeneutik, Carl Haymanns Verlag KG, Köln, 1968.

the one hand, the type allows to avoid the closed tyranny defining the norm on the changing reality enriching the applicative experience of the particolaristic suggestions coming from the multiform reality but also on the other side avoiding the vapid particolarism of an exasperated casuistry that ends often to lose contact with the significant essence of things.

The dialectical opposition between universalism and particularism is taken in an axiological ethical sense, it seems undoubted a strong tendency of current international criminal law to the increasingly imperative affirmation of universal values. The unequivocal continuation of the list of crimes against humanity is unequivocally increasing. The number of crimes originally written as offensive goods is substantially renewed, as is the appreciation of individual States that are today perceived as harmful even of values with a universalistic vocation and as such qualified as against humanity. Given also some cautions are necessary to avoid the risk of hasty and misleading misunderstandings.

In the historicized world of law the contrast between universalism and particularism must be understood not in an absolute but relative manner. In the sense that the same values can be presented as universal with respect to a given reference system, for example the European Union and details with respect to a wider current system such as that of United Nations and as a consequence the birth of international criminal courts. Nor is it said that the claim of universality is more in keeping with the values of geographically vast order. The universalistic vocation of the criminally protected values rather than being an ethical-evaluative axiom is, if anything, dependent on the will to power that values, are able to express and above all to achieve in disparate historical situations. So in the question of blacklists. These are lists of subjects suspected of being financiers of international terrorism formulated in the UN headquarters. The tendency towards the universalization of goods and the criminal intentional right that protects them must be disfigured by different or only partly analogous phenomena. One of these is the intensification of international cooperation in the pressure of crimes also provided by Chapter 9 of the StICC. This widespread and heartfelt need arises essentially from the transnational character of certain criminal phenomena. Sit-in of a character to dare to say extrinsic to the value of the offense and consistently at the bottom in a territorial datum of its realization. Judicial cooperation is always based on a relationship between states of a particular type, even though it is certainly now one of the main objectives of European Union. The need for international criminal cooperation goes hand in hand with the tendency and necessity of the harmonization of legislation of the various countries which is an indispensable prerequisite for the efficiency of cooperative instruments and is therefore assumed to be instrumental to caries international conventions.

In this perspective, the harmonization of the substantial discipline of international ratios does not cease to be instrumental in the proper interest of each State to the effectiveness of the repression made difficult by the territorial transnational dimension of criminal phenomena (such as drug trafficking, war crimes, crimes of genocide, aggression, etc.) and the dissimilarity of national laws.

Another phenomenon only akin to true universalization is the globalization of criminal law, *rectius* the birth/evolution of international criminal justice. We intend to refer to a process of homogenization of criminal repression of phenomena that tend to occur precisely homogeneous in different areas of the planet. It is not so much the territorial executive data but rather an intrinsic homogeneity of the facts to justify a corresponding process of homogenization of the criminal response. It could also be said that moving from the phenomenological homogeneity of the fact one arrives at the evaluative homogeneity of the normative forecast.

It is perhaps possible to identify the role of international criminal courts with an essential character of this globalized criminal law-or in any case homogeneous in large regions of the planet. As a rule, it is aimed at reinforcing the repressive response, not without some intent in the sense of the exclusion of international offender, as it is directed especially with regard to serious international crimes. It is not infrequent an orientation towards the anticipation of sanctioning answer to facts deprived in themselves of a real and substantial negative value but artificially elevated to crimes in order to realize a preventive protection of the final goods as recorded in particular in relation to crimes against the war. There is also a serious tendency triggered, in particular, by the repressive needs of terrorism, to a sort of militarization of international criminal law that can manifest itself in aspects of different intensity. Not all countries have gone to the same levels of repressive reinforcement in the internal sphere in this process of homogenization of the international penal law of the so-called post-modernity but there is no doubt that the trend exists and that it goes in a direction exactly opposite to the recognition of fundamental rights of the individual and the principle of humanity in international criminal law.

3. Towards the true universalization of international criminal justice.

The direction in which the true universalization of international criminal law is marched is the opposite. Historically it is placed in the sign of human rights. Despite the constant and problematic relationship with particularism, the universalization of international criminal law gives voice to the will to power that human rights have managed to express. Although universalistic veins have always existed in the international criminal law of modernity, perhaps less evident because they concern apparently more abstract profiles of penalties, *rectius* international responsibility. It is appropriate to distinguish the universal components that manifest them in terms of justification of international penalty from those that manifest themselves in terms of contents subject to national criminal protection.

To the eternal problem of justification of punishment, universalism has contributed to providing reassuring tranquillizers, confirming also that vocation of apparently irenistic universalism. There are essentially two universalistic paradigms that do not cease to be repeated: one referring to a metaphysical universalism of religious ancestry focuses on the idea of retribution, the other referring to a unitarian universalism of Enlightenment ascendancy focuses on the purpose of social defense. Both are basically two manifestations, certainly very different from a moral rationalism that has played an objective mystifying role-both without polemical ideology-of the reality of punishment, at least since legitimate violence has become a monopoly of the modern state. The universalistic paradigms of punishment have overshadowed the fact that the penalty is at the bottom an instrument of the power of social stabilization and a dependent variable of its social and institutional set-ups.

The justifying universalism of the punishment has ignored the concrete and existential particularism of the guilty man in flesh and blood. Certainly in the history of international criminal law there have been no movements of thought that have recovered the particularism of the individual man unrepeatable from the positive school of the late nineteenth century to the religious humanism of explanation, to the fleeting triumph of reeducational ideology of the second half of the last century. Today the so-called rehabilitative function of punishment continues to play a precious role, albeit re-dimensioned and surrounded by caution. Punitive rehabilitation rather than being able to found work, the punishment tries to re-establish and maintain a balance between rationalistic universalism and humanistic-solidaristic particularism giving voice to the concrete man who suffers it from his needs and his individual characteristics. And even fundamental rights with the abstractness of their human paradigm of reference can replace and substitute the richness of content and the nobility of the commitment that the rehabilitative idea attributes to punishment.

4. On the level of values and assets...protected by international criminal law

On the level of goods and values that are the object of international criminal protection, today's universalism is manifestly resounding in the upward parabola of human rights, which from the limits of criminal law become its content. A content that precisely because it derives from fundamental rights can not but tend to free itself from the particularism of individual states to trigger the great movement that in 1999 gave rise to the statute of Rome and ICC. The criminal law of human rights assumed full awareness that the greatest dangers for humanity come from states is constituted in a supranational order with a universal vocation incardinated in a permanent organ of justice which is finally the ICC. Realistically we must acknowledge that the particularly jealous of states is hard to die and the universalism of ICC must coexist with many limitations that also condition the effectiveness of its justice. Not only the lack of ratification of the statute of Rome by some great countries of the world in relation to their criminalistic attitude, the irenisitic universalism of rights reveals its ambivalence: on one hand it is a possible instrument of planetary cultural power. Another possibility is the recognition of a parity in which the will to power of the great ones is tempered, but also the complementary character of the jurisdiction of

ICC[691] destined to take over the protection of single States only when they have not been able or wished to exercise it. The lack of coercive power directly vested in the ICC with the consequent need to rely on the initiative of the States and their particular evaluations inspired by the Realpolitik of each of them. The universalistic vocation of this international justice is undeniable despite the coexistence with the irrepressible particularism of states.

The fundamental fact is that universalism of human rights and international criminal justice is rooted in something axiologically deeper and more meaningful. It is the discovery of a supreme value that at the basis of human rights calls for criminal protection per se, even in its various forms of manifestation. It is about the dignity of human person. And the humanistic essence of which it feeds can only push towards its universal protection. Then the multilateral international conventions proliferate that oblige of states to take particular incriminations but now assume a new relevance for their special content of negative value concerning just the dignity of the person. Here are the conventions against torture, slavery, trafficking, sexual exploitation.

In brackets we can see a significant inversion of tendency in the historical process of identification of personal legal assets to be protected by criminal law. If the fragmentation of other personality rights, which was necessary for the evolution in the international criminal sphere in relation to the specific needs of typification of offensiveness, had arisen in the middle of the last century, today the value of dignity plays a unifying role of different aggressive types of the person. This does not mean that the number of cases inspired by the protection of dignity is reduced in number and tends to unity. But it has two consequences which are by no means negligible for the international criminal lawyer. Many naturalistically different crimes find a common *raison d'être* and a unitary discipline in their containment of the dignity of which implies, for example, the subjection to a regime of special jurisdiction. These cases, inspired by the protection of dignity, are subject to a tendency of indeterminacy of the normative description due to the naturalistic evanescence of the property protected on a

---

691 D. ROBINSON, Three theories of complementarity: Charge, sentence or process?, in Harvard International Law Journal, 53, 2012, pp. 87ss. J. TRAHAN, Is complementarity the right approach for the International Criminal Court's crime of aggression-Considering the problem of overzealous National Court prosecutions, in Cornell International Law Journal, 45, 2012, pp. 576ss. K.J. HELER, A sentence-based theory of complementarity, in Harvard International Law Journal, 53, 2011, pp. 208ss. M.H. ZAWATI, The International Criminal Court and complementarity, op. cit., pp. 208-228. L.E. CARTER, The future of the International Criminal Court: Complementarity as a strength or a weakness?, op. cit., pp. 454ss. D. ROBINSON, The mysterious mysteriousness of complementarity, op. cit., pp. 6ss. C. STAHN, One step forward, two steps back? Second thoughts on a "sentence-based" theory of complementarity, op. cit., pp. 183-196. A. DAZA GONZÁLEZ, El principio de complementariedad en el derecho penal internacional, op. cit., D. SASCHA, D. BACHMANN, L. EDA NWIBO, Pull and push- Implementing the complementarity principle of the Rome Statute of the ICC within the AU: Opportunities and challenges, op. cit., pp. 464ss.

primary, if not exclusive, basis.

5. Towards a universalism of human rights...

Universalism of human rights and crimes against humanity and human dignity is jurisdiction, the terrain of major and persistent tensions with the particularism of states. On this very terrain the call of sovereignty is stronger. It is rather that the jurisdiction of ICC has a tendentially universal character but it nevertheless derives from a conventional act resulting from the will of the states and furthermore always presupposes an element of connection of the crime with a state party to the constitutional convention. The genuinely universalistic value of jurisdiction would be different if the state were entitled to exercise it independently of the existence of any connection to the crime. It would be the so-called absolute universal jurisdiction.

In this regard, the toric contrast between Grozio's thought and Beccaria's position still expresses with extreme clarity what tensions exist between universalism and particularism with regard to the hypothetical affirmation of a universal jurisdiction of states. We read in *De iure pacis ac belli* (Book II, chapter XX and XXI): "(..) the general care of human society is also incumbent on the sovereigns, regardless of the particular care of their states (...) the sovereigns and those who they have a power equal to that of kings, they have the right to inflict penalties not only for the crimes committed against them or their subjects, but particularly but which seriously violate the natural right or of the peoples with regard to anyone (..)". We read in some crimes and punishments (part XXI): "(...) the judges are not the avengers of the human race in general, they are the defenders of particular conventions that tie together a certain number of men. It must not be punished that in the country in which it was committed, because it is only there-it is not elsewhere-that men are driven to repair, by the example of punishment, the fatal effects that produced the example of crime (...)".

The general belief is that there is no principle of customary law that imposes universal jurisdiction on certain states for crimes. Only a customary principle would be able to overcome the particularism of States, thus deriving from a source substantially superior to their will and to the conclusion of natural law as it was in the Grozian perspective. But the fact that this radical retrenchment of the will of the states has not been achieved does not mean that there are no international conventions on torture, piracy and terrorism that impose or authorize states to assert their universal jurisdiction for such crimes[692]. It is a universal

---

[692]R.R. BAKER, Universal jurisdiction and the case of Belgium: A critical assessment, in ILSA Journal of International and Comparative Law, 16, 2009, pp. 4ss. M. HENZELIN, Le principe de l'universalitè en droit pènal international, Helbing & Licthenthan, Bâle, 2000. A. HUNEEUS, International criminal law by other means: The quasi-criminal jurisdiction of the human rights court, in American Journal of International Law, 107, 2013, pp. 6ss. T. KIRCHENHAST, Victims and the criminal trial, ed. Palgrave & Macmillan, London, 2016. ER. HANNA MORAWSKA, The complex structure of the absolute prohibition of torture. Comments in the light of the regulation of article 3 of the European

jurisdiction that does not impose itself on the states by an external will, but which still derives from its own act of self-determination as a conventional source. But this does not mean that for this reason only that universal jurisdiction is necessarily the expression still of the particularism of states, that is, of their nationalistic needs and interests. It is possible to distinguish the different substantive motivations that lead a state to affirm or accept its universal jurisdiction. The distinction arises between the so-called unilateral or delegated universal jurisdiction on one side and the so-called universal jurisdiction on the other.

The first form of universal jurisdiction reflects genuinely particularist interests of the state which affirms the application of its penal law beyond its territory or even beyond any other element of connection of the crime, as a repression of a will to power that in ita unfolding sovereign does not intend to recognize limits. In the delegated universal jurisdiction, it is the states that mutually attribute jurisdiction outside of connecting elements in order to ensure in the mutual interest of each and everyone the exercise of jurisdiction which otherwise would be impossible or difficult. Like international cooperation, this delegated jurisdiction also corresponds to the interests of the homogeneous states that belong to each one.

The absolute universal jurisdiction is attributed by the States conventionally, but by virtue of the universal nature of the protected good, which entails that the States assumes general care. All this in the name of an interest that is not particular of each State but common to all and equally shared in full. If these are the substantive motivations underlying the currently rare and conventional attribution of absolute universal jurisdiction, nothing excludes the possibility of the future customary formation of a general principle of the identical content.

Speaking of the universalization of international criminal law, it is necessary to mention the re-emergence of those trends which, by referring to the international legislator (that is to states!) Values of transcendent order, risk calling into question the conquest of the secular nature of international criminal law in today's democracies. Here the universalist aspiration of objects of criminal protection is not nourished by a historically verifiable cultural process of geographically planetary dimension such as human rights. But not for this the universalistic aspiration of these values is less strong. On the contrary, their

---

Convention on Human Rights, in Espaço Juridico Journal of Law, 17, 2016, pp. 769ss. S. GREER, Is the prohibition against torture, cruel, inhuman and degrading treatment realy "absolute" in international human rights law?, in Human Rights Law Review, 15, 2015, pp. 5ss. C. TOMUSCHAT, Universal criminal jurisdiction. Jurisdiction with respect to the crime of genocide, crimes against humanity and war crimes, in Yearbook of the Institute of International Law, 71, 2005, pp. 246ss. A. LETT, The meaningless existence of universal jurisdiction, in Michigan State International Law Review, 23, 2015, pp. 547ss. M. LANGER, The diplomacy of universal jurisdiction: The political branches and the transnational prosecution of international crimes, in American Journal of International Law, 105, 2011, pp. 1, 42ss.

universalism claims to be unconditioned in so far as it is founded on an axiologically unconditional imperative. These are values which, in order to be qualified as non-negotiable values, constitute and postulated to the states not only at least presumptuously of any socio-cultural historicism but also outside any democratic process of their formation. Nothing excludes that those values can not coincide with assets that are certainly worthy of criminal protection by the states but is their non-negotiation that makes them an expression of universalism antithetical to the principle of secularism of international criminal law as well as anti-historical with respect to the process of secularization of national criminal law.

It is easy to understand that in so far as the universalization of international criminal law deviates from the particular will of the legislator of individual States, the production of penal legislation is further strained from democratic participation. Whether this happens because of the complex procedures of conventional training of agreements with penal content, something that happens by virtue of the very original legal production system proper of European Union after the communitarization also of the criminal matter. Lastly, let it be that this happens even through the formation of customary principles having criminal content and scope. It is clear that this production of criminal law with a universal vocation tends to ignore the reality and needs of that national demos in whose name it was erected the guaranteed fortress of criminal law.

The dialectical interweaving between universalism and particularism leads to a sort of paradox. Since this national and democratic identity is established in the name of criminal legality in the context of individual rights, it follows that national representative democracy ends up crediting itself as the best way of protecting rights. Precisely those human rights that, on the other hand, represent the field of choice for criminal universalism, now worldwide.

6. The complex game between universalism and particularism...

In the complex game of contrast between universalism and particularism, the latter proposes his revenge not only by making the voice of demos feel in the irenic uniformity of the European and global criminal law in defense of the humanistic essence. But there is also a genuine revolt of the *etnos* against the claim of uniform compulsory nature naturally claimed by the legal order including the criminal. We refer to the phenomenon of the so-called multiculturalism that would seem to mark the triumph of particularism beyond all expectations, thus closing the circle of this ineluctable return and coexist with universalism/ particularism.

Let us leave aside the hypothesis unknown to western systems but also present in history and on the planet in which multiculturalism reaches the extreme of the coexistence between the legal juridical order and the ethnic juridical-criminal order that divide at least a part of the area of the criminal according to the ethnic identity of the responsible subjects.

In the field of international criminal law, multicultural particularism can lead to consequences both in *malam and in bonam partem*. In the first direction there are some special incriminations or especially aggravated by the motively cultural as for example the hypothesis of female genital mutilation with respect to the general case of lesions. These are manifestations of a criminal law evidently inspired by a completely assimilationist logic that most probably are not in themselves and in itself inevitably unconstitutional-but that does not mean that such incriminating hypotheses give rise to dangerous tensions within the legal system. Being a clear universalistic pretext because they signal the need for a strengthened protection of human rights in the face of the particularity of cultural motivation. On the other hand, they seem to conflict with instances of substantive democracy because they impose a poor treatment of the cultural factor deliberately ignoring the fact that populism is circulating in a now multi-ethnic demos.

In the second direction in *bonam partem,* the problem arises of identifying the juridical instrument, that is, the institute through which cultural motivation can find recognition and assume some relevance in the sense of the exclusion or attenuation of punishment, the culture defense of the Anglo-Saxon legal systems. It may perhaps be agreed that this place of the system in which cultural motivation becomes relevant is guilt based on the clear consideration that the cultural actor conditions precisely the motivational process in which the criminal decision is formed. There is no shortage of those who have understood that the conditioning of the cultural factor while operating on guilt must analyze its sparse intensity as the criminal determination is ultimately more rooted in the personality of the subject so as to manifest its greater hostility to the legal system. On the other hand, the most reasonable opinion to the contrary considers that the cultural motivation leads to a lower intensity of guilt on the consideration that the cultural orientation that is certainly not reprehensible to the subject makes psychologically more difficult, that is, less demanding the formation of a motivational determination in conformity with the sorting.

Probably for those who intend to reject those implicit preliminarist assimilationist and integrationist present in the first perspective and that that schematism inherent in the second, the best solution should be that of a concrete assessment. It should be the judge to verify from time to time whether and how much the cultural factor has affected the motivational process effectively hindering the formation of the will in accordance with the law. Apart from its considerable practical difficulties, however, if this were to be the operational solution accepted, it would seem that particularism would thus accelerate its triumph. In truth, through the importance given to the cultural factor, the judgment of responsibility would go deep into the labyrinths of the concrete motivations of the agent and the compulsory claim of the penal law would be conditioned more than the different socio-cultural values that are objectively coexisting in a same ordering to the peculiar major or minor difficulties of its subjectivation in the criminal motivation of individual.

Once again, the opposing poles of particularism and universalism would touch upon the vital spark that animates all the phenomena of the spirit. If this is a true universal criminal law this is the guilt: it is the principle of guilt to demand that in the violence of the punitive affair not lose the sense of value of the human person in flesh and blood. The extreme particularism for which the compulsory claim of the law must confront with the motivation processes the concrete agents of the agent, especially if culturally conditioned, reveals itself at the end functional to the full observance of the principle of guilt. Once again it is not possible to separate if not artificially what the nature of the human spirit conquers.

7. The future of the indictment in international criminal justice: A new dawn or an inevitable sunset?

The path of international criminal justice is not linear but karstic[693]. History shows, in fact, how, at moments of great enthusiasm, characterized by surprising accelerations towards the development of an autonomous system of rules and principles at the international level, alternating periods, even very long ones, of mistrust and stalemate, were due mainly to the diffidence and fear of certain States to renounce sovereignty spaces in such sensitive terrain as that of criminal justice[694].

---

[693]Some trace the origins of international criminal justice even in the late fifteenth century with the establishment in 1474 of the Breisach Court in Germany. It consisted of twenty-six judges from different states of the Holy Roman Empire and was competent to judge the crimes committed by Peter Van Hagenbach, a Dutch mercenary in the service of the Duke of Burgundy, who had hired him to collect the tributes of the city of Breisach. The excessive tax burden had led the population to rebel. For this reason, the Duke had ordered Van Hagenbach to loot Breisach. The circumstance had not gone unnoticed and the neighboring German municipalities denounced the incident to the Impressor, which established the court to prosecute those crimes that were then defined as contrary to the "laws of nature and of God". The mercenary, after having been subjected to torture according to the logic of the inquisitorial process, was condemned to the measure, while the Duke did not undergo the trial. This is perhaps an insignificant experience in the context of the evolution of international criminal justice, but there are already some fundamental elements in it: the creation of a court made up of judges coming from different geographical areas and its competence on crimes that cause a particular disapproval in the international community. These are characters that will be made from the most recent experiences of international criminal justice. For details see, G. SCHWARZEN-BERGER, International law: As applied by International Courts and Tribunals, Sweet & Maxwell, London, 1968, pp. 462ss. G.D. SOLIS, The law of armed conflict: International humanitarian law in war, Cambridge University Press, Cambridge, 2010, pp. 28ss.

[694]For more analysis see: R. GOLDSTONE, The future of international criminal justice: The crucial role of the United States, in ILSA Journal of International & Comparative Law, 18 (2), 2016, pp. 622ss. Y. SHANY, How can international criminal courts have a greater impact upon national criminal proceedings? Lessons from the first two decades of international criminal justice in operation, in Israel Law Review, 46, 2013, pp. 434ss. A. HIRAD, S. KOH, The emerging enforcement practice of the International Criminal Court, in Cornell International Law Journal, 45, 2012, pp. 8ss. G. ACQUAVIVA, Was a residual

ICC is the most significant result of this path, but today suffers a serious crisis due to the high running costs, the slow procedures and the scarce (if not completely absent) cooperation from the States. There is a growing mistrust of ICC. In particular, some African-supported countries of the African Union claim that ICC[695] has focused exclusively on the African continent[696]. In this context of widespread distrust, South Africa, Burundi and Gambia officially launched the procedure to exit the StICC, while other States (Kenya[697], Uganda, Namibia) have announced their intention to withdraw their support to ICC[698]. In addition, the African Union has adopted a draft Statute for the creation of a Criminal Court[699] within the African Court of Human Rights[700] responsible for judging international crimes[701] committed in Africa. These phenomena are the symptom of a centrifugal tendency which must not be neglected and which could effectively lead to an irreversible ICC crisis. It is essential to suggest perspectives for the reform of the indictment function which will allow to reduce costs and increase the efficiency

---

mechanism for international criminal tribunals really necessary?, in Journal of International Criminal Justice, 9 (4), 2011, pp. 790ss. M. DE HOON, The future of the International Criminal Court. On critique, legalism and strengthening the ICC's legitimacy, in International Criminal Law Review, 17 (4), 2017, pp. 596ss. C. DAVIS, Political consideration in prosecutorial discretion in the International Criminal Court, in Internatonal Criminal Law Review, 15 (1), 2015, pp. 182ss.

[695]C. EBOE-OSVJI, The ICC and the African Court and the extended notion of complementarity of international criminal jurisdictions, in Nigeria Yearbook of International Law, 2018.

[696]See, Communiqué of the 175th meeting of the Peace and Security Council of the African Union, PSC/PR/Comm (CLXXV), 5 March 2009, par. 2.

[697]According to the art. 127 of the Statute, the State which intends to exit (withdraw) from the system of the Court must notify the Secretary-General of the United Nations of a letter in which it communicates its withdrawal. In any event, that act does not undermine the duty of that State to fulfill the financial and cooperation obligations which arose before the letter was notified.

[698]L. NKANSAH, International Criminal Court in the trenches of Africa, in Africa Journal of International Criminal Justice, 2014.

[699]Seem Protocol on Amendments to the Protocol on the Statute of the African Court on Human and Peoples' rights, 2014. See for details, A. ABASS, Prosecuting international crimes in Africa: Rationale, prospects and challenges, in European Journal of International Law, 24, 2013, pp. 936ss.

[700]C.B. MURUNGU, Towards a criminal chamber in the African Court of Justice and man rights, in Journal of International Criminal Justice, 9, 2011, pp. 1067ss.

[701]In addition to genocide, war crimes and crimes against humanity, and the crime of aggression, a type of crime typical of international criminal justice, the preparatory document prepared by the African Union provides that the Tribunal can also judge the crimes of 'constitutional order, piracy, terrorism, mercenarism, corruption, recycling, trafficking in human beings, drug trafficking, trafficking in hazardous waste, illicit exploitation of natural resources. The extension of jurisdiction ratione materiae constitutes a fundamental aspect, which must also be taken into account in the prospect of a reform of the international criminal court system. (art. 28A par. 1, Protocol on Amendments to the Protocol on the Statute of the African Court on Human and Peoples' rights).

of the system. Therefore, it is necessary to imagine a new structure of ICC, also in light of the most recent experiences of international criminal justice that started from the 2000s to support the ICC a whole series of Courts with a typical characteristic: they are "mixed" or "internationalized" judicial systems[702], in which national and international components live together. These are experiences that deserve to be studied because they could be an effective alternative to the idea of a centralized international criminal justice, which today manifests considerable operational difficulties.

These Courts certainly represent one of the most advanced approaches to international criminal justice. They are established with the support, often also financial, of the United Nations and are constituted, in part, by national personnel, in part, by international personnel: judges and Office of national Prosecutors are joined by judges and Office of foreign Prosecutors. These courts apply both domestic law, which is specifically amended by the national legislature in order to include in its legal system these particular systems of justice, and international law. Some of them, such as Special Court for Sierra Leone (SCSL)[703] and the Special Tribunal for Lebanon (STL)[704], have been established with an

[702]K. AMBOS, M. OTHMAN (a cura di), New approaches in international criminal justice: Kosovo, East Timor, Sierra Leone and Cambodia. Max-Planck-Institut für ausländisches und internationales Strafrecht, Reihe Interdisziplinäre Untersuchungen aus Strafrecht und Kriminologie, 2003. C.P.R. ROMANO, A. NOLLKAEMPER, J.K. KLEFFNER (a cura di), Internationalized criminal Courts and Tribunals: Sierra Leone, East Timor, Kosovo and Cambodia, op. cit.,

[703]ICC, Prosecutor v. Thomas Lubanga Dyilo, Partly Dissenting Opinion of Judge Sang-Hyun Song, AC, ICC-01/04-01/06 A 4 A 6, 1 December 2014, par. 3ss. ICC, Prosecutor v. Thomas Lubanga Dyilo, Separate and Dissenting Opinion of Judge Odio Benito, TC, ICC-01/04-01/06, 14 March 2012, par. 6. N. VAN DER HAVE, The prevention of gross human rights violations under international human rights law, ed. Springer, Berlin, 2018. C. JALLOH CHEVROR, A. MARONG, A., Promoting accountability under international law for gross human rights violations in Africa. Essays in honour of prosecutor hasan Bubacar Jallow, ed. Brill, The Hague, 2015. L.A. CAMARGOS, A responsabilidade penal internacional dos individuos: Estudo do caso Darfur, in Revista de Direito Brasileira, 2013, pp. 199ss. R. NOLLEZ-GOLDBACH, J. SAADA, La justice pènale internationale face aux crimes de masse, ed. Pedone, Paris, 2014. A. BOWERS, International Criminal Court, Wolf Legal Publishers, The Netherlands, 2011. S. WHARTON, The evolution of international criminal law: prosecuting "new" crimes before the Special Court for Sienna Leone, in International Criminal Law Review, 11, 2011, pp. 218ss. K.A. RODMAN, Justice is interventionist: The political sources of the judicial reach of the Special Court for Sierra Leone, in International Criminal Law Review, 13, 2013, pp. 65ss.

[704]This justice system was created in 2007 with an international agreement incorporated in a UN Security Council resolution (1757/2007) to prosecute those responsible for the murder of Lebanese President Rafiq al-Hariri. The Court applies Lebanese law, but consists of judges and prosecutors appointed jointly by the State and the United Nations. See also: R. ROTH, Tribunal spècial sur le Liban: retour sur une expèrience, in Revue Belge de Droit International, 122 (1), 2018.

international agreement[705], others, such as the Special panels[706] of the Dili District Court[707], and the Hybrid Court for South Sudan constitute real state organs created by ordinary law[708]. There are also Tribunals created by international organizations

---

[705]In 2015, in the context of the peace negotiations between the Colombian government and the FARC, the Special Jurisdiction for Peace was also competent to judge the crimes committed by all the parties that took part in the civil war.

[706]More commonly called the Special Tribunal for East Timor, this jurisdiction was established in 2000. It dealt with the crimes committed during the civil war that broke out in 1999. This justice system was set up within the United Nations UNTAET mission, which assisted the government of East Timor in the reconstruction of the administrative and judicial apparatus. The Court is composed of internal judges and applies national law. S. CHESTERMAN, An altogether different order, defining the elements of crimes against humanity, in Duke Journal of Comparative and International Law, 10, 2002, pp. 332ss. G. HEINE, H. VEST, Murder/wilful killing, in G.K. MCDONALD, O. SWAAK-GOLDMAN (a cura di), Substantive and procedural aspects of international criminal law. Volume I: Commentary, Kluwer Law International, The Hague, 2000, pp. 175ss. In the same spirit see also from the giurisprudence from the Special Panels for Serious Crimes in Timor Est: SPSC, Prosecutor v. Marques (Los Palos), Judgment, 09/2000, 11 December 2001, par. 649 and SPSC, Prosecutor v. Agostinho Cloe, Judgment, 4/2003, 16 November 2004, par. 15.C. CHERNOR JALLOH, The Sierra Leone Special Court and its legacy: The impact for Africa and international criminal law, Cambridge University Press, Cambridge, 2013, pp. 234ss. V.O.O. NMEHIELLE, Africa and the future of international criminal justice, Eleven International Publishing, 2012.C. CHERNOR JALLOH, A. MORGAN, International criminal justice processes in Rwanda and Sierra Leone: Lessons for Liberia, in C. CHERNOR JALLOH, E. OLUFEMI, Shielding humanity. Essays in international law in honour of judge Abdul G. Koroma, ed. Brill, The Hague, 2015. Y. BEIGBEDER, Special panels for serious crimes in East Timor. Now Timor-Leste, in Y. BEIGBEDER, International criminal Tribunals, ed. Palgrave Macmillan, London, 2011.

[707]The Extraordinary Chambers of the Cambodian Tribunals were established in 2004 with the task of punishing the crimes committed by the Khmer Rouge between 1975 and 1979. This system of justice applies Cambodian law and consists of both national and international personnel.

[708]M. HOLVOET, The continuing relevance of the hybrid or internationalized justice model: The example of the Kosovo Specialist Chambers, in Criminal Law Forum, 27 (1), 2016, pp. 4ss. G.P. FLETCHER, The storrs lectures. Liberals and romantics at war: The problem of collective guilt, in Yale Law Journal, 111, pp. 2002ss. According to the author: "(...) there is no term fraught with greater ambiguity that that venerable phrase that haunts Anglo-American criminal law: mens rea". The confusion over the meaning of the term continues to exist in modern criminal law, which is fuelled by the perpetual theoretical debates on the nature of various mens rea standards and the principle of culpability (...)". 1514. P. GAETA, The history and the evolution of the notion of international crimes, in R. BELLELLI (a cura di), International criminal justice. Law and practice from the Rome statute to its review, Ashgate Publishing, Farnham, 2010, pp. 169-180. A. CASSESE, P. GAETA, Cassese's international criminal law, Oxford University Press, Oxford, 2013, pp. 37ss. For the Makrokriminalität see also: Art 6 Abs. 1 Statute of the Special Court for Sierra Leone, SCSL-Agreement v. 16.1.2002 (SCSL-Statut); Art. 29 Abs. 1 Law on the Establishment of Extraordinary Chambers in the Courts of Cambodia for the Prosecution of Crimes Committed during the Period of Dem-ocratic Kampuchea, ECCC-Agreement v.

operating at regional level, such as the Extraordinary African Chambers[709] and the Hybrid Court for South Sudan[710], both set up by the African Union. Finally, it is necessary to mention the so-called Regulation 64 Panels in the Kosovo Specialists Chambers[711], which constitute a budding of the ICTY.

6.6.2003 (ECCC-Statute). H. JÄGER, Makrokriminalität. Studien zur Kriminologie kollektiver Gewalt, ed. Suhrkamp, Berlin, 1989. W. JOECKS, K. MIEBACH (Hrsg.), Münchener Kommentar zum Strafgesetz-buch, C.H. Bech, München, 2017. S.U. BURKHARDT, Vergewaltigung als Verbrechen gegen die Menschlichkeit Sexualisierte Gewalt, Makrokriminalität und Völkerstrafrecht, LIT Verlag, Berlin, 2005. U. MURMANN, Problems of causation with regard to (potential) actions of multiple protagonist, in Journal of International Criminal Justice, 12, 2014, pp. 284ss. O. TRIFFTERER, K. AMBOS (a cura di), The Rome Statute of the International Criminal Court. A Commentary, C.H.Beck-Hart-Nomos, München, 2016. S. BOCK, Zurechnung im Völkerechtstrafrecht, in Zeitschrft für Internationale Strafrechtdogmatik, 7-8, 2017, pp. 414ss. C.F. STUCKENBERG, Vorstudien zu Vorsatz und Irrtum im Völkerstrafrecht: Versuch einer Elementarstrafrecht für eine übernationale Vorsatzdogmatik, ed. De Gruyter Recht, Berlin, 2011, pp. 6ss. K. KONLE, Makrokriminalitàt im Rahmen der jugoslawischen Sezessionskriege, Herbert Utz Verlag, 2010, pp. 49ss. C. GLOBKE, Die Auslieferung an den Internationalen Strafgerichtshof, Mohr Siebeck, Tübingen, 2009. N. QUICK, Forced transfer and customary international law: Bridging the gap between Nuremberg and the ICTY, in S.M. MEISENBERG, I. STEGMILLER (a cura di), The Extraordinary Chambers in the Courts of Cambodia. Assessing their contribution to international criminal law, ed. Springer, The Hague, 2016, pp. 291-319. H. KUCZYŃSKA, Changing evidentiary rules to the detriment of the accused? The Ruto and Sang decision of the ICC Appeals Chamber, in Polish Yearbook of International Law, n. 37, 2017. C. MARXSEN, What do different theories of customary international law have to say about the individual right to reparation under international humanitarian law?, in Zeitschrift für äuslandisches öffentliches Recht, n. 78, 2018 (3). S. MEISENBERG, The extraordinary Chambers in the Courts in Cambodia. Assessing their contribution to international criminal law, ed. Springer, Berlin, 2016. K. CHIEDU MOGHALU, International humanitarian law from Nuremberg to Rome: The weighty precedents of the international criminal Tribunal for Rwanda, in Pace International Law Review, 14, 2002, pp. 285ss. S. SIVAKUMARAN, Re-envisaging the international law of internal armed conflict, in European Journal of International Law, 22, 2011, pp. 240, 240.242. Y. DINSTEIN, Non-international armed conflicts in international law, Cambridge University Press, Cambridge, 2014, pp. 186ss. L. MAY, Z. HOSKINS, The extraordinary Chambers in the Courts of Cambodia. Assessing their contribution to international criminal law, ed. Springer, Berlin, 2016.

709 The Extraordinary African Chambers were established in 2012 in Senegal and are competent to judge the international crimes committed in Chad between 1982 and 1990. They apply both international criminal law and the Senegalese penal procedure. Chambers are made up of Senegalese judges and partly from other African Union countries.

710 The Hybrid Court for South Sudan were created in 2015 in South Sudan and are made up of national and international judges. They are competent to judge the serious violations of international law and South Sudan law committed from December 15, 2013 until the end of the peace process underway in the country.

711 For further analysis and details see: E. MUARREMI, The concept of hybrid courts revisited. The case of the Kosovo Specialist Chambers, in International Criminal Law Review, 18 (4), 2018, pp. 625ss.

These peculiar justice systems have been designed to cope with multiple needs. In fact, they aim not only to ascertain the criminal responsibility of those who have committed international crimes, but also to rebuild the judiciary, restore peace within the state and social cohesion. These justice systems offer, however, considerable advantages compared to ICC, because according to our opinion: a) they do not undermine the sovereignty of the State in criminal matters, since these Courts are part of the national judiciary and also apply internal law[712]; b) the mixed nature of such systems of justice allows a greater sensitivity to the specifics of the system in which they operate, as well as to the cultural, linguistic and social characteristics of the country in which they are established; c) the celebration of processes at the national level, on the one hand, allows a more immediate knowledge of the crimes committed and, for the other, favors the reconciliation of the parties in conflict, who are more easily recognized in the judicial system of their country[713]. In this sense, it is opportune to cite the example of SCSL, which has shown to operate effectively, not only creating a climate of consensus in relation to its work, but also promoting respect for human rights within the country. There are also positive effects on the procedural level. In fact, the proximity of the Courts to the place where the crimes were committed, on the one hand, makes it easier to collect evidence, which is not conditioned by the complex mechanisms of cooperation that the ICC must use, and, for the other , limits the movements of defendants and witnesses, with an obvious reduction of costs[714].

If these are the advantages, it is, however, appropriate to also account for the defects of these justice systems. Firstly, the establishment of "mixed" or "internationalized" courts leads to a fragmentation of international criminal justice[715], as a result of the creation of judicial systems operating in parallel with ICC. This inevitably prevents the realization of a unitary international law and

---

[712]Regulations 64 Panels in the Courts of Kosovo were set up in 2000 to prosecute perpetrators of international crimes committed in Kosovo and to alleviate the judicial burden of the International Criminal Tribunal for the former Yugoslavia. The staff of the panels is partly made up of local judges in part by international judges.

[713]S. LINTON, Cambodia, East Timor And Sierra Leone: Experiments In International Justice, in Criminal Law Forum, 12 (1), 2001, pp. 186ss. P.K. MENDEZ, The new wave of hybrid Tribunals: A sophisticated approach to enforcing international humanitarian law or an idealistic solution with empty promises?, in Criminal Law Forum, 20 (1), 2009, pp. 71-75.

[714]J.P. PHAM, A viable model for international criminal justice: The Special Court for Sierra Leone, in New York International Law Review, 86 (1), 2006, po. 38ss.

[715]See for details: J. NYAWO, Selective enforcement and international criminal law, ed. Intersentia, Oxford, Antwerp, 2017. A. CLAPHAM, Three tribes engage on the future of international criminal law, in Journal of International Criminal Justice, 9 (3), 2011, pp. 691ss. J. NICHOLSON, Strengthening the validity of international criminal Tribunals, op. cit., M. RANKIN, The future of international criminal evidence in new wars? The evolution of th Commission for International Justice and Accountability (CIJA), in Journal of Genocide Research, 20 (3), 2018, pp. 394ss. V. NMEHELLE, Africa and the future of international criminal justice, Eleven International Publishing, The Netherlands, 2012.

criminal procedure. Furthermore, it should be stressed that reconciling the national dimension with the international one is not always an easy operation, since it involves an interaction between people, rules and principles coming from different systems, whose outcomes can be unpredictable. This is a problem that has occurred in practice[716]. In fact, it is necessary to highlight how in the cases of Regulation 64-The ECCC and the Special Panels of the Dili District Court have not always found an adequate balance between domestic and international issues[717], as well as between the different legal traditions of the Office of the Prosecutors and the judges operating in these courts. A further critical profile of these justice systems is represented by their location within states. This exposes these Tribunals to significant risks to their security, given that the political and social tensions that the international crimes committee often causes last for many years.

It is necessary to highlight how these Courts, despite the mentioned defects, constitute an important resource for international criminal justice. In fact, it is true that a centralized system like ICC allows a uniform application of criminal law and international criminal procedure. Indeed, a central system has a greater impact at global level and allows the creation of a common legal culture at a supranational level, but it is also appropriate to underline as mixed judicial systems allow the overcoming of crucial problems, such as those concerning judicial cooperation.

8. The prospects for reform of the indictment function in the process before the ICC.

It therefore seems appropriate to suggest some prospects for reforming the system, with particular reference to the functions of the Office of the Prosecutor, which take into account the specific features of the ICC system, whose fundamental aspects need to be summarized briefly to highlight its strengths and weaknesses. In this system, the indictment function assumes, as we have seen, peculiar and often contradictory connotations. The Prosecutor is an independent body, but is subject to the political control of a body outside the ICC, which is certainly not judicial in nature, such as the United Nations Security Council. Moreover, he must impartially seek the truth, but he also plays the role of a procedural party. These are typical features of a system that must reconcile multiple needs, even of a meta-procedural nature: to ascertain the criminal responsibilities of the authors of international crimes, in fact, there are additional objectives such as the historical reconstruction of events, the protection of victims, for which the same celebration of the process before the ICC can represent in itself

---

[716]L.A. DICKINSON, The promise of Hybrid Courts, in American Journal of International Law, 97 (2), 2003, pp. 306ss.

[717]P.K. MENDEZ, The new wave of hybrid Tribunals: A sophisticated approach to enforcing international humanitarian law or an idealistic solution with empty promises?, op. cit., pp. 88ss. S. LINTON, Rising from the Ashes: The creation of a viable criminal justice system in East Timor, in Meburne University Law Review, 25 (1), 2001, pp. 146ss.

some form of compensation, the restoration of the social bonds of a people, assistance in the restoration of the judicial structures of a State, which could have been seriously damaging during a conflict.

The Prosecutor plays a key role in this context. He plays the delicate role of mediator between the-not always reconcilable-needs of international criminal justice and those of peace and security, of which the United Nations are carriers. The Prosecutor is a hybrid organ, which operates, on the one hand, as a judicial body to which the indictment function is entrusted, and, on the other, as an institution that endeavors to establish diplomatic relations with the States and international organizations. In this regard, the Rome Statute recognizes the Prosecutor's discretionary power to select the authors and the crimes to be prosecuted in order to guarantee at the same time a flexible and efficient action. It is certainly a discretion that meets the limits in the jurisdictional screening made by Chambers, but it is also true that the flexibility and vagueness of the normative parameters that constitute the assumption of the exercise of the indictment leave wide margins of appreciation to the investigating organ.

Despite the magnitude of these powers, the Prosecutor's action however encounters numerous obstacles due, on the one hand, to the lack of judicial police forces and, on the other, to the need to rely on personal precautionary measures and for the collection of evidence to the States, which do not always guarantee full cooperation. So we need to think about reform proposals that aim to reduce the scope of these problems. A viable solution could be to provide a structure that is not exclusively centralized by the ICC Office of the Prosecutor, but on two levels: one centralized and the other decentralized. In each State an Office of the Prosecutor responsible for international crimes should be established, which can directly dispose of the judicial police and gather evidence without the mediation of national government authorities. The prosecution body, therefore, should no longer depend on the ineffective judicial cooperation mechanisms envisaged by the StICC. In this way the cost of the investigations would be reduced and the territorial charge on the territory would be more rooted and more sensitive to the peculiarities of the legal system in which it operates. The central structure could be maintained, but streamlined, with an Office of the Prosecutor consisting of a number of Office of the Prosecutors elected by the Assembly of States Parties to the Rome Statute. These Office of the Prosecutor could play a controlling role, involving investigations in the event of inaction of the internal prosecution body, and of coordination, facilitating the exchange of documents and information and assisting the national prosecutors.

One could also think of a reform of the composition of the judge, promoting the creation within the States of mixed courts, partly constituted by national judges and partly by foreign judges, who could be selected according to the procedures laid down by the StICC. This composition, which would recall that provided for in the "internationalized" justice systems, would be justified by the peculiar nature of the crimes pertaining to ICC which, on the one hand, tear social ties and undermine the civil coexistence of a people and, for the other, they threaten global peace and security. It is necessary to highlight how such a structure risks re-proposing the mentioned critical issues related to the difficult reconciliation of the international dimension with the national one. But this problem would have a far more limited impact in a context in which judges, even though formed in countries with different legal traditions, operate in the unitary framework of StICC, which provides a set of rules and principles in which states recognize each other.

This two-level configuration of the Office of the Prosecutor and the establishment of "mixed" courts, which would certainly require a radical change in the Rome Statute and the Rules of Procedure and Proof, would allow, on the one hand, to overcome the distrust of many States towards international criminal justice and, on the other, to avoid conflicts caused by the application of the complementarity principle[718], which requires the ICC to assess the will and ability of the state to prosecute international crimes, creating an integrated justice system, less expensive and more efficient.

According to our opinion: "(...) if the Prosecutor becomes aware that national authorities have detained a person who could be considered a suspect falling under the respective international court/tribunal's jurisdiction, should inform the national authorities of its duty to ensure that the rights of this suspect-as set out in national legislation, applicable treaties, and customary international human rights law[719]-are respected. In particular: 1.Pre-Trial Chambers should monitor and uphold the rights of suspects during the investigative phase and should request the Prosecution to notify the judges if any investigative targets are being detained by national authorities, with a view to monitoring whether the proceedings are being conducted with due diligence (...) 2.Although the potential subjects of the Prosecution's investigations will generally be confidential, as demonstrated in particular from the SCTL, internal defense offices can also play a role in monitoring the rights of suspects prior to their transfer to the court/tribunal in question, and petitioning the Chamber to take appropriate measures (...) 3.In the absence of any applicable statutory provisions, the ICC, which has the duty to ensure that the processes before it comply with international fair trial standards, should clearly inform the defense in advance of the procedural requirements and deadlines for filing an application seeking a remedy for violations of their rights which have occurred prior to their arrest/detention.

---

[718]In this sense, the Sudanese case is emblematic. In fact, the failure to deliver to the Court of the President Al-Bashir constitutes one of the aspects that has contributed to aggravating the crisis in international criminal justice.

[719]UNGA "Text of the draft conclusions on identification of customary international law" in "Report of the International Law Commission" UN GAOR 73rd session Supp No 10, UN Doc A/73/10 (Advance) (2018) par. 65, Conclusion 2. See also in argument: C. TAMS, J. SLOAN, The development of international law by the International Court of Justice, Cambridge University Press, Cambridge 2013. S. DARCY, Law and war: The judicial development of international humanitarian law, Cambridge University Press, Cambridge 2014, pp. 64ss. N. ARAJÄRVI, Looking back from nowhere: Is there a future for universal jurisdiction over international crimes?, in Tilburg Law Review, 16, 2011, pp. 16ss. Y. TAN, The identification of customary rules in international criminal law, op. cit., pp. 94ss.

Where such procedural time limitations impact negatively on the suspect's rights, under the relevant rules, the fundamental fair trial guarantees under the Statute and under human rights law would mandate that discretion be exercised to favor upholding the rights of the suspect or accused (...) 4.The court should monitor the Prosecution's disclosure obligations to ensure that any information concerning the relationship between the Prosecution and national authorities which might be relevant to such an application is disclosed, and is not unduly withheld due to security reasons. In accordance with human rights jurisprudence, if any information concerning the defendant's claim is within the custody of the state and the state refuses to disclose this information, or the state has provided the information to the Prosecution on condition of confidentiality and refuses to lift the confidentiality vis-à-vis the defense-the court should draw the appropriate inferences of fact in favor of the defendant (...) 5.When evaluating whether the defendant's rights have been violated, the court should adopt a defendant-centric inquiry: the primary emphasis should be on whether the defendant's rights have been violated, rather than requiring the defendant to establish wrongdoing or responsibility on the part of an organ of the tribunal as a preliminary step. Prosecutorial/tribunal wrong doing should be an aggravating factor rather than a prerequisite (...) 6.Even if the violation in question does not meet the requisite threshold to justify a stay of the proceedings and the release of the defendant, the Chamber should also consider whether it is appropriate to grant alternative remedies (...) 7.It is questionable whether the severity of the alleged crime that the defendant has been charged with should be a deciding factor in determining the appropriate remedy. As stated by the ICC Appeals Chamber-a fair trial is the only means to do justice-this maxim holds true irrespective of whether the defendant has been charged with petty crimes or genocide[720]-the crime of crimes. If the

[720]H.D. BOSLY, D. VANDERMEERSCH, Gènocide, crimes contre l'humanitè et crimes de guerre face à la justice, ed. Bruylant, Bruxelles, 2012. H. ALONSO, Current trends on modes of liability for genocide, crimes against humanity and war crimes, in C. STAHN, L. VAN DEN HERIK (eds.), Future perspectives on international criminal justice, T.M.C. Asser Press, The Hague, 2010, pp. 522-524. S. MANACORDA, C. MELONI, Indirect perpetration versus Joint Criminal Enterprise: Concurring approaches in the practice of international criminal law?, in Journal of International Criminal Justice, 9 (1), 2011, pp. 165ss. In the Kvočka et al. case, the Appeals Chamber emphasized that it is the accused person's knowledge that is central, that is, what was natural and foreseeable to this person. More specifically, the Appeals Chamber held that: "(...) participation in a systemic joint criminal enterprise does not necessarily entail criminal responsibility for all crimes which, though not within the common purpose of the enterprise, were a natural or foreseeable consequence of the enterprise. A participant may be responsible for such crimes only if the Prosecution proves that the accused had sufficient knowledge such that the additional crimes were a natural and foreseeable consequence to him (...)". Kvočka et al., judgment, AC, ICTY, 28 February 2005, para. 86, in the same spirit: Limaj et al., judgment, TC, ICTY, 30 November 2005, par. 512. C. FOURNET, C. PÉGORIER, "Only one step away from genocide". The crime of persecution in international criminal law, in International Criminal Law Review, 10, 2010, pp. 714ss. L. MAY, Z. HOSKINS, The extraordinary Chambers in

violations have compromised the fairness of the judicial process, the proceedings should be stayed. Moreover, whilst the objective of eliminating impunity is a laudable raison d'être for these courts, it should also be borne in mind that arbitrary arrest and detention can be so egregious in nature and impact on an individual as to attract the moral and legal condemnation that we may properly call crimes against human rights. The remedy provided by the court must therefore be effective in deterring the Prosecutor/national authorities from engaging in such practices in the future (...).8.The courts/tribunals should also bear in mind that if the defendant is acquitted, financial compensation cannot fully compensate a person for the loss of his or her family life which he or she may have experienced during the period of arbitrary detention. For this reason, the court should include a period of domestic detention in its calculation concerning whether the defendant has been detained for an unreasonable length of time and should therefore be provisionally released. Similarly, if the defendant is convicted, this period of time should automatically be included in the credit for time served which is deducted from the sentence. Such credit is a right, however, and not a remedy for the violation itself. The defendant should therefore be granted a separate remedy in addition to a sentencing credit, for example, financial compensation or a further reduction of sentence (...)"[721].

9. Concluding remarks and outlook.

The Prosecutor in his role of discretion has made no decision on the basis of prosecutorial discretion to select the current situations. The African situations have been selected on the basis of the satisfaction of the legal requirements, but not prosecutorial discretion. In specimen, the situations that were rejected were

---

the Courts of Cambodia. Assessing their contribution to international criminal law, op. cit., C. TOMUSCHAT, Universal criminal jurisdiction. Jurisdiction with respect to the crime of genocide, crimes against humanity and war crimes, op. cit., pp. 246ss. A. LETT, The meaningless existence of universal jurisdiction, op. cit., pp. 547ss. M. JACKSON, A conspiracy to commit genocide. Anti-fertility research in apartheid's chemical and biological weapons programme, in Journal of International Criminal Justice, 13, 2015, pp. 933-950.C.J.M. SAFFERLING, The special intent requirement in the crime of genocide, in C.J.M. SAFFERLING, E. CONZE (a cura di), The Genocide Convention sixty year after its adoption, ed. Springer, The Hague, 2010, pp. 172ss. C. APTEL, The intent to commit genocide in the case law of the International Criminal Tribunal for Rwanda, in Criminal Law Forum, 13, 2002, pp. 277ss. G. KEMP, South Africa's (possible) withdrawal from the ICC and the future of the criminalization and prosecution of crimes against humanity, war crimes and genocide under domestic law: A submission informed by historical, normative and policy considerations, in Washington University Global Studies Law Review, 14, 2017, pp. 414ss.

[721]D. LIAKOPOULOS, International standards and responsibility competition according to the International Criminal Court: Anatomy, interpretation, proposals, in Revista Eletrônica de direito Penal e Polìtica Criminal-UFRGS, 6, 2018. D. LIAKOPOULOS, International Criminal Court: Impunity status and the situation in Kenya, in International and European Union Legal Matters, 2014.

dismissed on the basis of the non-satisfaction of the legal requirements. Accordingly, the focus of the examination of the charges of politicisation, derived from the exercise of selective justice, in fact, informs as technically the Prosecutor has not made any situational decision so far on the basis of prosecutorial discretion. For this reason, this study sought a different approach to analyse why the Prosecutor receives the charges of politisation, derived from the exercise of discretion. The problem may lie with the hidden sense of discretion that has been effectively and widely exercised by the Prosecutor when interpreting the legal requirements for initiating investigations or prosecuting cases. In particular, on the term "sufficient gravity" that constitutes the key legal admissible criterion for initiating investigations or prosecuting cases. "Sufficient gravity" is a legal admissible criterion and is supposed to be applied through a clear and consistent manner. The ICC also endorsed a low level for the assessment of "sufficient gravity", as the Appeals Chamber and the Pre-Trial Chamber decided in the *Lubanga* and *Ntaganda* cases and the Comoros situations respectively. The Prosecutor has used two different methods to interpret "sufficient gravity": a) the comparative method, and b) the judgment method (threshold). The Prosecutor took account of a wide range of factorial analysis to determine the issue of "sufficient gravity". The Prosecutor was picking from scale, impact, manner of commission, and nature of crimes. For example, in using the comparative approach, the Prosecutor heavily depended on the quantitative measure, namely the number of victims. In using the threshold judgment, the Prosecutor sometimes used one factor to reject a situation, the insistent use of the quantity measure to evaluate gravity does not only undermine the legitimacy of the ICC, but also the global character of the ICC. It also restricted the reach of the ICC to only big situations and cases instead the gravest ones. Thereafter, the Office of the Tribunal Prosecutor (OTP) adopt a relative meaning of the term scale instead of using an absolute one. The relative meaning of scale provides that the OTP should conclude the percentage of "the scale of the crime" according to the total number of the given society itself, compared to the total population of the country, and not to the other cases that might involve thousands of incidents and crimes[722].

As we can understand from the above analysis: 1.In terms of referrals, the prosecutor has no discretion-whether prosecutorial discretion or legal interpretive discretion-to initiate admissible referred situations, according to the Comoros's judgement, chich the Prosecutor can exercise prosecutorial discretion only at the stage of the assessment of "the interests of justice". In particular, gravity in its relative sense under the art. 53 StICC "interests of justice" provisions can be considered by the prosecutor when exercising prosecutorial discretion. Before the PTC's decision in the Comoros situation, it was established and emphasised that the prosecutor in effect exercised a broad discretion, which we could called legal interpretive discretion; 2. In relation to the prosecutor's proprio motu power, the extent of prosecutorial discretion the prosecutor can exercise is

[722]D. LIAKOPOULOS, International Criminal Court: Impunity status and the situation in Kenya, op. cit.,

not clear. Art. 15 (1) StICC clearly authorises the prosecutor to exercise prosecutorial discretion. However, paragraph (3) of the same Article contains an obligatory language enforcing the prosecutor to proceed with the investigation. The ICC has not made any clear judgment on this question, and the matter is still debated; 3. With respect to the selection of admissible cases, the StICC are silent. However, there is an explicit and common consensus among commentators and authors that the prosecutor has an implicit power to reject any case on the basis of "the interests of justice", in particular "relative gravity", whatever the trigger mechanism is. The OTP has just published a new policy document on the selection of cases and confirmed that it has broad prosecutorial discretion when selecting among legally worthy admissible cases. The paper particularly sets three criteria for this selection, namely: the gravity of the crimes, the degree of the responsibility of the alleged perpetrators, and the potential charges; 4.The prosecutor sits at the critical juncture of the efficiency and sufficiency of the ICC at furthering its institutional goals. Whilst the prosecutor is required to maintain the sufficiency of the ICC as a legal body, which works independently without concrete prescriptions, she is required as well to make the work of the ICC efficient and capable of achieving its institutional aims. Whilst the first stands for the value of independence, the latter refers to the value of discretion. The strict commitment to the legal rules does not necessarily render the work of the ICC efficient. The ICC is not yet an ideal resort to address all sorts of atrocities, and that its ability to deliver justice is considerably limited. There are often legitimate political questions that are necessary for making the work of the ICC efficient at furthering its institutional goals[723].

These set of considerations are vital to the success of the ICC in furthering its institutional aims, including justice, peace and security, and it recommends the OTP to follow them, given the current circumstances in which the ICC works. The decision to initiate investigations or proceed with prosecutions are not only contingent on the legal criteria of the Statute. There are always extra-legal factors and political circumstances necessary for the exercise of meaningful prosecutorial missions. The engagement of the prosecutor in the particularities of situations and cases is very important for enforcing meaningful justice that the ICC itself may not be able to do. The consideration of extra-legal factors is essential for the viability, efficacy, efficiency, and independence of the ICC. The consideration of these political circumstances within the decision making-process is because these kinds of political considerations are intrinsic to international justice.

The policy of denial rhetoric has mainly prevented the Prosecutor from delivering justice on several occasions. Applying the law in its rigid formula has not helped the Prosecutor to do meaningful justice in Sudan or Uganda. Several pragmatic considerations in these situations required the prosecutor to use her discretion to stop the ICC's proceedings as an option and allow for other

[723]D. LIAKOPOULOS, Schutz des angeklagten im Strafverfahren, in International and European Union Legal Matters, working paper series, 2013.

alternatives to replace the ICC's approach. The existence of these two poles established that the ICC is not yet an ideal approach to deal with all atrocities. Most situations under the ICC jurisdiction are still experiencing mass violation of human rights. Some conflicts are still in progress. The peace-related problems in Sudan, Uganda, and Kenya are, to a large extent, impeded by the policy of the Prosecutor.

Based on above recommendations, it was also found that contemporary international prosecutors have more roles to deliver. The development of the international criminal law, rectius justice and the jurisprudence of international prosecutors all contributed to developing the role of an international prosecutor, as a new international player within the international legal arena and international politics. For instance, when the prosecutor stops the criminal proceedings, using her discretionary power, based on "the interests of justice", the prosecutor, in fact, may be addressing other values, such as stability or peace-related considerations. This process confesses the prosecutor's new roles to play alongside with her main mandate in delivering justice. Accordingly, the current international Prosecutor can/should exercise a multifunction of roles in order to promote those values. With the establishment of the ICC, we have begun to see a dramatic development in the idea of the prosecution in terms of both the legal level and practical level. It is a multi-functional prosecution. The creation of the ICC witnessed a formal emergence of a new sense of prosecution, where the role of the prosecutor has been formally widened, accordingly. Article 53 StICC was a product of the historical development of the exercise of the discretionary power by the previous prosecutors. Although this form of power was not clear enough either theoretically or practically in the work of the Military Tribunals, it was clear enough in the practice of the Special Criminal Tribunals. With the arrival of the ICC, we have begun to see that these developments have been embedded in the law.

However, in considering the political considerations, the prosecutor must aim at achieving justice. The consideration of peace processes (a political influence) on the basis of "the interests of justice" can be accounted for only when such processes are associated with some sort of justice mechanisms. This is often the case when international justice of the ICC is not attainable due to some obstacles, then other justice mechanisms might be more meaningful and needed. The use of the apologist considerations as a tool to achieve the utopian end, which is justice, in its broad sense, is the approach that may legitimately help justify the consideration of political factors. As the prosecutor is expected to be independent, respecting the rule of law when exercising her discretion, she is also expected to be flexible, as discretion is in nature a power that stands outside the law. The prosecutor may need to give weight to considerations that are not warranted in law. The ignorance of one of these premises posed the prosecutor in the dyadic criticisms.

The long strife between the advocate of bringing criminal justice to perpetrators at any cost and those who call for the abandonment of criminal justice in favor of peace may just end with neither justice nor peace delivered to both victims and perpetrators. The tension between these two values is still yet to be sorted out. The impotent enforcement mechanisms that the ICC holds make the ability of the ICC as a main international protector of victims highly questionable, in particular that the ICC has achieved little since its operation in 2002. That means, that the ICC should abandon its proceedings whenever its ability to deliver its own justice is not possible. In fact, based on the practice of the Prosecutors of the ad hoc Tribunals, the ICC prosecutor is required to analytically and carefully examine potential effects and ability of the Court, before intervening in a certain situation. Although this is not an easy task, as the ICC prosecutor cannot predict every single circumstance of the future, however, there are still different strategies that the prosecutor can follow in case it appears that the Court's approach is not workable. The strategy of delaying an investigatory or prosecutorial decision is one of the most effective, as we have seen with regard to the practice of the ICTY. We made a distinction between the strategy of the ICTY Prosecutor and the ICC Prosecutor in relation to the decision of indicting *Milosević* and *Al-Bashir,* respectively, where the first was successfully brought to the Tribunal, whilst Al-Bashir remains at large. The results of the exercise of this strategy of prosecution were the blatant failure of the OTP to bring any alleged perpetrator to the Court, including the President, the refusal of many of African states, including those who are parties to the ICC, to cooperate with the Court to arrest Al-Bashir or to promote the fragile peace negotiations, and to put an end to humanitarian tragedy in Darfur. On the other hand, the Prosecutor of the ICTY did not initially make a decision against *Milosević,* although he was responsible for many atrocities. The Prosecutor instead took several pragmatic considerations such as the fact that *Milosević* was needed for the peace process at the time, and more importantly his power and role. Through the exercise of prosecutorial discretion, allowing enough time to build a strong case against a high ranking leader, by indicting lower indictees such as *Karadzić* and *Mladić*, and the others facilitated and paved the way for the Prosecutor to make the biggest decision. The ICC Prosecutor did not follow such a strategy and did not give any attention to the peculiarities of the situation of Darfur and the potential impacts that may result from indicting the most high-ranking official in Sudan-President *Al-Bashir*-in a rushed way. This simply ended with a zero achievement in Sudan. The ICC Statute and Rules of Procedure and Evidence emphasised the importance of the participation of victims in proceedings. Explicitly, Article 53 StICC requires the prosecutor to consider the voices of victims before proceeding with her investigation or prosecution. This particular factor is highly crucial to changing the type of the decision the prosecutor may make. If the local voices of a certain conflict favor a certain form of alternative other than the ICC, then the prosecutor is highly likely required to respect this particular demand. The Uganda situation has shown a typical example, where the majority of voices favored the peace demands ahead of justice. Even more to the point, the majority of Ugandans sought the local justice mechanism to replace the ICC. In such a scenario, the Prosecutor should have stepped back and allowed for the local alternatives to take place. Any potential failure of the prosecutor, therefore, to respond to every side of the argument does not mean that the prosecutor is in a crisis. The persistent criticism is a healthy phenomenon and does not nullify the good mission that the Court, and, in particular, the prosecutor has conducted so far. On the contrary, the dyadic criticisms helped us to find why the prosecutor faces criticisms, and also pushed us to look for solutions for some dyadic arguments. It is true that some dyadicisms cannot be resolved due to the strong legal arguments that each side uses, however, there has often been means to reduce others[724].

[724]D. LIAKOPOULOS, International Criminal Court: Impunity status and the situation in Kenya, op. cit.

Bibliography

ABASS, A., Prosecuting international crimes in Africa: Rationale, prospects and challenges, in European Journal of International Law, 24, 2013, pp. 936ss.

ABBAS, A., The competence of the Security Council to terminate the jurisdiction of the international criminal court, in Texas International Law Journal, 4, 2005, pp. 272ss.

ACQUAVIVA, G., Was a residual mechanism for international criminal tribunals really necessary?, in Journal of International Criminal Justice, 9 (4), 2011, pp. 790ss.

AINLEY, A., The international criminal court on trial, in Cambridge Review of International Affairs, 23 (3), 2011, pp. 320ss.

AKANDE, D., International law immunities and the international criminal court, in American Journal of International Law, 98 (3), 2004, pp. 416ss.

AKANDE, D., The effect of Security Council resolutions and domestic proceedings on state obligations to cooperate with the ICC, in Journal of International Criminal Justice, 12, 2012, pp. 310ss.

AKANDE, P., The legal nature of Security Council referrals, in Journal of International Criminal Justice, 7 (2), 2009, pp. 342ss.

AKHAVAN, P., Are international criminal tribunals a disincentive to peace? Reconciling judicial romanticism with political realism, in Human Rights Quarterly, 31 (3), 2009, pp. 624ss.

AKHAVAN, P., Reducing genocide to law: Definition, meaning and the ultimate crime, Cambridge University Press, Cambridge, 2012.

AKHAVAN, P., The rise and fall and rise of international criminal justice, in Journal of International Criminal Justice, 11 (3), 2013, pp. 528ss.

ALBERT, J., MERLIN, J.B., L'avenir de la justice pènale internationale, ed. Larcier, Bruxelles, 2018.

ALLAN, T.R.S., Constitutional justice: A liberal theory of the rule of law, Oxford University Press, Oxford, 2003, pp. 162ss.

ALONSO, H., Current trends on modes of liability for genocide, crimes against humanity and war crimes, in C. STAHN, L. VAN DEN HERIK (eds.), Future perspectives on international criminal justice, T.M.C. Asser Press, The Hague, 2010, pp. 522-524.

ALVAREZ, J., Nuremberg revisited: The Tadić case, in European Journal of International Law, 7 (2), 1996, pp. 248ss.

ALVAREZ, J., Tadić revisited, in Journal of International Criminal Justice, 16 (5), 2013, pp. 298ss.

ALVAREZ, J., The likely legacies of Tadić, in ILSA Journal of International and Comparative Law, 4, 1997-1998, pp. 614ss.

ALVAREZ, J.E., Judging the security Council, in American Journal of International

Law, 90 (1), 1996, pp. 8ss.

AMBOS, K., Expanding the focus of the African criminal court, in W.A. SCHABAS, MCDERMOTT, HAYES, The Ashgate research companion of international criminal law, Ashgate Publishing, The Hague, 2013, pp. 500ss.

AMBOS, K., OTHMAN, M., (a cura di), New approaches in international criminal justice: Kosovo, East Timor, Sierra Leone and Cambodia. Max-Planck-Institut für ausländisches und internationales Strafrecht, Reihe Interdisziplinäre Untersuchungen aus Strafrecht und Kriminologie, 2003.

AMERASINGHE, C.R.F., Jurisdiction of international tribunal, Martinus Nijhoff Publishers, The Hague, London, New York, 2003.

ANDENAS, M., BJORGE, E., A farewell to fragmentation: Reassertion and convergence in international law, Cambridge University Press, Cambridge, 2015, pp. 324ss.

ANTONOPOULOS, C., Whatever happened to crimes against peace?, in Journal of Conflict and Security Law, 6 (1), 2001, pp. 33ss.

APTEL, C., The intent to commit genocide in the case law of the International Criminal Tribunal for Rwanda, in Criminal Law Forum, 13, 2002, pp. 277ss.

APUULI, K.P., The ICC's possible deferral of the LRA case to Uganda, in Journal of International Criminal Justice, 6 (4), 2008, pp. 802ss.

ARAJÄRVI, N., Looking back from nowhere: Is there a future for universal jurisdiction over international crimes?, in Tilburg Law Review, 16, 2011, pp. 16ss.

ARCARI, M., De l'action parajudiciaire du Conseil de Sècuritè, in M. ARCARI, L. BALMOND, La sècuritè entre lègalitè et dèfies à la lègalitè, ed. Giuffrè, Milano, 2008, pp. 106ss.

ARSANJANI, M.H., Financing, in A. CASSESE, P. GAETA, J.R.W.D. JONES, The Rome statute of the international criminal court. A commentary, Oxford University Press, Oxford, 2002, pp. 325ss.

ARSANJANI, M.H., The Rome statute of the International Criminal Court, in American Journal of International Law, 93, 1999, pp. 22ss.

ASHIAGBOR, D., COUNTOURIS, N., LIANOS, I., The European Union after the Treaty of Lisbon, Cambridge University Press, Cambridge, 2012, pp. 109-135.

BABAIAN, S., The International Criminal Court. An international criminal world court? Jurisdiction and cooperation mechanisms of the Rome statute and its practical implementation, ed. Springer, Berlin, 2018, pp. 23ss.

BAETENES, F., Legitimacy of unseen actors in international adjudication, Cambridge University Press, Cambridge, 2019.

BAKER, R.R., Universal jurisdiction and the case of Belgium: A critical assessment, in ILSA Journal of International and Comparative Law, 16, 2009, pp. 4ss.

BARRIGA, S., BLOKKER, N., Conditions for the exercise of jurisdiction based on state referrals and propio motu investigations, in C. KRESS, S. BARRIGA, The crime of aggression: A commentary, Cambridge University Press, Cambridge, 2017, pp. 662ss.

BARRIGA, S., KRESS, C., The travaus preparatoires of the crime of aggression, Cambridge University Press, Cambridge, 2012.

BARROS, A.S., Governance as responsibility, Cambridge University Press,

Cambridge, 2019.
BECKER, T.A., The dispute that wasn't there. Judgments in the nuclear disarmament cases at the ICJ, in Cambridge International Law Journal, 6, 2017, pp. 4ss.
BEIGBEDER, Y., Special panels for serious crimes in East Timor. Now Timor-Leste, in Y. BEIGBEDER, International criminal Tribunals, ed. Palgrave Macmillan, London, 2011.
BEKOU, O., BIRKETT, D., Cooperation and the International Criminal Court: Perspectives from theory and practice, ed. Brill, Bruxelles, 2016.
BEKOU, O., The International Criminal Court, ed. Routlege, London & New York, 2017.
BELLAMY, A.J., WILLIAMS, P., Peace operations and global order, ed. Routledge, London, New York, 2014.
BELLELLI, R., International criminal justice: Law and practice from the Rome statute to its review, ed. Routledge, London & New York, 2016, pp. 40ss.
BENEDETTI, F., BONNEAU, K., WASHBURN, J., Negotiating the International Criminal Court: New York to Rome 1994-1998, Martinus Nijhoff Publishers, The Hague, 2013.
BENSOUDA, F., International justice and diplomacy: Partnering for peace and international security, in Acadèmie Diplomatique Internationale-Forum for new diplomacy, 20 March 2013.
BENZIG, M., Bilateral non-surrender agreements and article 98 of the statute of the international criminal court: An exercise in the law of treaties, in Max Planck Yearbook of United Nations Law, 8, 2004, pp. 200.
BERGSMO, M., KRUGER, P., BEKOU, O., Article 54, in O. TRIFFTERER, K. AMBOS, The Rome statute of the international criminal court. A commentary, B.C. Beck, Hart, Nomos, München, Oxford, Baden-Baden, 2016, pp. 1392ss.
BERGSMO, M., Occasional remarks on certain state concerns about the jurisdictional reach of the international criminal court and their possible implications for the relationship between the Court and the Security Council, in Nordic Journal of International Law, 69 (1), 2000, pp. 94ss.
BERGSMO, M., PEJIC, J., Article 16, in O. TRIFFTERER, Commentary on the Rome statute, observer's notes, article by article, Oxford, Baden-Baden, München, 2008, pp. 604ss.
BERGSMO, M., PEJIC, J., ZHU, D., Article 16, in O. TRIFFTERER, K. AMBOS, The Rome statute of the international criminal court. A commentary, C.H.Beck-Hart-Nomos, München, Oxford, Baden-Baden, 2016, pp. 774ss.
BERMAN, F., The international criminal court and the use of force by states, in Singapore Journal of International and Comparative Law, 3, 2000, pp. 480ss.
BERMAN, F., The relationship between the international criminal Court and the Security Council, in H.A.M. VON HEBEL, J.G. LAMMERS, J. SCHUKKING, Reflections on the international criminal court: Essays in honor of Adriaan Bos, T.M.C. Asser press, The Hague, 1999, pp. 174ss.
BERNER, K., Authentic interpretation in public international law, in Zeitschrift für ausländisches öffentliches Recht und Völkerrecht, 74, 2016, pp. 876ss.
BESSELINK, L., CLAES, M., REESTMAN, J.H., A Constitutional moment: Acceding to the ECHR (or not), in European Constitutional Law Review, 11,

2015, pp. 2ss.
BIANCHI, A., Assessing the effectiveness of the UN Security Council's anti-terrorism measures. The quest for legitimacy and cohesion, in European Journal of International Law, 17 (5), 2007, pp. 912ss
BIANCHI, A., International law theories: An inquiry into different ways of thinking, Oxford University Press, Oxford, 2016.
BILKOVÁ, V., The standard of equivalent protection as a standard of review, in L. GRUSZCZYNSKI, W. WERNER, Deference in international courts and tribunals, Oxford University Press, Oxford, 2014, pp. 282ss.
BILLING, F.M.W., The right to silence in transnational criminal proceedings. Comparative law perspectives, ed. Springer, Berlin, 2016, pp. 323ss.
BIRDSALL, A., The responsibility to protect and the ICC: A problematic relationship?, in Criminal Law Forum, 26 (1), 2015, pp. 26ss.
BJORGE, E., The evolutionary interpretation of treaties, Oxford University Press, Oxford, 2014.
BLAISE NGAMENI, H., Le droit international pènal à l'èpreuve des règimes politiques africaines, in Revue Quèbècoise de Droit International, 29 (1), 2016, pp. 10ss.
BLOKKER, N., A consensus agreement on the crime of aggression: Impressions from Kampala, in Leiden Journal of International law, 23 (4), 2010, pp. 892ss.
BLOKKER, N., KRESS, C., A consensus agreement on the crime of aggression: Impressions from Kampala, in Leiden Journal of International Law, 20, 2010, pp. 890ss.
BLOKKER, N., Outsourcing the use of force: Towards more Security Council control of authorized operations?, in M. WELLER (ed), The oxford handbook of the use of force in international law, Oxford University Press, Oxford, 2015.
BLOME, K., MARKARD, N., Contested collisions: Successful conditions management. The example of article 16 of the Rome Statute, in Leiden Journal of International Law, 29 (2), 2016, pp. 572ss.
BOAS, G., CHIFFLET, P., International criminal justice, Edward Elgar Publishing, Cheltenham, 2017.
BOCK, S., Zurechnung im Völkerechtstrafrecht, in Zeitschrft für Internationale Strafrechtdogmatik, 7-8, 2017, pp. 414ss.
BOEVING, J.N., Aggression, international law and the ICC: An argument for the withdrawal of aggression from the Rome Statute, in Columbia Journal of Transnational Law, 43 (2), 2005, pp. 538ss.
BÖHLAU, H., Competenz-competenz? Erörterungen zu artikel 78 der Verfassung des Nordeutschen Reichs, ed. Veit, Leipzig, 1869.
BOISSON DE CHAZOURNES, L., KUIJPER, P.J., Mr Kadi and Mrs Prost: Is the UN Ombudsman going to find herself between a rock and a hard place?, in H. RIETER, E. WAELE, Evolving principles of international law. Studies in honor of Karel C. Wallens, ed. Brill, Leiden, 2011, pp. 78ss.
BOISSON DE CHAZOURNES, L., The principle of compètence de la compètence in international adjudication and its role in an era of multiplication of courts and tribunals, in M.H. ARSANJANI, J.K. COGAN, S. WIESSNER, Looking to the future. Essays on international law in honor of W. Michael Reisman, Martinus Nijhoff Publishers, Leiden, 2011, pp. 1028ss.

BOLTON, J.R., The risks and weaknesses of the international criminal court from America's perspective, in Law and Contemporary Problems, 64 (1), 2001, pp. 168ss.

BONAFÉ, B., The relationship between state and individual responsibility for international crimes, Martinus Nijhoff Publishers, Leiden, Boston, 2009.

BOSCHIERO, N., The ICC judicial finding on non-cooperation against the DRC and no immunity for Al-Bashir based on UNSC Resolution 1593, in Journal of International Criminal Justice, 13, 2015, pp. 654ss.

BOSCO, D., Rough justice, Oxford University Press, Oxford, 2014.

BOSLY, H.D., VANDERMEERSCH, D., Gènocide, crimes contre l'humanitè et crimes de guerre face à la justice, ed. Bruylant, Bruxelles, 2012.

BOTHE, M., Les limites de pouvoirs du Conseil de Sècuritè, in R.J. DUPUY, The development of the role of the Security Council, Martinus Nijhoff Publishers, Dodrecht, 1993, pp. 70ss.

BOURGON, S., Jurisdiction ratione loci, in A. CASSESE, P. GAETA, J.R.W.D. JONES, The Rome statute of the international criminal court. A commentary, Oxford University Press, Oxford, 2002, pp. 560ss.

BOURGON, S., Ratione temporis, in A. CASSESE, P. GAETA, J.R.W.D. JONES, The Rome statute of the international criminal court. A commentary, Oxford University Press, Oxford, 2002, pp. 564ss.

BOWERS, A., International Criminal Court, Wolf Legal Publishers, The Netherlands, 2011.

BOWETT, D.W., Judicial and political functions of the Security Council and the International Court of Justice, in H. FOX, The changing constitution of the United Nations, British Institute of International Law, 22, 1973, pp. 84ss.

BREAU, S., The responsibility to protect in international law: An emerging paradigm shift, ed. Routledge, London & New York, 2016.

BRIGHTON, C., Unwillingness: Addressing the political pitfalls inherent in the complementarity regime of the international criminal court, in International Criminal Law Review, 2012, pp. 630ss.

BROCKMAN-HAWE, B.E., Questioning the UN's immunity in the Dutch Courts: Unresolved issues in the Mothers of Srebrenica litigation, in Washington University Global Studies Law Review, 10, 2011, pp. 727ss.

BRÖLMANN, C., RADI, Y., Research handbook on the theory and practice of international law making, Edward Elgar Publishing, Cheltenham, 2016, pp. 186ss.

BRÖLMANN, C.M., Specialized rules of treaty interpretation: International organizations, in D.B. HOLLIS, Oxford guide to treaties, Oxford University Press, Oxford, 2012, pp. 508ss.

BROOMHALL, B., International justice and the international criminal court: Between sovereignty and the rule of law, Oxford University Press, Oxford, 2003, pp. 162ss.

BROWN, C., The inherent powers of international courts and tribunals, in British Yearbook of International Law, 76 (1), 2005, pp. 196ss.

BROWNLIE, I., The decision of political organs of the United Nations and the rule of law, in R.S.J. MACDONALD, Essays in honor of Wang Tieya, Martinus Nijhoff Publishers, Leiden, Boston, 1993, pp. 102ss.

BUGA, I., Modification of treaties by subsequent practice, Oxford University Press, Oxford, 2018.

BURKE-WHITE, W.W., A community of courts. Toward a system of international criminal law enforcement, in Michigan Journal of International Law, 24 (2), 2002, pp. 5ss.

BURKHARDT, S.U., Vergewaltigung als Verbrechen gegen die Menschlichkeit Sexualisierte Gewalt, Makrokriminalität und Völkerstrafrecht, LIT Verlag, Berlin, 2005.

BUTT, D., Victor's justice? Historic injustice and the legitimacy of international law, in L.H. MAYER, Legitimacy, justice and public international law, Cambridge University Press, Cambridge, 2009, pp. 164ss.

ÇAKMAK, C., A brief history of international criminal law and International Criminal Court, ed. Springer, Berlin, 2017, pp. 161ss.

CAMARGOS, L.A., A responsabilidade penal internacional dos individuos: Estudo do caso Darfur, in Revista de Direito Brasileira, 2013, pp. 199ss.

CANNIZZARO, E., A Machiavellian moment? The UN security council and the rule of law, in International Organization Law Review, 3, 2006, pp. 190ss.

CANNIZZARO, E., PALCHETTI, P., Ultra vires acts of international organizations, in G. KLABBERS, E. WALLENDAHL, Research handbook on the law of international organization, Edward Elgar Publishers, Cheltenham, 2011, pp. 367ss.

CANNIZZARO, E., PALCHETTI, P., WESSEL, A., International law as the law of European Union, ed. Brill, Leiden, Boston, 2012, pp. 386ss.

CAPPS, P., PALMER OLSEN, H., Legal authority beyond the state, Cambridge University Press, Cambridge, 2018.

CARPENTER, A.C., The international criminal court and the crime of aggression, in Nordic Journal of International Law, 64, 1995, pp. 234ss.

CARTER, L.E., ELLIS, M.S., CHERNOR JALLOH, C., The International Criminal Court in an effective global justice system, Edward Elgar Publishers, Cheltenham, 2016, pp. 176ss

CARTER, L.E., The future of the International Criminal Court: Complementarity as a strength or a weakness?, in Washington University Global Studies Law Review, 12, 2013, pp. 454ss.

CASSESE, A., GAETA, P., Cassese's international criminal law, Oxford University Press, Oxford, 2013, pp. 37ss.

CASSESE, A., International criminal law, Oxford University Press, Oxford, 2008, pp. 312ss.

CASSESE, A., Is the ICC still having teething problems?, in Journal of International Criminal Justice, 4, 2006, pp. 434ss.

CASSESE, A., On the current trends towards criminal prosecution and punishment of breaches of international humanitarian law, in European Journal of International Law, 9, 1998, pp. 20ss.

CASSESE, A., The statute of the international criminal court: Some preliminary reflections, in European Journal of International Law, 10 (1), 1999, pp. 24ss.

CHALMERS, D., DAVIES, G., MONTI, G., EU law, Cambridge University Press, Cambridge, 2014.

CHANG, Y.T., The interpretation of treaties by judicial tribunals, Columbia University

Press, London, 1933.

CHENG, B., Pre-emptive or similar type of self-defense in the territory of foreign states, in Chinese Journal of International Law, 13, 2014, pp. 4ss.

CHERIF BASSIOUNI, M., (ed.), International criminal law, vol. I: Sources, subjects and contents, Martinus Nijhoff Publishers, The Hague, 2013.

CHERIF BASSIOUNI, M., The legislative history of the International Criminal Court: Introduction, analysis and integrated text. Volume I, ed. Brill/Martinus Nijhoff Publishers, New York, 2005, pp. 151ss.

CHERNOR JALLOH, C., BANTEKAS, I., The International Criminal Court in Africa, Cambridge University Press, Cambridge, 2017, pp. 198ss.

CHERNOR JALLOH, C., MORGAN, A., International criminal justice processes in Rwanda and Sierra Leone: Lessons for Liberia, in C. CHERNOR JALLOH, E. OLUFEMI, Shielding humanity. Essays in international law in honour of judge Abdul G. Koroma, ed. Brill, The Hague, 2015.

CHERNOR JALLOH, C., The Sierra Leone Special Court and its legacy: The impact for Africa and international criminal law, Cambridge University Press, Cambridge, 2013, pp. 234ss.

CHESTERMAN, S., An altogether different order, defining the elements of crimes against humanity, in Duke Journal of Comparative and International Law, 10, 2002, pp. 332ss.

CHIEDU MOGHALU, K., International humanitarian law from Nuremberg to Rome: The weighty precedents of the international criminal Tribunal for Rwanda, in Pace International Law Review, 14, 2002, pp. 285ss.

CHINKIN, C., Jus cogens, article 103 of the UN charter and other hierarchical tecniques of conflict solution, in Finnish Yearbook of International Law, 17, 2006, pp. 64ss.

CHINKIN, C., KALDOR, M., International law and new wars, Cambridge University Press, Cambridge, 2017, pp. 437ss.

CIAMPI, A., CONDORELLI, L., Comments on the security council referral of the situation in Darfur to the ICC, in Journal of International Criminal Justice, 3 (3), 2005, pp. 592ss.

CIAMPI, A., The proceedings against president Al Bashir and the prospects of their suspension under article 16 ICC Statute, in Journal of International Criminal Justice, 6 (5), 2008.

CLAPHAM, A., Three tribes engage on the future of international criminal law, in Journal of International Criminal Justice, 9 (3), 2011, pp. 691ss.

CLARK, J.N., Peace, justice and the international criminal court, in Journal of International Criminal Justice, 9 (3), 2011, pp. 522ss.

CLARK, P., Distant justice: The impact of the International Criminal Court on African politics, Cambridge University Press, Cambridge, 2018.

CLARK, R.S., Rethinking aggression as a crime and formulating its elements. The final work-product of the preparatory commission for the international criminal court, in Leiden Journal of International Law, 15 (4), 2002, pp. 860ss.

COLLINS, R., The institutional problem in modern international law, ed. Bloomsbury, New York, 2016.

COLLINS, R., WHITE, N.D., International organizations and the idea of autonomy:

Institutional independence in the international legal order, ed. Routledge, London & New York, 2011.

COMBACAU, J., Le chapitre VII de la charte des Nations Unies: rèsurrection ou mètamorphose?, in R. BEN ACHOUR, S. LAGHMANI, Les nouveaux aspects du droit international, ed. Pedone, Paris, 1994, pp. 148ss.

CONDORELLI, L., La soumission des organisations internationales aux normes internationales aux normes internationales realtives aux droits de l'homme: Journèe d'ètudes de Strasbourg, ed. Pedone, Paris, 2009, pp. 140ss

CONDORELLI, L., VILLALPANDO, L., Can the Security Council extend the ICC's jurisdiction, in A. CASSESE, P. GAETA, J.R.W.D. JONES, The Rome statute of the international criminal court. A commentary, Oxford University Press, Oxford, 2002, pp. 582ss.

CONDORELLI, L., VILLALPANDO, L., Les Nations Unies et les juridictions penales internationales, in J.P. COT, M. FORTEAU, A. PELLET, La charte des Nations Unies commentaire article par article, LGDJ, Paris, 2005, pp. 202ss

CONDORELLI, L., VILLALPANDO, L., Referral and deferral by the Security Council, in A. CASSESE, P. GAETA, J.R.W.D. JONES, The Rome statute of the international criminal court. A commentary, Oxford University Press, Oxford, 2002, pp. 634ss.

CORTEN, O., KLEIN, P., The Vienna Conventions on the law of treaties. A commentary, Oxford University Press, Oxford, 2011.

CORTEN, O., The law against war: The prohibition on the use of force in contemporary international law, Hart Publishing, Oxford/Oregon & Portland, 2010.

CRAWFORD, J., The ILC's Draft Statute for an international criminal tribunal, in American Journal of International Law, 88 (1), 1994, pp. 148ss.

CREEGAN, E., Justified uses of force and the crime of aggression, in Journal of International Criminal Justice, 10, 2012, pp. 60ss.

CREMONA, M., THIES, A., WESSEL, R.A., The European Union and international dispute settlement, Bloomsbury Publishing, New York, 2017, pp. 8ss.

CRUSZCZYNSKI, L., WERNER, W., Deference in international courts and tribunals: Standard of review and margin of appreciation, Oxford University Press, Oxford, 2014

CRYER, C., FRIMAN, H., ROBINSON, D., WILMSHURST, E., An introduction to international criminal law and procedure, Cambridge University Press, Cambridge, 2014, pp. 200ss.

CRYER, C., Sudan, resolution 1593 and international criminal justice, in Leiden Journal of International Law, 2006, 19, pp. 212ss.

CRYER, C., WHITE, N.D., The Security Council and the international criminal court: Who's feeling threatened?, in Journal of International Peacekeeping, 19, 2004, pp. 156ss.

CRYER, R., FRIMAN, H., ROBINSON, D., WILMSHURST, E., An introduction to international criminal law and procedure, Cambridge University Press, Cambridge, 2007, pp. 139ss.

CRYER, R., FRIMAN, H., ROBINSON, D., WILMSHURST, E., An introduction to international criminal law and procedure, Cambridge University Press,

Cambridge, 2014, pp. 231ss.
CRYER, R., ROBINSON, D., VASILIEV, S., An introduction to international criminal law and procedure, Cambridge University Press, Cambridge, 2019, pp. 152ss.
D'ASPREMONT, J., Epistemic forces in international law, Edward Elgar Publishers, Cheltenham, 2015, pp. 147ss.
D'ASPREMONT, J., The multifaceted concept of the autonomy of international organizations and international legal discourse, in R. COLLINS, N.D. WHITE, International organizaions and the idea of autonomy, ed. Routledge, London, New York, 2011, pp. 64ss.
DANNENBAUM, T., Translating the standard of effective control into a system of effective accountability: How liability should be apportioned for violation of human rights by member state troop contingents serving as United Nations peace keeping, in Harvard International Law Journal, 51, 2010, pp. 115ss.
DANNENBAUMN, T., The crime of aggression, humanity and the soldier, Cambridge University Press, Cambridge, 2018.
DARCY, S., Law and war: The judicial development of international humanitarian law, Cambridge University Press, Cambridge 2014, pp. 64ss.
DARQUES-LANE, F., MADEC, C., GODART, S., Article 54, in J. FERNANDEZ, X. PACREAU, Statut de Rome de la cour pènale internationale-Commentaire article par article, ed. Pedone, Paris, 2012, pp. 1256ss.
DAS, S., NARGAS, A., Mapping the Jadhav dispute at the world court. Evaluating India and Pakistan's arguments, in California Western International Law Journal, 48 (1), 2018, pp. 40ss.
DASKALOPOULOU-LIVADA, P., The principle of complementarity and Security Council referrals, in F. GIOIA, M. POLITI, The international criminal court and national jurisdictions, ed. Routledge, Aldershot, 2008, pp. 60sss.
DAU, C., Die völkerrechtliche Zulässigkeit von Selbstverteidigung gegen nicht-staatliche Aktueure, Nomos Verlag, Baden Baden, 2018.
DAVIES, S.E., TRUE, J., The oxford handbook of women, peace and security, Oxford University Press, Oxford, 2018
DAVIS, C., Political consideration in prosecutorial discretion in the International Criminal Court, in Internatonal Criminal Law Review, 15 (1), 2015, pp. 182ss.
DAZA GONZÁLEZ, A., El principio de complementariedad en el derecho penal internacional, ed. Universidad Catòlica de Colombia, Bogotà, D.C, 2015.
DE BRABANDERE, E., Immunity of international organizations in post-conflict international administrations, in International Organizations Law Review, 7, 2010, pp. 79ss.
DE FROUVILLE, O., Les juridictions pènales internationales et hybrides, in H. RUIZ-FABRI, J.M. SOREL, Indèpendance et impartialitè des juges internationaux, ed. Pedone, Paris, 2010, pp. 154ss.
DE GUZMAN, M.M., Choosing to prosecutor. Expressive selection at the international criminal court, in Michigan Journal of International Law, 33, 2012, pp. 267ss
DE HOON, M., The future of the International Criminal Court. On critique, legalism and strengthening the ICC's legitimacy, in International Criminal Law

Review, 17 (4), 2017, pp. 596ss.
DE VOS, C., KENDALL, S., STAHN, C., Contested justice: The politics and practice of International Criminal Court interventions, Cambridge University Press, Cambridge, 2015.
DE WET, E., From Kadi to Nada: Judicial techniques favoring human rights over United Nations Security Council sanctions, in Chinese Journal of International Law, 12 (4), 2013, pp. 788ss.
DE WET, E., NOLLKAEMPER, A., Review of the Security Council decisions by national courts, in German Yearbook of International Law, 45, 2002, pp. 168ss.
DE WET, E., Referrals to the International Criminal Court under chapter VII of the United Nations Charter and the immunity of foreign state officials, in ASIL Unbound, 112, 2018, pp. 36ss.
DE WET, E., The implications of president Al-bashir's visit to South Africa for international and domestic law, in Journal of International Criminal Justice, 13 (5), 2005, pp. 1050ss.
DE WITTE, B., Article 53, in S. PEERS et al. (eds.), The EU Charter of Fundamental Rights, A Commentary, Hart Publishing, Oxford & Oregon, Portland, 2014, pp. 1523-1538.
DE WITTE, B., European Union law: How autonomous is its legal order?, in Zeitscrhift für öffentiliches Recht, 65 (1), 2010, pp. 142ss.
DECAUX, E., DE FROUVILLE, O., Droit international public, ed. Dalloz, Paris, 2018.
DELEAU, O., L'examen du rôle de la CIJ par l'Assemblèe gènèrale des Nations Unies, in Annuaire Français de Droit International, 16, 1970, pp. 4ss.
DELMAS-MARTY, M., Le pluralisme ordonnè, Seuil, Paris, 2006.
DELMAS-MARTY, M., Libertès et sûretè dans un monde dangereux, Seuil, Paris, 2010, pp. 196ss.
DEPREZ, C., L'applicabilitè des droits humains à l'action de la Cour pènale internationale, ed. Larcier, Bruxelles, 2016.
DERMOTT, Y., The Ashgate research companion to international criminal law: Critical perspectives, ed. Routledge, London & New York, 2016.
DICKINSON, L.A., The promise of Hybrid Courts, in American Journal of International Law, 97 (2), 2003, pp. 306ss.
DINSTEIN, Y., Non-international armed conflicts in international law, Cambridge University Press, Cambridge, 2014, pp. 186ss.
DIREK, Ö.F., Responsibility in peace support operations: Revisiting the proper test for attribution conduct and the meaning of the "effective control" Standard, in Netherlands International Law Review, 61, 2014, pp. 7ss.
DORIA, J., Conflicting interpretation of the ICC statute. Are the rules of interpretation of the Vienna Convention still relevant?, in M. FITZMAURICE, O. ELIAS, P. MERKOURIS, Treaty interpretation and the Vienna Convention on the law of treaties: 30 years on, ed. Brill, Leiden, Boston, 2010, pp. 312ss.
DÖRR, O., Article 31. General rule of interpretation, in O. DÖRR, K. SCHMALENBACH (a cura di), Vienna Convention on the Law of Treaties. A commentary, Springer, Heidelberg-New York 2012, pp. 536ss.
DROUBI, S., Resisting United Nations Security Council resolutions, ed. Routledge,

London, New York, 2014, pp. 12ss.
DRUMBL, M., Atrocity, punishment and international law, Cambridge University Press, Cambridge, 2007, pp. 152ss.
DUBBLER, R., KALYK, M., Crimes against humanity in the 21st century: Law, practice and threats to international peace and security, ed. Brill, Bruxelles, 2018, pp. 222ss.
DUGARD, J., Obstacles on the way of an international criminal court, in Cambridge Law Journal, 56 (2), 1997, pp. 330ss.
DUPUY, P.M., The constitutional dimension of the charter of the United Nations revisited, in Max Planck United Nations Yearbook, 1997, pp. 5ss.
DUURSMA, A., MÜLLER, T.R., The International Criminal Court indictment against Al-Bashir and its repercussions for peacekeeping and humanitarian operations in Darfur, in Third World Quarterly, 40 (5), 2019.
DYANI-MHANGO, N., South Africa's dilemma: Immunity laws, international obligations and the visit by Sudan's President Omar al Bashir, in Washington International Law Journal, 26 (3), 2017, pp. 544ss.
EBOE-OSVJI, C., The ICC and the African Court and the extended notion of complementarity of international criminal jurisdictions, in Nigeria Yearbook of International Law, 2018.
ECKES, C., HOLLENBERG, S., Reconciling different legal spheres in theory and practice: Pluralism and constitutionalism in the cases of Al Jedda, Ahmed and Nada, in Maastricht Journal of European and Comparative Law, 20, 2013, pp. 218ss.
EECKHOUT, P., The EU's Common Foreign and Security Policy after Lisbon: From pillar talk to constitutionalism, in A. BIONDI, P. EECKHOUT, S. RIPLEY, (eds.), EU Law after Lisbon, Oxford University Press, Oxford, New York, 2012, pp. 265-291.
EECKROUT, P., LOPEZ-ESCUDERO, M., The European Union's external action in times of crisis, Blomsburry Publishing, New York, 2016.
EL AMINE, H., Article 16, in J. FERNANDEZ, X. PACREAU, Statut de Rome de la cour pènale internationale-Commentaire article par article, ed. Pedone, Paris, 2012, pp. 676ss.
EL SCHWÖBEL, C., Global constitutionalism in international legal perspective, Martinus Nijhoff Publishers, The Hague, 2011,
EL ZEIDY, M., The Ugandan government triggers the first test of complementarity principle: An assessment of the first state's party referral to ICC, in International Criminal Law Review, 5, 2005, pp. 100ss.
ELABY, K., The role of the Security Council and the independence of the International Criminal Court. A challenge of impunity, Taylor & Francis, New York, 2017.
ELAGAB, O.Y., Indicting the Sudanese president by the ICC: Resolution 1593 revisited, in International Journal of Human Rights, 13 (5), 2009, pp. 658ss.
ELGEBEILY, S., The rule of law in the United Nations Security Council, decision making process: Turning the focus inwards, ed. Routledge, London & New York, 2017.
ELIAS, J., QUAST, A., The relationship between the security council and the international criminal court in the light of resolution 1422 (2002), in Non-State Actors and International law, 3 (2-3), 2003, pp. 170ss.

ELLIS, M.S., DOUTRIAUX, Y., RYBACK, T.W., Justice and diplomacy: Resolving contradictions in diplomatic practice and international humanitarian and international humanitarian law, Cambridge University Press, Cambridge, 2018, pp. 102ss.

ESCARAMEIA, P., The ICC and the Security Council on aggression: Overlapping competencies, in M. POLITI, G. NESI, The International Criminal Court: A challenge to impunity, Ashgate Publishing, Aldershot, 2001, pp. 134ss.

ESCOBAR HERNÁNDEZ, C.E., Corte penal internacional, consejo de seguridad y crimen de agresiòn un equilibrio dificil e inestable, in F.M. MARIÑO MÉNENDEZ, El derecho internacional en los albores del siglo XXI. Homenaje al profesor Juan Manuel Castro-Rial Canosa, ed. Trotta. Fundaciòn Juan March, 2002, Madrid, pp. 262ss.

ESCUDERO ESPINOSA, J.F.E., Los poderes del Consejo de Seguridad y la corte penal internacional en el estatuto de Roma, in Annuario de Derecho Internacional, 19, 2003, pp. 257ss

FALLIGANT, J., The prosecution of Sudanese president Al Bashir: Why a security Council deferral would harm the legitimacy of the international criminal court, in Wisconsin International Law Journal, 27, 2010, pp. 748ss.

FASSBENDER, B., The United Nations charter as constitution of the international community, in Columbia Journal of Transnational Law, 36, 1998, pp. 530ss.

FERENCZ, D.M., Aggression in legal limbo: a gap in the law that needs closing, in Washington University Global Studies Law Review, 12, 2013, pp. 508ss.

FERNÁNDEZ DE GOURMENDI, S.A., The working group on aggression at the preparatory commission for the international criminal court, in Fordham International Law Journal, 25, 2001-2002, pp. 606ss.

FITZMAURICE, M., ELIAS, E., Contemporary issues in the law of treaties, Eleven Publishing International, The Hague, 2005, pp. 284ss.

FITZMAURICE, M., ELIAS, O., MERKOURIS, P., (eds), Treaty interpretation and the Vienna Convention on the Law of Treaties, 30 years on, Martinus Nijhoff, The Hague, 2010, pp. 9ss.

FLETCHER, G.P., OHLIN, J.D., The ICC-Two courts in one?, in Journal of International Criminal Justice, 4, 2006, pp. 432ss.

FLETCHER, G.P., The storrs lectures. Liberals and romantics at war: The problem of collective guilt, in Yale Law Journal, 111, pp. 2002ss.

FLETSCHER, L.E., WEINSTEIN, H.M., Violence and social repair: Rethinking the contribution of justice to reconciliation, in Human Rights Quarterly, 24, 2002, pp. 574ss.

FOKA TAFFO, F., Le pouvoir discretionnaire du procureur de la cour pènale internationale, Nomos Verlag, Baden-Baden, 2018.

FOLLESDALL, A., ULFSTEIN, G., The judicialization of international law: A mixed blessing?, Oxford University Press, Oxford, 2018.

FOURNET, C., PÉGORIER, C., "Only one step away from genocide". The crime of persecution in international criminal law, in International Criminal Law Review, 10, 2010, pp. 714ss.

FOUTER, M.E., SCHMIDT, J., WHITE, N.D., Security and international law, Bloomsbury Publishing, New York, 2016, pp. 106ss.

FRANCK, T., Is the UN Charter a constitution?, in J.A. FROWEIN, K. SCHARIOTH,

I. WINKELMANN, R. WOLFRUM, Verhandeln für den Frieden. Liber amicorum Tono Eitel, C.H. Beck, Berlin, 2003, pp. 96ss.

FRANCK, T., Political question, judicial answers, Princeton University Press, Princeton, 1992.

FRANCK, T.M., Fairness in the international legal and institutional system, in Recueil des cours, ed. Brill, Bruxelles, vol. 240, 1993, pp. 192

FRITSCHE, C., Security Council resolution 1422: Peacekeeping and the international criminal court, in J.A. FROWEIN, K. SCHARIOTH, I. WINKELMANN, R. WOLFRUM, Verbandeln für den Frieden. Liber amicorum Tono Eite, ed. Springer, Berlin, 2003, pp. 116

FRITSCHE, C., Security Council Resolution n.1422: Peacekeeping and the international criminal court, in J.A. FROWEIN, K. SCHARIOTH, I. WINKELMANN, R. WOLFRUM, Verbandeln für den Frieden. Liber amicorum Tono Eite, ed. Springer, Berlin, 2003, pp. 114ss.

FROWEIN, J.A., Issues of legitimacy around the United Nations Security Council, in J.A. FROWEIN, K. SCHARIOTH, I. WINKELMANN, R. WOLFRUM, Verbandeln für deb Frieden. Liber amicorum Tono Eite, ed. Springer, Berlin, 2003

FROWEIN, J.A., The international and external effects of resolutions by international organizations, in Zeitschrift für ausländisches öffentliches Recht und Völkerrecht, 49, 1989, pp. 790ss.

GAETA, P., Does president Al Bashir enjoy immunity from arrest?, in Journal of International Criminal Justice, 7 (2), 2009, pp. 324ss.

GAETA, P., Inherent powers of international courts and tribunals, in L.C. VOHRAH, Man's inhumanity to man. Essays on international law in honor of Antonio Cassese, Martinus Nijhoff Publishers, The Hague, London, New York, 2003, pp. 352ss.

GAETA, P., Is the practice of "self-referrals" a sound start for the ICC?, in Journal of International Criminal Justice, 4 (4), 2004, pp. 950ss.

GAETA, P., Official capacity and immunities, in A. CASSESE, P. GAETA, J.R.W.D. JONES, The Rome statute of the international criminal court. A commentary, Oxford University Press, Oxford, 2002.

GAETA, P., The history and the evolution of the notion of international crimes, in R. BELLELLI (a cura di), International criminal justice. Law and practice from the Rome statute to its review, Ashgate Publishing, Farnham, 2010, pp. 169-180.

GAJA, G., Rèflexions sur le rôle du Conseil de Sècuritè dans le nouvel ordre mondial, in Revue Gènèrale de Droit International Public, 97, 1993, pp. 316ss.

GAJA, G., The long journey towards repressing aggression, in A. CASSESE, P. GAETA, J.R.W.D. JONES, The Rome statute of the international criminal court. A commentary, Oxford University Press, Oxford, 2002, pp. 124ss.

GAJA, G., The protection of general interest in the international community, in Recueil des cours, ed Brill, Bruxelles, vol. 364, 2011, pp. 84ss.

GAJA, G., The respective roles of the ICC and the Security Council in determining the existence of aggression, in M. POLITI, G. NESI, The International Criminal Court: A challenge to impunity, Ashgate Publishing, Aldershot, 2001, pp. 124ss.

GAJA, G., The role of the United Nations in preventing and suppressing genocide, in P. GAETA, The UN Genocide convention, Oxford University Press, Oxford, 2009, pp. 400ss.

GARDINER, R.K., Treaty interpretation, Oxford University Press, Oxford, 2015, pp. 127ss.

GEGOUT, C., The International Criminal Court: Limits, potential and conditions for the promotion of justice and peace, in Third World Quarterly, 34 (5), 2014, pp. 800ss.

GIOIA, F., The International criminal Court and national jurisdictions, ed. Routledge, London & New York, 2016.

GISSEL, L., The International Criminal Court and peace processes in Africa: Judicialising peace, ed. Routledge, London & New York, 2018.

GLOBKE, C., Die Auslieferung an den Internationalen Strafgerichtshof, Mohr Siebeck, Tübingen, 2009.

GOLDSTONE, R., The future of international criminal justice: The crucial role of the United States, in ILSA Journal of International & Comparative Law, 18 (2), 2016, pp. 622ss.

GOLDSTONE, R.J., FRITZ, N., In the interests of justice and independent referral. The ICC prosecutor's unprecedent powers, in Leiden Journal of International Law, 13 (3), 2000, pp. 667ss.

GOVAERE, I. GARBEN, S., The interface between European Union and international law: Contemporary reflections, Bloomsbury Publishing, New York, 2019, pp. 19ss.

GOWLLAND-DEBBAS, V., The relationship between political and judicial organs if international organizations: The role of the Security Council in the new international criminal court, in L. BOISSON DE CHAZOURNES, C.P.R. ROMANO, R. MACKENZIE, International organizations and international dispute settlement. Trends and prospects, Martinus Nijhoff Publishers, 2002, pp. 108ss.

GOWLLAND-DEBBAS, V., The relationship between the Security Council and the projected ICC, in Journal of Armed Conflict, 3 (1), 1997, pp. 115ss.

GOWLLAND-DEBBAS, V., The role of the Security Council in the new international criminal court from a systemic perspective, in L. BOISSON DE CHAZOURNES, V. GOWLLAND-DEBBAS, The international legal system in quest of equity and universality. Liber amicorum Georges Abi-Saab, ed. Brill & Martinus Nijhoff Publishers, Bruxelles, The Hague, 2001, pp. 632ss.

GOWLLAND-DEBBAS, V., The Security Council and issues of responsibility under international law, in Recueil des cours, ed Brill, Bruxelles, vol. 353, 2012, pp. 298ss.

GRAEFRATH, B., International crimes and collective security, in E. SUY, K. WELLES, International law, theory and practice essays in honor of Eric Suy, Martinus Nijhoff Publishers, Hague, 1998, pp. 238ss.

GRAY, C., International law and the use of force, Oxford University Press, Oxford, 2018.

GREEN, J.A., Questioning the peremptory status of the prohibition of the use of force, in Michigan Journal of International Law, 32, 2011, pp. 216ss.

GREENWALT, A.K.A., Justice without politics? Prosecutorial discretion and the international criminal court, in International Law & Politics, 39, 2007, pp. 584ss.

GREER, S., Is the prohibition against torture, cruel, inhuman and degrading treatment realy "absolute" in international human rights law?, in Human Rights Law Review, 15, 2015, pp. 5ss.

GROVER, L., Interpreting crimes in the Rome statute of the International Criminal Court, Cambridge University Press, Cambridge, 2014, pp. 114ss.

GROVER, S., The responsibility to protect: Perspectives on the concept's meaning proper application and value, ed. Routledge, London & New York, 2018, pp. 101ss.

GRZEBYK, P., Criminal responsibility for the crime of aggression, ed. Routledge, London & New York, 2013.

HALBESTRAM, D., It's autonomy stupid. A modest defense of Opinion 2/13 on EU accession to the ECHR, and a way forward, in Michigan Law Paper, 105, 2015.

HALDEMANN, F., UNGER, T., The United Nations principles to combat impunity: A commentary, Oxford University Press, Oxford, 2018.

HALFF, M., TOLBERT, D., VILLACIS, R., Article 115. Funds of the court and of the Assembly of states parties, in O. TRIFFTERER, K. AMBOS, The Rome statute of the international criminal court. A commentary, C.H.Beck-Hart-Nomos, München, Oxford, Baden-Baden, 2016.

HALL, C.K., The first two sessions of the UN preparatory committee on the establishment of an international criminal court, in American Journal of International Law, 91 (1), 1997, pp. 1822ss.

HALLESLOV STORGAARD, L., European Union law autonomy versus European fundamental rights protection. On opinion 2/13 on EU accession to the ECHR, in Human Rights Law Review, 15 (3), 2015, pp. 487ss.

HAMONIC, A., Les relations entre l'Union europèenne et l'ONU dans le domaine de la gestion des crises, ed. Larcier, Bruxelles, 2018.

HANNA MORAWSKA, ER., The complex structure of the absolute prohibition of torture. Comments in the light of the regulation of article 3 of the European Convention on Human Rights, in Espaço Juridico Journal of Law, 17, 2016, pp. 769ss.

HASSEMER, W., Tabestand und Typus. Untersuchungen zur Strafrechtlichen Hermeneutik, Carl Haymanns Verlag KG, Köln, 1968.

HEINE, G., VEST, H., Murder/wilful killing, in G.K. MCDONALD, O. SWAAK-GOLDMAN (a cura di), Substantive and procedural aspects of international criminal law. Volume I: Commentary, Kluwer Law International, The Hague, 2000, pp. 175ss.

HELER, K.J., A sentence-based theory of complementarity, in Harvard International Law Journal, 53, 2011, pp. 208ss.

HENQUET, T., International organizations in the Netherlands: immunity from the jurisdiction of the Dutch courts, in Netherlands International Law Review, 49, 2010, pp. 267ss.

HENZELIN, M., Le principe de l'universalitè en droit pènal international, Helbing & Licthenthan, Bâle, 2000.

HEYDER, C., The UN Security Council's referral of the crimes in Darfur to the international criminal court in light of US opposition to the court: Implications for the international criminal court's functions and status, in Berkeley Journal of International Law, 24 (2), 2006, pp. 654ss.

HIGGINS, R., Policy considerations and the international judicial process, in The International and Comparative Law Quarterly, 17 (1), 1968, pp. 80ss.

HIGGINS, R., The place of international law in the settlement of disputes by the Security Council, in American Journal of International Law, 64 (1), 1970, pp. 16ss.

HIGGINS, R., WEBB, P., AKANDE, D., Oppenheim's international law: United Nations, Oxford University Press, Oxford, 2017.

HIGGINS, R., WEBB, P., AKANDE, D., Oppenheim's international law: United Nations, Oxford University Press, Oxford, 2018.

HINOJOSA MARTÍNEZ, L., Bad law for good reasons: The contradictions of the Kadi judgment, in International Organizations Law Review, 5 (2), 2008, pp. 342ss

HIRAD, A., KOH, S., The emerging enforcement practice of the International Criminal Court, in Cornell International Law Journal, 45, 2012, pp. 8ss.

HOGAN, N., Five sides of justice. The dangerous and disproportionate influence of the permanent five members of the United Nations Security Council in the International Criminal Court, in Brigham University of Prelaw Review, 32, 2018, pp. 234ss.

HOHMANN, J., JOYCE, D., International law's objects, Oxford University Press, Oxford, 2019, pp. 372ss.

HOLMES, J., Complementarity: National courts versus the ICC, in A. CASSESE, P. GAETA, J.R.W.D. JONES, The Rome statute of the international criminal court. A commentary, Oxford University Press, Oxford, 2002, pp. 684ss.

HOLVOET, M., The continuing relevance of the hybrid or internationalized justice model: The example of the Kosovo Specialist Chambers, in Criminal Law Forum, 27 (1), 2016, pp. 4ss.

HORSPOOL, M., HUMPHREYS, M., EU law, Oxford University Press, Oxford, 2012, pp. 552ss.

HUNEEUS, A., International criminal law by other means: The quasi-criminal jurisdiction of the human rights court, in American Journal of International Law, 107, 2013, pp. 6ss.

IMOEDEMHE, O.C., The complementarity regime of the ICC: National implementation, ed. Springer, Berlin, 2016.

INGADOTTIR, T., The financing of international adjudication, in C.P.R. ROMANO, K.J. ALTER, Y. SHANNY, The oxford handbook of international adjudication, Oxford University Press, Oxford, 2014, pp. 596ss

IOVANE, M., L'influence de la multiplication des juridictions internationale sur l'application du droit international, in Recueil des cours, ed. Brill, Bruxelles, vol. 383, 2017, pp. 322ss.

ISANGA, J.M., The International Criminal Court ten years later: Appraisal and prospects, in Cardozo Journal of International & Comparative Law, 21, 2013, pp. 238ss.

JACKSON, M., A conspiracy to commit genocide. Anti-fertility research in apartheid's chemical and biological weapons programme, in Journal of International Criminal Justice, 13, 2015, pp. 933-950.

JACOBS, D., The frog that wanted to be an ox: The ICC's approach on immunities and cooperation, in C. STAHN, The law and practice of the international criminal court, Oxford University Press, Oxford, 2015, pp. 282ss.

JACQUÉ, J.P., CJUE-CEDH: 2-0, in Revue Trimestrielle de Droit Européen, 40 (4), 2014 pp. 823ss.

JACQUÉ, J.P., La Cour de Justice de l'Union et l'application de la Charte dans les Etats membres: "Mehr Licht", in European Yearbook on Human Rights, 14, 2014 pp. 125-147).

JACQUÉ, J.P., The accession of the European Union to the European Convention on Human Rights and Fundamental Freedoms, in Common Market Law Review, 48 (4), 2011, pp. 995, 1005.

JÄGER, H., Makrokriminalität. Studien zur Kriminologie kollektiver Gewalt, ed. Suhrkamp, Berlin, 1989.

JAIN, N., A separate law for peacekeepers: The clash between the security council and the international criminal court, in European Journal of International law, 16 (2), 2005, pp. 248ss.

JALLOH CHEVROR, C., MARONG, A., Promoting accountability under international law for gross human rights violations in Africa. Essays in honour of prosecutor hasan Bubacar Jallow, ed. Brill, The Hague, 2015.

JALLOH, C.C., CLARKE, K.M., NMEHIELLE, V.O., The African court of justice and human and peoples' rights in context: Development and challenges, Cambridge University Press, Cambridge, 2019, pp. 730ss.

JANSSENS, C., The principle of mutual recognition in European Union law, Oxford University Press, Oxford, 2013, pp. 208ss.

JENKS, C.W., Some constitutional problems of international organizations, in British Yearbook of International Law, 11, 1945, pp. 12ss.

JO, H., SIMMONS, B., Can the International Criminal Court defer atrocity?, in International Organization, 70 (3), 2016, pp. 446ss.

JOECKS, W., MIEBACH, K., (Hrsg.), Münchener Kommentar zum Strafgesetz-buch, C.H. Bech, München, 2017.

JURDI, N.N., The International Criminal Court and national court: A contentious relationship, ed. Routledge, London & New York, 2016.

KAMTO, M., L'affaire Al Bashir et les relations de l'Afrique avec la cour pènale internationalke, in Liber amicorum Raymond Ranjeva. L'Afrique et le droit international: Variations sur l'organisation international. Africa and international law. Reflections on the international organizations, ed. Pedone, Paris, 2013, pp. 150ss.

KASTNER, P., Armed conflicts and referrals to the International Criminal Court, in Journal of International Criminal Justice, 12 (3), 2014, pp. 482ss.

KASTNER, P., International criminal law in context, Routledge, London & New York, 2017.

KAUL, H.P., KRESS, C., Jurisdiction and cooperation in the statute of the international criminal court. Principles and compromise, in Yearbook of International Humanitarian Law, 2, 1999, pp. 172ss.

KAUL, H.P., The ICC and international criminal cooperation. Key aspects and fundamental necessities, in F. GIOIA, M. POLITI, The international criminal court and national jurisdictions, ed. Routledge, Aldershot, 2008, pp. 86ss.

KAULK, H.P., Towards a permanent international criminal court, in Human Rights Law Journal, 7, 1997, pp. 172ss.

KAZADI MPIANA, J., La cour pènale international et la Rèpublique dèmocratique du Congo: 10 ans après. Ètude de l'impact du statut de la cour pènale international dans le droit interne congolais, in Revue Quèbècoise de Droit International, 26 (1), 2012, pp. 59ss.

KELSEN, H., The law of the United Nations: A critical analysis of its fundamental problems, ed. Praeger, London, 1951, pp. 294ss.

KEMP, G., South Africa's (possible) withdrawal from the ICC and the future of the criminalization and prosecution of crimes against humanity, war crimes and genocide under domestic law: A submission informed by historical, normative and policy considerations, in Washington University Global Studies Law Review, 14, 2017, pp. 414ss.

KENDALL, S., Modifying global justice. Economics of accountability at the international criminal court, in Journal of International Criminal Justice, 13 (1), 2015, pp. 113ss.

KERSTEN, M., Between justice and politics. The ICC's intervention in Libya, in C. DE VOS, S. KENDALL, C. STAHN, Contested justice. The politics and practice of international criminal court interventions, Cambridge University Press, Cambridge, 2015, pp. 462ss.

KERSTEN, M., Justice in conflict. The effects of the international criminal court's interventions on ending wars and building peace, Oxford University Press, Oxford, 2016.

KHERAD, R., La question de la dèfinition du crime d'aggression dans le statute de Rome. Entre pouvoir politique du Conseil de sècuritè et compètence judiciaire de la cour pènale internationale, in Revue Gènèrale de Droit International, 109 (2), 2005, pp. 355ss.

KING, F.P., The crime of aggression: Is it amenable to judicial determination?, in B.S. BROWN, Research handbook on international criminal court, Edward Elgar Publishers, Cheltenham, 2011, pp. 128ss.

KIRCHENHAST, T., Victims and the criminal trial, ed. Palgrave & Macmillan, London, 2016.

KIRSCH, P., ROBINSON, D., Reaching agreement at the Rome conference, in A. CASSESE, P. GAETA, J.R.W.D. JONES, The Rome statute of the international criminal court. A commentary, Oxford University Press, Oxford, 2002, pp. 68ss.

KIRSCH, S., Introduction to chapter VIII: The general framework, in N. WESSENDORF, B. SIMMA, D. ERASMUS KHAN, G. NOLTE, A. PAULUS, The charter of the United Nations. A commentary, Oxford University Press, Oxford, 2012, pp. 1264ss.

KLABBERS, J., WALLENDAHL, A., Research handbook on the law of international organizations, Edward Elgar Publishers, Cheltenham, 2011.

KLEIN, P., Responsabilitè pour les faits commins dans le cadre d'opèrations de paix et ètendue du pouvoir de contrôle de la cour europèenne des droits de l'homme: quelques considèrations critiques sur l'arrêt Behrami et Saramati, in Annuaire Français de Droit International, 53, 2007, pp. 44ss.

KNOOPS, J., An introduction to the law of international criminal Tribunals. A comparative study, ed. Brill. The Hague, 2014.

KNOTTNERUS, A.S., The Security Council and the international criminal court: The unsolved puzzle of article 16, in Netherlands International Law Review, 61 (2), 2014, pp. 198ss.

KOH, H.H., BUCHWALD, T.F., The crime of aggression: The United States perspective, in American Journal of International Law, 109 (2), 2015, pp. 260ss.

KOLB, R., L'article 103 de la charte des Nations Unies, in Recueil des cours, ed. Brill, Bruxelles, vol. 365, 2013, pp. 250ss.

KONLE, K., Makrokriminalitàt im Rahmen der jugoslawischen Sezessionskriege, Herbert Utz Verlag, 2010, pp. 49ss.

KORENICA, F., The EU accession to the ECHR: Between Luxembourg's search for autonomy and Strasbourg's credibility on human rights protection, ed. Springer, Berlin, 2015, pp. 282ss.

KOURSAMI, N., The contextual elements of the crime of genocide, ed. Springer, Berlin, 2018, pp. 126ss.

KOUTRAKOS, P., The EU Common Security and Defence Policy, Oxford University Press, Oxford, 2013.

KOUTROULIS, V., And yet it exists: In defence of the "equality of belligerents" principle, in Leiden Journal of International Law, 26, 2013.

KRENN, C., Autonomy and effectiveness as common concerns: A path to ECHR accession after Opinion 2/13, in German Law Journal, 16 (1), 2015, pp. 147ss.

KRESS, C., The International Court of Justice and the "principle of non-use of force", in M. WELLER (ed), The oxford handbook of the use of force in international law, Oxford University Press, Oxford, 2015.

KRESS, C., The international criminal court and immunities under international law of states not party top the court's statute, in M. BERGSMO, L. YAN, State sovereignty and international criminal law, ed. TOAEP, Beijing, 2012, pp. 232ss.

KRIEGER, D., A permanent international court and the United Nations systems, in N. AL-NAUMI, R. MEESE, International legal issues arising under the United Nations decade of international law, Martinus Nijhoff Publishers, Hague, 1995, pp. 774ss.

KRIEGER, H., Addressing the accountability gap in peacekeeping. Law-making by domestic courts as a way to avoid UN reform?, in Netherlands International Law Review, 62, 2015, pp. 262ss.

KRISCH, P., ROBINSON, D., Referral by states parties, in A. CASSESE, P. GAETA, J.R.W.D. JONES, The Rome statute o0f the international criminal court, Oxford University Press, Oxford, 2001, pp. 623ss.

KRZAN, B., International Criminal Court facing the peace vs. justice dilemma, in International Comparative Jurisprudence, 2 (2), 2016, pp. 84ss.

KRZAN, B., Prosecuting international crimes, ed. Brill, Martinus Nijhoff Publishers, The Hague, Bruxelles, 2016.

KUCZYŃSKA, H., Changing evidentiary rules to the detriment of the accused? The

Ruto and Sang decision of the ICC Appeals Chamber, in Polish Yearbook of International Law, n. 37, 2017.

KUIJER, M., The accession of the European Union to the ECHR: A gift for ECHR's 60th anniversary or an unwelcome intruder at the party?, in Amsterdam Law Forum, 4 (3), 2011, pp. 17-32.

KYLE, J., The "new legal reality"? Peace, punishment and Security Council referrals to the ICC, in Transational Law and Contemporary Problems, 109, 2015, pp. 134ss.

LA HAYE, E., The jurisdiction of the international criminal court: Controversies over the preconditions for exercising its jurisdiction, in Netherlands International Law Review, 46 (1), 1999, pp. 12ss.

LADENBURGER, C., Vers l'adhésion de l'Union européenne à la Convention européenne des droits de l'homme, in Revue Trimestrielle de Droit Européen, 47 (1), 2011, pp. 20-26.

LAGRANGE, P., Responsabilitè des Etats pour actes accomplis en application du Chapitre VII de la Charte des Nations Unies, in Revue Gènèrale de Droit International Public, 112, 2008, pp. 86ss.

LAMB, S., Legal limits to United Nations Security Council powers, in S. GOODWIN-GILL, S. TALMON, The reality of international law, Oxford University Press, Oxford, 1999, pp. 386ss.

LAMBRECHT, S., The sting is in the Tail: CJEU Opinion 2/13 objects to draft agreement on accession of the EU to the European Convention on Human Rights, in European Human Rights Law Review, 15 (1), 2015, pp. 185ss.

LANGER, M., The diplomacy of universal jurisdiction: The political branches and the transnational prosecution of international crimes, in American Journal of International Law, 105, 2011, pp. 1, 42ss

LATTANZI, F., Concurrent jurisdictions between primacy and complementarity, in R. BELELLI, International criminal justice. Law and practice from the Rome statute to its review, Ashgate Publishing, Farnham, 2010, pp. 202ss.

LAUTERPACHT, E., Partial judgments and the inherent jurisdiction of the international court of justice, in V. LOWE, M. FITZMAURICE, Fifty years of the international court of justice. Essays in honor of Sir Robert Jennings, Cambridge University Press, Cambridge, 1996, pp. 466ss.

LAUTERPACHT, E., The legal effect of illegal acts of international organizations, in Mcnair, Essays in honor of lord McNair, ed. Stevens, London, 1965, pp. 89ss.

LAVALLE, R., A vicious storm in a teacup: The action by the United Nations Security Council to narrow the jurisdiction of the International Criminal Court, in Criminal Law Forum, 14 (2), 2003, pp. 212ss

LAVERS, T., Aggression, intervention and powerful feminist methodologies on peace and security issues, in Amsterdam Law Forum, 5 (2), 2013, pp. 127ss.

LENAERTS, K., DE SMIJTER, E., The United Nations and the European Union. Living apart together, in E. SUY, K. WELLENS, International law. Theory and practice. Essays in honor of Eric Suy, Martinus Nijhoff Publishers, The Hague, Boston, London, 1998, pp. 454ss.

LENTNER, G.M., The role of the United Nations Security Council towards the International Criminal Court. Resolution 1970 (2011) and its challenges to international criminal justice, in International Criminal Law Review, 14 (2), 2014, pp. 9ss.

LENTNER, G.M., The United Nations Security Council and the International Criminal Court. The referral mechanism in theory and practice, Edward Elgar Publishers, Cheltenham, 2018, pp. 1644ss.

LETT, A., The meaningless existence of universal jurisdiction, in Michigan State International Law Review, 23, 2015, pp. 547ss.

LIAKOPOULOS, D., International Criminal Court: Impunity status and the situation in Kenya, in International and European Union Legal Matters, 2014.

LIAKOPOULOS, D., International standards and responsibility competition according to the International Criminal Court: Anatomy, interpretation, proposals, in Revista Eletrônica de direito Penal e Polìtica Criminal-UFRGS, 6, 2018.

LIAKOPOULOS, D., La tutela cautelare nella Corte internazionale di giustizia. Aspetti processuali e comparati, ed. Amon, Firenze, 2012.

LIAKOPOULOS, D., Schutz des angeklagten im Strafverfahren, in International and European Union Legal Matters, working paper series, 2013.

LIANG, J., The inherent jurisdiction and inherent powers of international criminal courts and tribunals: An appraisal of their application, in New Criminal Law Review. An International and Interdisciplinary Journal, 15 (3), 2012, pp. 378ss.

LIANG, Y., Notes on legal questions concerning the United Nations. The establishment of an international criminal jurisdiction. The second phase, in American Journal of International Law, 46 (2), 1953, pp. 640ss

LINTON, S., Cambodia, East Timor And Sierra Leone: Experiments In International Justice, in Criminal Law Forum, 12 (1), 2001, pp. 186ss.

LINTON, S., Rising from the Ashes: The creation of a viable criminal justice system in East Timor, in Meburne University Law Review, 25 (1), 2001, pp. 146ss.

LOCK, T., The ECJ and the ECtHR: The future relationship between the two European Courts, in The Law and Practice of International Courts and Tribunals, 8, 2010, pp. 375-398.

LOCK, T., The future of EU accession to the ECHR after Opinion 2/13: Is it still possible and is it still desirable?, in Edinburgh School of Law Research Paper Series, 2015.

MAC AMHLAIGH, C., Harmonizing global constitutionalism., Cambridge University Press, Cambridge, 2016.

MACDONALD, A., In the interests of justice? The International Criminal Court, peace talks and the failed quest for war crimes accountability in Northern Uganda, in Journal of Eastern African Studies, 11 (4), 2017, pp. 630ss.

MACDONALD, R., The charter of the United Nations in constitutional perspective, in Australian Yearbook of International Law, 20, 1999, pp. 206ss.

MALONE, D.M., The Security Council in the post-cold war era: A study in the creative interpretation of the UN charter, in Security Dialogue, 28 (4), 1997, pp. 489ss.

MALUWA, T., DU PLESSIS, M., TLADI, D., The pursuit of a brave new world in international law. Essays in honor of John Dugard, ed. Brill, Bruxelles, 2017, pp. 256ss.

MANACORDA, S., MELONI, C., Indirect perpetration versus Joint Criminal Enterprise: Concurring approaches in the practice of international criminal law?, in Journal of International Criminal Justice, 9 (1), 2011, pp. 165ss.

MANDANI, M., Responsibility to protect or right to punish?, in Journal of Intervention and State Building, 4 (1), 2010, pp. 56ss.

MARC DE LA SABLIÉRE, J., Le Conseil de sècuritè des Nations Unies, ed. Larcier, Bruxelles, 2018.

MARSCHIK, A., Legislative powers of the Security Council in R.S.J. MACDONALD, D.M. JOHNSTON, Towards world constitutionalism. Issues in the legal ordering of the world community, ed. Brill, Leiden, Boston, 2005, pp. 464ss.

MARXSEN, C., What do different theories of customary international law have to say about the individual right to reparation under international humanitarian law?, in Zeitschrift für äuslandisches öffentliches Recht, n. 78, 2018 (3).

MATHIAS, D.S., BOEVING, J.N., Aggression, international law and the ICC: An argument for the withdrawal of aggression form the Rome Statute, in Columbia Journal of Transnational Law, 43, 2005, pp. 576ss.

MATHIAS, D.S., Remarks on the definition of aggression and the ICC, in ASIL Proceedings, 96, 2002, pp. 182ss.

MAUNGANIDZE, O.A., DU PLESSIS, A., The ICC and the AU, in C. STAHN, The law and practice of the international criminal court, Oxford University Press, Oxford, 2015, pp. 67ss.

MAY, L., HOSKINS, Z., The extraordinary Chambers in the Courts of Cambodia. Assessing their contribution to international criminal law, ed. Springer, Berlin, 2016.

MCCABE, M., Balancing aggression and compassion in international law: The crime of aggression and humanitarian intervention, in Fordham Law Review, 83 (2), 2014, pp. 999ss.

MCDOUGALL, C., The crime of aggression under the Rome statute of the International Criminal Court, Cambridge University Press, Cambridge, 2013, pp. 215ss.

MCKNIGHT, J., Accountability in Northern Uganda: Understanding the conflict, the parties and the false dichotomies in international criminal law and transitional justice, in Journal of African Law, 59 (2), 2015, pp. 194ss.

MCLACHLAN, C., The principle of systemic integration and article 31 (39 (c) of the Vienna Convention, in International & Comparative Law Quarterly, 54 (2), 2005, pp. 282ss.

MCPHERSON, B.F., Building an international criminal court for the 21st century, in Connecticut Journal of International Law, 13, 1998, pp. 54ss.

MEISENBERG, S., The extraordinary Chambers in the Courts in Cambodia. Assessing their contribution to international criminal law, ed. Springer, Berlin, 2016.

MENDEZ, J.E., KELLEY, J., Peace making justice and the International Criminal Court, Cambridge University Press, Cambridge 2015, pp. 480ss.

MENDEZ, P.K., The new wave of hybrid Tribunals: A sophisticated approach to enforcing international humanitarian law or an idealistic solution with empty promises?, in Criminal Law Forum, 20 (1), 2009, pp. 71-75.

MENON, R., The conceit of humanitarian intervention, Oxford University Press, Oxford, 2016.

MERKOURIS, P., Article 31 (3) (C) VCLT and the principle of systems integration: Normative shadows in Platon's cave, ed. Brill, The Hague, 2015.

MERON, T., Defining aggression for the International Criminal Court, in Suffolk Transnational Law Review, 25, 2001, pp. 2ss

METTRAUX, G., DFUGARD, J., DU PLESSIS, M., Heads of state immunities, international crimes and president Bashir's visit to South Africa, in International Criminal Law Review, 18 (4), 2018.

METTRAUX, G., International crimes: Law and practice genocide, Oxford University Press, Oxford, 2019.

MEYER, J., (ed.), Charta der Grundrechte der Europäischen Union, ed. Nomos, Baden-Baden, 2014, pp. 813-826.

MILANOVIC, M., Al-Skeini and Al-Jedda in Strasbourg, in the European Journal of International Law, 23 (1), 2012, pp. 124ss.

MILANOVIĆ, M., Norm conflict in international law: Whither human rights?, in Duke Journal of Comparative and International Law, 20, 2009, pp. 70ss.

MILLS, K., International responses to mass atrocities. Responsibility to protect, prosecture and palliate, University of Pennsylvania Press, Pennsylvania, 2015.

MISKOWIAK, K., The international criminal court: Consent, complementarity and cooperation, ed. Djøef, Copenhagen, 2000, pp. 172ss.

MOCHOCHOKO, P., International cooperation and judicial assistance, in S.K. LEE, The international criminal court. The making of the Rome statute. Issues, negotiations, results, Martinus Nijhoff Publishers, The Hague, 1999, pp. 306ss

MOELLE, M.P., The international responsibility of international organizations, Cambridge University Press, Cambridge, 2017, pp. 7ss.

MOFFETT, L., Justice for victims before the International Criminal Court, ed. Routledge, London & New York, 2014.

MOKHTAR, A., The fine art of arm-twisting. The US resolution 1422 and security council deferral power under the Rome statute, in International Criminal Law Review, 3 (4), 2003, pp. 305ss.

MÖLLERS, C., The three branches, Oxford University Press, Oxford, 2013.

MORANO-FOADI, S., VICKERS, L., (eds.), Fundamental Rights in the EU-A matter for two Courts, Oxford University Press, Oxford, 2015.

MORRIS, V., Prosecutor v. Kanybashi, Decision on jurisdiction, case n. ICTR-96-15-T: International criminal tribunal for Rwanda, June 18 1997, in American Journal of International Law, 92 (1), 1998, pp. 67ss.

MUARREMI, E., The concept of hybrid courts revisited. The case of the Kosovo Specialist Chambers, in International Criminal Law Review, 18 (4), 2018, pp. 625ss.

MÜLLER-SCHIEKE, I.K., Defining the crime of aggression under the statute of the international criminal court, in Leiden Journal of International Law, 14 (2), 2001, pp. 428ss.

MURMANN, U., Problems of causation with regard to (potential) actions of multiple protagonist, in Journal of International Criminal Justice, 12, 2014, pp. 284ss.

MURPHY, S.D., The crime of aggression at the international criminal court, in M. WELLER, The oxford handbook of the use of force in international law, Oxford University Press, Oxford, 2015, pp. 542ss.

MURUNGU, C.B., Towards a criminal chamber in the African Court of Justice and man rights, in Journal of International Criminal Justice, 9, 2011, pp. 1067ss.

NAERT, F., International law aspects of the EU's Security and Defence Policy, with a particular focus on the law of armed conflicts and human rights, Hart Publishing, Oxford & Oregon, Portland, 2010.

NASU, H., Chapter VII powers and the rule of law. The jurisdictional limits, in Australian Yearbook of International Law, 26, 2007, pp. 109

NATHANIÉL, K.H., La Cour Pènale Internationale (CPI) à l'èpreuve des poursuites en Afrique, in Afrique et Dèveloppement, 41 (2), 2016, pp. 134ss.

NICHOLSON, J., Strengthening the validity of international criminal Tribunals, ed. Brill, Leiden, 2018.

NIKOLOVA, M., VENTURA, M.J., The Special Tribunal for Lebanon declines to review UN Security Council action. Retreating from Tadić's legacy in the Ayyash jurisdiction and legality decisions, in Journal of International Criminal Justice, 11 (3), 2013, pp. 626ss.

NKANSAH, L., International Criminal Court in the trenches of Africa, in Africa Journal of International Criminal Justice, 2014.

NMEHELLE, V., Africa and the future of international criminal justice, Eleven International Publishing, The Netherlands, 2012.

NMEHIELLE, V.O.O., Africa and the future of international criminal justice, Eleven International Publishing, 2012.

NNABUIKE MALU, I., The International Criminal Court and peace processes. Côte d'Ivoire, Kenya and Uganda, ed. Springer, Berlin, 2019.

NOLLEZ-GOLDBACH, R., SAADA, J., La justice pènale internationale face aux crimes de masse, ed. Pedone, Paris, 2014.

NOLLKAEMPER, A., Concurrence between individual responsibility and state responsibility in international law, in International and Comprative Law Quarterly, 52 (3), 2003, pp. 616ss.

NOLTE, G., Subsequent practice and treaties, Oxford University Press, Oxford, 2013.

NOUTE, G., Treaties and subsequent practice, Oxford University Press, Oxford, 2013, pp. 224ss.

NOUWEN, S.M.H., WERNER, G., Doing justice to the political: The international criminal court in Uganda and Sudan, in European Journal of International Law, 21 (4), 2010, pp. 942ss.

NOWAK, C., Europarecht nach Lissabon, ed. Nomos, Baden-Baden, 2011.

NSEREKO, D.N., Aggression under the Rome statute of the international criminal court, in C. MCDOUGALL, The crime of aggression under the Rome Statute of the International Criminal Court, Cambridge University Press, Cambridge, 2013, pp. 517ss.

NSEREKO, D.N., Article 18, in O. TRIFFTERER, K. AMBOS, The Rome statute of the international criminal court. A commentary of the international criminal court. A commentary, C.H.Beck-Hart-Nomos, München, Oxford, Baden-Baden, 2016, pp. 836ss

NSEREKO, D.N., The ICC and complementarity in practice, in Leiden Journal of

International Law, 26 (2), 2013, pp. 432ss
NTUBE NGANE, S., The position of witnesses before the International Criminal Court, ed. Brill, Bruxelles, 2015.
NYAWO, J., Selective enforcement and international criminal law, ed. Intersentia, Oxford, Antwerp, 2017.
O'BRIAN, M., Prosecutorial discretion and obstacle to prosecution of United Nations peacekeepers by the international criminal court. The big fish/small fish debate and the gravity threshold, in Journal of International Criminal Justice, 10 (3), 2012, pp. 526ss.
O'DONOGHUE, A., Constitutionalism in global constitutionalism, Cambridge University Press, Cambridge, 2014.
O'MEARA, N., A more secure Europe of rights? The European Court of Human Rights, the Court of Justice of the European Union and EU Accession to the ECHR, in German Law Journal, 12, 2011, pp. 1813-1832.
OHLIN, J.D., Peace, security and prosecutorial discretion, in C. STAHN, G. SLUITER, The emerging practice of the international criminal court, ed. Brill, Bruxelles, 2009, pp. 186ss.
OKOWA, F., The Security Council, the African Union and the international criminal court. Anatomy of a problematic relationship, in J. EBBESSON, M. JACOBSSON, M.A. LAMBERG, D. LANGLET, P. WRANGE, International law and changing perceptions of security. Liber amicorum Said Mahmoudi, Hotei Publishing, The Hague, 2014, pp. 226ss.
OLASOLO, H., The prosecutor of the ICC before the initiation of investigations. A quasi judicial or a political body?, in International Criminal Law Review, 3 (2), 2003, pp. 88ss.
OLASOLO, H., The triggering procedure of the International Criminal court, Martinus Nijhoff Publishers, Leiden, Boston, 2005, pp. 122ss.
OOSTHUIZEN, G.H., Some preliminary remarks on the relationship between the envisaged international criminal court and the UN Security Council, in Netherlands International Law Review, 46 (3), 1999, pp. 314ss.
OPPERMANN, T., CLASSEN, C.D., NETTESHEIM, M., Europarecht, C.H. Beck, München, 2016.
ORAKHELASHVILI, A., Collective security, Oxford University Press, Oxford, 2011, pp. 340ss.
ORELLANA ZABALZA, G., The principle of systemic integration. Towards coherent international legal order, Lit Verlag, Münster, 2012, pp. 236ss.
ÖSTERDAHL, I., The exception as the rule: Law making on force and human rights by the UN Security Council, in Journal of Conflict and Security Law, 10 (1), 2005, pp. 5ss.
OTIM, O., WIERDA, M., Justice at Juba: International obligations and local demands in Northern Uganda, in N. WADDELL, P. CLARK, Courting conflict? Justice, peace and the ICC in Africa, Oxford University Press, Oxford, 2008, pp. 23ss.
PAUST, J.J., The U.N. is bound by human rights: understanding the full reach of human rights, remedies, and non immunity, in Harvard International Law Journal, 51, 2010, pp. 4-9.
PAVONI, R., Human rights and the immunities of foreign states and international

organizations, in E. DE WET, J. VIDMAR, Hierarchy in international law: The place of human rights, Oxford University Press, Oxford, 2012, pp. 71ss.

PEAT, D., Comparative reasoning in international courts and tribunals, Cambridge University Press, Cambridge, 2019, pp. 50ss.

PEAT, D., Comparative reasoning in international courts and tribunals, Cambridge University Press, Cambridge, 2019.

PEERS, S., The EU's Accession to the ECHR: The dream becomes a nightmare, in German Law Journal, 16, 2015, pp. 213, 222.

PESCHKE, K., The ICC investigation into the conflict in norther Uganda: beyond the dichotomy of peace versus justice, in B.S. BROWN, Research handbook on international criminal court, Edward Elgar Publishers, Cheltenham, 2011.

PESKIN, V., The international criminal court, the Security Council and the politics of impunity in Darfur, in Genocide Studies and Prevention: An International Journal, 4 (3), 2009, pp. 316ss.

PETCULESCU, I., The review of the United Nation Security Council decisions by the International Court of Justice, in Netherlands International Law Review, 52 (2), pp. 194ss.

PETERS, A., Global constitutionalism revisited, in International Legal Theory, 11, 2005, pp. 65ss.

PETERSMANN, E.U., Multilevel constitutionalism for multilevel governance of public goods: Methodology problems in international law, Bloomsbury Publishing, New York, 2017, pp. 338ss.

PETITE, M., The battle over Strasbourg: The protection of human rights across Europe has suffered a setback, thanks to the Court of Justice of the European Union, in Competition Law Insight, 2015, pp. 10ss.

PHAM, J.P., A viable model for international criminal justice: The Special Court for Sierra Leone, in New York International Law Review, 86 (1), 2006, pp. 38ss.

PICHON, J., Internationaler Strafgerichtshof und Sicherheitsrat der Vereinten Nationen, ed. Springer, Heidelberg, 2011, pp. 352ss.

PICOD, F., La Cour de justice a dit non à l'adhésion de l'Union européenne à la Convention EDH, in La Semaine Juridique, Édition Générale, 2015, pp. 230, 234.

PIERCE, R., Which of the preparatory commission's latest proposals for the definition of the crime of aggression and the exercise of jurisdiction should be adopted into the Rome Statute of the International Criminal Court?, in Brigham Young University Journal of Public Law, 15, 2000-2001, pp. 282ss.

PIERIK, R., ERNER, W., Cosmopolitanism in context. Perspectives from international law and political theory, Cambridge University Press, Cambridge, 2010, pp. 206ss.

POLAKIEWICZ, J., EU law and the ECHR: Will the European Union's accession square the circle?, in European Human Rights Law Review, 6, 2013, pp. 592-605.

POLITI, M., NESI, G., The international court and the crime of aggression, ed. Routledge, Burlington, 2004.

POLITI, M., NESI, G., The International Criminal Court: A challenge to impunity, Ashgate Publishing, Aldershot, 2001, pp. 46ss.

POTTEAU, A., Quelle adhésion de l'Union Européenne à la CEDH pour quel niveau

de protection des droits et de l'autonomie de l'ordre juridique de l'UE?, in Revue Générale Droit International Public, 115, 2011, pp. 77-111.
PRANDLER, A., The Security Council and international law, in Acta Juridica. Academiae Scientiarum Hungaricae, 15, 1973, pp. 179ss.
PROULX, V.J., Institutionalizing state responsibility: Global security and UN organs, Oxford University Press, Oxford, 2016.
QUICK, N., Forced transfer and customary international law: Bridging the gap between Nuremberg and the ICTY, in S.M. MEISENBERG, I. STEGMILLER (a cura di), The Extraordinary Chambers in the Courts of Cambodia. Assessing their contribution to international criminal law, ed. Springer, The Hague, 2016, pp. 291-319.
QUIGLEY, J., International Court of Justice as a forum for genocide cases, in Case Western Reserve Journal of International Law, 40, 2008-2009, pp. 244ss.
QUIRICO, O., International criminal responsibility. Antinomies, ed. Routledge, London & New York, 2019.
RAAB, R., BEVERS, H., The international criminal court and the separation of powers, in International Organizations Law Review, 3(1), 2006, pp. 94ss.
RACHOVITSA, A., The principal of systemic integration in human rights, in International & Comparative Law Quarterly, 66 (3), 2017, pp. 560ss.
RALPH, J., The international Criminal Court, in A.J. BELLAMY, T. DUNNE, The oxford handbook of the responsibility to protect, Oxford University Press, Oxford, 2016.
RAMSDEN, M., Uniting against impunity: The United Nations General Assembly as a catalyst for action at the International Criminal Court, in The International & Comparative Law Quarterly, 66 (4), 2017, pp. 98ss.
RANGANATHAN, S., Strategically created treaty conflicts and the politics of international law, Cambridge University Press, Cambridge, 2014.
RANKIN, M., The future of international criminal evidence in new wars? The evolution of th Commission for International Justice and Accountability (CIJA), in Journal of Genocide Research, 20 (3), 2018, pp. 394ss.
RASTAN, R., Situation and case. Defining the parameters, in C. STAHN, M. EL ZEIDY, The international criminal court and complementarity, Cambridge University Press, Cambridge, 2011, pp. 432ss.
RATNER, S.R., The thin justice of international law: A moral reckoning of the law of nations, Oxford University Press, Oxford, 2015.
REALE, E.P., Chronicles from Kampala amending the Rome statute, in Revue Internationale de Droit Pénal, 82, 2011, pp. 258ss.
REISMAN, W.M., Reflections on the judicialization of the crime of aggression, in The Yale Journal of International Law, 39, 2014, pp. 72ss.
REYNAMS, L., WOUTERS, J., RYNGAERT, C., International prosecutors, Oxford University Press, Oxford, 2012, pp. 538ss.
ROBINSON, D., The mysterious mysteriousness of complementarity, in Criminal Law Forum, 21, 2010, pp. 6ss.
ROBINSON, D., Three theories of complementarity: Charge, sentence or process?, in Harvard International Law Journal, 53, 2012, pp. 87ss.
RODMAN, K.A., BOOTH, P., Manipulated commitments: The International Criminal Court in Uganda, in Human Rights Quarterly, 35 (2), 2016, pp. 274ss.

RODMAN, K.A., Justice as a dialogue between law and politics: Embedding the International criminal Court within conflict management and peace-building, in Journal of International Criminal Justice, 12 (3), 2014, pp. 442ss.

RODMAN, K.A., Justice is interventionist: The political sources of the judicial reach of the Special Court for Sierra Leone, in International Criminal Law Review, 13, 2013, pp. 65ss.

ROMANO, C.P.R., INGADOTTIR, T., The financing of the international criminal court, in C. ROMANO, A. NOLLKAEMPER, J. KLEFFNER, Internationalized criminal courts and tribunals. Sierra Leone, East Timor and Cambogia, Oxford University Press, Oxford, 2004.

RONZITTI, N., Coercitive diplomacy sanctions and international law, Martinus Nijhoff Publishers, The Hague, 2016, pp. 234ss.

ROPER, S.D., BARRIA, L.A., State co-operation and international criminal court bargaining influence in the arrest and the surrender of suspects, in Leiden Journal of International Law, 21 (2), 2008, pp. 458ss.

ROSENTRETER, D., Article 31 (3) c) of the Vienna convention on the law of treaties and the principle of systemic integration in international investment law and arbitration, ed. Nomos, Baden-Baden, 2015, pp. 217ss.

ROSS, C., Contribution of the United Nations: Analysis of structure and functions, ed. Rinehart, New York, 1950.

ROTH, R., Tribunal spècial sur le Liban: retour sur une expèrience, in Revue Belge de Droit International, 122 (1), 2018.

ROYER, C., The Bête Noire and the Noble Lie: The International Criminal Court and politics, in Criminal Law & Philosophy, 13 (2), 2019, pp. 230ss.

RUDA, M., Nulidad de los tratados, in Y. DINSTEIN, M. TABORY, international law at a time of perplexity. Essays in Honour of Shabtai Rosenne, ed. Springer, Dordrecht, Boston, London, 1989, pp. 150ss.

RUIZ VERDUZCO, D., The relationship between the ICC and the United Nations Security Council, in C. STAHN, The law and practice of the International Criminal Court, Oxford University Press, Oxford, 2015, pp. 32ss.

RUIZ-FABRI, H., SOREL, J.M., Indèpendence et impartialitè des juges internationaux, ed. Pedone, Paris, 2010

RUYS, T., CORTEN, O., HOFER, A., The use of force in international law: A case-based approach, Oxford University Press, Oxford, 2018, pp. 397ss.

RYNGAERT, C., Apportioning responsibility between the UN and member states in UN peace-support operations: An inquiry into the application of the effective control standard after Behrami, in Israel Law Review, 45, 2012, pp. 152ss.

SADAT, L.N., The Nuremberg paradox, in The American Journal of International Law, 58 (1), 2010, pp. 154ss.

SAFFERLING, C.J.M., The special intent requirement in the crime of genocide, in C.J.M. SAFFERLING, E. CONZE (a cura di), The Genocide Convention sixty year after its adoption, ed. Springer, The Hague, 2010, pp. 172ss.

SAMSO, M., High hopes, scant resources: a word of scepticism about the anti-fragmentation function of article 31(3)(c) of the Vienna Convention on the Law of Treaties, in Leiden Journal of International Law, 24, 2011, pp. 5ss.

SARI, A., Jurisdiction and international responsibility in peace support operations the Behrami and Saramati cases, in Human Rights Law Review, 8, 2008, pp.

152ss.

SAROOSHI, D., (ed.), Remedies and responsibility for the actions of international organizations, Martinus Nijhoff Publishers, The Hague, 2014, pp. 444ss.

SAROOSHI, D., Aspects of the relationship between the international criminal court and the United Nations, in Netherlands Yearbook of International Law, 32, 2001, pp. 28ss.

SAROOSHI, D., Some preliminary remarks on the conferral by states of powers on international organizations, in New York University Jean Monnet working paper, 11, 2004, pp. 11ss.

SAROOSHI, D., The peace and justice: Paradox. The international criminal court and the UN Security Council, in D. MCGOLDRICK, P. ROWE, E. DONNELLY (ed. by), The Permanent International Criminal Court. Legal and policy issues, Hart Publishing, Oxford & Portland, Oregon, 2004, pp. 114ss.

SAROOSHI, D., The United Nations and the development of collective security, Oxford University Press, Oxford, 1999, pp. 20ss.

SASCHA, D., BACHMANN, D., EDA NWIBO, L., Pull and push- Implementing the complementarity principle of the Rome Statute of the ICC within the AU: Opportunities and challenges, in Brooklyn Journal of International Law, 43, 2018, pp. 464ss.

SATZGER, H., International and European criminal law, Hart Publishing, Oxford & Oregon, Portland, 2017.

SCHABAS, W.A., An introduction to the international criminal court, Cambridge University Press, Cambridge, 2017, pp. 144ss.

SCHABAS, W.A., BERNAZ, N., Routledge handbook of international criminal law, ed. Routledge, London & New York, 2010.

SCHABAS, W.A., Complementarity in practice: Creative solutions or a trap fro the court?, in F. GIOIA, M. POLITI, The international criminal court and national jurisdictions, ed. Routledge, Aldershot, 2008, pp. 32ss.

SCHABAS, W.A., Follow up to Rome: preparing for entry into force of the international criminal court Statute, in Human Rights Law Journal, 20, 1999, pp. 158ss

SCHABAS, W.A., PECORELLA, G., Article 13, in O. TRIFFTERER, K. AMBOS, The Rome statute of the international criminal court. A commentary of the international criminal court. A commentary, C.H.Beck-Hart-Nomos, München, Oxford, Baden-Baden, 2016, pp. 700ss.

SCHABAS, W.A., Prosecutorial discretion v. Judicial activism at the International Criminal Court, in Journal of International Criminal Justice, 6 (4), 2008, pp. 732ss

SCHABAS, W.A., Selecting situations and cases, in C. STAHN, The law and practice of the international criminal court, Oxford University Press, Oxford, 2015, pp. 375ss.

SCHABAS, W.A., The International Criminal Court: A commentary on the Rome statute, Oxford University Press, Oxford, 2016, pp. 846ss.

SCHABAS, W.A., The international criminal court. A commentary to the Rome statute, Oxford University Press, Oxford, 2010, pp. 302ss.

SCHABAS, W.A., The rise and fall of complementarity, in C. STAHN, M. EL ZEIDY,

The international criminal court and complementarity, Cambridge University Press, Cambridge, 2014, pp. 152ss.

SCHABAS, W.A., The unfinished work of defining aggression: How many times must the cannonballs fly, before they are forever banned?, in D. MCGOLDRICK, P. ROWE, E. DONNELLY (ed. by), The Permanent International Criminal Court. Legal and policy issues, Hart Publishing, Oxford & Portland, Oregon, 2004.

SCHACHTER, O., International law in theory and practice. Developments in international law, ed. Springer, Berlin, 2001, pp. 208ss.

SCHEFFER, D., Amending the crime of aggression under the Rome Statute, in C. KRESS, S. BARRIGA, The crime of aggression: A commentary, Cambridge University Press, Cambridge, 2012, pp. 1480ss.

SCHEFFER, D.J., Staying the course with the international criminal court, in Cornell International Law Journal, 35 (1), 2001-2002, pp. 90ss.

SCHMALENBACH, K., Preserving the gordian knot: UN legal accountability in the aftermath of Srebrenica, in Netherlands International Law Review, 62, 2015, pp. 313ss.

SCHUSTER, M., The Rome statute and the crimes of aggression. A gordian knot in search of a sword, in Criminal Law Forum, 14 (1), 2003, pp. 36ss.

SCHWARZEN-BERGER, G., International law: As applied by International Courts and Tribunals, Sweet & Maxwell, London, 1968, pp. 462ss.

SHAMSI, N., The International Criminal Court: A political toll? How the Rome statute is susceptible to the pressures of more power states, in Willamette Journal of International Law and Dispute Resolution, 24 (1), 2016, pp. 88ss.

SHANY, Y., How can international criminal courts have a greater impact upon national criminal proceedings? Lessons from the first two decades of international criminal justice in operation, in Israel Law Review, 46, 2013, pp. 434ss.

SHANY, Y., Questions of jurisdiction and admissibility before international courts, Cambridge University Press, Cambridge, 2016, pp. 12ss.

SHARP, D.N., Re-thinking transitional justice for the 21st century, Cambridge University Press, Cambridge, 2018, pp. 54ss.

SHEERAN, S., BEVILACQUA, C., The UN Security Council and international human rights obligations. Towards a theory of constraints and derogation, in S. SHEERAN, N. RODLEY, Routledge handbook of international human rights law, Routledge, London & New York, 2013, pp. 390ss.

SHELTON, D., International law an "relative normativity", in M. EVANS, International law, Oxford University Press, Oxford, 2006, pp. 178ss.

SHIHATA, I.F.I., The power of the international court of determine its own jurisdiction, ed. Springer, The Hague, 1965.

SHIRAM, C.L., BROWN, S., Kenya in the shadow of the ICC: Complementarity, gravity and impact, in International Criminal Law Review, 12, 2012, pp. 220ss.

SIEVERS, L., DAWS, S., The procedure of the United Nations Security Council, Oxford University Press, Oxford, 2014.

SIMON, D., L'interpretation judiciaire des traitès d'organisations internationales, ed. Pedone, Paris, 1981.

SIVAKUMARAN, S., Re-envisaging the international law of internal armed conflict,

in European Journal of International Law, 22, 2011, pp. 240, 240.242.
SKANDER GALAND, A., United Nations Security Council referrals to the International Criminal Court: Legal nature, effects and limits, ed. Brill, The Hague, 2018, pp. 206ss
SLUITER, G., FRIMAN, H., LINTON, S., International criminal procedure: Principles and rules, Oxford University Press, Oxford, 2013.
SLUITER, G., International adjudication and the collection of evidence: Obligations of states, Antwerp, Oxford, New York, 2002, pp. 172ss.
SLUITER, G., Obtaining cooperation from Sudan-Where is the law?, in Journal of International Criminal Justice, 6, 2008, pp. 874ss.
SOHN, M.C., The UN system as authoritative interpreter of its law, in O. SCHACHTER, C. JOYNER, United Nations legal order, Cambridge University Press, Cambridge, 1995, pp. 204ss.
SOLER, C., The global prosecution of core crimes under international law, ed. Asser Press, The Hague, 2019.
SOLERA, O., The definition of the crime of aggression: Lessons not learned, in Case Western Reserve Journal of International Law, 42, 2010, pp. 808ss.
SOLIS, G.D., The law of armed conflict: International humanitarian law in war, Cambridge University Press, Cambridge, 2010, pp. 28ss.
SOREL, J.M., BORÉ EVENO, V., Article 31, O. CORTEN, P. KLEIN, The Vienna conventions on the law of treaties, Oxford University Press, Oxford, 2011, pp. 822ss.
SPAVENTA, E., A very fearful Court? The protection of fundamental rights in the European Union after Opinion 2/13, in Maastricht Journal of European and Comparative Law, 22, 2015, pp. 51ss.
SPIJKERS, O., The immunity of the United Nations in relation to the genocide in Srebrenica in the eyes of a Dutch District Court, in Journal of International Peacekeeping, 13, 2009, pp. 197ss.
SPRINGROSE, L.G., Aggression as a core crime in the Rome statute establishing an international criminal court, in Saint Louis-Warsaw Transnational Law Journal, 99, 1999, pp. 152ss
SQUATRITO, T., YOUNG, O.R., FOLLESDAL, A., ULSTEIN, G., The performance of international Courts and Tribunals, Cambridge University Press, Cambridge, 2018.
STAHN, C., Libya, the international criminal court and complementarity, in Journal of International Criminal Justice, 10 (2), 2012, pp. 327ss.
STAHN, C., One step forward, two steps back? Second thoughts on a “sentence-based” theory of complementarity, in Harvard International Law Journal, 53, 2012, pp. 183-196.
STAHN, C., The "end", the "beginning of the end" or the "end of the beginning"? Introducing debates and voices on the definition of aggression, in Leiden Journal of International Law, 23, 2010, pp. 880ss.
STAHN, C., The ambiguities of Security Council Resolution 1422, in European Journal of International Law, 14 (3), 2003, pp. 87ss.
STAHN, C., The geometry of transitional justice, in Leiden Journal of International Law, 18 (3), 2005, pp. 426ss.
STAHN, C., The law and practice of the International Criminal Court, Oxford

University Press, Oxford, 2015.

STEIN, M.S., The Security Council, the international criminal court and the crime of aggression: How exclusive is the Security Council's power to determine aggression?, in Indiana International and Comparative Law Review, 16 (1), 2005, pp. 4ss.

STEINFELD, M., When ethnic cleansing is not genocide: A critical appraisal of the ICJ's ruling in Croatia v. Serbia in relation to deportation and population transfer, in Leiden Journal of International Law, 28, 2015, pp. 938ss.

STERIO, M., SCHARF, M., The legacy of ad hoc tribunals in international criminal law, Cambridge University Press, Cambridge, 2019.

STOVER, E., PESKIN, V., KOENIG, A., Hiding in plain sight: The pursuit of war criminals from Nuremberg to the war on terror, in University of California Press, California, 2016.

STRAPATSAS, N., The practice of the Security Council regarding the concept of aggression, in C. KRESS, S. BARRIGA, The crime of aggression: A commentary, Cambridge University Press, Cambridge, 2012, pp. 184ss.

STROMSETH, J.E., Law and force after Iraq: A transnational movement, in American Journal of International Law, 97, 2003, pp. 634ss.

STUCKENBERG, C.F., Vorstudien zu Vorsatz und Irrtum im Völkerstrafrecht: Versuch einer Elementarstrafrecht für eine übernationale Vorsatzdogmatik, ed. De Gruyter Recht, Berlin, 2011, pp. 6ss.

SUNGA, L.S., The crimes within the jurisdiction of the international criminal court (Part II, Articles 5-10), in European Journal of Crime, Criminal Law and Criminal Justice, 6, 1998, pp. 64ss.

SUQATRITO, T., Resourcing global justice: The resource management design of international courts, in Global Policy, 8 (5), 2017, pp. 67ss.

SWART, B., Arrest and surrender, in A. CASSESE, P. GAETA, J.R.W.D. JONES, The Rome statute of the international criminal court. A commentary, Oxford University Press, Oxford, 2002, pp. 1678ss.

SWART, B., In the eye of the storm: The Keynatta case and the dispute between the African union and the international criminal court, in African Yearbook of International Humanitarian Law, 20, 2015, pp. 134ss.

SWART, B., SLUITER, G., The ICC and international criminal co-operation, in H.A.M. VON HEBEL, J.G. LAMMERS, J. SCHUKKING, Reflections on the international criminal court: Essays in honor of Adrian Bos, T.M.C. Asser Press, The Hague, 1999, pp. 902ss.

SWEENEY, J.A., The elusive right to truth in transitional human rights jurisprudence, in International & Comparative Law Quarterly, 67 (2), 2018, pp. 359ss.

TALMON, S.A.G., Security Council treaty action, in Revue Hellenique de Droit International, 62, 2009, pp. 10ss.

TAMS, C., SLOAN, J., The development of international law by the International Court of Justice, Cambridge University Press, Cambridge 2013.

TAN, Y., The identification of customary rules in International Criminal Court, in Utrecht Journal of International and European Law, 34 (2), 2018, pp. 96ss.

TANNER, F., Addressing the perils of peace operations. Toward a global peacekeeping system, in Global Governance, 16 (2), 2010, pp. 212ss.

TAVERNIER, J., La responsabilité des Etats au regard de la Convention européenne des droits de l'homme pour la mise en oeuvre de résolutions adoptées dans la cadre du chapitre VII de la Charte des Nations Unies, in Revue Générale de Droit International Public, 117, 2013, pp. 102ss.

THAKUR, R., The United Nations, peace and security: from collective security to the responsibility to protect, Cambridge University Press, Cambridge, 2010, pp. 280ss.

THÉVENOT-WERNER, A.M., Le droit des agents internationaux à un recours effectif: Vers un droit comun de la procèdure administrative international, ed. Brill, Bruxelles, 2016.

THIRLWAY, H., The law and procedure of the international court of justice 1960-1989, in British Yearbook of International Law, 72 (1), 1996, pp. 29ss.

THOUVENIN, J.M., Article 103, in J.P. COT, A. PELLET, M. FORTEAU, La charte des Nations Unies, ed. LGDJ, Paris, 2005, pp. 2134ss

TILLOTSON, J., FOSTER, N., Text, cases and materials on EU law, Gavedish Publishing, New York, 2013.

TLADI, D., The international criminal court and the duty to arrest and surrender. The case of Omar Al-Bashir in South Africa, in Zeitschrift für Internationale Strafgerichtsdogmatik, 10, 2015, pp. 498ss.

TOMUSCHAT, C., International law as a coherent system. Unity or fragmentation?, in M.H. ARSANJANI, J.K. COGAN, R.D. SLOANE, S. WIESSNER, Looking to the future: Essays on international law in honor of W. Michael Reisman, ed. Brill, The Hague, 2011, pp. 338ss.

TOMUSCHAT, C., The European Court of Human Rights and the United Nations, in A. FØLLESDAL, B. PETERS, G. ULFSTEIN, Constituting Europe: The European Court of Human Rights in a national, European and global context, Cambridge University Press, Cambridge, 2013, pp. 334ss.

TOMUSCHAT, C., Universal criminal jurisdiction. Jurisdiction with respect to the crime of genocide, crimes against humanity and war crimes, in Yearbook of the Institute of International Law, 71, 2005, pp. 246ss.

TORRES PEREZ, A., Too many voices? The prior involvement of the Court of Justice of the European Union? in European Journal of Human Rights, 40, 2013, pp. 565-583.

TRAHAN, J., Defining "aggression": Why the Preparatory Commission for the International Criminal Court has faced such a conundrum, in Loyola of Los Angeles International and Comparative Law Review, 24, 2002, pp. 462ss.

TRAHAN, J., Is complementarity the right approach for the International Criminal Court's crime of aggression-Considering the problem of overzealous National Court prosecutions, in Cornell International Law Journal, 45, 2012, pp. 576ss.

TRIFFTERER, O., AMBOS, K., (a cura di), The Rome Statute of the International Criminal Court. A Commentary, C.H.Beck-Hart-Nomos, München, 2016.

TRIFFTERER, O., BURCHARD, C., Article 27, in O. TRIFFTERER, K. AMBOS, The Rome statute of the international criminal court. A commentary of the international criminal court. A commentary, C.H.Beck-Hart-Nomos, München, Oxford, Baden-Baden, 2016, pp. 1054ss.

TSAGOURIAS, N., Conceptualizing the autonomy of the European Union, in R. COLLINS, N.D. WHITE, International organizations and the idea of autonomy, ed. Routledge, London, New York, 2011, pp. 340sss.

TSAGOURIAS, N., WHITE, N.D., Collective security. Theory law and practice, Cambridge University Press, Cambridge, 2013

TZANAKOPOULOS, A., Collective security and human rights, in E. DE WET, J. VIDMAR, Hierarchy in international law: The place of human rights, Oxford University Press, Oxford, 2012, pp. 56ss.

TZANAKOPOULOS, A., Transparency in the Security Council, in A. BIANCHI, A. PETERS, Transparency in international law, Cambridge University Press, Cambridge, 2013, pp. 368ss.

UERPMANN-WITTZACK, R., Rechtsfragen und Rechtsfolgendes Beitritts der Europäischen Union zur EMRK, in Europarecht, 2012, pp. 167ss.

USACKA, A., Building the international criminal Court, in Global Business & Development Law Journal, 23 (2), 2011, pp. 228ss.

VAGIAS, M., DUGARD, J., The territorial jurisdiction of the International Criminal Court, Cambridge University Press, Cambridge, 2014, pp. 46ss.

VAN DER HAVE, N., The prevention of gross human rights violations under international human rights law, ed. Springer, Berlin, 2018.

VAN DER VYVER, J.D., Prosecuting the crime of aggression in the ICC, in University of Miami National Security & Armed Conflict Law Review, 2010-2011, 1, pp. 17ss.

VAN DER VYVER, J.D., The Al Bashir debacle, in African Human Rights Law Journal, 15 (2), 2015.

VAN DER WILT, H., PAULUSSEN, C., Legal responses to transnational and international crimes, Edward Elgar Publishing, Cheltenham, 2017.

VAN MULLIGEN, J.G., Global constitutionalism and the objective purport of the international legal order, in Leiden Journal of International Law, 24 (2), 2011.

VAN ROSSEM, J.W.C., The autonomy of EU law: more is less?, in A.R. WESSELS, S. BLOCKMANS, Between autonomy and dependence. The EU legal order under the influence of International organizations, ed. Springer, The Hague, 2013, pp. 14ss.

VAN SLIEDREGT, E., VASILIEV, S., Pluralism in international criminal law, Oxford University Press, Oxford, 2014

VERDIRAME, G., Breaches of the European Convention on Human Rights resulting from the conduct of international organizations, in European Human Rights Law Review, 8, 2008, pp. 220ss.

VERDIRAME, G., The UN and human rights. Who guards the guardians?, Cambridge University Press, Cambridge, 2011, pp. 316ss.

VILLIGER, M.E., The Vienna convention on the law of treaties-40 years after, ed. Martinus Nijhoff Publishers, The Hague, 2009, pp. 124ss.

VINUESA, R.E., La jurisdicciòn del Tribunal penal internacional para la ex Yugoslavia segùn la decisiòn de la Càmara de Apelaciones en el caso Tadić (sobre competencia), in Hèctor Gross Espiell Amicorum Liber, human person and international law, ed. Bruylant, Bruxelles, 1997, pp. 1802ss.

VIRALLY, M., Les Nations Unies et l'affaire du Congo en 1960, in Annuaire Français de Droit International, 6, 1960, pp. 572ss.

VON BOGDANDY, A., VENZKE, I., In whose name? A public law theory of international adjudication, Oxford University Press, Oxford, 2014.

VON GLAHN, G., TAULBEE, J.L., Law among nations: An introduction to public international law, ed. Routledge, London & New York, 2015.

VON HEBEL, H.A.M., LAMMERS, J.G., SCHUKKING, J., Reflections on the international criminal court: Essays in honor of Adriaan Bos, T.M.C. Asser Press, The Hague, 1999, pp. 432ss.

VON HEBEL, H.A.M., ROBINSON, D., Crimes within the jurisdiction of the court, in S.K. LEE, The International Criminal Court. The making of the Rome statute. Issues, negotiations, results, Martinus Nijhoff Publishers, The Hague, Boston, London, 1999, pp. 80ss.

VOULGARIS, N., Rethinking indirect responsibility: a study of article 17 of the Draft Articles on the Responsibility of International Organizations, in International Organizations Law Review, 11, 2014, pp. 8ss.

WARBRICK, C., ROWE, C., The international criminal tribunal for Yugoslavia: The decision of the appeals chamber on the interlocutory appeal on jurisdiction in the Tadić case, in International and Comparative Law Quarterly, 45 (3), 1996, pp. 692ss.

WARRICK, T.S., Organization of the international criminal court. Administrative financial issues, in Denver Journal of International Law & Policy, 25, 1997, pp. 334ss.

WATSON, G.R., Constitutionalisms, judicial review and the world court, in Harvard International Law Journal, 34, 1993, pp. 22ss.

WATSON, K.W., Behrami v. France: constructive blue helmets protect KFOR nations from accountability, in Tulane Journal of International and Comparative Law, 16, 2007-2008, pp. 576ss.

WEBB, P., International judicial integration and fragmentation, Oxford University Press, Oxford, 2013.

WEDGWOOD, R., The international criminal court: an American view, in European Journal of International Law, 10, 1999, pp. 94ss.

WEGNER, P.S., The International criminal Court in ongoing infra-state conflicts: Navigating the peace-justice divide, Cambridge University Press, Cambridge, 2015.

WENAWESER, C., Reaching the Kampala compromise: The chair's perspective, in Leiden Journal of International Law, 23 (4), 2010, pp. 888ss.

WENQI, J., On co-operation by states not party to the international criminal court, in International Review of the Red Cross, 88, 2006, pp. 92ss.

WERLE, G., JESSBERGER, F., Principles of international criminal law, Oxford University Press, Oxford, 2014, pp. 35ss.

WERLE, G., ZIMMERMANN, A., The International criminal Court in turbulent times, ed. Springer, Berlin, 2019.

WESSEL, R.A., Division of international responsibility between the EU and its member States in the area of Foreign, Security and Defence Policy, in Amsterdam Law Forum, 3 (3), 2011, pp. 34-48.

WESSEL, R.A., ŁAZOWSKI, A., When Caveats Turn into Locks: Opinion 2/13 on Accession of the European Union to the ECHR, in German Law Journal, 16, 2015, pp. 179ss.

WEXLER, L.S., The proposed permanent international criminal court. An appraisal, in Cornell International Law Journal, 29 (3), 1996, pp. 667ss.

WHARTON, S., The evolution of international criminal law: prosecuting "new" crimes before the Special Court for Sienna Leone, in International Criminal Law Review, 11, 2011, pp. 218ss.

WHITE, N., CRYER, R., The ICC and the Security Council. An uncomfortable relationship, in J. DORIA, H.P. GASSER, M. CHERIF BASSIOUNI, The legal regime of the international criminal court. Essays in honor of professor Igor Blishchenko. In memory of professor Igor Pavlovich Blishchenko (1930-2000), Martinus Nijhoff Publishers, Leiden, 2009, pp. 462ss.

WHITTLE, D., The intervention brigade, Monusco, and the application of international humanitarian law to United Nations forces, in Georgetown Journal of International Law, 6, 2014-2015, pp. 838ss.

WHITTLE, D., The limits of legality and the United Nations Security Council: Applying the extralegal measures model to chapter VII action, in European Journal of International Law, 26 (3), 2015, pp. 674ss

WILLIAM, S.A., SCHABAS, W.A., Article 13, in O. TRIFFTERER, Commentary on the Rome statute, observer's notes, article by article, Oxford, Baden-Baden, München, 2008, pp. 572ss.

WILMSHURST, E., (ed), International law and the classification of conflicts, Oxford University Press, Oxford, 2012.

WILSON, G., The United Nations and collective security, ed. Routledge, London & New York, 2014, pp. 192ss.

WITSCHELL, G., Financial regulations and rules of the court, in Fordham International Law Journal, 25, 2002, pp. 668ss.

WOOD, M., Constitutionalization of international law. A skeptical voice, in K.H. KAIKOBAD, BOHLANDER, International law and power. Perspectives on legal order and justice. Essays in honor of Colin Warbrick, ed. Brill, Dordrecht, 2009, pp. 96ss.

WOOD, M.C., Security Council working methods and procedure. Recent developments, in International and Comparative Law Quarterly, 45 (1), 1996, pp. 150ss.

WOOD, M.C., The interpretation of Security Council resolutions, in Max Planck Yearbook of the United Nations, 2, 1998, pp. 73ss

WOUTERS, J., The judgment in the arrest warrant case: Some critical remarks, in Leiden Journal of International Law, 16 (2), 2003, pp. 259ss.

YEE, L., Not just a war crimes court: the penal regime established by the Rome statute of the International Criminal Court, in Singapore Academy of Law Journal, 10, 1998, pp. 322ss.

YEE, S., A proposal to reformulate article 23 of the ILC draft statute for an international criminal court, in Hastings International and Comparative Law Review, 19, 1995-1996, pp. 534ss.

YEE, S., The international criminal court and the Security Council, in S.K. LEE, The International criminal court: The making of the Rome statute. Issues, negotiations, results, Martinus Nijhoff Publishers, The Hague, 1999, pp. 150ss.

ZAPPALÁ, S., Are some peacekeepers better than others? UN Security Council resolution 1497 (2003) and the ICC, in Journal of International Criminal

Justice, 1 (3), 2003, pp. 674ss.
ZAPPALÁ, S., Reviewing security council measures in the light of international human rights principles, in B. FASSBENDER, Securing human rights? Achievements and challenges of the UN Security Council, Oxford University Press, Oxford, 2011, pp. 180ss.
ZAPPALÁ, S., The reaction of the US to the entry into force of the ICC statute: Comments on UN SC Resolution (2002) and article 98 agreements, in Journal of International Criminal Justice, 1 (1), 2003, pp. 115ss.
ZAWATI, M.H., The International Criminal Court and complementarity, in Journal of International Law and International Relations, 12, 2016, pp. 208-228.
ZEMANEK, K., The legal foundations of the international system, in Recueil des cours, ed. Brill/Martinus Nijhoff Publishers, Bruxelles, vol. 269, 1997, pp. 96ss.
ZIMMERMANN, A., "Acting under chapter VII (...)": Resolution n.1422 and possible limits of the powers of the Security Council, in J.A. FROWEIN, K. SCHARIOTH, I. WINKELMANN, R. WOLFRUM, Verbandeln für den Frieden. Liber amicorum Tono Eite, ed. Springer, Berlin, 2003, pp. 262ss.
ZIMMERMANN, A., SENER, M., Chemical weapons and the International Criminal Court, in American Journal of International Law, 108 (3), 2014, pp. 438ss.
ZIMMERMANN, A., The creation of a permanent international criminal court, in Max Planck Yearbook of United Nations Law, 2, 1998, pp. 236ss.
ZIMMERMANN, A., TOMUSCHAT, C., OELLERS-FRAHM, K., TAMS, C.J., KASHGAR, M., DIEHL, D., The statute of the International Court of Justice. A commentary, Oxford University Press, Oxford, 2019, pp. 1418ss.
ZWANENBURG, M., The statute for an international criminal court and the United States: Peacekeepers under fire?, in European Journal of International Law, 10, 1999, pp. 131ss.

www.ingramcontent.com/pod-product-compliance
Lightning Source LLC
LaVergne TN
LVHW070743240926
848802LV00001B/2
9781680531305